Cultural Studies in Question

Cultural Studies in Question

edited by

Marjorie Ferguson and Peter Golding

SAGE Publications
London • Thousand Oaks • New Delhi

SAGE Publications Ltd
6 Bonhill Street
London EC2A 4PU

SAGE Publications Inc
2455 Teller Road
Thousand Oaks, California 91320

SAGE Publications India Pvt Ltd
32, M-Block Market
Greater Kailash – I
New Delhi 110 048

British Library Cataloguing in Publication data

A catalogue record for this book is
available from the British Library

ISBN 0 8039 7923 1
ISBN 0 8039 7924 X (pbk)

Library of Congress catalog record available

Typeset by M Rules
Printed in Great Britain by The Cromwell Press Ltd,
Broughton Gifford, Melksham, Wiltshire

Contents

Notes on Contributors

Michael Billig is Professor of Social Sciences at Loughborough University, where he was a founder member of the Discourse and Rhetoric Group. His recent books include *Talking of the Royal Family* (1992), *Arguing and Thinking* (rev. edn 1996) and *Banal Nationalism* (1995). He is Associate Editor of *Discourse and Society.*

James W. Carey is Professor of Journalism at the Graduate School of Journalism, Columbia University, New York. He was Dean of the College of Communications, University of Illinois. He is author of *Communication as Culture: Media Myths and Narratives* (1989) and *James Carey: A Conversation* (1997).

John D.H. Downing is John T. Jones Jr. Centennial Professor of Communication in the Department of Radio-Television-Film at the University of Texas at Austin. His books include *The Media Machine* (1980), *Questioning the Media* (rev. edn 1995) and *Internationalizing Media Theory* (1996). He has a forthcoming book on alternative media and political movements. He has written widely on racism and the media, and on 'Third World' cinemas.

Marjorie Ferguson is Associate Professor and Director of Graduate Studies in the College of Journalism, University of Maryland at College Park. Her books include *Forever Feminine: Women's Magazines and the Cult of Femininity* (1985), the edited volumes, *New Communication Technologies and the Public Interest* (1986) and *Public Communication, the New Imperatives* (1990), and *Media Globalization: Myths, Markets and Identities* (1997).

Nicholas Garnham is Professor of Communication and Director of the Centre for Communication and Information Studies at the University of Westminster, London. He is the author of many works on media and communication issues, including *Capitalism and Communication* (1990) and *The Economics of Television* (1988). He is an editor of the journal *Media, Culture and Society.*

Todd Gitlin's books include *The Twilight of Common Dreams: Why America is Wracked by Culture Wars* (1995), *The Sixties: Years of Hope, Days of Rage*

(1987), *Inside Prime Time* (1983) and *The Whole World is Watching* (1980), along with a novel, *The Murder of Albert Einstein* (1992), and an edited volume, *Watching Television* (1987). Formerly a professor of sociology and director of the mass communication programme at the University of California, Berkeley, he is now a professor of culture, journalism, and sociology at New York University.

Peter Golding is Professor of Sociology and Head of the Department of Social Sciences at the University of Loughborough, where he is also co-director of the Communication Research Centre. His books include *Images of Welfare* (with Sue Middleton, 1982), *Communicating Politics* (edited with Philip Schlesinger and Graham Murdock, 1986), and *Taxation and Representation: Political Communication and the Poll Tax* (with David Deacon, 1995). He is co-editor of the *European Journal of Communication*.

Joli Jensen is Associate Professor of Communication at the University of Tulsa, Oklahoma. Her publications include *Redeeming Modernity: Contradictions in Media Criticism* (1990) and articles on American cultural thought, the typewriter, and country music production. She is currently writing a book on beliefs about the social power of the arts among American intellectuals.

Douglas Kellner is Professor of Philosophy at the University of Texas at Austin. His books include *Camera Politica: The Politics and Ideology of Contemporary Hollywood Film* (with Michael Ryan, 1988), *Critical Theory, Marxism and Modernity* (1989), *Jean Baudrillard: From Marxism to Postmodernism and Beyond* (1989), *Television and the Crisis of Democracy* (1990), *Postmodern Theory: Critical Interrogations* (with Steven Best, 1991), *The Persian Gulf TV War* (1992), and *Media Culture* (1995).

Jim McGuigan teaches communication, culture and media at Coventry University, UK. He is the author of *Cultural Populism* (1992) and *Culture and the Public Sphere* (1996), and co-editor of *Studying Culture* (1993, 2nd edition 1997). His forthcoming publications include *Cultural Methodologies* and *Technocities*.

Denis McQuail is Professor Emeritus of Mass Communication at the University of Amsterdam. His many books include *Mass Communication Theory* (3rd edition 1994), *Media Performance: Mass Communication and the Public Interest* (1992) and *Communication Models* with Sven Windahl (2nd edition 1993). He is an editor of the *European Journal of Communication*.

Angela McRobbie teaches sociology at Loughborough University and is author of *Postmodernism and Popular Culture* (1994) and *Fashion and the Image Industries* (1997). She has published widely on popular and youth culture and on feminist and cultural theory.

David Morley is Professor of Communications, in the Department of Media and Communications, Goldsmith's College, University of London. He is the author of *The 'Nationwide' Audience* (1980), *Family Television* (1986), *Television, Audiences and Cultural Studies* (1992) and *Spaces of Identity* (with Kevin Robins, 1995). He is the co-editor (with Kuan-Hsing Chen) of *Stuart Hall: Critical Dialogues in Cultural Studies* (1996) and (with James Curran and Valerie Walkerdine) of *Cultural Studies and Communications* (1996).

Graham Murdock is Reader in the Sociology of Culture at Loughborough University. He has been visiting professor at several universities including, currently, the University of Bergen. He has written widely on sociological aspects of media and communications and his books include *Mass Media and the Secondary School* (with Guy Phelps, 1973), *Demonstrations and Communications: A Case Study* (with James Halloran and Philip Elliott, 1970) and *Televising Terrorism* (with Philip Schlesinger and Philip Elliott, 1983).

John J. Pauly is Professor of Communication and American Studies, and Chair of the Communication Department at Saint Louis University. His research on the history and sociology of the mass media has appeared in many journals, and from 1989 to 1993 he was editor of *American Journalism*, the scholarly quarterly of the American Journalism Historians' Association.

Sari Thomas is Professor of Communication, Chair of Mass Media and Communication, and Director of the Institute of Culture and Communication, Temple University. She is the former editor of *Critical Studies in Mass Communication*, and has published numerous articles in leading journals.

Preface

This volume was borne of a deep sense of unease. The continuing growth, and apparent vitality, of media and cultural studies have brought a vibrant and cutting edge to interdisciplinary work in the social sciences and humanities over the past three decades. At the same time, the worldwide expansion of the media and information industries has superimposed on the flourishing study of popular culture an added area of intellectual exploration which has captured the imagination of large numbers of students and scholars.

Yet, as teachers and researchers in this field, we gradually became aware of an anxiety about the intellectual direction of much work labelled cultural studies, that was patently shared by many others. This seemed to stem from two specific concerns. First, the balance of intellectual labour seemed to us to have moved away from the still live and critical issues at the heart of the social sciences, towards those aspects of the study of cultural forms inherited primarily from the humanities. As social scientists ourselves, this was not only a matter of territorial paranoia, but the cause of a deepening sense that important issues and debates were being hopelessly elided by a field of study increasingly isolated from nourishing streams of work elsewhere. Secondly, we were becoming puzzled by the emergence of an orthodoxy, a canon of founding fathers, defining work and myths of origin, which was beginning to ossify an intellectual and academic community that insistently advocated openness, dialogue and interdisciplinarity.

Such concerns could very easily become intensified. On both sides of the Atlantic we found aspiring graduate students emerging from cultural studies programmes able to offer the most elegant and detailed discourses on Derrida or Lacanian theory, yet seemingly unaware of current threats to public-service broadcasting or legislative and industrial trends eroding media plurality and democratic diversity. At times, the first and impatient response is somewhere between regret and despair. In North America, the work of British cultural studies pioneers was becoming the object of almost fanzine regard, a new iconography for American graduate students. On to this was grafted French postmodernism and American pragmatism in a new but distinctly dissociated *mélange* of interests and approaches.

With these common concerns, the editors decided to organize a 'theme session' at the May 1993 annual meeting of the International Communication Association in Washington, DC. The session was entitled

'Interfaces: culture and structure in communications research', and its panel members (all contributors to this volume) were set the task of bringing together 'in constructive debate, contrasting intellectual research traditions which have attempted critically to address the changing social and political character of communications'. The session was, to say the least, lively. It was both heartening, and at times not a little alarming, to witness the passions and commitment aroused by the debate as issues raised, deliberately or innocently by the panel, touched a number of nerves in the distinguished assembly. At one level the session rubric seemed straightforward enough, seeking to explore contrasts between 'approaches broadly under the "cultural studies" umbrella, whose primary concern has been with texts, meaning and signification, and on the other hand, social and political science approaches more extensively interested in those features of social structure which shape communication processes and cultural products'. Indeed, only too easily did it get boiled down to another familiar bout between something neat and tidy called cultural studies and something equally contained called political economy, in which neither recognized its image in the glassy caricature conjured up by the other. Clearly, something more was required.

Thus, as the debate moved on, and as current academic and media debates about collective identity, postcolonialism and postmodernism attest, the boundaries and topography of our areas of study had become almost terminally, and certainly frustratingly, obscure. The ferocity of the ICA panel debate, and its terms and tenor, have subsequently replayed in the literature, notably in the growing secondary literature in cultural studies of a more critical and introspective cast, suggesting perhaps a loss of certainty as to direction and destinations.

That is the backdrop to the professional, philosophical and pedagogical aims and purposes of this book: to offer media scholars thoughtful and critical reflection on a set of crucial debates in contemporary social and cultural analysis. Inevitably, we cannot be comprehensive or global in scope, whether understood culturally or geographically. But we are confident that these aims have been richly realized by the outstanding and original essays contributed by a distinguished set of scholars. We are deeply grateful for the time and energy they have devoted to this common task.

The production of such an anthology will always owe debts to many beside its contributors. We are grateful to those whose hospitality and forbearance made editorial work on both sides of the Atlantic more congenial: in Leicester, Jen, Ben and Ruth Golding; in Washington, Laura Ferguson and Caryl Kerollis; in London, John Carrier and the London School of Economics; in Vancouver, Simon Fraser University and summer session colleagues. We gratefully acknowledge, too, the patient support and advice of our editor at Sage, Stephen Barr.

Last but not least, our warm thanks and appreciation to Erik Bucy at Maryland who tracked down elusive references and data with his customary verve; Wendy Monk at Loughborough provided efficient research, editorial and bibliographical support, and not least, the index, with her usual good cheer and diligence; and David Murphy at Simon Fraser University who kept the editors connected in cyberspace over the last lap.

Marjorie Ferguson
Peter Golding
Washington/Vancouver/Loughborough, July 1996

Cultural Studies and Changing Times: An Introduction

Marjorie Ferguson and Peter Golding

It is a curiosity of cultural and media analysis that cultural studies is not infrequently caught in the act of reinventing itself. There is a certain critical groundswell that suggests this process may again be under way. The spectacle of epistemological tails being swallowed and methodological skins being shed, while a matter of interest to others, appears to be neither novel nor noteworthy for an 'intellectual project' that extols the virtues of eclecticism, relativism, and the moving target as research agenda.

This propensity towards metamorphosis seems to fuel the current high level of cultural studies' internal debate and, millennial angst apart, goes somewhere towards explaining the current restless dynamic abroad in the field as a whole. In an environment where retrospectives on the cultural studies 'project' have become something of a scholarly (and publishing) *mode du jour*, the task of critical analysis is one the editors and authors of this volume join with some fervour and pursue from a variety of perspectives, including cultural studies itself.

Three forces appear to be driving the wheels of re-evaluation and reinvention. The first is cultural studies' high visibility, the consequence of its international advance, academic institutionalization and disciplinary colonization through the proliferation of professional associations, conferences, celebrity theorists, journals and texts. The second force derives from cultural studies' penchant for a pedagogy of infinite plasticity, with interests that include, apart from its own history, gender and sexuality, nationhood and national identity, colonialism and postcolonialism, race and ethnicity, popular culture and audiences, science and ecology, identity politics, pedagogy, the politics of aesthetics and disciplinarity, cultural institutions, discourse and textuality, as well as 'history and global culture in a postmodern age' (Grossberg et al., 1992: 18–22).

The third force pushing cultural studies along the path of revisionism stems directly from external critique. The substantive issue was, and is, cultural studies' failure to deal empirically with the deep structural changes in national and global political, economic and media systems through its eschewing of economic, social or policy analysis. Notably missing from the whole-earth intellectual catalogue noted above are references to political and economic system change, such as the collapse of the former Soviet empire, employment consequences of a global market or their impact on information or entertainment access or production. Even farther removed are questions about the politics of the voting booth or public policy. The question remains, and merits repetition, where do claims of inclusivity stand when issues of changing media technology, ownership, regulation, production and distribution are shrugged off and only those of consumption are addressed?

Along the way, cultural studies has produced a new professional sub-species, that of the 'practitioner', a semantic stroke that transforms a scholarly state of 'doing' critical media and cultural analysis, to an imperial state of 'being' its own subject-object, while heeding a calling. As ontology replaces epistemology and interpretation replaces investigation, the embrace of textualism, discursive strategies, representation and polysemic meanings accelerates the elevation of the theoretical over the empirical and the abstract over the concrete.

Chronicles of a transnationalizing academic enterprise

Both intellectually and spatially, the story of the cross-national and cross-disciplinary growth of cultural studies has been something of a traveller's tale. Chronicling an odyssey more Hollywood than Homeric, we can trace the movement of ideas, theories, methods and people – patron saints, superstars, hot gospellers and true believers – around the globe. In the process, national, regional and diasporic differences in ways of working, as well as particular interests, are grounded in specific experiences of history, geography, culture and politics. Inter-national and intra-group differences were always present, but only recently demonstrate a fragmentation potential as cultural studies reaches that '40-something' age.

What is indisputable is the scale and speed of growth in cultural studies activity. Some measure of these developments can be traced in the citation indices of the humanities and social science literature. Indicators of the extraordinary growth of cultural studies, the centrality of popular culture to its concerns and recent tendency to introspection are illustrated by the parallel growth and expansion of 'popular culture' and 'cultural studies' citations in the indices of two major social science, humanities and media data bases – Worldcat and ERIC, 1960–95. From 1960 with just 23 and 34 mentions for 'cultural studies' and 'popular culture' respectively, to their trebling and quadrupling in 1970 (100 and 77), citations have accelerated at broadly similar rates. But by far the largest jump occurred between 1985 (156 and 145 respectively) and the high point of 1991 (431 'cultural studies', 314 'popular culture'), since when there has been a steady downturn.

The changing temper of this output is also indicated in the output of leading publishers in cultural studies. Taking the 234 current titles in the 1995–96 catalogues of the five leading publishers' cultural studies lists on both sides of the Atlantic, we divided books into substantive studies and books reviewing, critiquing or providing didactic overviews of the field. Roughly one in four fell into the second category. As cultural studies grew as a market, it would seem the appetite for titles outgrew the capacity of the field to undertake new work. While wary, as editors of this volume, of the charge of occupying a glass house with large and fragile windows, we cannot but reflect on the view that the imperative driving much cultural studies work derives, at least in part, from 'the fantasies of the marketing managers of a handful of anglophone publishing houses' (Schwarz, 1994: 386). The line between productivity and superfluity is a thin one. The problem is not mere redundancy, but the inward-looking narcissism that threatens innovativeness, openness and sensitivity to other fields of work. Indeed, realization of this may be contributing to the current revisionist climate and calls for a 'return' to a more social science approach.

Divergences in underlying assumptions and analytical categories are manifest in the different routes cultural studies has pursued in the UK, the USA, Latin America, Australia and elsewhere. Each reflects its particular history and zeitgeist, and, perhaps surprisingly, nowhere is this more evident than when work in the UK and the USA is compared. The notion that shared language, literature and theoretical gurus have produced an Anglo-American cultural studies hegemony is questionable, if not inaccurate.

Few would dispute that cultural studies' 'myths of origin' were made in Britain, or that their 'founding fathers' were Raymond Williams, Richard Hoggart and E.P. Thompson, and subsequently Stuart Hall. The enduring influence of Williams, in particular, on the sociology of culture as well as cultural studies, is explored here, notably by Carey, Gitlin and Murdock. The pioneer generation's British New Left origins profoundly influenced their quest to effect change. As Gitlin notes: 'the grid of meaning that was discerned within (or imposed upon) popular culture was imported from radical politics. It had a teleology. It was not simply conflict but "contestation", or confrontation' (Chapter 2: 29). Reflecting further on Williams's political commitment to gain intellectual acceptance for examining everyday cultural practice, Murdock (Chapter 6: 87) adds that Williams recognized that: 'The problem of how to build a shared culture that spoke to the needs of a complexly divided society, however, could not be properly addressed without a detailed engagement with concrete issues of policy', though he also adds how Williams's theoretical demands never produced in his own work the detailed empirical inquiries this engagement required. But support for cultural studies in the UK also grew from frustration with American-style positivism and perceptions of sociology as 'bourgeois' science (a critique already begun by American sociologists such as Alvin Gouldner). The abandonment of sociology was not without problems, however. As Harris (1992: 15) concludes, 'what is extraordinary about the break with sociology is how selective the treatment of sociology has been', citing the invisibility of early formative Giddens in the cultural studies canon as an example.

The later travels of cultural studies in the UK roamed from Leavisism through phenomenology, enthnomethodology, Lévi-Strauss structuralism,

Althusser, Gramsci, post-Marxism, psychoanalytic and other strands of French literary theory, postmodernism and, most recently, the politics of identity, postcolonialism and post-nationalism. Defending the record of a field that clearly believes it is better to travel than arrive, Hall (cited in Morley and Chen, 1996: 150, 263) affirms that inclusivity is one of cultural studies' most positive, primary characteristics seen in a teleological light as a necessity for cultural studies to remain "open-ended". A thought Fiske echoes in lauding refusal 'to produce or accept canonized criteria for defining either its boundaries or its center: while the field is not formless, its topography is far from fixed, so that any position within it can claim to occupy higher or more central ground than others' (Fiske, 1996: 370). Such fancy epistemological footwork and incredible lightness of practitioner-being, 'eclecticism' and 'relativism' are not without their critics (see, for example, Eagleton (1996) and several essayists here).

In the USA the picture was and is different. In America, as in the UK, the area of media and cultural analysis that called itself cultural studies sprang from concerns specific to its own history. Reflecting on the genesis of American cultural studies and its roots in Dewey and American pragmatism, James Carey stresses its particularity, because 'the culture, intellectual and otherwise, in which it was embedded was distinctive', cautioning further that the US model is 'useful only in those places where positive science had become paradigmatic of the culture as a whole' (Chapter 1: 4).

American cultural studies differs further on the basis of its political culture and national mythology. The dualism embedded in a core culture of pluralism and 'e pluribus unum' still marks ethnicity or race as the deepest cleavage lines. Whereas class *qua* class is text and subtext in the UK (from the Registrar General's five population 'classes' to 'EastEnders', the BBC's most-watched television soap), and class relationships and regional identities are the foundation of social life, class is a largely absent category in American public, private or scholarly discourse. Its elision is due in part to the lingering legacy of the Red Menace, Marx and the Evil Empire, but also to shared beliefs that (almost) everyone is 'middle class' and only a residual category of non-persons qualify as the 'underclass'. Class in the American context is seen primarily as the product and consequence of individual enterprise rather than that of a complexly configured historical, social and political economic location. The absence of class analysis also is attributed to American 'exceptionalism' as defined by the absence of a strong labour movement or socialist party (Lipset, 1996: 23). A situation that goes someway towards explaining why US cultural studies gives 'class' such a wide berth.

What is unquestionable is that the USA is where cultural studies has achieved its greatest institutional following in terms of student numbers, courses and book sales, but not without some cost of reification. As Davies asserts (1995: 158), 'the way in which cultural studies as a Thing has been co-opted in the United States raises quite a different issue from those in the UK . . . taken everywhere as an academic development, rather than a political or educational one, forgetting that many of the debates in Britain took place in the pages of *New Left Review*, *Marxism Today*, and a host of non-academic magazines and journals'.

The transatlantic differences and intersections in cultural studies concerns highlights the importance of noting, however briefly, other national and regional traditions in doing cultural and media analysis under the cultural studies umbrella. A body of work has grown apace but which only partially, or tangentially, follows the same topics, tropes or frames of the USA or the UK.

Two cases that illustrate the richness of cultural studies work beyond the Anglo-American axis are those of Latin America and Australia. In Latin America, scholars have traced the distinctive image of their countries' popular cultural practice based on adaptation and transformation of a mixture of indigenous and imported (largely American) popular culture products. Much of the research and theoretical literature developed is in response to the search for answers to questions about media and democracy, and the creation of a more multi-vocal public sphere (Fox, 1996). Avoiding old theoretical dualisms of power-holders and powerless, Latin American scholars such as García Canclini (1995) and Martín-Barbero (1993, 1988) have proposed analytical categories such as syncretism, hybridization and *mestizaje* (mixing of Indian and Spanish heritage) to clarify processes of cultural appropriation, adaptation and vocalization in the mediation between cultural practice, popular culture, democratic media and politics.

Australia offers another site of location-specific theory and method. Uncharacteristic of the wider dearth of cultural and media policy analysis, pointedly critiqued by McQuail in Chapter 3, the policy literature is a substantial strand in Australian cultural studies. Leading cultural theorist, Tony Bennett has consistently called for a more widespread policy practice in reminding cultural studies that it is 'committed to examine cultural practices in terms of their intrication with and within relations of power' (Bennett, 1992a: 23) an injunction both Cunningham (1992) and O'Regan (1993) observe in demonstrating the relevance of policy study for understanding the politics, economics and total culture of Australia's media and cultural industries, journalism and regulatory regime.

Disquiet within: cultural studies' debate with itself

The mid-1990s southern hemisphere is also the site of what might be called an emergent 'alternative' cultural studies (see, *inter alia*, Chen, 1996). Diasporic dissatisfaction at the Anglo-American focus of much debate is reflected more centrally in the ongoing 'whither cultural studies' debate and the literature explosion that has accompanied it from the late 1980s to the present. And while no direct causal connection can be made between the considerable critical mass (in both senses) of texts and articles, some correlation exists between cultural studies' current condition of publicly re-examining its own entrails and the momentum of sociological revisionism under way. Cultural studies' debates with itself and growing unease with the textualist and postmodernist trends that facilitated the moving away of cultural analysis from its substantive political, social and material roots raise further questions. As internal dust storms continue to swirl, perhaps the notion of a cross-national, like the notion of cross-disciplinary, cultural studies is oxymoronic. When all boundaries are 'essentialist' and epistemological eclecticism is canonical, out of many throats does not always come one clear chorus.

The propensity to produce amending formulae is congruent with doctrinal attachment to methodological eclecticism. As the earlier strand of progressive and left-leaning political-empirical work was superseded by the 'turn' to popular culture and textualism, a patchwork of methods was stitched together from the 'new' ethnography, phonemic analysis, semiotics, deconstruction, rhizomatics, psychoanalysis and more recently, autobiography (a development returned to later). Only in recent times has there been a move among the cognoscenti to return to more social science, empirical modes of inquiry. In the spirit of what might be called 'episto-methodological nostalgia', there is a growing argument for resurrecting the sociological methods of the 1970s for rediscovery in the 1990s.

This volume contains two thoughtful contributions to this internal debate. Angela McRobbie (Chapter 11), calling upon feminist theory to reconnect with more sociological and policy-relevant questions, urges a more applied feminist cultural studies armed with data and empirical facts as 'a prerequisite for engagement in certain kinds of political discussion, however precious little attempt has been made so far to explore how poststructuralism can be made use of more productively' (Chapter 11: 170), and argues for a return to the 'three Es': the empirical, the experiential and the ethnographic. David Morley (Chapter 8) offers a critical examination of cultural studies' orthodoxies and makes a case for 'putting sociology back in'. The pursuit of ethnography, postmodernity, constructivist epistemology, textualist form of discourse theory with 'little regard for questions of socio-economic determination' has been problematic, he concludes, and North American cultural studies notably so, with its tilt to postmodernism and deconstructionist literary theory. He makes a powerful case for a cultural studies based on the combination of 'sociological materialism, epistemological realism and methodological pragmatism' (Morley, Chapter 8: 122).

One of the most celebrated, if perhaps least likely, practitioners to come out of the sociological closet is John Fiske, proponent of 'semiotic democracy' and audience empowerment. While not abandoning earlier positions, recent work suggests something of a founding father's revisionism. Fiske (1994a: 9) cites Williams's call for 'culture is a whole way of life' and calls for closer attention to be paid to the media's social agency role in the material world. In recommending policy analysis of cultural studies' texts, Fiske demonstrates the wheels of epistemological reinvention in motion.

Whatever lies ahead, it is clear the era of cultural studies expansionism of the past decade is ending. In part this has been foreshadowed by discontent within and crossfire around the edges of the diaspora. Although the facility to reinvent by means of grafting critique on to earlier interests, methods or theories is regularly saluted as a sign of internal vitality by its proponents, for those outside it can also signal clear signs of factionalism and fragmentation.

Disquiet without: the watching disciplines pose questions

Alongside this introspective debate there has been a continuing rumble of concern, occasionally spilling over into exasperation, from outside cultural studies. Traditional disciplines, not unexpectedly, have expressed distaste for the upstart pretensions of a field of study which has commanded such enviable affection from students and publishers alike. On occasion, the malice and vehemence of such hostility has been startling. But the underlying commentary was to the effect that cultural studies was ignorant of significant developments elsewhere in academia, thus very often self-importantly re-inventing the conceptual wheel of cultural analysis.

Wolff (1993), writing from within sociology, regrets that sociology itself has had little to say about art and culture. However, in filling the vacuum, cultural studies has moved to an idealist 'over enthusiastic abandonment of structure, causality, and the "real" world'. In her view, 'the expansion of cultural studies, especially in the United States, is to some extent based on this textualising shift, whose consequences are both a depoliticisation of the original project of cultural studies, and the transformation of what should be a sociological critical study into a new hermeneutic' (Wolff, 1993: 149–50). Important to the puzzled commentary of many sociologists, especially in the UK, was the apparent retreat from class as an axial principle of social analysis. The close, and sometimes exclusive, attention paid to questions of gender, sexuality or race by an analytical tradition still in some kind of debate with Marxism seemed to others to have lost sight of fundamental questions of structured inequality (see Murdock, Chapter 6; Garnham, Chapter 4).

The deepening frown on the forehead of a number of neighbour pursuits was prompted by impatience with the insularity and apparent ignorance of their own endeavours within the increasingly self-enclosed and self-defined world of cultural studies. Audience researchers were astonished at claims that the discovery of qualitative work with cultural consumers was wholly new, when they thought they had been doing it for years. Anthropologists, especially those engaged in the 'new ethnography', were puzzled by the variety of practices labelled 'ethnographic' by cultural studies in its 'turn' to the audience and to empirical work (see Morley, Chapter 8). In social psychology, the remaking of the discipline around notions of discourse has still to enter into the vision of writers using a much looser notion of discourse within cultural studies (see Billig, Chapter 13). Similarly, as Jameson notes, 'the historians seem particularly perplexed by the somewhat indeterminable relationship of the cultural people to archive material', and cites Catherine Hall's anxiety that cultural history has been ignored by cultural studies with serious consequences (Jameson, 1993: 18). Only slowly, however, was this work seeping into the cultural studies' consciousness, at least among its toiling multitudes.

The critique from without has not been restricted, of course, to the conference hall and journal debate. Academia is itself in the political fray, and in the utilitarian temper of both UK and US politics of recent years the expansive success of cultural studies has inevitably drawn fire. The recent expansion of cultural studies in the UK has been part of the deliberate force-fed increase in the number of full-time university students from 563,000 to 930,000 between 1988 and 1994. At the same time the atrophy of some traditional disciplines in the humanities and social sciences has left a space for newer, and superficially glamorous fields, to mop up student demand. The expansion of these popular areas of study has not been without its opponents, and the subject continues to struggle for legitimacy in a political culture which is now almost obsessively utilitarian in its approach to education. One Minister for Education proclaimed 'I have ordered an inquiry . . . to try to find out why some young people are turned off by the laboratory, yet flock to the seminar room for a fix of one of those contemporary pseudo-religions like media studies . . . For the weaker minded, going into a cultural Disneyland has an obvious appeal' (Patten, 1993: 14). In 1995 and 1996 a flurry of articles in the national press attacked media and cultural studies when it was revealed that university applications to study in these areas continued to rise.

In the UK this attack has not indulged in the luxury of differentiating the sub-areas of cultural and media studies. While those in the field may enjoy demarcation disputes, to the new utilitarianism such subtleties had little substance, and it became clear that there was a necessity for the recurrent defence of a broad body of scholarship against an offensive which had little patience for the delicacies of dissent examined here.

In the USA criticism of the academy in the 1990s has focused more on questions of curriculum change and cultural diversity than journalism, communication or cultural studies enrolments. The debates around the so-called 'culture wars' have centred on positions for or against issues such as 'Western greats', 'identity politics', 'eurocentrism' or 'ethnic studies' (see, for example, Gitlin, 1995; Shohat and Stam, 1994). In a land where 'freedom' is iconic and individualistic, and where students (not the government) pay the fees, attacks on degree choices *per se* are rare.

The critics converge: questions of method, motive and meaning

So, as criticism, both from within and without, of the 'cultural studies project' began to mount, the central features of this critique became clearer. First, the charge of 'textualism' acquired a wider currency as a wholesale concern about the apparent idealist epistemology of much cultural studies analysis. Despite discussion of culture as a way of life, bequeathed by the Raymond Williams's legacy, most cultural studies' work focused on media artifacts, or the output of cultural practice rather than its conduct. Williams's own injunction that 'we should look not for the components of a product but for the conditions of a practice' (Williams, 1980: 48) was seldom heeded. Production in particular vanished from view, to such an extent that by 1992 a notable exponent of the musicological end of cultural studies, Simon Frith, could reflect regretfully that the study of popular music was only thriving because of the input from anthropology and sociology, work whose importance is 'because it focuses on an area and issue systematically (and remarkably) neglected by cultural studies: the rationale of cultural production itself, the place and thought of cultural producers' (Frith, 1992: 178). Cultural activities became texts to be read, rather than institutions or acts to be analysed. As ever there are exceptions. Reception, as distinct from production, of culture, came to occupy a major place in the cultural studies vision. In a reawakened enthusiasm for empirical work, studies of the audience for cultural goods reflected an 'ethnographic turn' in the route-march of cultural studies. Indeed, cultural production was now seen to occur in the engagement of reader with text; the 'moment of cultural production' was in its reading. Yet somehow this was too easy a rewriting of social dynamics. As Stuart Hall put it, it was time to 'return the project of cultural studies from the clean air of meaning and textuality and theory to the something nasty down below' (Hall, 1992: 278).

It was as though culture had entirely lost its moorings from the bedrock of history. Social structure, political force, economic dynamics, all appeared to have been evaporated by the intense heat of textual 'interrogation'. Of course, much of this arose, especially in the UK, from the ticklish business of dealing with the base-superstructure analogy so troubling for the Marxist legacy (see Chapters 4 and 6 by Garnham and Murdock, respectively). But this debate was seldom in mind in the mass production of ever more evanescent readings of popular culture from Madonna to mall. Allied to this was the critical observation that the texts being pursued with such analytical energy were, in the main, limited in scope, most especially to the moving image media. Newspapers and printed texts generally seemed of less and less interest. Occasional forays into the popular novel or teenage magazine aside, the overwhelming mass of attention was to popular television, cinema and video.

The second strand of criticism attached to the theoreticism of cultural studies work. In part this was a familiar jibe about jargon and language, only too regularly encountered by anyone working in theoretical mode in the humanities or social sciences. But the justification for jargon is that it provides for a precision of description, a battery of concepts or terms allowing more accurate and meaningful analysis. In cultural studies, too often the opposite was true, the language facilitating a looseness and imprecision only too easily masked by the opacity of the syntax and vocabulary deployed. The indigestible mix which emerged as ingredients were selected from French structuralism, Gramscianism and psychoanalysis provided an easy target for critics ready to deflate any rising balloon of academic pretension. The apparent use of 'a pointlessly obscure and convoluted style' (Howe, 1994: 40), allied to a cunning use of inverted commas to convey a notion that terms used carried complex and expanded meanings hidden to all but the tutored reader, produced a literature of growing opalescence and diminishing clarity. Certain terms became the coded cant of imprecise analysis. Such concepts as 'terrain', 'site of struggle', 'problematic' (as a noun), 'configuration', 'articulation', 'moment', 'project', 'turn', all lost any focus with which they had been endowed in the literatures from which they were borrowed, and became merely the calling cards of the cognoscenti.

But theoreticism is a harsher charge than mere affectation. Looking back on cultural studies' anti-empiricist attempt to engage with power, which it found not in the citadels of capital and oaklined chambers of state, but in the mysteries of language and meaning, Schwarz notes how 'a dazzling and on the whole fruitful eclecticism was shadowed by fantasies of intellectual omniscience in which theory itself would unlock the deep secrets of 'the totality'' (Schwarz, 1994: 383). The constant distancing from the material simplicities of history and politics seemed to compel a retreat into levels of abstraction in which theory was an end in itself. Endless appeals to an unexplicated 'complexity' remind the reader that nothing is as it seems, that the cultural studies text signals, but cannot for the moment deliver, a limitless elaboration of what had previously seemed self-evident.

Third, and not unrelated to linguistic affectation, was a form of analysis highly dependent on metaphor. Davies (1995: 116) has noted the recurrence of horticultural and military metaphors in Gramsci's work, and the elaboration of this usage in cultural studies is discussed productively in Chapter 10 by Jensen and Pauley. Now, as Hall reminds us, 'metaphors are serious things. They affect one's practice' (Hall, 1992: 282). But the metaphor as second order construct, without which no form of analysis is possible, is different from the metaphor as mere likeness, the suggestive semblance of reality but not its analytical construction. What is one to make of the claim, for example, that 'Cultural practices are places where a multiplicity of forces (determinations and effects) are articulated' (Grossberg, 1993: 90)? The use of physical and spatial metaphors is always fraught, of course; the endless difficulties unleashed by the widespread adoption and exposition of Habermas's notion of the public sphere is a case in point. But analysis by metaphor poses exceptional problems within cultural studies, precisely because of the uneasy drift into theoreticism and idealism already noted.

Take such a major text as *Policing the Crisis* (Hall et al., 1978), one of the most creative and incisive of early UK works in the field and still a much cited cultural studies' seminal text. Yet, insightful though its unpicking of British political developments in the post-war period to 1975 undoubtedly is, almost any selection at random reveals a dependence on analysis by metaphor, which is bound to sound alarm bells in the mind of the reading historian or sociologist. Can we really depend on appeals to 'the spirit of the times' (ibid.: 237) as a historical or materialist explanandum? What are we to make of the repeated appearance of abstract nouns as the subjects of sentences, and thus as the apparent agencies of history? 'Intellectual liberalism threw in the sponge without a fight' (ibid.: 242). Who, how, when, one immediately wants to know. 'The counter culture was . . . directed at the superstructures of modern capitalism. . . . It demanded, above all, a revolution in consciousness' (ibid.: 254). What was this 'it' that did the demanding?

Now this is a dangerous game, and perhaps too easy, and few of us could escape similar selective exposure. At the other end of this rope lies the possibly apocryphal but appealingly indicative, supposed response of Paul Lazarsfeld to Wright Mills's famous first sentence in *The Sociological Imagination* (1959). To Mills's opening flourish, 'Nowadays men often feel that their private lives are a series of traps', Lazarsfeld is held to have responded with a query as to 'how many men, which traps, how often do they feel this?' in a charmingly ironic capture of the empiricists' impulse (though without a more recent sensitivity as to issues of gender). Nonetheless the issue is what kind of explanation of cultural and social process cultural studies is able to offer. The idealism and imprecision inherent in analysis by metaphor pose particular questions for the status of the cultural studies text.

The political and the popular: pleasure, resistance and power

During the 1980s cultural studies' embrace of a new form of political populism, predicated on the power of popular culture and its consumers, began to raise the first serious questions about the scope and utility of its modes of media and cultural analysis. This period, in retrospect, demonstrated cultural studies at the outermost point of its trajectory from a starting point in the cultural practices of the material world. As 'style' triumphed over economy and society as mediating agencies, a new politics of meaning and 'resistance' was discovered in accounts acclaiming audience power to read meaning into television and other texts. The impact of what Mukerjee and Schudson (1991) call 'the power of the ordinary' on the intellectual agenda of cultural studies is difficult to overstate. Indeed, the substantive questions remain those of correctly identifying 'the ordinary' and whether power and the social are appropriately analysed, a caution Silverstone (1994: 992) points out is relevant for both cultural studies and the sociology of culture. The triumph of cultural choice and aesthetics over issues of inequality and democracy, the 'realpolitik' of government and market practices, widening structural inequalities between nations or groups or the impact of an infotainment ethic on news journalism appears to be total. The impact of all these mediating factors on cultural choice, cultural fashion and consumption had little or no place in the cultural studies theoretical universe.

By making audience popularity a criterion of worth, and raising consumer choice to the status of holy writ, it proved difficult to avoid the conclusion that cultural studies was offering an academic echo of the neo-Adam Smith philosophy as retailed by supply-side Reaganomics. This confusion, according to Gitlin (Chapter 2), 'while seeming to defend the people against capitalism comes to echo the logic of capitalism . . . the model of contemporary politics inherent in cultural studies is, finally, self-confirming' (Chapter 2: 37). This is a judgement Jim McGuigan (Chapter 9) extends when he notes how economic theory has been transposed 'on to a cultural plane, a plane that tended to be seen as almost entirely autonomous from any actual economy and polity . . . a transposition . . . with no recourse to an economy conceived in terms of the circulation of wealth is a curious form of theoretical repression' (Chapter 9: 140).

Thus the contradictions of cultural studies' power-to-the-people style of populism juxtaposes its hurrahs for cultural choice and audience empowerment with a *non sequitur* conclusion: pleasure alone constitutes resistance to its sources, a position difficult to sustain given the prior media and cultural market interventions by infotainment organizations or government policies. Arguing that cultural studies is in fact conformist, Mulhern (1995: 34–5) correctly observes, a form of populism that insists on 'the active and critical element in popular cultural usages . . . tends to overlook the overwhelming historical realties'. In this case, the shaping and packaging of most urban popular culture today results from sophisticated celebrity and product marketing on the part of media organizations before any element of consumer choice enters the marketplace.

The second dimension in the political critique is the inevitable suppressing force on the energies and innovation of a field which comes with institutionalization. Success breeds inertia and insularity. The establishment of the full apparatus of associations, journals, conferences, departments and networks reinforces both a siege mentality and at the same time a loss of interaction and engagement with work elsewhere. The least productive aspect of this has been cultural studies' growing fascination with its own life story, a continuous rehearsal of foundation myths and intellectual biography, which has all the appeal and significance of the premature memoirs of an adolescent prodigy. As Barker and Beezer point out, cultural studies, 'rather like a football star at twenty five, is busy writing its autobiography' (Barker and Beezer, 1992: 3). There seems a certain *folie de grandeur* in the incessant disinterring of the founding fathers, and a picking over the ground of 1960s Birmingham. Detailed histories of who moved where, and taught whom, are respectfully narrated as if unveiling the mysteries of daily life in Plato's Academy (see, for example, Bennett, 1996).

Third, and perhaps more fundamental to the political critique of cultural studies, is its ironic retreat from politics *per se*. The 'project' of cultural studies has always and explicitly been as an intervention in political life, as a contribution to the unmasking of ideology and as the liberation from oppression of those subject to its repressive power. The journal *Cultural Studies* proclaims its mission as

> propelled less by a theoretical agenda than by its desire to construct possibilities, both immediate and imaginary, out of historical circumstances; it seeks to give a better understanding of where we are so that we can create new historical contexts and formations which are based on more than just principles of freedom, equality, and the distribution of wealth and power.

Now this is a brave and compelling standard to fly, and much courageous and effective work has been prompted by it. Yet to many observers the actual practice of cultural studies, especially in recent years when its distant origins in the British New Left of the 1960s, the workers' education movement, or the radical politics of US pioneers discussed by Carey in Chapter 1, seems almost invisible, and has largely departed from such an engagement. To the American radical historian Robert McChesney, 'cultural studies has given us much hype, but little action . . . due to the marginalization of explicitly radical politics' (McChesney, 1995: 2).

Cultural studies has always been resolutely focused on the links between culture and power, especially as detectable in popular culture. But this credo seems little evident in the torrent of dissection of the epiphenomena of popular culture and everyday practice in which the dynamics of power, inequality and oppression seem obscured. In retreat from the crudities of economic reductionism and the base-superstructure model, cultural studies' construction of culture has become entirely detached from economics, and largely from politics too. Downing, in Chapter 12, questions the curious absence of cultural studies from any critical assessment of the epochal changes in Eastern Europe over the last decade, despite, as he explains, the centrality of cultural processes and institutions in the seismic shifts experienced in those societies. Thomas, in Chapter 5, returns us to the central concept of dominant ideology, which, she argues, has been misunderstood and misused by both cultural studies and its critics.

The guilty dilemma of the intellectual is always that of commentator, of witness, unsure that the pen really is the mightier. Cultural studies is not alone in this. But the contrast between proclaimed mission and practice has acute difficulties for cultural studies. Partly this is the fruits of its debate with Marxism, at least in the UK context, and with the axial principle of class as the locus of primary social difference. In wresting itself from that canon, cultural studies often loses all purchase on the institutional and structural context of cultural practice. Thus, even when dealing with other fault-lines in social stratification, the loss of political dynamic has been a source of intense irritation. Sivanandan, reflecting on recent work on race, pours scorn on 'theoretical practitioners', working simply on textuality, who have lowered their sights 'from changing the world to changing the word' (Sivanandan, 1990: 49).

Concrete instances of this arise in the debate about cultural studies' failure to impact on, or even engage with, matters of cultural policy. At a time when debates such as those over the contradictory imperatives of state policy to unleash market forces but to contain cultural licence, the current uncertainty in much of the world over the definition and institutional future of public service broadcasting, the continuing advance of multinational corporate control of cultural production, the dithering attempts to arrive at cultural policy that matters in bodies national, regional and global are all at the forefront of political dispute, but where are the insights and interventions of cultural studies?

This question has indeed been posed from inside cultural studies, as noted earlier, but is discussed from a different perspective by McGuigan in Chapter 9, where he calls for a policy perspective that engages with macro processes.

'Cultural studies must be imaginative, it must propose alternatives, different ways of ordering the social and cultural worlds' (McGuigan, Chapter 9: 153). McQuail, in Chapter 3, develops this theme. His aim is 'to speak up for the need to revive an "applied" version of critical cultural study' which he contrasts with the dominant version of cultural studies which claims to fulfill a critical role but chooses not to engage with cultural issues on the policy agenda (McQuail, Chapter 3: 41).

This line of critique is not unrelated, of course, to the difficult business of value. As McQuail reminds us, value matters. In Frow's words, 'There is no escape from the discourse of value' (Frow, 1995: 134). The discovery, in the name of resistance, of an inexhaustible capacity for subversion and selective reception among audiences does not remove the obligation and analytical necessity of addressing the question of value. McGuigan, too, in castigating such an approach as populist, notes that the call for a return to questions of cultural value has yet to receive a response, and most probably requires concrete sociological research to provide one. Most of all, he insists, 'questions of value, quality, and truth are necessary to ask' (McGuigan, Chapter 9: 148). Cultural studies has to face this particular problem because of the awkward double realization of the notion of value derived from both aesthetic and also economic analysis. Torn between the two, too often cultural studies has evaded both.

Beyond cultural studies: the way forward, or more than one way forward?

If, indeed, cultural studies is in transition, its current stage of evolution is much preoccupied with questions of collective identity. Now identity is a notoriously slippery and multi-dimensional concept, that ranges in this case from the identity of cultural studies itself to those of its theorists and constituencies: the dialogues of difference or sameness within the discourses of feminism, ethnicity, sexual orientation, Eurocentrism, the diasporic, the post-colonial and the post-national. The embrace of identity, and its excavation from the bedrock of personal history, adds perhaps another mile or two to cultural studies' movement away from its own intellectual 'roots', roots once firmly planted in the social and material, not the self-actualizing, world.

This latest interest-shift sometimes comes dangerously close to establishing an intellectual autarchy, where autobiography can become its own auto-didactic method cum theory within a self-sufficient conceptual environment. A focus on the micro rather than the macro, coupled with an introspective fascination with the practice rather than the outcomes of cultural studies as a mode of inquiry, can be seriously constrictive, not least in creating a self-validating logic that has the added convenience of permitting inferences to be drawn about nationalism, colonialism, inter-group or transnational power relations and the global market, without reference to empirical (as opposed to personal–historical) data. Cultural studies' populism rightly stands accused of Blake's Folly, or becoming what it beheld.

In this introduction to the collection of essays that follows we have attempted to trace the main routes of cultural studies' travels thus far, and signal some of the successes and problems that have arisen along the way. We have also attempted to clarify some of the major issues at the heart of current internal and external debates about cultural studies' ends and purposes, very much in evidence inside and outside its ranks. If the current spasm of re-evaluation in the field as a whole is one reason for this book's appearance, it is also a phase that provokes a certain aura of *déjà vu* as cultural studies struggles with signs of 'bringing sociology back in' (and economics) to its conceptual purview. Having said that, it is not possible to generalize where there are exceptions to every one within each national, regional or difference group. Each sees itself through the prism of a different history, cultural tradition and political context. Criticized for doing what it does best – responding to the questions of the moment from multiple starting positions – can lead to some understandable defensiveness among cultural studies' advocates.

Despite these caveats, the problems with cultural studies, adumbrated by its growing army of critics, do represent a substantial charge sheet. But it is important to recognize the limits and dangers to such critique. The myopia of which cultural studies sometimes stands accused is not unique to that field alone. Many critics are frequently, and often with some justice, accused in turn by cultural studies of ignoring both the breadth and diversity of work within the field, and its own readiness to respond to identified lacunae or partiality. Here, the evolution and history of cultural studies in North America, the UK, Latin America, Asia and elsewhere is highly distinctive, and more attention needs to be given to their particularities.

Equally, it has become clear that new forms of analysis are needed to energize research and theory in an era of new communication technologies and global–local information and entertainment exchange. As a number of authors argue here, the least satisfactory approach is to perpetuate a false dichotomy between a cultural studies fixated on populism and difference and a monotheistic political economy fixated on class and economics. Kellner, in Chapter 7, explores the possibilities of what he terms a 'multiperspectival' approach which overcomes such dichotomies, one among several proposals designed to move beyond a perennial mutual caricature that allows each side to mount the barricades and declare itself the Saviour of critical research while labelling the other a False God.

The definitive history of cultural studies and its contribution to critical discourse remains to be written, but growing pessimism about its future has made this an exciting time to work with the distinguished contributors whose chapters follow. Although we can make no claims that they cover all the issues currently on the critical agenda, we can and do claim that they offer a provocative and productive analysis of cultural studies' contributions to our field of media and cultural analysis. There are lessons here for all our scholarly and research agendas on the eve of the twenty-first century.

PART I

QUESTIONS AND CRITIQUE

1

Reflections on the Project of (American) Cultural Studies

James W. Carey

This is a real revolution . . . I am a genuine revolutionary; they (the Democrats) are the genuine reactionaries.

Newt Gingrich

The democrats thought the enemy had been overcome when they had conjured him away in imagination, and lost all understanding of the present in their inactive glorification of the anticipated future, and of the deeds they had up their sleeves but did not yet wish to display publicly.

Marx, *The Eighteenth Brumaire*

A clash of doctrines is not a disaster but an opportunity.

Alfred North Whitehead

A predictable but nonetheless disquieting outcome of three decades of political change and agitation is that conservatives are in the political saddle virtually everywhere, forcing all political positions to contest on terrain they have defined. When Newt Gingrich, the Republican House leader, describes himself not as a conservative but a revolutionary, he presents the ultimate political oxymoron: the first self-styled American radical to occupy a position of genuine power in Washington is on the right wing of a right-wing party.

This perverse outcome did not result from anything done on the campus (with one critical exception to be mentioned later) or from any academic movement or 'theory'. Still there is a paradox to be confronted: over the period that cultural studies, as a take on media and many other things, was establishing itself in the American university and coming to a dominant position in the humanities, and while political economy was going through something of a revival in academic studies, American culture, political and otherwise (and not America alone), was turning sharply toward the right. The culture, as a whole, was, to twist some lines of Marx, undertaking a world-historical necromancy, cloaking itself in the mantle of a revolutionary past as the way to make the poetry of its future (Marx, 1974: 147–9). But the poet of that future, the prophet of the withering away of the state and the new technological (and mediacentric) civilization emerging from its ashes 'which blind men everywhere are trying to suppress' is not Marx but, hold on, Alvin Toffler. This alone gives substance to the late Christopher Lasch's remark, '. . . we are winning the argument but losing the culture'.

All the Western democracies have entered the post-communist period less confident about their basic institutions and values than at any time since the end of World War II. In continental Europe there is deep estrangement from established political elites and antiliberal movements mindful of interwar fascism enjoy levels of support not seen since the 1930s. There is a deep political cynicism in the United States that lurks behind conservative triumphs, and American citizens have decided to go it on their own, to seek market-driven, private solutions to every collective problem and thereby to eliminate the need of the state or public life in every way possible.

The only cheery aspect of the paradoxical relation of the academy and the society is that it provides us with a propitious moment for some reflection and stocktaking, a moment to reconsider cultural studies and political economy as a means of grasping and understanding the mass media and, simultaneously and inevitably, a way of being in the world. This will require my speaking out of some parochial experience (and revealing a heady amount of naivete), not because that experience is privileged, but only because it provides a convenient peg on which to hang a story. The reflection will also require some history, however implicit and truncated, of the American political ambience of the last 35 years.

I

Cultural studies these days embraces an astonishing number of people and positions (no one has managed to register the trademark) but can be divided, if only as an initial convenience, into two broad camps: one that draws primarily on continental sources and regularly invokes names like Althusser, Derrida, Foucault, Deleuze and Guttari; and one that draws primarily on American sources and regularly invokes names like Dewey, James, Rorty, and Geertz. Virtually everyone in the English-speaking world appeals to the founding British triad of Williams, Hoggart and Thompson, but different groups draw quite variant lessons from them. Whichever wing of cultural studies we examine, it must be remembered they represent loose, shifting and occasional coalitions of scholars, particularly in communications. While British cultural studies had an identifiable locus at Birmingham with Richard Hoggart and Stuart Hall for a couple of decades, cultural studies today is pretty much a nowhere college, a pattern of cross-reference and mutual citation spanning a couple of continents but hardly intellectually dominating on any campus.

I want to tell one small part of the story of cultural studies in the United States and use it as a peg for a commentary and critique. Somewhere around the Fall of 1963, I suggested that it made sense to group together as an intellectual and political position a wide variety of work under the label 'cultural studies'. The term was neutral – just a name – and the suggestion innocent and practical at once. Political economy, historical studies, work that flowed out of pragmatism and the Chicago School, such as symbolic interactionism, were being rapidly eroded, displaced and marginalized in the American academy by the power of the formal and behavioral sciences which were colonizing intellectual life with the active support of the National Science Foundation and other funding agencies. Church and state had been officially and often antagonistically divorced by constitutional mandate in the United States. Unfortunately, there was no constitutional provision prohibiting a union of science and the state. During World War II, and even more in the post-war world, that marriage had been consummated with, I thought, I still think, devastating effects on intellectual work in communications and in most other areas.

This union, and the displacement it occasioned, had more than academic consequences in the United States for it created a formidable coalition, implicitly uniting commerce, the state and the academy in a project of social reconstruction. The task of cultural studies was, then, simultaneously intellectual and political: to contest a body of theoretical and empirical work carried forward in the name of positive science *and* to contest the project of social reconstruction carried forward, implicitly or otherwise, in the name of positive knowledge.

The first task in the contest was necessarily a modest one: the creation of something of a wedge discipline: a body of work that had sufficient weight and reach to clear a space, a legitimate and central space, in the academy for work that was, broadly, historical, critical, interpretive and empirical. No one of the strands I identified, not political economy or marxism or pragmatism, had the clout to do it alone. Moreover, it would be necessary to clear this space, not an easy task, across the historical divide of the humanities and social sciences for neither of those two rough academic groupings had a purchase on the intellectual resources necessary for a general defense of a humane and progressive culture.

The project and the formation, to use Raymond Williams's phrase, had, of course, a parochial and ethnocentric twist; it might not have been necessary in any other country to initiate the contest on the scientific, as opposed to the political, front. However, science played (and plays) a role in the legitimation of social relations and possessed a moral authority in the United States that was not necessarily typical elsewhere. Within the academy, the behavioral and positive sciences dominated intellectual discourse to a degree not encountered elsewhere. This may not be immediately apparent from a distance. Many American intellectual figures who influenced social theory and communications studies around the world – C. Wright Mills, Erving Goffman, Peter Berger and post-Schutzian ethnomethodologists, Alvin Gouldner, Kenneth Burke, David Riesman, the Frankfurt School, including Herbert Marcuse – were, in the early 1960s, virtually without influence within the American academy, their devotees confined within isolated enclaves or cult followings without impact on the curriculum or the general intellectual outlook of the culture. Within communications studies in particular, these figures were decidedly marginal and offered no threat to the rigorously positivist outlook of the 'discipline'. Mills, in particular, was a tragic and isolated figure at the time of his death. While he and others mentioned above became more prominent in the Vietnam era, they did not have a decisive and shaping influence on their respective disciplines and, more to the point, did not shape public discourse on fundamental questions of social life.

The project of American cultural studies had to be distinctive because the culture, intellectual and otherwise, in which it was embedded was distinctive. The project of American cultural studies was limited because the formation which gave rise to it was unusual, and it would be useful only in those places where positive science had become paradigmatic of the culture as a whole.

However, for the project of cultural studies to be effective it would be necessary to suppress some immediate theoretical differences in the interest of a wider intellectual coalition, and, in Whitehead's words, to treat the inevitable clashes among resulting viewpoints as an opportunity rather than a disaster. While the task seemed to me primarily intellectual at the outset, it aimed, or so I hoped, at creating a political coalition as well: a revival of the republican and progressive tradition of American politics through wider, more powerful alliances. Those alliances, while largely on the left, had to incorporate the equally strident opposition of conservative forces – at least those forces whose sense of culture and of the economy was defined outside of the orbit of conventional liberal/capitalist thought. After all, it was conservatives who had made the sharpest critiques of media and mass culture, as even Raymond Williams admitted.

I say the suggestion was innocent and neutral because I had no particular program in mind. The term cultural studies was not in widespread use at the time in the United States or anywhere else, and had a more or less pacifistic meaning; it was an attractively impartial phrase. I picked up the phrase through Max Weber's notion of 'cultural science' (perhaps the first sign of trouble), as interpreted through Ernst Cassirer, though I thought 'science' was a horribly pretentious and misleading word for so speculative an enterprise and the word had already been colonized by the very group with which it was necessary to contest.

I had read the usual suspects, Raymond Williams and E.P. Thompson, corresponded with Richard Hoggart and was following the early work of the Centre for the Study of Contemporary Culture. It seemed that a broadly similar project was in the making and one that was not afraid, astonishing for a left-wing outlook, to acknowledge the power and influence of conservative thinkers and even to be willing to argue with them and, when they were right, to incorporate them into the project. The Centre was undertaking a broadly similar project: the creation of a wedge into the academy, the clearing of a space for a new subject that would unite marxism and political economy with modern studies in history, literature and social theory. From my initial correspondence and reading it also seemed there was room for the Canadian work of Harold Innis and even for some of the speculations of Marshall McLuhan before he went round the bend. It appeared there might be some common ground to stake: Williams and Hoggart were being widely read in the United States, though in political and social theory and not in literature departments. The Birmingham Centre had worked through the scholarship of the Chicago School, particularly in 'labeling theory', and found it useful in its early formulations of central issues in the analysis of subcultures and deviance. Even political economists had shown interest in Harold Innis and issues of space and time that derived from the urban ecology of Robert Park.

There were many intellectual divisions, of course. The Birmingham group had to wedge their way into the academy through literary studies and did not confront the overwhelming dominance of the behavioral sciences. While marxism was more prominent in their studies, just as it was and is throughout Europe, they were relatively untouched by the Frankfurt School which dominated the largely nonacademic speculation on mass culture in America. *Culture and Society* and *The Uses of Literacy* were, I thought, attempts to constitute a tradition in English studies, largely from literary sources, that was similar to what Lewis Mumford and John Dewey, among many others in the American studies movement, had done earlier, though with less satisfactory results. Williams had shown an openness to political economy in *The Long Revolution* and the Birmingham group were actively mining the social sciences, even if they did not like certain American variants thereof. Certainly, a major problem was that the tradition of pragmatism and symbolic interactionism was relatively unknown in the UK and rather too ethnocentric for British taste. Finally, there had been skirmishes between pragmatists and marxists during the 1930s that had left some bitterness in the intellectual atmosphere.

The worst possible outcome of the transatlantic influence and borrowing would be a diversionary contest over the shape of a universal theory of culture, as if everything had to be settled in order to agree on something. That contest, however futile and divisive, has been a major consequence of cultural studies. But, on my reading, cultural studies is necessarily plural, for such studies emerge within diverse conditions and must speak to the pulse, pace and texture of the cultures they seek to explain. Any attempt to dissolve cultures in the acid of culture would forfeit the capacity to form coalitions both within and without the academy. You cannot address a culture for which you lack the terms of conversation. Despite the easy talk about capitalism as a quasi-universal formation, capitalism is not only an economy but a culture. Indeed, while we can dispute the numbers, capitalism comprises, on one rendition, at least seven distinctive cultures (Hampden-Turner and Trompenaars, 1993), even in the era of globalization and global culture. While today much business is hypermobile, moving information and capital over vast distances at blinding speeds by fax and modem, such organizations still rely on geographically rooted infrastructure – legal, financial and other services – that tends to cluster in cities within nations. The continued importance of national currencies – even though such currencies are freely converted and traded – as the European Union discovers, is enough to restrain the vision of globalization. The global, in fact, is not out there; it is embedded in national regimes. As Paul Krugman (1996) has recently put it, corporations come and go but nations, whether happy or unhappy with their economic performance, do not go out of business for they have no well-defined bottom line. While nations are formed or dissolved for many reasons, economic conditions are not predominant among them. Indeed, despite all the forces seeking to transcend the nation, nations remain the sturdiest of collectivities and nationalism the most rampant ideology of the current era whether we think of it as late modern or postmodern.

Despite those reservations, and speaking only for myself, I felt at the outset, and still feel, that there was nothing in principle or in theory that prevented an integration of a variety of intellectual positions, though not necessarily the ones I mention here, under the wider and more inclusive banner of cultural studies. That coming together did not presume a merger but merely a coalition of people who had read some common books and had certain common concerns; scholars who shared a willingness to talk and a common stake in opening up academic discourse to positions which were, as I said, historical, critical and interpretive. Most of the positions I've mentioned here were antifoundational and anti-essential in outlook and there were certainly ways of reading Marx into those same assumptions. The terms of such a formation could never have been, then or now, reconciliation or divorce, to use Nick Garnham's (1995b) recent phrase, for the options open to us. If that was the choice, the result could only be an official estrangement. However, there are more relationships within academic life than consensual and antagonistic ones, a fact that the widespread influence of Thomas Kuhn's notion of a paradigm may have obscured. Intellectual positions can also be symbiotic, complementary, generously parasitic; they can feed off and into diversely unified positions, exist in happy contradiction, without attempting to secure a monopoly of knowledge.[1] Indeed, monopoly is the enemy in academic work as elsewhere, as my 'teacher' Harold Innis warned; intellectual work fruitfully advances only through diversity, the route of monopoly is the route to short-run power and long-run extinction – a lesson the academic right had to learn and still awaits the academic left.

All that was required – a tall order as it turned out – was a minimal level of consensus that would plane off sharp elbows and permit a generous measure of discursive civility. In short, it was necessary to defeat the attitude, widespread among the left then and now, that intellectual life is primarily a matter of lining up opposing teams in clearly identifiable jerseys representing smaller and smaller communities and permitting no defection from either side without screams of apostasy and talk about the true political religion. I thought of cultural studies not as a new vocabulary developed in opposition to political economy for which either reconciliation or divorce were the necessary options, but as the name of the attitude itself, a reconciling tolerance that might come about once we managed to combine in different parts of the same brain's systematic economic analysis with a new attentiveness to cultural processes.

An instructive example comes from the history of the conservative movement in the United States. For decades conservatism had been an intellectual and political movement without a social base for it understood nothing about such a social base. Conservatives lacked concrete understanding of those phenomena central to sociology and anthropology. Conservatism took-off as a political movement, rather than merely an intellectual and ideological outlook, when it actively courted, recruited and invited social scientists into the tent to correct and complete obvious deficiencies in the basis of their knowledge. In short, conservatism found that without concrete knowledge of the social (and cultural) it floundered and was ineffective when addressed to all but the congenitally committed. In incorporating sociologists, the conservative movement did not wait around until every epistemological, ontological and theoretical difference that could be conjured up among practitioners of different disciplines had been settled. Nor did they dally, at the outset, over political and temperamental differences with its new recruits. It got on with the work of the project: the development of a base of knowledge that would permit and justify the dismantling of the welfare state, the defeat of forces of collectivism and the restructuring of industry and politics. They were not deterred by concrete political differences but showed a ready willingness at accommodation, at learning from friends and foes alike, in the prosecution of larger objectives.[2] The outlines of the conservative project were evident during the very years that cultural studies was forming and certainly was beyond dispute as early as 1964 with the founding of *The Public Interest*, the first of the journals expressing this new outlook, and devoted to bringing together, at the level of public intellectual life, the resources of a broad-based, comprehensive, conservative movement.

Nothing similar happened on the left. However, and at last to get to the point, I can think of no *theoretical* reason preventing the creation of a general, generous and inclusive position on the left by whatever name. If one doesn't want to call it cultural studies, call it something else. There are no necessary intellectual differences between cultural studies and political economy (to cite only two relevant fault lines) – differences that cannot be managed as long as there is broad agreement on goals and certain civil commitments. The differences that count, as I have experienced them, the ones that made and make a difference in case after case, are not intellectual but political. The theoretical debates through which we have lived – idealism vs materialism, discourse vs structure, economy vs culture, and, most famously, base vs superstructure – seem to me to be beside the point. They are vehicles for arguing political differences in a deflected and disguised way or for competing for status within a constantly constricting and powerless intellectual orbit, for privileging one discipline (economics or literature) over another, for defending one occupational psychosis and practice over another to the impoverishment of both intellectual and political life. That has been the shared and sad outcome of both cultural studies and political economy, although there are significant exceptions.

II

Cultural studies on my reading and on the American side of the Atlantic, then, was first, and by necessity, a critique of positivism and the behavioral sciences – a critique that had less to do with scoring epistemological and methodological points than with loosening the grip of those sciences, along with the general positivistic outlook, on the culture as a whole. The critique had as its central thrust the authority of positive science as a symbolic form and its role in legitimating social action and policy. The importance of positivism was, and is, less in its narrow philosophical outlook than in the fact that it had permeated and shaped American culture as a whole, establishing the ground conditions for discourse and social policy. The failure of cultural studies (and political economy as well) from my standpoint is its inability to sustain and make effective that critique. Indeed, cultural studies by and large incorporated the most basic and troubling assumptions of the positivist tradition into its own thinking.

The difficulty here is the failure to understand the rich and contradictory nature of the positivist inheritance and its internal dialectic. Talcott Parsons's (1949) rendition of the tradition of rationalistic positivism still provides a useful starting point. The basic assumption of this tradition, most vividly expressed in classical economic theory, is also the basic belief encoded into American culture as a whole and into the political culture in particular. The assumption is the following: the ends or goals of human action are random, unknowable or, more technically, exogenous. We cannot gain rational knowledge of human ends or purposes; rational action and knowledge is necessarily confined to the fitting together of ends and means. While one can attain knowledge of the rational allocation of resources among means and toward given ends, neither the actor nor the scientist can have rational knowledge of ends: we literally cannot know why we want what we want; these wants are as given to us as to the society. All that can be determined is the rational means to satisfy subjective and arational desire. These subjective and given preferences are expressed in human action as an attempt to maximize individual pleasure or happiness in which knowledge of the 'other' emerges only as a means to that end.

One might argue that such an assumption is common to capitalism wherever the social form takes root. True enough. But the uniqueness of the United States is that such assumptions form the virtually uncontested basis of the political culture and the culture of daily life as well. Moreover, they cut across the conventional divisions of left and right. As Michael Sandel (1996a) has put it, such assumptions inform not only the economy but also the public philosophy by which we live and the conception of citizenship that informs our political debates. The central belief in such debates is that freedom consists in our capacity to choose our ends for ourselves – exogenously as it were. Politics, therefore, should not try to form the character or cultivate the virtue of its citizens, for to do so would be to legislate morality. Neither government nor any other collective form of life should affirm through law, policy or persuasion any particular conception of the good life; instead the state and other collective forms should provide only a neutral framework of rights, the means, within which people can choose their own values and ends. Where left and right tend to disagree in the United States is not on this point but on which institution – market or state – ought to be the neutral means to individual ends. Both are committed to a political economy of citizenship, to adopt Sandel's term, that is resolutely individualistic, not only in the de Tocquevillian or sentimental sense of that term, but individualistic in the technical and programmatic sense as well.

The dialectic within the positive sciences emerges at the margins of this rationalistic theory of action. At the inevitable moment that questions arise as to the source of the presumptively exogenous ends or values of action, there is but one strategy available: to drive these values out of the individual mind and locate them in the objective world – genetics, environment, society or in culture, the latter understood not as the ether within which meaning is actively constituted but as a force, generally called ideology, determining conduct. Social darwinism, which has made a hydra-headed comeback in our time as, for example, sociobiology, is an example of the first strategy; behaviorism and sociological functionalism are examples of the second and third; and much, though far from all, of cultural studies exemplifies the fourth.

The internal dialectic of positivism has played itself out notably within communications studies as periodic shiftings back and forth between power-ful effects and uses and gratifications or, in another guise, between the determining power of ideology and the active resistance of audiences. But this history, whether in the large or small, has had a common effect: the constitu-tion of the self as a subject so driven by individual need and desire or so determined by external forces as to be in principle incapable of participating in democratic life. The behavioral sciences legitimated what Jacques Ellul (1980) called a technological society: at best a managed democracy controlled by a technical elite on behalf of a citizenry rendered incapable of more ardu-ous forms of political participation. But the self within the tradition of rationalistic positivism is equally unfit for democracy. For the self so con-ceived, freedom consists solely in the capacity of people to choose their own ends and all social arrangements as mere means to be manipulated in satisfy-ing individual desire. Against this minimalist sense of a procedural democracy, one must insist on the idea central to republican theory, namely that liberty depends on sharing in self-government (see, for example, Sandel, 1996b: 58).

In summary, both poles of the positivist analysis of conduct lead to the proclamation of the end of ideology and the end of the public sphere: in one case by extolling the market as the arena of individual choice unconstrained by collective obligation; in the other by transforming the state into the col-lective source of individual desire.

But where to begin? It was my belief then that as far as communications were concerned the necessary ground for a beginning was in the niche of lan-guage and meaning, for they represented an opportunity to attack the behavioral sciences on the ground they were weakest – the analysis of culture. Therefore, it was language and meaning, not in the narrow and constricted sense of these terms but in a sense both Weberian and Wittgensteinian – language as a form of life and meaning as the constitution not merely of representation but of significance – that provided the point of origin with the greatest chance of success for it provided an opportunity to speak to both the question of determination and the question of choice.

At the outset I should declare what I hope is obvious: the emphasis on language, culture and meaning does not exclude issues of power and conflict; instead, it attempts to locate them. All societies are riddled by antimonies and contradictions: ecological, structural, and cultural. They are riddled as well by differentials of class, status and power which are as ineradicable as the biological programming and cultural resources on which they are based. The trick is to locate the mechanisms by which differentials of power and intractable conflict are buried, deflected, resolved, exercised and aggregated into interests. I remain convinced, however, that the critical relationship in societies is between centres and margins. While national borders define the critical margin in the minds of most people and nations retain the monopoly on legitimate coercion and violence (though, as importantly, nations also rely on highly ritualized forms of conduct and ceremony), national consciousness will continue to be deeper and more powerful than class consciousness and nations more solid and enduring realities than classes. Furthermore, a nation is a cultural rather than an ideological prototype; its character is the outcome of history and culture, including the history and culture of its economy, rather than of ideology. The principal power among men and women, like it or not, is still nationalism. As early as the late middle ages this began to displace religion as the strongest bond of community among large numbers of people, as Benedict Anderson (1983) has emphasized.

There are a number of forms of cultural analysis consistent with a general program of critique of positivism and the behavioral sciences. There were five moves within my own general outlook that it is helpful to note in passing. The first was to de-naturalize communication, to take it out of nature, where it had been placed by positivism, and secure it within culture, that is as a practice, hardly the only one, through which a meaningful world is constructed, deconstructed, transformed, etc. To de-naturalize communication required, in turn, that science be reconceived as a symbolic form, one among many, without a priori claims to truth and legitimacy. If science was a symbolic form constituting the world through practice, no different in principle than, say, religion, then the test of science could be the contingent, nonfoundational, nonrepresentational, pragmatic sense of truth: does science get us, in its present form, to where we want to go. On this ground alone, the anti-democratic tendencies in received views of the science of communication could be exposed when representations of communications could be seen both as a model *of* and a model *for* reality: not merely the constitution/representation of an object – this is what it is – but as a model for a social practice – this is how you do it.

Secondly, as a model of a practice, communication was conceived within the behavioral sciences as a form of transmission for the pursuit of power (influence was what it was called) or the release of anxiety. When this model of transmission was reconceived as a ritual, it stood revealed not as a means of sending messages but as the constitution of a form of life. Communication was a device for constituting the world that science pretended it merely displayed: the construction within the shell of nature of an actual body of lived experience, an invitation to live a life defined by power and anxiety as opposite sides of the same cultural coin. To reduce it to chronotopes, and to link it to an argument made somewhat differently by Raymond Williams, the space of the social became dominated by the advertising agency and the psychic garage shop, two of the practical institutions that emerge in the behavioral science dispensation.

Thirdly, the constitution of ritual form through communication is pulled off, first of all, by embedding conceptions of time and space, duration and extent, history and geography, into the model and artifacts of the process and then living, in a consummatory fashion, the very conceptions therein embedded. Far from being neutral or natural agents of a benign process, technology is an imaginative anticipation and realization of social relations embedded within a time-space container. This moves technology from a neutral and natural instrument of either progress or possibility to a determinant form of a social relation.

Fourthly, communication requires a mode of understanding actions and motives, not in terms of psychological dispositions or sociological conditions but as a manifestation of a basic cultural disposition to cast up experience in symbolic forms that are at once immediately pleasing and conceptually plausible, thus supplying the basis for felt identities and meaningfully apprehended realities. There is a normative and dialogic dimension to culture. We are not just neutral observers of cultural texts. Rather, they confront us with claims and arguments about truth and rightness to which we must give our assent or dissent. That one must begin from this phenomenological assumption does not mean that one is required to accept every identity and every version of the real that is cast up, however. It does require that one recognize that human activity, by the very nature of the human nervous system, is cultural, involving the construction of a symbolic container that shapes and expresses whatever human nature, needs or dispositions exist. (See Max Weber, 1946, for an example of such an argument made in the context of religion.)

Finally, and derivatively, human action needs to be linked with culturally constructed 'tastes' for specific styles and forms – to expressive rather than cognitive or instrumental forms of symbolism. Communication expresses, then, alternative styles of life by social groups created within the communication process itself wherein social character and identity is integrated: as a need to ritualize the unfamiliar and disconnected; a means of steadying the world, not changing it, of transforming it into satisfying drama in which one finds a meaningful life through structures of significance. From these resources one can begin to construct a phenomenology of experience around its consummatory moment. The key issue is the constitution of taste, style and form of life.

You will note that these arguments say nothing about texts. The metaphor of the text is a useful one for it emphasizes that the entire human environment can and must be read and interpreted, that all objects, technologies and places have no real existence before they are encased in symbolic forms. But my effort was not to substitute a literary, textual model of analysis for an economic one. Rather it was directed toward the construction of the forms of social relations into which people enter rather than the messages transacted within those forms. The choice of ritual over text points to practices and practical reason against poststructuralism's reduction of society to discourses. As a style of analysis, ritual was more dependent on the microsociology of Erving Goffman than the literary analysis of the critic, new or otherwise. In fact, it was an attempt to avoid the dead ends in which, it seems to me, an encoding/decoding model always ends. Beyond that it attempted to make problematic the formation of social movements bearing new social relations that form not only in relation to the state and the economy but *autogenetically* within the social process, and to emphasize that the meaning of these movements must be understood not on the model of instrumental or rational action but as the consummations of the search for identity and the formation of alternative forms of life. There are, in short, social movements and relations that form outside of production and consumption that must be circumspectly analysed.

III

It seemed to me that the program sketched above offered enormous possibilities to those scholars pursuing the political economy of the media, not possibilities in the sense of displacement but, as said earlier, the possibility of a broader based intellectual movement with strength deriving from the complementarity of positions. While my own version of cultural studies was less radical and more open to conservative voices than was political economy, it was nonetheless tendentially headed in the same direction – toward a progressive politics – and could only strengthen the hand of political economy. Nowhere did it originate in a critique of political economy. By opening up and widening the critique of behavioral science, it supplemented the tired charge of 'administrative research' with a more effective critique while at the same time widening the space in which political economy could operate. Cultural studies also offered the possibility of systematic commentary on a range of phenomena – symbolic forms, meanings, motives, technologies, social movements, popular culture – on which political economy was inevitably silent – or at least relatively so. That reach could, of course, be sacrificed to yet another debate about the base-superstructure, and so it was, as if differences of emphasis and interest, as well as strategy, could be reduced to philosophical questions. There is no resolution to such questions and so the alternative must be, not to engage the question but to outflank it, not to reformulate the base and superstructure, to find newer and cleverer ways to express 'interrelations' and 'last instances' but to side step the question entirely. The only reason I can figure for retaining either the distinction or the argument is as a pious genuflection to the past and to feel morally upright, convinced we are on the right side of history.

As I said earlier, there were no theoretical reasons why the reach of political economy could not be expanded to a more open accommodation with cultural phenomena or cultural analysis could not have become more attuned to economic complexities. But there were, alas, political reasons, reasons I would very much like to finesse, for little is to be gained by waking up the dead only to sing them a lullaby. But perhaps one episode can represent the general problem.

Earlier in the century political economy in the form of classical marxism co-existed fairly well with the cultural analysis that emerged out of pragmatism and the progressive and populist movements as represented by John Dewey. It was never an easy relationship, for Dewey had concluded, as a result of observing the Pullman strike, that in any direct confrontation between labor and capital in the United States, labor would lose. Moreover, he had, as I will outline in conclusion, great reservations about class-based political and intellectual movements. If a direct confrontation would not work and if class-based struggles were bound to deform the working class, Dewey's alternative, reforming strategy, was to struggle on the ground of culture, particularly in education and the mass media. Because he did not feel that capitalism could be defeated, perhaps he didn't want it defeated, he felt that the best we could do was contain it, check it off, prevent its characteristic social relations from infecting every sphere of the social. This was not so much a program of amelioration, though it easily could be construed as such, but a program to contain, in the words of Harold Innis, the penetrative powers of the price system. It was also an attempt to contain the persistent but dreamy belief of the left that an ideal social order – perfect equality, abolition of all authority and elites, a universal reign of love and altruism – could be achieved through political revolution.

Dewey was, of course, a dominating figure in American intellectual life both as a professional philosopher and public intellectual. He was also one of many early supporters of the experiments of the Soviet Union and during the 1930s was a frequent ally of the radical left. The trouble began, as we all know, with Trotsky and the Stalin Trials. Dewey chaired a Commission of Inquiry into the trials – his old antagonist Bertrand Russell borrowed the form during the Vietnam War – and, in the course of that investigation, traveled to Mexico City to take testimony from Trotsky. The Communist Party brought all the forces of persuasion and intimidation to bear on Dewey that it could muster in order to convince him to abandon the inquiry for the party realized that it was only through Dewey that it could reach wider currents of American sentiment and political belief. Dewey undertook the investigation anyway and the report painted a very grim and portentous portrait of the course of life in the Soviet Union and the possibilities of accommodation with the Stalin regime.[3] As a result, Dewey was visited with a campaign of vilification and the accusation of being a social fascist and, among certain elements of the left, including some in communications, that campaign of vilification never ended and spread out to anyone intellectually associated with pragmatism and American progressivism. Of course, Dewey was in good company, surrounded by other 'running dogs of capitalism' such as Norman Thomas and A. Phillips Randolf, consigned to the apostate community of social fascists (Hook, 1987).

The point is not to rehearse old grievances – though some of that inevitably creeps in – but to identify a persistent Stalinist or stalinist tendency in leftist discourse that consistently rules out of consideration issues of practical politics and social policy which have not received the imprimatur of orthodoxy. In the United States, where everything on the left is minuscule, Stalinism and stalinism remain proportionately significant presences. They have led to ingrained discursive habits of the left. It is simply unable to grapple with any intellectual issue without first of all backgrounding it in proper opinion. And so, the left has been split ever since by issue after issue: the cold war, American imperialism, Israel, race relations, Vietnam – you name it. Anti-communism and anti-anti-communism are the names often given to this division that sparked the belief that the moral support provided totalitarian and repressive regimes, and the toleration of anti-democratic practices on campus bespoke an obligatory alienation and contempt for Western political institutions. I am not going to produce yet another orthodoxy on these matters except to record the obvious fact: by putting politics outside of discussion, and insisting that intellectual work proceed within an a priori view of proper leftist belief – conveyed between the lines, parenthetically, or with knowing glances and smiles – all sorts of intellectual alliances have been foreclosed at the outset, most importantly in this case an alliance between political economy in the United States, where these habits were finely wrought, and cultural studies.

The issue of course is the obligatory marxism or neomarxism that in different forms provides the background for both political economy and cultural studies as they today are conventionally understood. But marxism, neo or otherwise, is not only an intellectual movement but a political and ideological one as well. In the concrete practices of daily life it is a movement that has permitted relatively narrow ranges of deviance, not only on primary questions such as the capitalist economy but on secondary ones as well. Political economy has come to an interest in the public sphere rather late in its life and cultural studies has generally been hostile from the outset. The anti-democratic practices that have emerged from these assumptions offered an opportunity to the right through the construction of the category of 'political correctness', and, despite the general mendacity of these attacks, they unfortunately capture enough of the truth to produce a wake of political devastation. These are genuinely fundamental disagreements as to the daily practices of politics, on which more by way of conclusion.

IV

Where are we today? I will speak only of the troubles that beset cultural studies, even though the sales of books and the number of students belies this conclusion. I think this is a false prosperity. Intellectually and politically cultural studies is not very healthy and I believe its days are numbered except as an irrelevant outpost in the academy. The encounter between British cultural studies and French structuralism and poststructuralism has been, I think, a deeply deforming episode. When the well-known culturalism–structuralism divide was reached, the wrong road was taken and the price was an abandonment of the progressive program developed by Williams and Hoggart and also the virtual preclusion of any alliance between cultural studies and political economy (cf. Carey, 1995). While one can be properly appalled at the extreme polemics of *The Poverty of Theory* (1978), I think E. P. Thompson pretty much got it right, as did Raymond Williams (1989c) in the last essays he wrote on the subject. Williams argued that the tendency to treat cultural studies as a derivative of a group of *texts*, rather than as the interaction of a project and its formation, was not only a retreat to a type of what he called idealist history, but also the point at which cultural studies was lost as a project: it forgot its purposes and alliances. Williams argued that the recrudescence of formalism within cultural studies came through the contact with Althusser and structuralism and was an accommodation with a self-consciously modernist marxism that offered new forms of human reduction as the cutting edge of theory and significantly altered the intentions of cultural studies as a practice. While Williams uses the word agent in this regard, he clearly means the loss of agency:

> . . . the theories which came – the revival of formalism, the simpler kinds (including Marxist kinds) – of structuralism tendered to regard the practical encounters of people in society as having relatively little effect on its general progress, since the main inherent forces of that society were deep in its structures and – in the simplest forms – the people who operated were mere agents. (Williams, 1989c: 57)

Williams's argument was that cultural studies emerged as a particular project within a given social formation. I have emphasized how necessary and inevitable it was that the project and the formation would have to differ between the United Kingdom and the United States, indeed differ in any two countries. Williams's emphasis was almost completely ethnocentric. Cultural studies emerged in Britain, not via an engagement with the behavioral science and positivism, but in opposition to the formalism common to much marxism and literary theory. The subject and project was British cultural studies and both modifiers were crucial. The project was the elucidation of British culture, not the offering of covering laws that could be stretched across time and space. The founding texts were about the making and expression of the English working class, about the debate between culture and society in Britain. They were developed in adult education (part of their formation), via an encounter with and an attempt to speak to the kinds of people who enrolled in those courses in the 1940s and 1950s. Of course, it was an attempt to counter an increasingly abstract and, in that sense, economistic marxism as well, one stipulating general laws of social development, but it was offered not in opposition to political economy as such but in an attempt to develop something closer to a vernacular that could be hooked into the rhythm of national idioms and meanings. An indispensable part of the formation of cultural studies is the desire to speak to, to engage in common deliberation, a wider public.

The strength of cultural studies in Williams's hands, and the same applies to Hoggart and Thompson, was precisely its ethnocentrism. Intellectual work, including both cultural studies and political economy, is always and everywhere decisively touched and shaped by the national formation (and the sub-formations of class, race, gender, etc.) within which it is produced. This does not deny the importance of transnational and diasporic sites of culture, but suggests that such sites are understood only relative to the sovereign states which produce, enable, inhibit, warp or merely tolerate such formations. Cultural studies at its best attempts to take account of this fact and turn it into a strength. It is an exercise, to use Clifford Geertz's phrase, in 'local knowledge'. Nothing discredited the behavioral sciences and classical marxism more than a rigid inability to adapt to local circumstances, which meant in practice an inability to understand local knowledge whether of a religious, familial, aesthetic or political sort.[4]

The form this commitment to the vernacular and local knowledge assumed in Williams left him open to the charge of laborism. He commented early in his writings on cultural studies that 'in what I am calling the politics of culture certain virtues are valued, in particular that complex of irony, tolerance and charity which most working class communities have kept as a saving grace'. He asks himself the question of why the insistence on the working class and answers as follows:

> It is not a matter of any temporary way of living but of fundamental ideas of *the nature of social relationships*. We base our values on the working class movement because it is the main carrier of the principle of common improvement against individual advantage. The working class movement, in its characteristic institutions, offers the example of community, collective action and substantial equality of condition, as again the prevailing ethos of opportunity and hierarchy. We believe in fact that the spirit of these working class institutions – the cooperatives, the trade unions, the numerous voluntary associations – is the best basis for any future British society. This is the British working class culture we value: the institutions of democracy, equality and community. (Williams, 1959: 11; emphasis added)

While I have reservations, to be developed later, about this emphasis on class, I do not know how it can be confused with laborism. Williams is not arguing that the working class ought to be privileged as a historical agent and they just happen to hold to certain values. Rather, I assume he is arguing that there is no historical agent. However, certain values should be privileged and, at the moment, without necessity or determination, the working class is the best embodiment of those values available. However, in privileging those values Williams argues against the grain, against the assumption dominant in the United States that republican politics had to be neutral toward the values and ends its citizens espouse.

While Williams came to cultural studies through literature, he did not restrict its scope to the literary as many of his essays attest. By the time British cultural studies reached the United States, after a fateful detour through France, it acquired a number of characteristics, including a certain philosophical tone and obsession, that led to its absorption into literature departments and transformed its study in communications into an analogue of literary study.

There were a number of unfortunate consequences that flowed from this transformation, including the fact that it took on the fashionableness that is an endemic characteristic of the French academy: the desire to be up to date by moving on from the latest author on the bestselling list before he or she has been absorbed or understood. There was also an implicit and invisible reconciliation with the argument over high culture and mass culture that earlier versions of cultural studies sought to escape. More importantly, it led to abandoning the critique of positivism. French thought, operating in a particular intellectual milieux formed by the *ecoles*, assumes that the struggle with the positive sciences is over and reform or revolution can come from philosophical critique alone. Nothing is further from the situation in the United States where scientists simply found poststructuralism to be silly and beside the point and promptly allowed their work to be incorporated into a more explicit and aggressive conservative agenda. Cultural studies took up residence in the English common rooms and confused the domination of discussion there with an influence on political culture and policy. As a corollary, it meant that cultural studies abandoned contact with the social sciences and transformed the poststructuralist belief that the critic is more important than the author into the comfortable but disputable assumption that the philosopher had become more important than the scientist. Thirdly, it assisted the general tendency to reduce social phenomena to interactions with a text. While the metaphor of the text had a certain usefulness, its literalization and imperial ambitions tended to reduce human interactions, however elaborated, to an encoding-decoding model. This turned out to be the same reduction, paradoxically, engineered in behaviorism and uses and gratifications theory, and led to the same result: the artificial detachment of social relations from the transactions in which they were embedded. This reached absurd extremes when the inevitable gap between encoding and decoding was transformed into a site of resistance and the birth of counter but democratic political movements. Every outbreak of American individualism was typically transformed into the beginnings of collective political assault on the citadels of capitalism even though such assaults assumed the characteristic forms of individual choice and market exchange.

The emergence of the text further reduced the entire domain of culture to ideology and all social relations into surrogates for power, a vicious self-fulfilling prophecy. The complex culture of a people and an adequate understanding of its formation was exhausted by grasping one limited part of its formulation. Moreover, by discovering ideology in the texts of popular culture, by searching for it in the enacted ideas of the popular practices of everyday life – shopping, commodities, music, television and leisure – political culture was reduced to the most managed and instrumental parts of life and the common-sense understandings of politics were completely evacuated. This strategy invited us to attend to the self-conscious construction of culture by the media and the modern state and away from culture in relation to community and tradition. In other words, it took the media and the state on their own terms.

There is, however, an American political culture that is not to be discovered in the artifacts of the mass media or in the domain of consumption practices alone, which is a major part of the reason that cultural studies as ideological analysis has been such a failure. Culture as a way of life means that political and legal institutions, and their specificity historically and comparatively, are important in any society's unique way of life and are not marginal to the popular arts or daily practices in the realm of consumption. The latter account for limited dimensions of the former. Every society has a distinct political culture formed in relation to a unique history and geography. A comparison between the United States and Canada reveals a wide sharing of quotidian practice and popular culture and yet vastly different political/legal/ideological cultures. Further, the absurdist concentration on ideology largely served to undermine confidence in basic democratic institutions and values. The politics of difference which it encouraged only further splintered the progressive movement and enormously strengthened conservatism and, paradoxically, the power of state.

A particular misfortune was the encounter with Michael Foucault. While Foucault's historical work contained some extraordinary and extraordinarily useful scholarship, the framework within which it was encased was a bad prescription for democratic politics. His attempt to establish a new periodization, bringing the classical period to a close only in 1800, served to eliminate the Enlightenment entirely and with it the political values of the Age of Reason. He concentrated his heaviest weapons on humanism in all its forms for humanism was everything in Western civilization that *restricts the desire for power*. Despite the technical ingenuity of his work, his project masked a doctrine of total liberation from all social and moral constraints in order to act out our most violent instincts: our cruelest phantasms 'should be freed from the restrictions we impose on them . . . and allowed to conduct their dance' (Miller, 1993: 223–4). Foucault's appeal in the United States rests partly on his affinity with a liberal individualist political culture that sees society and our fellow citizens only as constraint or coercion. In writing an allegory of endless domination, Foucault constructed a hymn to the pleasure of exercising power, and, paradoxically enough, a reverence toward the state of nature as a justification for cruel and murderous practices. He constituted not only an analysis of power, but a lust and idolatry towards it, for he spurned any middle ground between total power and total anarchy.[5] In short, in Foucault's rendition, power is simply another name for culture, for the webs of significance and meaning, in which the self is suspended, but that web is one of intrinsic cruelty. This is where the conversion of culture into ideology and power inevitably leads.

V

And that brings us around to what is the least satisfying but most necessary aspect of American cultural studies. I have already evinced a considerable discomfort with class analysis or more precisely, partisanship, that I need to clarify. That takes us back to the subject of John Dewey and pragmatism.

Perhaps one of the more disquieting things about pragmatism is that it bears within it a somewhat tragic view of life that contrasts sharply with the utopianism of much marxist thought. That sense was not unearned but forged within the events of the twentieth century. For Marx, every interest is a class interest. His view was constructed to oppose a central idea of liberalism, namely that interests are merely the expression of individual desire. If interest equals whatever individuals desire, then individuals are the best judge of their own interests. While conflicts of interest inevitably occur, they evidence merely an expression of competing desires rather than the collision of collective interests rooted in antagonistic ways of life. Therefore, individuals should be willing to compromise in order to maximize self-interest. If interests collide in the real world, the adjustments are compromises which, by addition and cancellation, maximize the realization of individual desires through a mechanically constructed agreement. Markets are to be prized because they effect these compromises and maximizations automatically and without the need of resort to politics and persuasion. Markets, then, are instruments of compromise, mechanisms which construct an instrumental as opposed to a mutual reciprocity.

Because Marx believed that all ideas and action are reflections of partisan interest, the task was to discover some partisan interest that could act as the agency for human emancipation. In this sense, partisanship is functional in the effort to improve society, for it substitutes a more comprehensive for a less comprehensive notion of social interest. Such a view led not only to the opposition of markets as an expression of a social will, but to compromise as a social institution. All compromise was merely tactical, a method to reach a more comprehensive but still partisan interest.

What makes partisanship such a conspicuous feature of marxism is the thesis that the working class represents a reconstructive universal interest such that the realization of the interests of the working class simultaneously abolishes the condition that makes all interests destructive interests: 'a class that can only redeem itself by a total redemption of humanity' (Marx, 1963: 56, quoted in D'Amico, 1981).[6]

This is a deeply appealing idea, not only because of the near total absence of ambiguity, but, for anyone with roots in the working class, it is deeply flattering and contains certain elements of the truth. As I mentioned earlier,

Raymond Williams saw in the working class the realization of what he took to be quasi-transcendental values. Whatever the truth – and the pre-industrial character of much of the working class lends it a truth – these values were surrounded by, and infected with, other notions, some ancient prejudices, some modern accretions, that would make the working class on occasion after occasion a disappointment to those who looked to them as an agent of emancipation.

Despite the growth of cynicism about the working class, a cynicism which by my experience was more prejudicial than earned, the notion of class redemption has not disappeared. It is periodically transferred on to new groups, a new universal class defined by race or gender or age, who are implicitly conceived as a reconstructive universal class by virtue of their suffering. Inevitably, each of these groups fails the test of politics, each turns into a special interest, a class for itself or, in the United States more often, a class dedicated solely to the satisfaction of the desires of its individual members.

It was the element of class privileging that Dewey most forcefully rejected in Marx. He did not reject classes or class interest; he rejected the notion that intellectual inquiry should adopt a class point of view. He argued that the norms of critical inquiry should be tied to no particular interest but to a social interest, to a public interest in an inclusive way of life and that no particular class realized or expressed this interest. In making this argument Dewey anticipated Hannah Arendt's (1958) claim that Marx reduced politics to economics and 'action' to labor and interests. In short, during a critical period in our history, Dewey argued that the controlling framework of ideas should be derived from a more comprehensive social interest than the working class could provide. Because social pluralism, not class, is the chief characteristic of society, as it is of nature, the framework of ideas needed to construct a comprehensive framework could not identify in an a priori way with the interests and outlooks of any particular group (Dewey, 1927).

What completed Dewey's break with marxism is his denial that 'partisan political activity on behalf of any one group can supply the human being with the character structure needed for the moral advance of society' (D'Amico, 1981: 662). The dramatic structure of marxism was deeply deforming and implicated in the carnage of the twentieth century. That structure is contained, for example, in passages like the following:

> For a popular revolution and the emancipation of a particular class of civil society to coincide, for one class to represent the whole of society, another class must embody and represent a general obstacle and limitation. A particular social sphere must be regarded as the notorious crime of the whole society so that emancipation from this sphere appears as a general emancipation. For one class to be the liberating class par excellence, it is necessary that another class should be openly the oppressing class. (Marx, 1963: 56, quoted in D'Amico, 1981)

For all the other changes in the rhetorical structure of modern marxism this is the one constant, the one belief that the experience of modern history has been unable to dislodge and is one of the things that gave revolution a bad name. For once the revolution has been realized, the dramatic structure of ideas could not disappear and demanded the production of a new enemy of the people and, unlike some symbolic demands, this one was easily realized, as cultural marxists like Gramsci and Alvin Gouldner recognized.

If Marx is correct concerning the nature of interests and if there is no reconstructive universal interest, for all the obvious candidates have failed, we are left with a good description of society as it concretely operates but with a morally empty vision of it as well. In such a circumstance all we can do is advance our own individual interests, find a demonized class on which to heap all our obloquy and scorn or constitute a wider partisan interest without hope or pretense that it can become a public interest. That strikes me as a decent description of how social life is constructed these days and represents a more adequate, if depressing, framework than that offered through most versions of cultural studies.

For Dewey, and for cultural studies, there must be a different starting point and, given the critique of positivism outlined above, it must be from the logical norms of trial and error rationalism. How we 'link theory and practice, knowing and doing, is the sign of what kinds of people we are to become as a result of the doing' (D'Amico, 1981: 662). The basic need is to try on intellectual outlooks and see how, in Kenneth Burke's lovely phrase (in Gusfield (1989)), we hop around as a result of the spirit we chose to inhabit us, to see what given positions commit us to. Dewey made norms of critical inquiry the decisive standard in guiding his arguments. His outlook was a vehicle for a reconstructed theory of education, communication and culture in which having experiences that promote the habits and disposition of a 'pragmatic', an experimental, a trial-and-error mind are crucial. This reconstruction informs his account of 'democracy as a way of life in which the art of inquiry, communication and community are blended together' (D'Amico, 1981: 662).

The end or what is to be done must always be considered from the 'angle of how individuals are to do it and *what kind of people they are becoming as a result of the doing.* If the end is community and commitment to the norms of mutuality and reciprocity that signify the realization of a more adequate society', then the partisanship, common to the left since Marx, runs the risk of breeding, and has in fact bred, antidemocratic practices. When Dewey identifies the substance of community with communication, his critics miss the point when they charge him with ignoring power and inequality. The individual is a social being, shaped in large measure by the pressures of society – yes. But

> changing conditions alone will not alter this natural causality operating in the social order. Overcoming this dependence requires new forms of experience guided by an intelligence cultivated to enable the individual to better judge how what he is doing affects him and his association with others. Dewey's experimentalism, not less than Marx's radical practice, is an autogenetic category. Through open inquiry, communication, trial-and-error action, the individual can better shape conditions,

thereby expanding control over his own shaping.

Communication, open inquiry, are still needed if individuals are to be open to those experiences and actions that will enable them to solve problems from a more general perspective, one that does not just calculate private advantage but considers the consequences for maintaining relationships of mutual reciprocity. Not partisan interests, but the social interest must be controlling; not radical politics, but the politics of trial-and-error rationalism is the school that teaches us how to reconstruct society in mutual interest. (D'Amico, 1981: 665)

Dewey preached a theory of praxis of course and shared with Marx the belief that the task was not to reflect society in thought but to change it in practice. However, no class by itself, not even an intellectual one, has the knowledge necessary to effect such change. All classes and social groups are necessarily imprisoned by their partial outlook, by knowledge limited and constrained by social location. This applies with equal force to intellectuals who, in the words of Saul Bellow, are often high IQ morons, due to their unwillingness to recognize that the knowledge necessary to their own self-fulfillment lies with the other, in the equally hard won knowledge of other, and frequently, less elevated groups. It was this fact, not some sentimentality, that led to a central principle of Dewey's ethics that communication is a good unto itself.

As D'Amico concludes:

Marx is most persuasive in arguing that partisanship plays a crucial role in the changing of conditions. Dewey on the other hand is most persuasive when defending the role of the norms of critical inquiry in the constitution of a democratic personality. The strengths and weaknesses of each theory are complementary. Or to put it somewhat differently, the quarrel between liberal amelioration and radical politics is not just a historical episode in political thought, but a fundamental quality of the individual's political experience as a conscious being. (1981: 665)

This is part of the complementarity between cultural studies and political economy I mentioned at the outset: the complementarity between conditions of existence and norms of open inquiry that alone provide the basis for such a relationship. I know no way of choosing between changing conditions of existence and changing the norms of critical inquiry in terms of a more comprehensive social interest. One is useless without the other. If I started at Dewey's end of the scale, it was only because it was the end that needed support in order to restore a balance to progressive politics.

I have staged Hamlet without the prince; cultural studies without the public sphere. I know I have not allayed the fear, and perhaps cannot, that I have again neglected the facts of power, that I have placed too much emphasis on inquiry, community and communication. Still, I hope these last remarks point toward a more defined notion of a public sphere and why much of the post-Dewey, post-Habermas analysis of such a sphere – the working-class public sphere, the feminist public sphere – for all its empirical truth, simply is another appropriation of public life for reinsertion in the traditional marxist problematic of partisanship or the typically positivist version of pluralism and special interests. Perhaps Dewey's vision is an impossibly utopian one. The most effective recent, though indirect, critique of it is by the French scholar

Pierre Manent (1994) who claims that attempts to revivify civic associations – families, communities, etc. – are doomed to failure because of the problem of representation. A key notion of every argument we've examined is that the exercise of power is legitimate only if it is based upon the voluntary and rational consent of those who will be governed by it. This was the dilemma of liberal societies that de Tocqueville formulated in 'the most extensive and profound way' (Manent, 1994: 114). But this Promethean ambition to be free of all social ties demolishes all influences, even public and rational ones, by which people act on each other. Because the modern self wants to be an ever freer individual; he wants the fewest commands or influences; he wants to be an increasingly more equal individual and therefore attempts to 'construct a social mechanism where he is governed ever more exclusively by a state that governs less . . .' (Manent, 1994: 116). The most powerful motivation among us is the desire to escape from culture, from the shaping influence of others and the consent thus demanded and 'the no less natural desire to escape the mechanism man conceived to satisfy the first desire' (Manent, 1994: 116). Or as I have often put it, rather more colloquially: Americans are a people who are always creating new communities and then trying to figure a way to get out of town. Because all authority over the self is illegitimate, we now have movements opposing all authority, including that of parents and family, not grounded in consent. Representation is only possible when consent is given, but there is never a reason for granting consent. We now have a consumer politics as well as a consumer culture as people expect to buy from the state with a vote what they can't buy from the market with a dollar. The only authority that appears to be freely chosen is that of which celebrity to admire and emulate.

The principle of representation erodes the self-sufficiency and power of sub-political units, which are, however, necessary to the health of civil society. This, Manent explains, is the paradox of representation: it tends to dominate and atomize the society it claims to represent. Now that is an argument that really bothers me for it is also a description of what has happened to most leftist movements in our time and most civic associations as well. If true, both marxism and pragmatism, political economy and cultural studies, are quite beside the point.

To end on a cheerier note, there remain areas of accommodation or complementarity between cultural studies and political economy that can form around Michael Sandel's (1996a) notion of the political economy of citizenship. To do this one has to at least share the Deweyan point that large national and global corporations, and the even more massive centralized state, threaten democracy not only through the concentration of power and their resistance to public control but also, and just as importantly, through the erosion of the moral and civic capacities – the capacity to think beyond individual desire – that enable people to act as citizens. This erosion, however, is not a consequence of the state and the corporation alone for, as I have argued elsewhere, though the late Christopher Lasch (1995) is the most gifted exponent of the view, elites in the professions, including the academic professions, have been equally intent on appropriating these civic capacities of the general population and turning them to their own ends. We do not have to choose between the creation of greater economic equality and the creation of citizens capable of self-government, for, if we so choose, we will get neither.

We have finally to rouse ourselves, in the United States at least, from the long sleep of reason in which we have chosen to set ourselves free of all moral and communal ties that we have not chosen after infancy. However liberating this idea was when we were all back on the farm, it is now our great liability for it prevents the formation of the wide range of moral and political obligation that will allow us to act to form a democratic culture outside both the market and the state.

Notes

1 For example, one must accept the fact, without too much hand-wringing, that economics and communications are based on different and contradictory fundamental principles: all economics must begin from the principle of scarcity; communications begins from a principle of abundance. That difference does not rule out a political economy of communications but it does constrain its reach. I try to characterize that contradiction and constraint in an essay 'Communications and Economics' (Carey, 1994).

2 The contrast with cultural studies is instructive. When cultural studies took up residence in literature departments, one was visited with the spectacle of literary scholars pronouncing on all sorts of matters – the economy, morality, population, crime, race and ethnicity etc. – to which they had never devoted any study, including the most cursory examination of the basic literature. And, in general, they were not interested in listening to any one who had studied these matters unless they first jumped the barrier of ideological correctness. This was far from universally true but was a tendency unopposed by the discursive norms of the left. Genovese (1994) may exaggerate when he claims that right-wing audiences are generally more courteous to left-wing scholars than the reverse but he does identify a tendency. Conservatives more often support civil discourse and think that one may be actually able to learn something from the opposition and thus forswear asking the questions that would end the conversation. The party of difference cannot, in general, tolerate difference whereas the party of hegemony can, which is, of course, why they are the party of hegemony.

3 I take this account from Sidney Hook's autobiography (1987).

4 The most decisive argument along these lines came from Paul Feyerabend in a number of distinguished books, particularly *Science in a Free Society* (1978).

5 My views of Foucault, always skeptical, have been much influenced by James Miller's remarkable biography, *The Passion of Michael Foucault* (1993). The quotations come from Miller, pp. 199, 223–4. See also Shattuck (1995).

6 I take this formulation, and paraphrases throughout (along with much of the quoted material) from Alfred D'Amico's (1981) exceptional article on Marx and Dewey.

2

The Anti-political Populism of Cultural Studies

Todd Gitlin

Cultural studies did not spring full-blown from its object of study, culture. No surprise: it emerged in history. Cultural studies arose in a moment that, like all others, had political, economic, social and cultural dimensions. It has survived and ballooned into a different moment. These observations are not as simple as they sound, though they are necessary. The relation between ideas and their institutional settings is a complex subject, and not one to be settled too easily. Still, students of cultural studies should not be surprised to discover that cultural studies is susceptible to analysis as an object of cultural study. For of all the human sciences, cultural studies has the least claim to – and for that matter, the least interest in – an Archimedean point of view. It fiercely disbelieves in unmoved movers.

In all its variations, this intellectual movement distinguishes itself by seeing culture as an activity, a set of values and practices, undertaken by particular people who live particular lives in particular settings and try to make sense of them, to reach particular goals, solve particular problems, express particular sentiments. For the field of cultural studies to fail to see itself through the same lens would be myopic. Cultural studies is itself a sort of culture performed by people who live particular lives in particular settings, trying to solve, or surpass, or transform particular problems.

I do not wish to dwell on problems of definition, whose tedium is matched only by inconclusiveness and circularity. The interminable examination of what exactly constitutes cultural studies – or its subject, 'culture' – is itself part of the problem I seek to diagnose. Rather, I hope to slip (if not cut) the Gordian knot with the simple statement that cultural studies is the activity practiced by people who say they are doing cultural studies.

Stanley Aronowitz observed in 1990 that 'cultural studies is a social movement'.[1] If this was meant as a recommendation, I take it to be self-serving and tautological. But as a statement of fact, it is accurate. There is something more going on in cultural studies than the pursuit of tenure and self-promotion by young and no-longer-so-young academics. In North America, at the very least, there has been a tremendous growth in the number of practitioners who identify with cultural studies, claim to be doing it, publish in it, aim to establish programs of it, recruit for it, debate purposes and methodologies in it. There is energy at work. There is conviction, *élan*, passion. This could only be because cultural studies is a form of intellectual life that answers to passions and hopes imported into its precincts from outside. Cultural studies may not be a significant social movement beyond the precincts of certain academies, but it certainly responds to the energies of social and cultural movements – and their eclipse.

In part, the ascendancy of cultural studies derives from the growth of its object of attention – the boom in the scale of popular culture, and its significance in the lives of Western societies, especially from the 1960s on. Measure this significance in units of time (television is watched by the average American for more than four hours a day, and most other industrial societies are not far behind) or the emotional loyalty of its audiences, or in the volume of money at stake, and the significance is plain. No economic determinism is needed to sustain the observation that one necessary condition for the growth of the commercial youth market was the economic boom that followed World War II. With the success of Keynesian policies, high employment, and collective bargaining came a boom in disposable income among the young in the more privileged countries. Moreover, the growing significance of popular culture derives from the secular decline of work and the salience of what used to be called 'leisure time' – not necessarily quantitative growth, but growth in its emotional weight, the sheer volume of popular culture in the imaginative life of the young. It is not simply that the market in popular culture grew enormously in scale after World War II, but that from the 1960s on, the young have come to define themselves by their taste, especially their taste in popular music. They relate not only to the music, but *through* the music to a sense of cultural membership. In part, too, the bulking up of popular culture and the connected phenomenon of celebrity stem from the declining grip of the institutions that traditionally imparted identity to the young: occupation, class, religion. The 'other-directed' character first described by David Riesman (1950), the youth taking his or her cues of membership and morality from the mass media and peer groups, has for half a century been entrenched as the normal Western type.[2]

It is incontrovertible, then, that the growth of disposable income and the proliferation of media specific to youth have increased the weight of popular culture and its significance in national life. And the weight of popular culture has grown outside the world of youth as well. One need not endorse the misleading slogan that we live in an 'information society' to recognize that electronics and telecommunications are central to the industrial economies. The transfer of images is a core feature in so-called advanced economies; after aerospace, entertainment is America's next most remunerative export.

Politics, too, seems inconceivable outside the flows and eddies, the pumping stations and sewers of industrialized culture. Whether for left, right, or center, for center or margins, the intersections of popular culture and politics are so frequent, the interconnections so dense, as to raise the exaggerated claim that the two domains have collapsed into each other. Think of the political core: in the course of the twentieth century, the star marched out of the biographies in popular magazines (Lowenthal, 1961[1943]) into the Reagan White House. Think of the margins: before the American-based 'counterculture' was a mark*et*, it was a mark*er* of collective identity. Loved by its partisans, loathed by its enemies, popular culture in the 1960s became a touchstone for controversy and a fulcrum of political debate. In the United States, and then elsewhere, issues of the legitimacy of various ways of life – questions of sexuality, abortion, drugs, multiculturalism – came to loom large in political discourse. 'Culture wars' became routine (Gitlin, 1995).

The academy's intellectual matrix in the 1970s was conducive to an interest in the new cultural tendencies. The premise of the prevailing style of thought was that human beings make sense of their world actively, collectively, and in specific historical circumstances. Historians of 'mentalité' and anthropologists of culture were already staking out the territory that cultural studies would claim as its own. 'History from the bottom up' was insurgent. Under the influence of E.P. Thompson (1963), classes were 'made', not born. There was in progress an upsurge in social history, especially in the study of historically subordinated populations – women, African-Americans, workers, the colonized. For their part, anthropologists were bringing ethnographic methods to bear on cultural life in the 'home countries'. Insurgent sociologists were turning away from the dismissive 'collective behavior' diagnosis of social movements as, in effect, neurotic symptoms, and taking seriously the professed intentions of activists, presuming them to be not only explicable but rational. The early cultural studies group at Birmingham employed academic methods from all three fields to investigate the social history of the present – of working-class and dissident youth populations (Hall and Jefferson, 1976; Willis, 1977, 1978), television personages (Hall et al., 1976) and viewers (Morley, 1980), among others. Cultural activity was, for all these researchers, *activity* – not the absence of something (civilization, literature, politics) but the presence of a form of engagement in the here-and-now. To these projects in the social sciences were added, crucially, the postmodernist turn in philosophy and 'theory' – the rejection of hierarchies of value; the devaluation of 'center' in favor of 'periphery'; the emphasis on the active production (or 'construction') of meaning; the search for 'local knowledges' as opposed to truth; the insistence on self-challenging reflexivity.

But the tenor of cultural studies was set, crucially, by the political circumstances of the first waves of cultural students, if I may call them that. The founding generation were deeply involved with the British New Left. Two of their formative elders, Richard Hoggart and Raymond Williams, derived from the industrial working classes, and so did many of their students. Others came from the once colonized periphery, and/or were women and/or gays and lesbians. They were frequently the first members of their families to go ('go up', as they say at Oxbridge) to university. Designated meritocratically for the replenishment of ruling classes and elite institutions, they encountered condescension alongside encouragement. Especially in Britain, they also encountered programs in literary studies which had little place for the culture these students – let alone their families – actually lived. They did not see why they should have to check their form of life at the gates. Reverence for cultural authority was not their generational spirit. They had grown up in a youth culture of enormous ambitions and, let it be said, achievements. By the late 1960s, they were imbibing a youth culture itself saturated by syncretic, high-cultural masterworks of modernism – the Beatles with their puns, their sitars, their echoes of Stockhausen; Bob Dylan with his reference to 'Ezra Pound and T.S. Eliot'. They may have been taught to revere Beethoven, but at least equally came to revere Chuck Berry telling the selfsame Beethoven to roll over and tell Tchaikovsky the news. Into the universities, they carried not only their cultural points of reference but a certain texture of popular-culture experience. If reading, study sessions, rallies, and love-making took place against a background of rock music, they wanted to know, why shouldn't the academy pay attention?

They, like the rest of their societies, were saturated with popular culture at a time when leftist commitments were tinged with poignancy. In the United States, in the early to mid-1970s, many veterans of the American student movement found themselves in an impasse. In the late 1960s, riding the wave of the student movement, they had committed themselves to something of a revolutionary breakthrough in the politics of the Western world. As the tide went out, they now found themselves beached. In so far as they had overrated the radical potential of students as such, yet were attached to the idea of a transformation of social life, they sought to compensate for the error by seeking out 'radical chains' among other social groups. Marxist traditionalists found hope in a redefinition if not revival of a unitary 'working class' – a hope that events failed to reward. Theorists of a 'new working class' were quickly outdistanced by theorists and advocates of a – or 'The' – 'Third World Revolution', with the majority of humanity (never mind that the very category 'Third World' was named by a Frenchman) cast in the role of surrogate world proletariat.

The radical upsurge of the late 1960s had culminated, then, in anticlimax and undertow. In Britain, Labour, union, feminist and antiracist momentum continued through the 1970s, though the conspicuous manifestations masked the fact that they had become the property of a minority – a fact that became clear with the election of Margaret Thatcher in 1979. In the United States, despite sectoral gains among women and gays, the 1970s were largely a time of defeat for the left, for the working class and the political movements of the 1960s. What was setting in, at these different paces, was a twilight of Labour and Democratic power. For leftists, the spirit of an insurgent class was no longer available. Instead, they were left with nostalgia, even at some remove, for eras of cogent struggle they knew only at second or third hand. The general student movement was finished, leaving beyond a range of identity-based movements, feminist, gay, and race-based, each vigorous, in its own right, yet lacking experiences of everyday practices which would amount to embryonic prefigurations of a reconstituted world.

It was this lack that riveted academic attention to popular culture. If one thought about youth culture properly, perhaps some sort of Marxist vision of history might be preserved! Perhaps it was youth culture that would invigorate, cement, ennoble the rising class that inevitably would displace and overcome the ruling groups! At least popular culture had vitality, rebelliousness, oppositional spirit – and then, by implication, so could the people who made it popular. If political power was foreclosed, the battlements of culture still remained to be taken! Or perhaps – if one really believed that the personal was the political – they had already been taken. Or perhaps the only reason politics looked unavailing was that the wrong culture was in force. Whatever the case, an obsession with popular culture might take the sting out of political defeat.

Cultural experience, then, dovetailed with the leftover political quest for a class, or its equivalent, that might lead the way to radical change. On the heels of a decade of youthful rebellion, it was easiest to look first to youth subcultures in the industrial countries for the emergence of disaffections that might be mobilized, or better, might mobilize themselves, into effective opposition to capitalism and racism. Culture, in this view, was a field of combat. The spirit of the moment was to survey the field and define the combat in terms imported from political struggles. The grid of meaning that was discerned within (or imposed upon) popular culture was imported from radical politics. It had a teleology. It was not simply conflict but 'contestation', or confrontation. It was not simply contestation but *the* stark and classic contestation between forces of liberation and forces of established repression. The early work of the Birmingham Centre for Contemporary Cultural Studies in the 1970s, especially their study of the 'mugging' phenomenon, concentrated on this coupled relationship: the meanings of rebellious youth activity experienced by the rebels themselves, alongside the repressive definitions imposed upon these activities by dominating media. If the bourgeois culture of the suites was hegemonic, therefore oppressive, then the angrily anti-bourgeois culture of the streets was counterhegemonic, resistant, and the class struggle was alive. Paul Willis's early work (1977, 1978) was saturated with ironic awareness that stances of dissidence among working-class boys might serve to integrate them all the more closely into lives of on-the-job subordination. But the still greater influence radiated from Dick Hebdige (1978), who took a tendency already visible in earlier Birmingham work and codified it into a virtual equating of style with politics. Hebdige's enthusiasm refused to dampen radical hopes in baths of irony. In Hebdige, style was insurgency because it was bricolage, and because bricolage pried symbols away from their original contexts, it was self-defining activity, or 'resistance'.

From the late 1960s onward, as I have said, the insurgent energy was to be found in movements that aimed to politicize specific identities – racial minorities, women, gays. More generally, cultural studies set itself to discern 'agency' among either marginalized or 'ordinary' people – initiative and creativity on the part of people whom, it was said, academicians of conventional stripes overlooked or underestimated. If the 'collective behavior' school of once-conventional sociology had grouped movements on behalf of justice and democratic rights together with fads and fashions (Smelser, 1962), cultural studies now set out to separate movements from fads, to take seriously the accounts of movement participants themselves, and thereby to restore the dignity of the movements – only to end up, in the 1980s, reaggregating movements with fads by finding equivalent dignity in both spheres, so that, for example, dressing like Madonna was upgraded to an act of 'resistance' equivalent to demonstrating on behalf of the right to abortion, and watching a talk show on family violence was positioned on the same plane. In this way, cultural studies extended the New Left symbiosis with popular culture (Gitlin, 1987). Eventually, the popular culture of marginal groups (punk, reggae, disco, feminist poetry, hip-hop) was promoted to a sort of counter-structure of feeling, and even, at the edges, a surrogate politics – a sphere of thought and sensibility hypothetically insulated from the pressures of hegemonic discourse, of instrumental reason, of economic rationality, of class, gender, and sexual subordination.

The other move in cultural studies was to claim that culture continued radical politics by other means. The idea was that cultural innovation was daily insinuating itself into the activity of ordinary people. Perhaps the millions had not actually been absorbed into the hegemonic sponge of mainstream popular culture! Perhaps they were free, or actually dissenting – even if at home, sitting on sofas. If 'the revolution' had receded to the point of invisibility, it was depressing to contemplate the victory of a hegemonic culture imposed by strong, virtually irresistible media. How much more reassuring to detect 'resistance' saturating the pores of everyday life! The specialized coloration of the word 'agency' – a term whose academic meaning was obscure to anyone outside the precincts of the academy – underscores the preciousness of the quest. Eager to be persuaded that the populace retained a potential for the right – that is, left – political engagement, academics of the left resorted to a term that, if it meant anything outside the academic glossary, smacked of advertising and public relations, or employment, or travel.

In this spirit, there emerged a welter of studies purporting to discover not only the 'active' participation of audiences in shaping the meaning of popular culture, but the 'resistance' of those audiences to hegemonic frames of interpretation in a variety of forms – news broadcasts (Morley, 1980), romance fiction (Radway, 1984), television fiction (Liebes and Katz, 1990; Press, 1991), television in general (Fiske, 1987), and many others. Thus, too, the feminist fascination with the fictions and talk shows of daytime 'women's television', seen to be generating a 'discourse' of women's problems that men derogated as 'merely' personal but were now revealed to be collective and therefore 'political'. In a certain view, the conventional dismissal of these shows as 'trivial', 'banal', 'soap opera', etc., follows from the patriarchal premise that what takes place within the four walls of the home is of less public significance than what takes place in a public sphere that was not so coincidentally established for the convenience of men. Observing the immensity of the audiences for Oprah Winfrey and her legions of talk-show imitators, many in cultural studies upended the phenomenon by turning the definitions around. The largely female audiences for these shows would no

longer be dismissed as distracted voyeurs, etc., but praised as active participants in the surfacing and therefore politicizing of crimes like incest, spousal
abuse, sexual molestation. These audiences would no longer be seen simply as
confirming their 'normality' with a safe, brief, well-bounded, vicarious
acquaintanceship with deviance. They could be understood as an avant-garde
social movement.

Above all, in a word, cultural studies has veered into populism (McGuigan,
1992). Its achievements and limits are rooted in an appreciation of popular
culture precisely because of one and only one of its outstanding attributes:
popularity. The defining premise is that popular culture, having been held
worthy of attention by its practitioners, is worthy of attention by its students.
If this is not an explicit premise, it is a large shadow cast by the work of cultural studies. Against the unabashed elitism of conventional literary and art
studies, cultural studies affirms an unabashed populism that derives intellectually from Weberian, symbolic interactionist, phenomenological, and
similarly derived schools of the social sciences, in which all social activities
matter, all can be understood, all contain cues to the social nature of human
beings. But this powerful tendency in cultural studies goes further than noting
the flows of popular culture and interpreting them. It seeks a particular kind
of interpretation: a political potential. The object of attention is certified as
worthy of such not by being 'the best that has been thought and said in the
world' but by having been thought and said by or for 'the people' – period. Or
rather, by being thought or said (or played or sung or built or . . .) in one of
two senses. First, it may be thought or said or followed or liked or taken to
heart by a vast population. Secondly, it may be thought or said, etc., by a subculture – in particular, by a marginal group, often, though not always, a
group with which the cultural student herself or himself identifies.
(Increasingly, the student wishes to overcome shame, is outspoken about this
preference, and interested in the whole phenomenon of fandom as such.)

In either case, the popularity of popular culture is what makes it interesting – and not only as an object of study. It is the populism if not the taste of
the analyst that has determined the object of attention in the first place. The
sociological judgment that popular culture looms large in the lives of people
blurs into a critical judgment that popular culture would not succeed in doing
so unless it were valuable. To use one of the buzzwords of 'theory', there is a
'slippage' from analysis to advocacy, defense, upward 'positioning'. Cultural
studies often claims to have overthrown hierarchy, but it is closer to the truth
to say that what it actually does with hierarchy is invert it. What now certifies
worthiness is the popularity of the object, not its formal qualities. What certifies (or 'valorizes') the subject as a subordinated person certifies the value of
the subject's cultural choices. If the people are on the right side, then what
they like is good. In this intellectual milieu, defenders of traditional categories
of 'literature' or 'art' are defensive, since cultural studies either jettison or toy
with questions of value, which are always slippery in the first place. The very
words 'literature' and 'art' stick in the throat of cultural studies' advocates,
who can rightly point to shifting definitions of high and low art in the work

of literary and art historians like Ian Watt (1957), to say nothing of Michel
Foucault on the 'genealogy' of frames of discourse (1970) or Raymond
Williams on etymology (1983a).

This tendency in cultural studies – I think it remains the main line – lacks
irony. One purports to stand four-square for the people against capitalism,
and comes to echo the logic of capitalism. The consumer sovereignty touted
by a capitalist society as the grandest possible means for judging merit finds
its reverberation among its ostensible adversaries. Where the market flatters
the individual, cultural studies flatters the group. What the group wants,
buys, demands is *ipso facto* the voice of the people. Supply has meshed with
demand. Popular creativity has found its forms. The people are already in the
process of liberation! Where once Marxists looked to factory organization as
the prefiguration of 'a new society in the shell of the old', today they tend to
look to sovereign culture consumers. David Morley, one of the key
researchers in cultural studies, and one of the most reflective, has himself recognized and deplored this tendency in recent audience studies (1992: 10–41).
He maintains that to understand that 'the commercial world succeeds in producing objects . . . which do connect with the lived desires of popular
audiences' is 'by no means necessarily to fall into the trap . . . of an uncritical celebration of popular culture' (Morley, 1992: 35). But it is not clear
where to draw the line against the celebratory tendency when one is inhibited
from doing so by a reluctance to criticize the cultural dispositions of the
groups whom one approves. No wonder there is an arbitrariness to the assessments embedded in much published work in cultural studies – as if the
researcher were straining to make the results conform to political needs.
Academic studies charged with boosting morale may not serve the cause of
enlightenment.

Here lies the danger of letting academic study serve as a vehicle for political identification. Indeed, unabashedly, the populism of cultural studies
prides itself on being political. In the prevailing schools of cultural studies, to
study culture is not so much to try to grasp cultural processes but to choose
sides or, more subtly, to determine whether a particular cultural process
belongs on the side of society's ideological angels. An aura of hope surrounds
the enterprise, the hope (even against hope) of an affirmative answer to the
inevitable question: Will culture ride to the rescue of the cause of liberation?
There is defiance, too, as much as hope. The discipline means to cultivate
insubordination. On this view, marginalized groups in the populace continue
to declare exceptions to hegemonic culture, if most of the academy remains
hidebound, cultural studies will pry open its portals, and hope to constitute
itself a sort of representative force. By taking defiant popular culture seriously, one takes the defiers seriously and furthers their defiance. Cultural
studies becomes 'cult studs'. It is charged with surveying the culture, assess-
ing the hegemonic import of cultural practices and pinpointing their
potentials for 'resistance'. Is this musical style or that literary form 'feminist'
or 'authentically Latino'? The model tends to be two-toned. The field of possibilities is frequently – usually, I would estimate – reduced to two: for or

against the hegemonic. But the nature of that hegemony, in its turn, is commonly defined tautologically: that culture is hegemonic which is conducive to, or promoted by, 'the ruling group' or 'the hegemonic bloc', and, by the same token, that culture is 'resistant' which is affirmed by groups assumed (because of class position, gender, race, sexuality, ethnicity, etc.) to be 'marginalized' or 'resistant'. The process of labeling is circular, since it has been predetermined whether a particular group is, in fact, hegemonic or resistant.

The populism of cultural studies is fundamental to its allure, and to the political meaning its adherents find there, for cultural studies bespeaks an affirmation of popularity *tout court*. To say that popular culture is 'worth attention' in the scholarly sense is, for cultural studies, to say something pointed: that the people who render it popular are not misguided when they do so; not fooled; not dominated; not distracted; not passive. If anything, the reverse: the premise is that popular culture is popular because and only because the people find in it channels of desire, pleasure, initiative, freedom. It is this premise that gives cultural studies its aura of political engagement – or at least, if nothing else, political consolation. To unearth reason and value, brilliance and energy in popular culture is to affirm that the people, however embattled, however divided, however battered, however fearful, however unemployed, however drugged, have still not been defeated. The cultural student, singing their songs, analysing their lyrics, at the same time in effect sings their praises. However unfavorable the balance of political forces, people succeed in living lives of vigorous resistance! Are the communities of African-Americans or Afro-Caribbeans suffering? Well, they have rap! (Leave aside the question of whether all of them want rap in equal measure.) The right may have taken possession of 10 Downing Street or the White House or Congress – and as a result of elections, embarrassingly enough! – but at least one is engaged within the English department.

Consolation: here is an explanation for the rise of academic cultural studies during precisely the years when the right has held political and economic power longer and more consistently than at any other time in the previous half-century. Or are other interpretations possible? Might it be, for example, that cultural studies for all its frailty amounts to a force combating right-wing control of the State? Perhaps it has been defeated, but through no fault of its own? But to believe this, one must embrace a vulgarization of the feminist idea that 'the personal is political'. Now, in effect, 'the cultural is political', and more, it is regarded as central to the control of political and economic resources. Regardless of the disposition of the agencies of force and the allocation of capital, the control of popular culture is held to have become decisive in the fate of contemporary societies – or at least it is the sphere in which opposition can find footing, find breathing space, rally the powerless, defy the grip of the dominant ideas, isolate the powers that be, and prepare for a 'war of position' against their dwindling ramparts. On this view, to dwell on the centrality of popular culture is more than an academic's way of filling her hours, it is a useful certification of the people and their projects. To put it more neutrally, the political aura of cultural studies is supported by something like a 'false consciousness' premise: the analytical assumption that what holds the ruling groups in power is their capacity to muffle or deform or paralyse or destroy contrary tendencies of an emotional or ideological nature. By the same token, if there is to be a significant 'opposition,' it must first find a base in popular culture – and first also turns out to be second, third, and fourth as well, since popular culture is so much more accessible, so much more porous, so much more changeable than the economic and political order.

In other words, to a considerable degree, cultural studies came into prominence as a compensation for the embattled position of the English-speaking left. With time, what began as compensation hardened – became institutionalized – into a tradition. Younger scholars gravitated to cultural studies because it was to them incontestable that culture *was* politics. To do cultural studies, especially in connection with identity politics, was the only politics they knew. The contrast with the rest of the West is illuminating. In varying degrees, left-wing intellectuals in France, Italy, Scandinavia, Germany, Spain and elsewhere retain energizing attachments to Social Democratic, Green, and other left-wing parties. There, the association of culture with excellence and traditional elites remains strong. But in the Anglo-American world, including Australia, these conditions scarcely obtain. Here, in a discouraging time, popular culture emerges as a consolation prize. (The same happened in Latin America, with the decline of left-wing hopes.) The sting is off the fragmentation of the organized Left, the metastasis of murderous nationalism, the twilight of socialist dreams virtually everywhere. Throughout the Anglo-Saxon world of Europe, North America, and Australia, class inequality may have soared, ruthless individualism may have intensified, the conditions of life for the poor may have worsened, racial tensions may have mounted, unions and social democratic parties may have weakened or reached an impasse, but never mind. Attend to popular culture, study it with sympathy for the rewards that minorities at least attempt to find there, and one need not dwell on unpleasant – to use an old-fashioned word – realities. One need not be unduly vexed by the most recent electoral defeat. One need not be preoccupied by the ways in which the political culture's center of gravity has moved rightward – or rather, one can put this down to the iron grip of the established media institutions. One need not even be rigorous about what one opposes and what one proposes in its place. Is capitalism the trouble? Is it the particular form of capitalism practiced by multinational corporations in a deregulatory era? Is it patriarchy (and is that the proper term for a society that has seen such an upheaval in relations between women and men in the course of a half-century)? Racism? Anti-democracy? Practitioners of cultural studies, like the rest of the academic left, are frequently elusive. Speaking cavalierly of 'opposition' and 'resistance' permits – rather, cultivates – a certain sloppiness of thinking. There it is possible to remain 'left' without having to face the most difficult questions of political self-definition.

Here is an interesting convergence with cultural studies' apparent rival among left-wing versions of media studies. The 'propaganda model' of news media popularized by Noam Chomsky and Edward Herman (Herman and Chomsky, 1987), much in favor on the left, purports to provide a political-economy alternative to cultural studies populism *vis-à-vis* the media. At first blush, the bleakness of the Chomsky–Herman 'propaganda model' would seem diametrically counterposed to the populist enthusiasms of cultural studies. But in structure the two approaches complement each other. In the Chomsky-Herman model, the uniform news media (this school does not much address the rest of popular culture) succeed in persuading educated elites (though not, *mirabile dictu*, the sensibly insulated *plebs*) that the ruling groups have the right to rule as they do – by conveying systematic propaganda for reasons of profitability and political influence, especially with respect to America's foreign activities. Chomsky and Herman are frequently right about the American media's disposition to find anti-communist victims (as in Cambodia) vastly more 'deserving' than victims who are communists or persecuted by regimes supported by Washington (as in East Timor or Guatemala). But they aim to do more than deplore the media skew. They aim to account for the power of the powerful and the submission of intellectuals. In their view, for example, if the press, following the Republican lead in the 1980s, demonized Nicaragua's Sandinistas, this explains why intellectuals went along with government policy.

The problem with this widely approved argument is that things didn't happen that way. American opinion did not favor the Reagan administration's support of the 'contras' (this, in fact, is why the administration went to extraordinary lengths to keep that support secret). Neither did television attention to Serbian and Croatian aggression and atrocities in Bosnia, in 1992–95, arouse an interventionist mood in either educated or general opinion, or among the political classes, although it must have tilted sympathies to the side of the Sarajevo government (generally known as 'the Muslims'). Now, one may legitimately argue that the establishment news media are generally comfortable in the arms of political power – their energetic servility during the Gulf War is a case in point – and yet at the same time recognize that the explanation for why political events take place as they do must be rather more complicated than are dreamed of in the Big Brother model of the media. In particular, there are other reasons, and substantial ones, for the ineffectuality of the left besides the fact that the media are rigged against its views. But to take seriously the occasions when Washington propaganda fails, to make room for these moments in one's analysis, would be to complicate a world view in which 'the enemy' is distinct and malevolent and the people noble (though ever and automatically doomed to the margins of power).

In my view, the skew of the news media matters less than the trivialization of public affairs altogether, the usurpation of public discourse by soap opera, the apparent breakdown of mechanisms for forming a public will and making it effective. Trivialization – infotainment and the like – works against the principled right and left alike. The incoherence of news, the fragmentation of vision, the personalization of public space militates against all consistent political mobilizations. But Chomsky and Herman appeal to the pleasure of self-marginalization: *we* possess the truth, *they* possess power. If only *we*, the righteous and smart, were in charge of filling the public mind with *correct* ideas, we would prevail. But this is Chomsky's rationalism overriding all bounds. It cannot admit the possibility that there is a popular will to be distracted and deceived, a will *not to know* – that is, not to know whatever might jolt one's routines – and that this passion for illusion was integral to Western civilization long before giant corporations became the centers of news and entertainment.

For present purposes, I wish simply to note the interesting complementarity joining cultural studies populism to Chomsky–Herman paranoia. The emotional tempers are different: cultural studies tends to be buoyant where the propaganda model tends to be gloomy. But both find the discourse of conventional politics deceptive and frozen, so that the choice to secede from it is rational. Both find the institutions of conventional politics irrelevant to the lives and passions people actually live. Both, in effect, abandon the play of parties, the play of working-class organization, the play of political alliance, for the play of interpretation. Cultural studies uses the propaganda model, in effect, to justify ceding official public discourse to the political powers that be – for within that suffocating climate there is no space for real work. In the end, where both detect genuinely dissonant and promising politics is in the sphere of culture, especially where culture expresses the sensibilities of the same social movements that animate the students of cultural studies themselves. But the political consequence is to cede majorities to big capital and its allies.

I return to my starting point. The situation of cultural studies conforms to the contours of this political moment. It confirms – and reinforces – the current paralysis: the incapacity of social movements and dissonant sensibilities to imagine and actualize forms of public engagement that would acquire institutional weight, feel effective, take power. It substitutes an obsession with popular culture for coherent economic–political thought or a connection with mobilizable populations outside the academy across identity lines. One must underscore that this is not simply because of cultural studies' default. The default is an effect more than it is a cause. It has its reasons. The odds are indeed stacked against serious forward motion in conventional politics. Political power is not only beyond reach, but majorities – at least in the United States – disdain it, finding the government and all its works contemptible. In the United States, too, none of the central problems of contemporary civilization are seriously contested within the narrow band of conventional discourse. Unconventional politics, such as it is, is mostly fragmented and self-contained along lines of racial, gender, and sexual identities. Presuming that the cultivation of dissonant sensibilities is the main (perhaps the only) useful activity for rebels, one cannot say that cultural studies diverts energy from a vigorous politics that is already in force across class, gender, racial and generational lines.

Still, in so far as cultural studies makes claims for itself as a framework for an insurgent politics, the field is presumptuous and misleading. Its attempt to legitimize the ecstasies of the moment confirms the collective withdrawal from democratic hope. For the model of contemporary politics inherent in cultural studies is, finally, self-confirming. Seeking to find political energies in audiences who function *qua* audiences, rather than in citizens functioning as citizens, the dominant current in cultural studies stamps its seal of approval upon what is already a powerful tendency within industrial societies: the diffusion of popular culture as a surrogate for politics. It confirms the futility of trying to – indeed, needing to – organize for the public control of mass media. Moreover, it is pressed willy-nilly toward a rapture of technological progress. It offers no resistance to the primacy of visual and nonlinear culture over the literary and linear. To the contrary: it embraces technological innovation as soon as the latest developments prove popular (at least with students of cultural studies themselves, or approved groups). It embraces the sufficiency of markets – at least of markets that have fragmented as a result of the pairing of technological innovation and audience segmentation, as with cable television. Its idea of the intellect's democratic commitment is to flatter the audience.

Or is there a chance of a modest redemption? Perhaps, if we imagine a harder-headed, less wishful cultural studies, free of the burden of imagining itself to be a political practice. A chastened, realistic cultural studies would divest itself of political pretensions. It would not claim to *be* politics. It would not mistake the academy for the larger society. It would be less romantic about the world but also about itself. Less would be more. Rigorous practitioners of cultural studies should be more curious about the world that remains to be researched – and changed. We would learn more about politics, economy, and society, and in the process, appreciate better what culture, and cultural study, do *not* accomplish. If we wish to do politics, let us organize groups, coalitions, demonstrations, lobbies, whatever; let us do politics. Let us not think that our academic work is already that.

As things stand, cultural studies tends to trump Hegel. What is real may not be rational, but that is only because it is better. In its disdain for elitism, cultural studies helps erode the legitimacy of the intellectual life that cultivates assessments of value that have the audacity to stand outside the market. In this way, cultural studies integrates itself nicely into a society that converts the need for distraction into one of its central industries, and calls 'critics' those arbiters of taste whose business is to issue shopping advice to restless consumers.

Notes

1 Present on the occasion when Aronowitz made this announcement at a conference organized through the History of Consciousness Program at the University of California, Santa Cruz was Adam Michnik, a major intellectual figure in the Polish movement against Communism, who held a drastically different idea of what constitutes a social movement, and found the proceedings for the most part something between incomprehensible and laughable. His astonishment at what passed for political debate among American academics was more than

idiosyncratic. It reflected an Eastern European's understanding of where the fundamental dividing line falls in politics: between civil society and the State.

2 Teaching *The Lonely Crowd* in the 1980s, I found that Berkeley students had trouble making intuitive sense of the transition from 'inner-' to 'other-direction'. It dawned on me that the category of 'inner-direction' had fallen outside their experience. They took other-direction for granted. *Of course* the young formed a sense of themselves from peer groups; of course they found companions and heroes in the mass media; where else might they have looked?

3

Policy Help Wanted: Willing and Able Media Culturalists Please Apply

Denis McQuail

Introduction: media culture still matters

We find ourselves at a confusing stage in the development of mass media and of their relationship to society. The media have acquired greater autonomy and an institutional dynamic of their own. 'Society' also appears more self-conscious than ever about the power of the media, yet with less power to influence their content and direction. The very notion of cultural policy has a dubious ring to many ears, on both the liberal and conservative wings of the mainstream political spectrum. It connotes commissars, preachers and regu-lators, cultural correctness backed by thought police or armies of middle-aged, middle-class bureaucrats. No doubt there are very divergent agendas for regulating the media, but the current political climate is not really favourable to either, even if the right wing seems to have the upper hand. Nevertheless, every society still exercises, openly or covertly, some branch or brand of media cultural policy, varying in reach, intrusiveness and precise goals.

Concern about media culture is not confined to one country or one class. Public rows about the quality of American television, extending from at least Federal Communication Commission (FCC) Chairman Newton Minnow's controversial 'Vast Wasteland' speech in 1961 (see Minnow, 1991) to the renewed assault in the mid-1990s by politically conservative forces, suggest a permanent condition of alarm in influential quarters (for instance, Senator Dole's outburst against Time-Warner and the Communications Decency Act in Spring 1995). The perceptions of American media failings are not funda-mentally very different from those voiced in Europe, West and East, as the commercialization of television gathers pace. Bogart (1995) extensively doc-uments what he refers to as the 'banality, sensationalism and corruption in commercial culture' and declares the market on its own to be inadequate to the task of redemption. Even fears about the effects of globalization on national culture are heard in the United States, the supposed cultural colo-nizer of the rest of the world.

According to Monroe Price, American broadcasting, despite its many channels, has signally failed to reflect or sustain the fundamental diversity of

the country: 'The United States, internally, could be viewed as the first example of globalization, a test run for some of the technological consequences
now felt throughout the world' (Price, 1994: 694). Price cites Jay Leno's joke
during the inauguration of NBC's European Super Channel, 'We're going to
ruin your culture just like we ruined our own'. George Gerbner (1995) has
noted that America's role as chief producer of global audiovisual fiction has
distorted its own domestic film and television supply because 'violence "travels well" on the global market'. In cultural terms, there are no winners, it
seems, from media concentration and conglomeration.

The mass media have increasingly been able to escape from the hand of
policy control, partly, although not solely, as a result of unplanned but 'liberating' trends in technology and economics. Although media policy retains
some mandate to regulate media structure and some aspects of media markets, regulation of content, and thus of *culture*, has widely been weakened,
delegitimated or even abandoned. The current condition is one of tension
between an expanding media world and a shrinking capacity by 'society' to
control it (not least because of a reduced national sovereignty in relation to
communication flows). It also reflects a more fundamental uncertainty and
disagreement over cultural standards and values in the modern world and
over the desirable direction and scope for any cultural politics. Culture, as far
as the mass media are concerned, has been cut loose, left to its own fortunes
and to the marketplace. Now it is for producers and consumers, buyers and
sellers to determine what it should be like and also what is better or worse,
what should survive or go under.

The *raison d'être* of the one-time alliance between those concerned with
media policy and theorists of culture and society has also been weakened,
leaving media policy with few cultural goals which are clear and undisputed,
let alone realizable. Older models of critical cultural theory which once provided support for policy have been largely abandoned. The study of media
culture has progressed steadily from a critique of mass culture, by way of a
recognition of cultural diversity and the integrity of popular forms, to a near-
celebration of the ephemeral and superficial.

Despite all this, the agenda of potential cultural policy issues grows, if anything, longer and more urgent. The new conditions of the media have
accentuated the 'threats' to culture, as formerly conceived. The perceived
problems associated with 'globalization', 'commercialization' and loss of
(national or local) autonomy and identity receive more and more attention
from socially concerned critics. Ethical issues arising from the conduct of
journalism and the operations of new forms of television in public life become
more and more troubling. In many countries, anxieties about displays of violence and pornography, which are perceived to be proliferating on the wave of
commercial media expansion, are not confined to the right of the political
spectrum but can be found among libertarians, communitarians, feminists,
socialists and just ordinary people who care about their children.

A continuing role for cultural theory

Against this background, one may locate the central point of this chapter. Its aim is to speak up for the need to revive an 'applied' version of critical cultural study which might shed continuing light on what is happening to media culture and give intellectual aid to reasoned defenders of cultural standards, cultural rights and also some informed support for policy, where this still has a role to play. The context is not encouraging. Societies are undergoing profound cultural changes, in which mass media are deeply implicated, while both the authority of cultural theory and also the scope and influence of media cultural policies is diminishing.

Nothing can be done to reverse the underlying social and cultural trends, but something can be done about the role of cultural theory, unless one wants just to sit back and enjoy the postmodernist ride to nowhere in particular. At the very least, we still need directions and signposts which could inform choices of individuals as well as public action. The chances of exerting any real influence are modest, but they still exist, especially if efforts are directed at the core of the problem, which lies in distorted media structures and (often self-serving) refusals to acknowledge a positive cultural role for public policy and the rights of citizens.

To argue that media culture matters is not necessarily to make a case for regulating the cultural role and content of the media in any particular way. There are few, if any, agreed goals to aim for and what regulation can ever achieve is limited. Freedom of expression and freedom from government or regulatory intervention have primacy over any particular claim for cultural rectitude. The available models for implementing cultural policy are limited and technological inventiveness, and with it media expansion, have easily outrun the slow pace and limited capacity of regulation.

Most societies still engage in a continuing, albeit changing, public debate about the good or harm caused by mass media. Such debates are an intrinsic part of the process of cultural change, exchange, negotiation and conflict. The standards at issue vary a good deal from one country to another, as do the means available for implementing change. Within the European model there has been a tendency to favour traditional notions of culture as held by social and educational elites. A premium has been placed on redistributive policies, designed to widen the horizons of the supposedly culturally underprivileged.

Such goals are less visible in the United States, although the institution of public broadcasting in 1967 reflects much the same project of public educational and cultural improvement, in order to serve the general good. Europe has also been more exercised by questions of national language and the need to maintain separate cultural identities, while the United States was historically more concerned, until recently, with establishing an (effectively) Anglo-Saxon cultural uniformity and hegemony in the interests of assimilation. In any democracy, cultural policy cannot be separated from the rest of politics and arguments for public interventions and subventions in relation to culture and media need to be advanced and defended. Increasingly, the task of supplying arguments and invigorating debate has been disregarded, sometimes denigrated, by cultural theory. This is where the help mentioned in the title of this chapter is wanted.

Media politics, policy and policy analysis

Media politics refers to the struggle for power over media, over the course of their development and over normative definitions of their role in society. The term *media policy* refers to any societal project of control, intervention, or supervision in relation to the mass media, for the ostensible benefit of some section of society, or in the general 'public interest'. Media policies are formed as an outcome and an instrument of media politics. In a sense, media policy, is the 'content', the product and concrete expression of media politics. Policy can apply to both the legal and economic structure of media and also to the nature of content produced and distributed. Media policies have to respond to changes in technology and to political–economic circumstances.

Media politics has traditionally been conducted at two levels. There is the official or formal level, where laws and regulations are made to protect or control the media and hold them publicly accountable. At this level we can speak of an 'administrative' approach to cultural issues, with an associated logic of action. This presumes the possibility of achieving objectified cultural goals by administrative means – measures applied to structure or rules set out for the conduct and content of media. It implies a systematic, bureaucratic approach, which sits uneasily with the uncertainty, inconsistency and contradictions of actual cultural production and consumption. The nature of this logic accounts in part for the increasing incompatibility between media policy and current streams of cultural analysis.

There is another sphere and another kind of media politics, informal and sometimes subversive, expressed in continuous criticism of, and debate over, the aims and outcomes of official media politics and about the performance of dominant media. This sphere is typically occupied by a disparate group of more or less critical thinkers and activists, of the left or the right, with the media themselves increasingly playing a part. It is here that radical change is likely to be proposed, debated or promoted. In the early days of mass media, cultural theorists and critics were often optimistic about the potential for achieving desirable cultural objectives by legal and economic intervention. This is characteristic of what is sometimes now referred to as a 'modernist' outlook, an extension of the 'enlightenment' project. For a good many current thinkers, this attitude has had its day.

The identity of the field of *media policy analysis* is somewhat uncertain and its boundaries unclear. Nevertheless, as media politics has become more institutionalized in the form of enquiries, policy proposals, as well as in media regulations and agencies for their implementation, a gap has opened up between the 'official' branch and its informal, critical and dissident counterpart. The former is more likely to adopt the concepts and language of law, administration, economics and management. In this, it reflects the degree to which the media have become a much more significant economic activity (closer to business than to culture), based on increasingly complex technology and organized on a global scale.

The recent rise of attention around the world to the 'electronic multi-media super-highway' in political rhetoric as well as in journalistic hype and marketing-newspeak is one indicator of the changed nature of public debate about the media and of the sidelining of old and maybe old-fashioned cultural concerns. The academic variant of media policy analysis is now typically long on 'realism', anxious to appear economically and technologically literate, and rather short on idealism, fundamental criticism and visions of a communication future which does more than service the global market and post-industrial state ever more efficiently and profitably.

Issues for media cultural policy

Despite the changed climate, there are numerous cultural issues which are a potential object of media policy and which call for sophisticated policy analysis. The cultural consequences of international media flow (sometimes with specific reference to 'cultural imperialism', 'globalization', 'americanization', etc.) still exercise some governments, cultural producers and concerned intellectuals. The cultural implications of a massive increase in advertising, which is often part of the transnational flow, matter to those whose ideal society is not totally devoted to getting and spending as well as to those who value the integrity of art and communication.

The perceived increase in the sensationalism, trivialization and arrogance of popular journalism worries many politicians. Older concerns about portrayals of violence and pornography are still vocally aired. Claims for minority access in the face of yet more homogeneous and concentrated media are as relevant as they ever were, as are the objections often voiced to unfair or demeaning portrayals of many minority and outgroups. There are still faint voices regretting that potentially enlightening and educational means of public communication are so rarely put to positive purposes.

It is noticeable that most of the 'issues' named are in fact also 'problems', implying perhaps that, left to themselves, without policy or its instruments of control and guidance, the media naturally gravitate to socially harmful practices and effects. This reflects a traditional bias of the policy field – a tendency to view the media as more culturally threatening than promising – displaying a susceptibility to 'media panic' ways of thinking (Drotner, 1991). This bias does not sit easily with the spirit of the times, nor with the optimistic and self-regarding attitude of the media themselves. There is a danger of problematizing too readily, just as there is a danger in adopting the administrative attitude to solving perceived problems.

Newer media cultural theory has the merit of avoiding both pitfalls, since it is more inclined to celebrate than to problematize. While this does help to accentuate the gulf between theory and policy, it is also a necessary and important corrective. There is no merit in advocating policy which goes back to an outdated mode of thinking, but there is, nevertheless, scope for cultural policy with constructive rather than repressive objectives.

Historical goals and assumptions of media cultural policy

Before the latest communications revolution, several basic assumptions were widely shared by those who expressed the 'conscience of society' in matters of cultural politics. The most influential model, aside from the critical thinking of the Frankfurt School, was probably that provided by the British school of cultural studies represented, among others, by Raymond Williams (*Culture and Society*, 1958a) and Richard Hoggart (1957). In the 1960s, the *Universities and Left Review* (later *New Left Review*), edited by Stuart Hall, and the Centre for Contemporary Cultural Studies at Birmingham University were active in formulating goals and means for media policy in matters of culture. Many others shared similar ideas, especially on the left and among intellectuals.

One basic assumption was that culture and society are inescapably interconnected and that a 'good society' must entail a widely shared cultural life (a 'common culture') which should promote and support the vital and also the 'virtuous' aspects of the society. A holistic view of culture and society of this kind is not unique to post-war, left-leaning, Britain. Similar ideas have been expressed in relation to very different versions of the good society, for instance: the newly independent nation state of the late nineteenth century, with its revived or invented national culture; the socialist form of society with its progressive, realist and humanistic culture; the new nations which emerged from colonialism.

Even aberrant visions of the good society like that of fascism in nazi Germany and stalinist Russia were incomplete without an ideal of cultural life to go with the radically new political and structural forms. This way of thinking, depending on circumstances, can be viewed as utopian, idealistic, paternalistic or totalitarian. But even in the liberal-democratic societies of post-war Europe, there was a measure of agreement that social progress should also entail cultural progress and that economic progress would be hollow, if marked by cultural regression. The idea lives on in official thinking about a European Union which looks after social, cultural as well as economic aspects of the 'public good'. The loss of some coherent and integrating vision of society and culture appears to be one of the elements now missed with regret in the former Soviet Union.

The assumption of a necessary interconnection between economic, social and cultural development is also open to challenge. The results of such cultural projects are not always happy and the planned connections not always necessary, even when they can be realized. Nationalist movements, old and new, have often found it hard to reconcile goals of modernization and material progress with the traditionalism required for social mobilization and cohesion. 'Progressive' socialism was unable to solve the problem of discordant cultural survivals, nor did it ever invent a satisfactory or viable alternative socialist culture. The advocates of public broadcasting in Europe have found it hard to reconcile diverse cultural goals with a bureaucratic and elitist institutional means (Burgelman, 1986). Left to themselves, the paths of economic, political and cultural developments often go their separate ways.

A second assumption of cultural media policy, in general, has usually been that culture can be changed and improved, desirable forms promoted and the undesirable suppressed. In any case, there is a commitment to the potential improvability of collective cultural experience. Cultural engineering, if only in modest forms, is thought to be possible, provided one has a clear and realistic vision of the goals to be pursued.

The assumptions named presume that culture really does or should matter to everyone and is central to the quality of life. This view underlies the concern with cultural redistribution – the need for more cultural equality as well as 'higher' cultural quality for the minority. The British variant of the cultural project, as described above, went beyond the wish to promote traditional hierarchical notions of aesthetic quality. Cultural quality also embraced social-moral concepts of 'integrity', authenticity, relevance, participation and community. A desirable culture as a way of life, with locally or regionally shared values and forms of expression was the (albeit somewhat vague) ideal, forged out of older materials, including romanticism, the arts and crafts movement, communitarian thinking, socialism, elements of modernism.

Generally speaking, capitalist commercialism was identified as the main enemy of the good cultural life and much media policy was concerned with finding alternatives to the market or ways of modifying its influence and making up for its deficiencies. The numerous and large cultural costs of commerce were identified in terms of: the commodification of culture itself, destroying its critical and creative force; the artificial stimulation of 'false needs' – the exploitation and manipulation of people by encouraging them to consume cheap and superficial products, designed for the interests of the production system rather than related to the 'real' social and cultural needs of people; the promotion of a homogenized and one-dimensional cultural experience; the flooding of the media cultural marketplace with intrinsically degenerate products, especially violent, nasty, pornographic, etc.

Cultural studies as a field and its discontents

Reference has already been made to a state of dissonance within the ranks of the present-day 'guardians' of cultural standards. This large and diverse category includes policy makers, academics, observers, critics, definers and even producers of culture. A once radical critique of the media (along the lines described above) seems to have been largely silenced or diverted. Some of the most prominent and vocal representatives of cultural theory are no longer giving any lead to media policy. They are even undermining it. The result *seems* to be an increasingly threadbare and ineffective cultural media policy project on the one hand and, on the other, a disengaged, uncommitted and self-indulgent project for the study and critique of (mainly popular) culture.

In the not-so-distant past, cultural critics were typically also supporters or designers (often self-appointed) of media policy. They were at least vigorously engaged in debates about media policy. The visions and ideas of critical thinkers inspired the politically minded and both groups pursued goals of cultural quality allied to social progress. Students of media culture and shapers of media cultural policy had common origins in a long history of efforts to reform and ameliorate the cultural conditions of modern society by way of social policy. The present-day successors of these former cultural critics are now largely to be found either in the academic field of policy analysis or in the burgeoning terrain of cultural studies.

Cultural studies is now firmly established as an academic discipline and major publishing project. It exists within and also independently of communication studies (Grossberg, 1993). It is expanding in numbers of its practitioners and students and is reaching out to new territories. It is not easy to define, pin down or capture the cultural studies project by any single definition and its adherents would probably resist any attempt to do this. Ang (1990) cites Geertz (1983) as calling cultural studies a 'blurred genre', being both 'cultural work and cultural criticism'. Ang's own description of cultural studies includes the following : '[it means] participating in an on-going, open-ended, politically-oriented debate, aimed at evaluating and producing critique on our contemporary cultural condition' (1990: 240).

In a broadly consistent analysis, Grossberg (1993) names three key features of the 'practice' which is cultural studies: it is 'committed to the fact that reality is continually being made by human action and thought and that, therefore, there are no guarantees in history. As a result, contestation . . . is a basic category' (Grossberg, 1993: 89–90). Secondly, 'cultural studies is continuously drawn to the "popular", not as a sociological category . . . but as a terrain on which people live and political struggle must be carried out' (ibid.: 90). Thirdly, cultural studies is 'committed to a radical contextualism, a contextualism that precludes defining culture, or the relations between culture and power, outside of the particular context' (ibid.: 90).

Most accounts of the nature of 'cultural studies', for instance those by Real (1989) and Carey (1989), identify its origins as an alternative (to the dominant, empiricist and social-scientist) mode of enquiry and as a critical approach to mass media. Most also identify European (primarily English) intellectual origins, although currently it flourishes in the New World(s). A broader view of cultural studies sees mass media as only one object of interest among many and then not even as central. The starting point of the developed 'culturalist' perspective is the subjective and shared experience of everyday life, shaped by circumstances of one's own biography and social location.

What matters are the practices engaged in and the giving and taking of meanings from daily life. The media enter into the picture as one source of meaning and one practice to which meaning is given. The media are not unimportant but they are not necessarily any more important than other aspects of daily life, such as work, personal relations, shopping, games and other entertainments. Nor do media form the only relevant sources of communication from our environment. Other people, locations, clothes, buildings, events may be equally relevant. The mass media, like these other forms of communication, are essentially subordinate, non-determining, open in meanings both as texts and as phenomena.

In the 'mainstream' cultural studies view, the media are open to multiple interpretations and lacking in fixed, given meanings (they are said to be 'polysemic'). They provide the basis for certain rituals of social life mixed with other staple ingredients. The 'texts' of mass media are neither independent of each other nor of other texts and other languages which we encounter in daily life, for instance those of clothing, fast-food dinners, football games, discos, betting shops, public libraries, churches. This fundamental principle of cultural studies means that we cannot legitimately or meaningfully identify the unique cultural message or content of the mass media and it is therefore pointless to make policies for media culture.

Equally important in the cultural studies perspective is the denial of objective cultural merit or value as embodied in a particular text or performance. The assignment of cultural value is the prerogative of the 'people', of those who take meaning or pleasure from the experience, whatever it may be. Cultural value resides in enjoyment and recognition, and cannot be programmed or legislated for. In his conclusion to an influential and ground-breaking study of television, Fiske makes fairly explicit some of the implications of 'semiotic democracy' for media cultural policy:

> The attempt to produce culture for others, whether that otherness be defined in terms of class, gender, race nation, or whatever, can never be finally successful, for culture can only be produced from within, not from outside. In a mass society the materials and meaning systems out of which cultures are made will almost inevitably be produced by the cultural industries. (1987: 322)

Against the grain of the classic approach to cultural criticism and policy outlined above, Fiske argues that '. . . attempts to produce or defend a national culture, whether by a national broadcasting system or other means, have historically been dominated by middle class tastes and definitions of both nation and culture' (1987: 324). Fiske is typical in directing attention to the sympathetic understanding of popular tastes. He proposes that cultural values deemed to be in the public interest need to be submitted to the 'test of popular pleasure and subcultural pertinence' (1987: 324).

The empowerment of the receiver/consumer as the arbiter of meaning and value transcends or sidelines such concepts as 'commercialization' or 'inauthenticity' which are still used by old-style cultural critics and advocates of media policy (see, for example, Blumler, 1992). Those who practise this kind of criticism are regarded as trapped in the same system of hierarchy, deprivation and cultural snobbery and inequality which they claim to oppose.

The position so outlined is theoretically rather well-founded and its liberating potential should be recognized. It introduces a much wider range of criteria as relevant to the analysis and understanding of cultural experience, including considerations of gender, race, age, locality and the specificity of things that can be culturally possessed and enjoyed, even in the absence of 'cultural capital' (Bourdieu, 1984). It opens a genuinely subversive view on the world of culture. It is fundamentally out of sympathy with the older kind of cultural politics which it caricatures as a sort of charity work for the deserving but ill-educated poor (though the beneficiaries are often the impoverished middle class). It provides a clean break with former, often patronizing as well as empty, debates about high and low culture and about the varying heights of people's brows.

Coming to terms with failing policy and lost critical support

This discussion leads at this point to a number of provisional conclusions. First, it does seem that the 'new culturalism' has definitively parted company with the traditional media cultural policy programme. There is almost total lack of theoretical common ground or sympathy between the two former allies against the common enemy of philistine and exploitative commercialism. The central tenets of cultural studies theory, deriving as they do from the idea that life as experienced and seen through the eyes of 'the people' is the only true source of authority in cultural matters, are not reconcilable with the idea that there are universal, external, more or less fixed standards of cultural 'merit'. It follows that goals of policy cannot be set in terms of 'quality' and that commercial media cannot be unequivocally faulted.

A second conclusion is that the policy project is itself deeply flawed, both theoretically indefensible and impracticable in many of its objectives and aspirations. It depends on assumptions which cannot be sustained and conditions which cannot be realized (especially in respect of the 'improvement' of popular taste). It is a translation of a political programme into cultural terms which are themselves of dubious validity. Many of the regulatory prescriptions for cultural quality appear arbitrary and lacking any consistent logic except that of maintaining an existing cultural order, often hierarchical, maternalistic or traditional. Policy is often implemented in a ritual manner, with little expectation that it will actually make much difference to the cultural experience of many people. Some of the most eloquent critics of media failings and commercialism, like Bogart (1995) are unable or unwilling to draw any fundamental conclusions concerning interference in the marketplace.

Thirdly, although there has not been space to demonstrate the point, the direction which has been taken by 'cultural studies', despite its own critical rhetoric and claim to true political engagement, appears to lead towards playful irrelevance and disengagement from any application of cultural politics in policy terms.

Despite these provisional conclusions, it is hard to see how the conditions of media operation and the central issues of culture and society have themselves fundamentally changed in the last 20 years. The media remain in the hands of owners and actors whose purposes are totally self-interested and whose methods of domination and expansion are crude and unashamed. The only alternative to considered and coherent media policy seems to be the patently messy and intellectually incoherent attempt to uphold somewhat arbitrarily chosen values (with sometimes dubious undercurrents and allies). Crude attempts to divert, dam and contain the flow of commercial influences seem to be the only way left to redress, in some small way, the balance of power between weak and strong cultural producers and weaker and stronger cultural consumers.

The weaker cultural producers in mass media are perceived not only as the despised elite but also as working against the grain or majority tendency of society and times, whose aims are not for profit but for some ideal, artistic, aesthetic or social goal which is not likely to be rewarded in social prestige or the marketplace. There is little consistency in social or value terms within this category. In order to protect them it may be necessary to invent or exaggerate some valued goal or to travel under some more acceptable flag (for example, that of national cultural autonomy). From the point of view of audiences, weak cultural 'producers' in mass media markets are barely audible or visible and are therefore not likely to be missed if they disappear. Thus there is no popular redress against market forces. Without 'artificial' support, they cannot extend or potentially enrich the cultural environment.

The weaker cultural consumers are also a diverse and fragmented set of individuals whose needs are either not recognized or who are underserved by the main commercial media and other purveyors of culture. This *may* not be accounted a great loss, but it reduces choice for all and leads to 'making do' with possibly irrelevant, unsuitable or inadequate symbolic and other cultural goods. Policy for media and other cultural services has always tried, albeit in a rough and ready and possibly manipulative and maternalistic way, to make up some of these deficits and at least to speak up for those involved.

The limits of contemporary culturalism and the poverty of populism

Despite theoretical validity and considerable achievement, the dominant version of the cultural studies approach now in circulation and claiming to fulfil a critical role is choosing not to engage with cultural issues on the policy agenda. It is now a pursuit, followed by and for intellectuals and not addressed to, or likely to benefit, the 'people' who actually constitute the 'popular'. It is also a postmodern pursuit in a world which has not yet fully reached modernity, ahead of its time and with the allure which often goes with that condition. It is not less valid for that in its own terms, but not especially relevant on account of it either.

Its theory, despite the literary origins and bent of many of its practitioners de-privileges the 'written' cultural 'text' in favour of the autonomy of every

reader as a creator of meanings, denying the authority of any expert interpretation or valuation. In doing so, it largely eliminates the need for any
'study' of culture, except as pastime.

By contrast, media cultural policy depends on the assumption that authoritative readings of media texts are still possible and called for. Intended
meanings are seen to have validity as the voice of the artist, with varying
degrees of significance and truth value. The purpose is to benefit both producer and recipient by promoting more authentic, 'desirable' or more
'meaningful' texts, according to various criteria.

One of the most often cited maxims of cultural studies writing, taken originally from the ideas of Raymond Williams (1958a, 1958b) is that culture is
'ordinary'. In its time and context this was an important statement, designed
to reclaim everyone's equal stake in making and enjoying their culture. But its
truth becomes a half truth by obscuring the fact that culture is also at times
extraordinary. Cultures, through signifying systems, order components
according to value and to degrees of significance for shared social life, independent of individual choice or subjective 'reading'. Cultural artifacts may be
invested with an aura of power and of the 'sacred'.

Culture varies in significance as invested in texts, when appropriately read.
Questions of differential reading and meaning–giving are only part of the
story. Texts have differentially encoded significance, recognizable to skilled
readers, or simply to the *appropriate* readers (for instance, the religious believers reading the sacred book). Most of the texts of popular entertainment are
not really regarded as deeply significant either by their producers or their
readers. They are generally seen as optional and disposable.

Much cultural studies' research confirms the marginal significance of the
media message in everyday concerns (for example, Hermes, 1995). It is easy to
exaggerate the significance of popular works by selective quotation, concentrating on 'fans' and devotees. The theory and practice of contemporary
cultural studies does not take away from the fact that some texts are differentially more valued, powerful, enduring and invested with special and wider
significance, especially by appropriate readers in appropriate contexts. Such
texts include many national songs, poems, religious rites, classical music and
much more.

The new populist version of cultural studies has developed around the
study of mass media and popular entertainment (even though it now claims
a much wider remit), and these are indeed ordinary provisions for ordinary
people in their everyday lives. No doubt this particular bias is a healthy
redressing of the balance of academic attention, but it does not change the
fundamental order of things.

Even this acknowledgement of the 'ordinariness' of the popular arts and
entertainment is flawed and incomplete, since the world of media entertainment, however accessible and incorporated into daily life (at a price of time
and money that everyone has to pay), is not necessarily experienced as ordinary by ordinary people. It too is structured by actual and perceived
differences of fame and fortune which indicate success and status and are

sometimes confused with real power and significance in the world. The new elite of popular entertainment may, strictly speaking, be 'powerless' (Alberoni, 1972), but it exerts considerable influence on devotees of popular arts.

Cultural studies has helped in recognizing and analysing aspects of this phenomenon, but it also tends to ignore the implication that this new hierarchy within popular culture is not much different in configuration or consequence from the hierarchy of cultural value associated with older systems of class and power. The limits of popular empowerment are encountered sooner or later and individual consumers of popular culture are subject to the dictates of a more powerful (commercial) system of publicity and the pressure of established and aggregated popular taste, often exerted through peers and the immediate social context.

The drift of these remarks is that cultural studies is not fully engaging with the reality and imbalance of power in the cultural marketplace. It wants to escape from what may be outworn class systems and worn out cultural theory, but the material realities of class are tenacious in their hold. In a world of 'semiotic power', there is personal satisfaction in having the freedom to interpret, select and put together the materials for cultural competence and enjoyment. Cultural studies may help us to escape from tired aesthetics (and to some extent, tired politics) which automatically devalue and disempower those outside the charmed circle of the 'cultivated' (and politicized). But it does so by exalting consumerism and implicitly denying the potential autonomous force and depth of artistic creation and expression.

Still needed: a policy-relevant branch of cultural studies

One might conclude from earlier remarks that media cultural policy as practised deserves no future and, even if acquitted of more serious charges, is no longer viable under current conditions. It is certainly true that cultural policy goals, as, for instance, those which are allocated to public broadcasting in Europe, can be interpreted as representing the interests of one minority or as serving one-sided political goals. Similarly, the various projects in defence of national cultural integrity often reflect or conceal underlying political and economic aims which are given a cultural coat to wear, but cannot bear close analysis according to a strict cultural logic (Schlesinger, 1987). This is not to dismiss such claims, but to locate them where they (may) properly belong. Much the same could be said of the way in which purveyors of commercial culture have taken comfort from postmodernism and the 'redemption' of popular culture.

In our own time (the 'times' get shorter and shorter) theorists of cultural studies have reacted against old-fashioned social–cultural problematization and tried to set a new agenda (though it is not one for action). Meanwhile, the world has also changed and cultural policy issues have been transformed by new conditions of media and society. The mission to spread cultural enlightenment to the benighted poor of industrial societies has been sidelined by the rumoured (but not witnessed) defeat of poverty and ignorance.

Even so, the structural deprivation of a very sizeable minority of members of industrial societies makes it hard to be optimistic about the pace of material and cultural progress for the many, left to (in this case) media market forces alone. The media market will not solve a problem in which it is deeply implicated as purveyor of a (still) mass-produced culture in which violence and various kinds of ugliness are widely discernable. This is not the place to examine these assertions nor to propose policy solutions (there may be none), but if they are taken seriously, there is a case for committed attention from an academic pursuit which takes the name of 'cultural studies' and carries social critical credentials.

Another contemporary issue concerns the survival and vitality of many threatened features of (sub)cultural life – especially the ways of life and symbolic representations of social groups which are being dispersed, broken up, or incorporated into the industrial consumer society. This applies to many migrant groups and displaced ethnic minorities, but also to surviving cultural minorities in Western industrial society. It is an issue shared across the globe and it matters in varying degrees and different ways to very many people. It is quite true that social and environmental forces will take their course and change and decay are essential to cultural vitality. Even so, the many small but valued manifestations of human cultural heritage and identity deserve at least as much notice as do endangered species of birds and plants.

The relative poverty of the dominant policy discourse, stuck in an old groove, is an open invitation to an extension of the field of cultural studies. The latter should be able, as a first step, to undertake a constructive critical analysis of the concerns and the discourses of cultural policy, of the kind just mentioned. Making judgements about media quality is not confined to elites (see Alasuutari, 1992). It is a practice which merits sympathetic attention along with other discourses and practices which have developed around the consumption of popular culture. Culture is itself a device for the ordering and ranking of different things, including concepts, people, practices, values and artifacts.

This leads to a second proposal – that cultural studies broaden its scope to include the larger framework in which cultural issues are problematized and in which varieties of culture are defined and ordered in a social process of production and distribution (as well as reception). The analysis of culture is not an end in itself, but it is a necessary component in formulating policy and it is a task which policy-makers are not especially qualified to undertake.

Thirdly, cultural studies (or some of its practitioners) could beneficially resume the mantle of commitment worn by the founders of the field and take a constructive look at the whole process of making cultural judgements and formulating policy goals and means. The over-simplified notions of media 'quality' as deployed until now in policy are often limited, ideological, manipulative and questionable. Nevertheless, cultural activities do have varying significance and there are degrees of skill, execution and performance in all cultural activities. People behave as if this is the case and speak as if they could perceive difference of value (aesthetic, ethical, social, personal). These remarks identify a minefield on which much intellectual blood has been shed for little good but some clearance work is still possible.

One can envisage a branch of cultural studies which makes an intelligent attempt to formulate some of these issues for research and for policy action in a viable way. It can also translate evaluative principles, which belong legitimately to the broader media/communication policy discourse, into more operational propositions and terms. The kind of enquiry envisaged would need to work with diverse value commitments (albeit suitably explicated and distanced). It would require conceptual tools for analysing value choices and would need to recognize that defensible notions of 'quality' and/or 'significance' in matters of culture do exist, beyond what can be deduced from reception alone.

A framework for cultural policy issues

One way of mapping out the territory of enquiry for an applied form of cultural studies could be as indicated in Figure 3.1, where a number of criteria have been reworked in a way more specifically relevant to media cultural policy. The proposed scheme begins with the broad question of whether or not there is any 'public interest' in the media, in the sense of there being any claim against the media on behalf of the longer term, or deeper, good of society. To answer 'Yes' is not necessarily to vote for government regulation, but to say 'No' closes the door on any further discussion of media accountability to society and on the need for cultural policy of any sort. However, the range of matters on which a public interest might arise is so broad that a total and unequivocal 'No' answer at this point is unlikely, except as an ideological statement of unalloyed libertarianism. Those on the right, as well as those on the left, are more likely to see a selective need for some form of action on one or other media-related issue.

If one goes beyond this stage to consider the specific 'cultural' grounds on which the media might be thought to matter to society, the situation becomes more complicated. There are diverse reasons for concern with media culture and, in line with issues discussed already, we can summarize the main grounds under one or other of the following headings: social equity (which is also a political issue); aesthetics and art; cultural or national identity; ethics and morals; taste and decency. The bases and directions of policy are very extensive and divergent. Within each category, as indicated, there are many further choices of criteria for making judgements, setting objectives and formulating lines of action.

In Figure 3.1, 'equity' stands for the many questions of cultural distribution, which can be addressed in terms of access and real chances to enjoy and participate, taking account of material circumstances. The heading 'aesthetics' refers to innumerable questions of quality, mainly but not only assessed

Figure 3.1 *Media cultural policy: a guide to further analysis*

according to traditional artistic standards. As indicated, there are criteria derived from professionalism and related to the need to innovate and create in a living culture. The term 'identity' is a code word for a wide range of matters which are currently in dispute, but especially concerning the survival of cultural identities of many kinds affecting whole nation states as well as small minorities. The problems created by media globalization mentioned above are only part of a much wider range.

'Ethics' covers all questions of what are considered to be right or wrong in human behaviour, individual or collective, ranging from hate propaganda to cruel and inhuman actions by individuals. The universe of moral judgements is vast and concern for morality remains a human trait. Finally, the entry 'taste' refers to the more superficial territory of public display, where fine distinctions of what is seemly and proper in language or representation in a given cultural setting continue to be made. The 'public interest' may be shallow and short-term, but questions of manners and appearance exercise us as much as morality. The last entry in Figure 3.1 is simply a reminder of the wide range of voices that might legitimately claim to rule on matters of culture in the media, inevitably drawing on very divergent and often contradictory criteria.

The approach to identifying media cultural 'problems' and relevant criteria represented by this framework acknowledges that there are many alternative perspectives and priorities. There is also a place for the view that there is no problem because these things take care of themselves or do not really matter. Even in this very simplified presentation, it is clear that cultural evaluation and policy-making is an extremely complex business and it is even more so if one takes account of the different levels at which work might need to be done (of system, channel, specific content or performance) and of the different roles involved in assessment. These can involve the standpoint of the professional, the (self-)appointed moral guardian, the independent expert, not to mention the audience in all its multiplicity.

It should be apparent, nevertheless, that there is a viable and a potentially valuable task for a field of cultural studies, which is both critical and willing to lend itself to practical (and political) purposes. A more modest and self-reflexive media cultural policy project working in collaboration with a less flighty and opinionated cultural studies programme can easily be envisaged.

In conclusion

Policy of any kind has to be about both means and ends. The means are likely to be interventions in matters of structure, partly because they are most likely to go to the core of problems, partly because they are the most acceptable kind of interventions where information and culture are concerned. Nevertheless, interventions in structure have often to be guided and justified by content-related goals. If modifications of structure have no effects on content, they are of little use. Policy and cultural analysis need each other.

At the core of this chapter is a belief that media cultural policy still has an important part to play in monitoring and guiding changes in communication systems. It appears, however, that the means of implementing policy have, worldwide, become less legitimate and effective. At the same time, the ends of policy, which have to be expressed in terms of cultural services, contents, experiences and influences have also become both less self-evident and more contested. The belief just expressed about the need for policy itself needs to be tested. Without a relevant apparatus of cultural analysis, the desirability and possibility of a role for policy will remain unclear and a matter of unexamined faith. The type of cultural analysis required to rescue (or to scrutinize and criticize) policy will need to be able to deal with matters of social equality and inequality, of ethics and of aesthetics, cultural identity and autonomy, as well as of popular meanings and pleasures. The challenge posed by this author is for cultural studies to join in this task.

4

Political Economy and the Practice of Cultural Studies

Nicholas Garnham

Cultural studies has experienced a remarkable growth within the humanities and social sciences over the last decade. It has mounted an increasingly powerful challenge to the traditional humanities for their elitism, cultural chauvinism and neglect of the relations of social power embedded in texts and their interpretation and to empirical, positivist sociology for its neglect of qualitative factors in general and of culture and agency in particular. The success of this challenge can in part be explained by the elective affinity of cultural studies to the postmodern moment in theory and in some forms of cultural and political practice, a moment that cultural studies itself did much to construct.

The success of cultural studies' challenge has undoubtedly brought with it many gains in our understanding of the complexity of the process by which the determinations of social structure and the effects of social power are mediated through systems of symbolic representation; of the ways in which human individuals and social groups come to understand their world, to endow it with meanings, and then to act upon it in the light of that understanding. But I want to argue here that this success has been bought at a price; that the way in which cultural studies has developed has brought it to positions from which it is difficult, if not impossible, either to analyse effectively current developments within our systems of symbolic representation and associated shifts in cultural power or to engage politically with them. To move on and fulfil the promises of its original project, cultural studies now needs to rebuild the bridges with political economy that it burnt in its headlong rush towards the pleasures and differences of postmodernism. In particular, I want to argue that, without such a reconciliation, cultural studies will be radically disabled from making its potentially valuable contribution to our understanding of the nature and impact of current changes in the mode of production of culture. These changes involve three interrelated processes: the restructuring of cultural production and exchange on a global scale, in part associated with radical developments in the means of production with new technologies of information and communication; the restructuring of the relations of cultural production, involving in particular a social and economic repositioning of intellectuals, the specialists of symbolic representation; the restructuring of the relationship between political and cultural power, involving a potential redefinition of the role, and potential powers, of both state and citizen. Only on the basis of a fuller understanding of the nature and impact of these changes can an appropriate political response then be constructed.

The purpose of this chapter is to explore the implications of what leading cultural studies scholars such as Hall (1992) and McRobbie (1992) identify as the origins of British cultural studies in a critique of economism and reductionism, seen as intrinsic to Marxism and to the base-superstructure model. I will argue that the consequent antagonism between political economy and cultural studies is based on a profound misunderstanding, and that the project of cultural studies can only be successfully pursued if the bridge with political economy is rebuilt.[1] I say 'rebuilt' because cultural studies as an enterprise came out of a set of political economic assumptions. It continues to carry that paradigm within itself as its grounding assumptions and sources of legitimation as a 'radical' enterprise, even if this paradigm is often suppressed or disguised behind a rhetorical smoke-screen in order to avoid the dread accusation of economism or reductionism.

What do I mean? The founding thrust of cultural studies in the work of Raymond Williams and Richard Hoggart, was, first of all, the revalidation of British working-class or popular culture as against elite, dominant culture, as part of an oppositional, broadly socialist political movement. Thus cultural studies took for granted a particular structure of domination and subordination and saw its task as the ideological one of legitimation and mobilization. It viewed itself clearly as part of a wider political struggle, even if many of its practitioners saw education as a key site for their contribution to that struggle. It knew both who the enemy was and who its friends were.

I want to argue that cultural studies as a meaningful political enterprise is unsustainable outside this founding problematic. One can clearly see in contemporary writing in both British and US cultural studies that most of its current practitioners still assume, indeed assert, that it is a broadly oppositional political enterprise. It is to this that Stuart Hall refers when he talks about cultural studies' 'worldly vocation' and argues that 'I don't understand a practice which aims to make a difference in the world, which doesn't have some points of difference or distinction which it has to stake out, which really matter' (Hall, 1992: 278). It is to this that the cultural studies literature constantly refers in its mantric repetitions of struggle, empowerment, resistance, subordination and domination.

Two developmental turns

In the history of cultural studies there have been two main subsequent developments within this paradigm: first, the question of ideology, complicated by the analysis of textuality, has posed the difficult but unavoidable problem of the relationship between symbolic representations and social action, and secondly, and crucially, the concept of domination and subordination has widened out from class to include race and gender. The implications of these developments require an initial clarification of political economy.

The roots of political economy in the writings of Adam Ferguson and Adam Smith lie in the analysis of societies' 'modes of subsistence'. For them, modes of subsistence had key structural characteristics, whether in terms of the dominance of pastoral, agricultural or industrial modes of production or in terms of differing relations of production (feudal and capitalist or a combination of the two). Here, the crucial differences between analytical traditions has been and remains between those who stress technology and organizational forms of production and those who stress social relations as the key defining characteristic of different modes and the source of historical change. Further, on their view, these modes of subsistence or production are necessarily collaborative social forms.

Three crucial aspects of political economy follow from this. First, such collaboration requires a set of institutional forms and cultural practices – legal and political forms, family structures and so forth (what became known as the superstructure) – in order to function. Moreover, different modes of production will have a different set of such superstructural forms and practices. It is important to stress, however, that this does not make political economy necessarily either reductionist or functionalist, as practitioners of cultural studies tend to claim. Thus the mode of production is indeed the bottom line because it sets the terms for individual and social survival and reproduction. But this does not lock anything into place or guarantee anything. The construction of a mode of production is historically contingent. It is also unstable in the sense of being subject to crisis and contradiction, the sources of which may be either internal or external. While created through an analysable historical process of trial and error and struggle, it does nonetheless have a certain historical stability – like all social institutions – because of the social investment, and thus cultural and psychic investment, made in its construction and because of the social dangers which stem from its dissolution. It is also, as the historians of technology say, path dependent – the choice of a particular set of institutions and practices cumulatively blocks off other choices within what is a social learning process.

There certainly have to be necessary correspondences between what the Regulation School term the mode of regulation and the regime of accumulation in the sense that the mode is historically constructed in order to support the functioning of the particular regime of accumulation. But there may, historically, be a range of possible modes functional for a given regime – indeed it is arguable that the USA, Western Europe and Japan all developed distinct modes of regulation for their Fordist regimes. Nor is this a functionalism in the sense that it argues that a crisis in the regime of accumulation, for instance Fordism, a crisis which may originate in either the regime or the mode, will necessarily be smoothly resolved or that a new, nascent regime of accumulation has in advance either a single or indeed any stable necessary corresponding mode of regulation. This again is historically contingent.

The second crucial argument of political economy is that this necessary structure of social collaboration is the form through which individual social agents are shaped and relate to one another. Thus identity formation and culture practices are not random. They are, in some sense to be analysed, determined. Cultural studies, in its fear of economic determinism, has placed overwhelming stress on cultural consumption at the expense of cultural production. It is not that, as cultural studies often claims, political economy prioritizes production at the expense of consumption, but it does argue that in a market economy characterized by extensive division of labour and where the production and consumption of commodities is the increasingly dominant form of production and consumption, including within the realm of culture itself, such production and consumption takes place on different sites which are articulated in specific ways. That, to take one example pertinent to the argument, peoples' identities as wage earners are articulated differently from their identities as consumers and that those differences are culturally and politically problematic and important. Thus, political economy is concerned with the articulation of production and consumption at both macro and micro levels. Of course, in a market system producers are forced to respond in determinate ways to peoples' needs and desires, just as in important ways peoples' needs and desires are formed by what the production system makes available. And this articulation will operate differently in different realms of production and consumption. I have been at pains in my own work to show how the production of commodified culture differs from other areas of consumption precisely because cultural consumption differs from other types of consumption. Nonetheless, a hierarchical structure of power is involved. First, because of their position within production, the resources available to people for cultural consumption will differ, resulting in observable differences in patterns of cultural consumption – to use Amartya Sen's concept in a differential distribution of cultural capabilities. The extent to which this makes a difference to the meanings circulated and to the possibilities of forms of political mobilization is a matter for analysis. But that it makes no difference is hardly, in my view, credible. It is true that there are probably no meanings that are 'unthinkable' within a system of commodity production. But there are certainly some meanings that are thought and others that are not and all political economy would argue is that this pattern is not entirely random or culturally determined in the narrow sense. I would go further and argue that it is meaningful to talk, as Williams did, of a structure of feeling related to a given stage of capitalist development. Certain problems become more pertinent, certain forms of social relation (or articulation) become more or less possible and therefore likely. To take a classic example, in Williams's *The Country and the City* (1973) the meaning of nature and its cultural mobilization for political ends shifts as the mode of production shifts from agriculture to urban manufacturing.

The third crucial argument of political economy is that, given the necessarily collaborative and supra-individual nature of the mode of production, the normative question of justice cannot be avoided. That is to say, how can inequitable distributions of the resources produced by the mode of production be either justified or changed. Both Smith and Marx attempted to develop a labour theory of value, in order to explain the existing pattern of distribution and the ways in which it diverged from the ideal of social justice.

It was further appreciated throughout classical sociology, from Smith through Marx to Weber, that the distribution of social resources was not natural but resulted from a political struggle. The question for our purposes here is whether this notion of class is any longer valid, and is it compatible with the project of cultural studies?

Most cultural studies' practitioners do in fact accept the existence of a capitalist mode of production. Fiske, for instance, constantly refers to something called capitalism, and argues that 'the social order constrains and oppresses the people, but at the same time offers them resources to fight against those constraints. The constraints are, in the first instance, material, economic ones which determine in an oppressive, disempowering way, the limits of the social experience of the poor. Oppression is always economic' (Fiske, 1992: 157). This sounds dangerously economistic to me. Similarly, Larry Grossberg, while arguing for radically distinct 'economies of value' – money, meaning, ideology and affect – with no necessary determining relationship, at the same time argues that the fact 'people cannot live without minimal access to some material conditions ensures only that economics (in a narrow sense) must always be addressed in the first instance' (Grossberg, 1992: 100). He talks elsewhere in the same book, in a very determinist manner, of the 'tendential forces' of capitalism, industrialism and technology (1992: 123).

The first problem in the relation between political economy and cultural studies, then, is the refusal of cultural studies to think through the implications of this apparent recognition that forms of subordination and their attendant cultural practices are grounded within a capitalist mode of production. One striking result of this has been the overwhelming focus on cultural consumption rather than cultural production and on the cultural practices of leisure rather than those of work. This in its turn has played politically into the hands of a Right whose ideological assault has been structured in large part around an effort to persuade people to construct themselves as consumers in opposition to producers.

By focusing on consumption and reception, and on interpretation, cultural studies has exaggerated the freedoms of daily life. Yes, people are not in any simple way manipulated. Yes, people can and often do reinterpret and use for their own purposes the cultural material, the texts, that the system of cultural production and distribution offers them. Yes, it is important to recognize the affective investment people make in such practices and the pleasures they derive from them. But does anyone who has produced a text or a symbolic form believe that interpretation is entirely random or that pleasure cannot be used to manipulative ends? If the process of interpretation were entirely random, and, therefore, we had to give up entirely the notion of intentionality in communication, the human species would have dropped the activity long ago.

There is no simple relationship between the unequal power relations embedded in the production, distribution and consumption of cultural forms as commodities – which is the overwhelming focus of cultural studies analysis – on the one hand, and the use-value of that commodity to the consumer on the other. But there is some relationship. A delimited social group, pursuing economic or political ends, determines which meanings circulate and which do not, which stories are told and about what, which arguments are given prominence and what cultural resources are made available and to whom. The analysis of this process is vital to an understanding of the power relationships involved in culture and their relationship to wider structures of domination.

As Grossberg rightly argues: 'Daily life is not the promised land of political redemption. . . . By separating structure and power it [the focus on daily life] creates the illusion that one can escape them. But such fantasies merely occlude the more pressing task of finding ways to distinguish between, evaluate and challenge specific structures and organizations of power' (1992: 94). Certainly the cultural industries are such specific structures and organizations of power. Where in the contemporary cultural studies' literature or research program are the studies of the cultural producers and of the organizational sites and practices they inhabit and through which they exercise their power?

Political economy does not claim that certain superstructures will be created because the mode of production requires them. Political economy does argue that once a mode is established, the general interest of the human agents living within it in their own material survival and reproduction will tend to ensure that human actions are so co-ordinated as to maintain it. For this reason, critics of the dominant ideology thesis have argued that the 'dull compulsion of economic relations', not ideological domination, explains the relative stability of the capitalist structure of domination, in spite of manifest inequalities. Thus there is a strong inertia in modes of production. This in its turn will entail the modification of cultural practices to this end. Where these stresspoints between base and superstructure will come and the forms of cultural change entailed are a matter for historical analysis.

It is important to note that an entailment of the relative autonomy of cultural practices from the mode of production is that, from the perspective dear to cultural studies of resisting, challenging or changing the structure of domination based upon that mode of production, many cultural practices will simply be irrelevant. One of the problems with much cultural studies writing is that in fact it assumes a very strong form of the base/superstructure relationship, such that all the cultural practices of subordinate groups necessarily come into conflict with the structure of domination. As Fiske puts it, 'popular differences exceed the differences *required* by elaborated white patriarchal capitalism. . . . Without social difference there can be no social change. The control of social difference is therefore *always* a strategic objective of the power bloc' (Fiske, 1992: 161, 163; emphasis added).

Globalization and culture

Cultural studies has brought us undoubted gains in our understanding of the ways in which people use the cultural resources at their disposal to make sense of their lives and of the ways in which that process of meaning construction influences their patterns of action, including, importantly, political action. But at the same time, in its desire to distance itself from political economy, cultural studies has been as much symptom as analysis of a cultural and political period now on the wane. In hindsight it is easy to see cultural studies, and the postmodern with which it has been complicit, not as the herald of the new post-industrial society and politics, but as the last gasp of Fordism and its accompanying American cultural hegemony. The intellectual presuppositions of cultural studies, its stress on consumption, on the pleasures and liberating potential of popular culture, on a new left politics springing from the ashes of the working-class movement, on multi-culturalism and the diasporic culture of postcolonialism, were born of the long Fordist boom and the social and cultural restructuring it gave rise to. Unless it rebuilds its bridges to political economy cultural studies will remain locked within that paradigm, increasingly unable to understand and respond to the ways in which the economy is now being restructured on a global scale and the accompanying changes in the spheres of culture and politics.

What is the nature of this restructuring? The general context is the process sometimes described as globalization. This is, of course, not a new process. It is an integral part of the history of both capitalism and modernism with its origins in the process of commercial expansion and conquest beginning in the late fifteenth century by which the European powers spread their economic and political power around the globe. But in the last 20 years or so this process has entered a new phase of transnationalization. In pursuit of the classic goals of economies of scale and scope, the major corporations in each sector of primary, secondary and now increasingly tertiary production have broken loose from their moorings within their national markets and under the regulatory control of their national governments. They have reconceptualized and restructured their input markets for capital, for raw materials, for intermediary products and for labour and their final product markets on a global scale. This process has been made possible by improvements in information and communication technology and has powered the widespread deregulation of telecommunication markets. This in its turn is part of a general weakening of the power of national governments to regulate their domestic economies.

In addition to this weakening of national states, globalization has been accompanied by a number of other crucial developments. The first is what has been dubbed the 'financialization' of the economy, that is to say an increasing delinkage between the deregulated global flows of finance capital and the necessarily more geographically fixed industrial capital. The second is heightened competition as the protection offered to local markets by the barriers of distance as well as tariffs crumble. The negative impact of this competition on labour and the social fabric more generally is not only increasingly beyond the power of national governments to mitigate, but is actually exacerbated by competition between states for the inward investment of globally mobile capital. This heightened competition has also lead to the rapid restructuring of corporations and the labour process within them, and thus of the labour market, in search of ever heightened productivity. This has had two effects: first, the reinforcement of a dual labour market with a small core of relatively well-paid and secure skilled workers surrounded by a penumbra of insecure, part-time, low paid workers – a reserve army of labour whose wage rates are increasingly determined by a global labour market; and secondly, powered by the exploitation of information and communications technologies, the spread of this dual labour market to managerial and white-collar labour. For the purposes of my argument here this development is of particular importance. The original post-industrial and post-Fordist thesis argued that the shift in the centre of economic gravity from manufacturing to services would lead to the growth of a new service class of information workers, or what has been more recently called symbolic analysts, and that this would lead to more flexible and liberating types of work and with it demands for greater social and cultural autonomy. This is supposedly a key feature of the post-industrial society, an analytical paradigm that lies, usually unacknowledged, behind so much cultural studies' analysis.

In fact what is happening through the process, in the jargon of management speak, of business process re-engineering, with its accompanying delayering and outsourcing, is the coming to fruition of Marx's forecast of general proletarianization, a forecast which the actual historical development of capitalism and accompanying growth of the middle class was supposed to have falsified. In Daniel Bell's *The Coming of Post-Industrial Society* (1976a) and *The Cultural Contradictions of Capitalism* (1976b), in the 'End of History' thesis it was the middle class in effect that took over the proletariat's role as the universal class, the harbingers of the future. This is particularly important for the field of cultural and communication studies because this class was also identified with the intelligentsia. Current statistics seem to me unequivocal. In the USA the average weekly earnings of the lower 80 per cent of working Americans fell, in real terms, by 18 per cent between 1973 and 1995, while, in contrast, between 1979 and 1989 the real annual pay of corporate chief executives increased by 19 per cent and by 66 per cent after tax (US Bureau of Statistics, in Head, 1996). Figures for the UK show a similar narrowing of the social pyramid. The percentage changes in real income between 1979 and 1992 for each income decile group have seen a drop in real terms for the lowest decile of 18 per cent, contrasted with a rise in real terms for the wealthiest decile of 61 per cent (Oppenheimer and Harker, 1996: 167).

Throughout Western Europe there are now persistent and high levels of unemployment, while for those in work, especially in managerial employ-ment, the level of exploitation is rising. In the UK average working hours fell steadily from 57 hours per week in 1860 to a low in 1975. Had that rate of decline continued, the average working week would now be 35 hours. In fact, more than a quarter of the workforce work over 45 hours per week, with white-collar hours rising between 1982 and 1993 from an average of 41 hours to 43 hours per week, in spite of a massive rise in part-time working and with 41 per cent of managers working over 50 hours and 13 per cent over 60 hours per week. In general I would want to argue that it is barely credible that these profound changes in the economic, and particularly labour market, structure will not have relatively direct cultural and political effects. Indeed, in the USA surveys have shown that while the political symptoms of this trend may take cultural forms – pro-life or school prayers for instance – the protest vote first against Bush and for Clinton and then against Clinton and for the New Republicanism is closely correlated with loss of economic status. Thus I think it can credibly be argued that identity politics is an increasingly thin disguise for a ferocious battle for access to the means of production and that a politics that fails to address this will be increasingly threadbare. Whether such a politics will be of the left or of the populist and nationalist right is of course another question.

These general trends that I have referred to as globalization are reflected in the sphere of cultural and communication proper. That is to say the cul-tural resources people have with which to confront politically the changes outlined above will themselves be made available within a globally restruc-tured system of cultural production and distribution. Again these trends are not new and their extent can be exaggerated. Indeed, they often are for their own political purposes by the representatives of the global media cor-porations themselves. The US film industry was one of the pioneers of transnationalization and the specific characteristics of the market for cul-tural commodities favours the maximization of economies of scale and scope. Nonetheless, rising production costs, allied to the saturation of national markets and assisted by developments in communication technol-ogy, have lead in the last decade to the creation of major cross-media global conglomerates, such as Time-Warner, News International and Bertelsman, with a growing share of the global market in cultural commodities. Accompanying this process, and in part a symptom of it, we have witnessed the progressive withdrawal of nation states from their regulatory role over communications (see McQuail in this volume). Indeed, in most cases the state actively encouraged processes of commercialization, liberalization and privatization. This process has in its turn been accompanied within the sphere of cultural production by the labour market restructuring outlined above. Cultural workers have been subjected to increased levels of proletar-ianization. The casualization endemic to the sector has increased and journalists, television programme makers, and other cultural workers are subject to increasingly rationalized processes of production within which any room for resistance to the crudest commercial pressures, whether in the name of truth or imagination, has been drastically reduced. This has been accompanied by a similar process within education.

This is of course a contradictory process. The work of cultural creation can never be entirely rationalized and if cultural commodities are to continue to have a use-value to consumers some roots within their life world must be maintained. It is also the case that language and cultural specificity raise very real barriers to the effortless expansion of global markets, as the failure of pan-European satellite channels and Murdoch's recent experience with STAR in Asia have amply demonstrated.

Nonetheless, there do seem to be three central aspects of these trends which are undeniable and which will powerfully influence both the ways in which we approach problems of cultural analysis and the assessment of possible political interventions. First, the distance between cultural producers and consumers is increasing. Consumers at the local level retain an unsuppressible margin of interpretative autonomy but the nature of the cultural resources at their disposal will be in increasingly concentrated and distant hands at the global level. Second, the relation between producer and consumer will become increasingly a serial one in the Sartrian sense. Cultural difference will increasingly be subject to strategies of market segmentation. This is not to praise automatically the local and its cultural autonomy, and often chauvinism, in contrast to the global, as some versions of both the cultural imperialism thesis and of cultural studies tend to do. The impact of the global may well be liberating. But the point is it will make a difference which is not under the unilateral control of the consumer at the local level. This difference is analysable and open to potential political intervention. The relation, in short, is one of differential power. First the impact needs analysis and then a value judgement needs to be made about that impact which does not accept a priori either pure local autonomy or the beneficence of market competition. In short, the analysis of, and political intervention in, these shifting relations of cultural production and consumption on a global scale requires us to discriminate between cultural practices on the basis of their likely contribution to the general project of the overthrow of domination.

If the aim of cultural studies remains, as its contribution to the general project of the overthrow of domination, the analysis of, and political intervention in, these shifting relations of cultural production and consumption, then it must meet two conditions. It must be able to discriminate between cultural practices on the basis of their emancipatory potential and thus unavoidably confront the question of false consciousness. And it must take seriously the mediated nature of the process and thus the crucial role played by the specialized agents of cultural production whom I will term intellectuals. The historical development of cultural studies now radically disables it in its approach to these two issues.

Intellectuals, cultural studies and false consciousness

Cultural studies was founded on a turn from the analysis of dominant or elite cultural practices towards the analysis of popular cultural practices. First, it aimed to give the working class a sense of the value of its own experience, values and voices as against those of the dominant class, as a contribution to a classic Gramscian hegemonic struggle. But it assumed that the values embedded or enacted in these cultural practices were progressive and sprung directly from the experience of subordination. This was a classic Marxist view. A revolutionary consciousness would be produced by the direct experience of subordination. The problem was to mobilize it. This model was later used in the context of colonialism and race by Fanon and his followers and within the feminist movement. It still runs powerfully through cultural studies, in particular through its increasing stress on the study of daily life. The project is then to give a voice to subordinate groups, a voice which because it stems from experience is, by definition, both authentic and progressive.

The second reason for the turn to popular culture derived from the preoccupations of the Frankfurt School with the demonstrable lack of revolutionary consciousness. The purpose of cultural studies was to analyse the mechanisms by which people are mobilized or not behind those emancipatory projects that aid progressive and combat reactionary mobilization. But once political and cultural values are divorced from the necessary authenticity of experience, some grounds for identifying positions as either progressive or reactionary must be found. In short, we have to discriminate between cultural practices. This in turn requires an analysis of the structure of domination which may be distinct from the perception of that domination by the social agents subject to it. The concept of false consciousness makes people uncomfortable because it seems to imply a rejection of the cultural practices of others as inauthentic and the granting to intellectuals – or, more pertinently in the history of cultural studies, a vanguard party – a privileged access to truth. However, once one accepts the idea both that our relations to social reality are mediated via systems of symbolic representation on the one hand and that we live within structures of domination the mechanisms and effects of which are not immediately available to experience on the other, then a concept like false consciousness becomes necessary. Moreover, only such a concept gives intellectuals a valid political role in the widest sense of that word. First, organic intellectuals, in a necessary and legitimate division of labour, create the consciousness of a class out of the fragments of that class's experience. Secondly, intellectuals provide a political strategy by providing a map of the structure of domination and the terrain of struggle.

In fact, most practitioners of cultural studies tacitly accept this intellectual role and task; otherwise their practice would be incomprehensible. But they have a debilitating guilty conscience about it. Of course, this is not to say that the consciousness of subordinate groups is necessarily false. That would be absurd. Whether a given consciousness is false or not is a matter for analysis and demonstration and, politically, it entails acceptance by a given subordinate group. For that moment of recognizing false consciousness is the basis for empowerment. At this moment one lifts oneself out of one's immediate situation and the limits of one's own immediate experience and begins to grasp the structure that dominates one. In this sense the model of the intellectual as a social psychoanalyst is both powerful and useful. And it is indeed strange that a tradition of thought such as cultural studies that has been and remains so deeply influenced by psychoanalytical modes of thought should refuse to recognize false consciousness while recognizing repression in the psychoanalytical sense.

The refusal to recognize the possibility of false consciousness, the associated guilt about the status of intellectuals, and the fear of elitism have all contributed to undermining cultural studies' role within education. In its British origins – and not just because its practitioners were located in academia – it saw education as a key site for its intervention and educational policy and reform were a key focus for many of its early practitioners.

Unfortunately, in my view, the educational influence of cultural studies has become potentially baleful and far from liberating, not because it has pursued the role of introducing popular cultural practices as objects of analytical study into the class room, but because in pursuit of superficial relevance and an uncritical acceptance of both 'experience' and 'the popular' as grounds for critical judgement it has divorced them from wider frameworks of analysis within social science. Thus the choice of both the forms of popular culture to be studied and the modes of analysis to be used have been at the expense of the wider political and emancipatory values of intellectual inquiry and of teaching.

The, in Stuart Hall's words (1992: 279), 'necessary and prolonged and as yet unending contestation with the question of false consciousness within cultural studies' goes along with the rejection of truth as a state of the world, as opposed to the temporary effect of discourse. But without some notion of grounded truth the ideas of emancipation, resistance or progressiveness become meaningless. Resistance to what, emancipation from what and for what, progressing towards what? The cultural studies' literature makes much play with the word power. The problem is that the source of this power remains, in general, opaque. And this vagueness about power and the structures and practices of domination allows a similar vagueness about resistance.

Here we need to make a distinction between resistance and coping. Much cultural studies' literature focuses, quite legitimately and fruitfully, on the ways in which cultural practices can be understood as responding to and coping with people's conditions of existence. For Angela McRobbie and others, shopping grants women a space for autonomous self-expression. For others, romance literature and soap operas provide the same function through fantasy. In the bad old days, we called this escapism and in those ascetic puritan socialist days that was a bad thing. Now, while it may be an understandable response to constrained social circumstances, and while it is clearly not either manipulated or merely passive, and while these social subjects are not given any other options, it does little, it seems to me, to resist the structure of domination in which they find themselves. In fact, it may, understandable as the practice is, contribute to the maintenance of that structure of power. This surely is Foucault's main theme – the widespread complicity of victims with the systems of power that oppress them. It is not a question of either patronizing this group or imposing one's own cultural standards on them, but of recognizing the systemic constraints within which they construct their forms of cultural coping and how unemancipative these can be. Surely the aim should not be to bow down in ethnographic worship of these cultural practices, but to create a social reality in which there are wider possibilities for the exercise of both symbolic and – in my view more importantly – material power. Can we not admit that there are extremely constrained and impoverished cultural practices that contribute nothing to social change? We may wish to salute the courage and cultural inventiveness shown in such circumstances and still wish to change the circumstances.

Changing circumstances

Once the question of changing our social circumstances is raised we confront the inevitable question of the nature of social power and the structure of domination within which such power is exercised. The way it has developed has given cultural studies a distorted view of the nature of such power and its relationship to political structure and action. This makes it difficult for it to engage with what has become one of the key issues for both research and political action in our field, namely the future of democratic politics in a world in which, on the one hand, global economic developments are undermining the power of the nation state to intervene to control the economic fate of its citizens, in particular to effect the distribution of the surplus, while, on the other, the cultural developments to which cultural studies has quite correctly pointed – the shift from class-based, party politics to identity-based, single-issue politics, a turn to local, more particularistic forms of solidarity, organization and campaigning and a general decline in levels of conventional political participation – are undermining the legitimacy of our inherited forms of representative democratic politics.

At the heart of political economy lies a concern with the relationship between justice on the one hand and the structural inequalities of the mode of production on the other. In working with this problem it has deployed, either implicitly or explicitly, a model of the State. The State acts first as the necessary enabling container or foundation for economic activity, providing the structural guarantees of both legality and legitimacy without which an effective market-based mode of production would be unsustainable. Secondly, the State acts as the ground upon which the struggle over justice is fought out and through which a just social order might be realized. The State is then related to the mode of production through a politics based ultimately, whether in Smith, Ricardo, Marx or Weber, upon economic interest, however those interests may be culturally mediated. Thus the questions are both what is political struggle ultimately about and what are the appropriate levers of power to effect the outcome? Cultural studies finds it difficult to confront either of these questions both because it has a deep inherited suspicion of the State and, for the same reasons as I have outlined in relation to intellectuals, a related suspicion of representation and thus of representative politics.

Cultural studies developed within the British New Left in reaction against the bureaucratic Stalinism of the Communist Party, within that international movement of thought and feeling for which the year 1968 has now become a symbol. It carried into its blood stream a romantic revolt against all institutions of organized power which drew strongly on the anarchist, syndicalist, direct democracy, ' withering away of the State' tradition within socialist thought. This tendency was then powerfully reinforced by cultural studies' move to the USA with its peculiar legalistic political culture where, as John Gray has recently argued, 'rights discourse is the only public discourse that retains any legitimacy' (Gray, 1995: 6) and 'the Enlightenment project . . . has the status of a civil religion' (ibid.: 144). This completed the move in the politics of cultural studies away from a concern with organized class-based party politics, redistributive justice and the State and their relationship to solidarity and a 'common culture' to an almost exclusive concern with the shifting coalitions of identity politics, with rights, with the validation of ever more fragmented 'differences' and with the local and the single issue. This, in particular, means that cultural studies has much to say about consumption but nothing about the economic policies that structure that consumption, much to say about the reception of cultural products but nothing about the national and international communication policies that structure that production. In particular, cultural studies has nothing to offer to a classic issue within media studies and one which is increasingly central in thinking about the future of democracy in general, namely the relationship between the structures and practices of public communication on the one hand and the structures and practices of democratic politics on the other. This problem is currently posed within the post-Habermasian tradition as that of the Public Sphere and of how such a concept and such a practice might be made meaningful in a world with weak nation states and globalized commercial media. It is not necessary to accept either the details of its historical analysis or the excessive rationality of its ideal model of public communication and democratic politics, to recognize that it is focused on the right problem, because it places at the centre of its analysis the relation between the economy on the one hand and the modes and issues of democratic politics on the other.

Here I think is possibly the main point of contention between political economy and cultural studies as it is presently constituted. To put the matter simply, it is argued that political economy sees class – namely, the structure of access to the means of production and the structure of the distribution of the economic surplus – as the key to the structure of domination, while cultural studies sees gender and race, along with other potential markers of difference, as alternative structures of domination in no way determined by those of class.

That patriarchal and ethnically based structures of domination pre-existed the capitalist mode of production and continue to thrive within it is not in question. To say the least, it is equally plausible to argue that forms of domination based on gender and race could survive the overthrow of capitalist class domination. Nor is the fact in question that until recently much political economic and Marxist analysis was blind to such forms of domination. But to think, as many cultural studies practitioners appear to do, that this undermines political economy and its stress on class is profoundly to misunderstand political economy and the nature of the determinations between economic and other social relations for which it argues.

There are two issues here. First, in what ways are the forms of this racial and gendered domination and the awareness of and struggle against them shaped in determinate ways by the mode of production? Secondly, what might be the connections, if any, between the struggles against class, gender and race-based forms of domination? Might there be any strategic priorities between them. Another way of putting this question is to ask whether the overthrow of existing class relations would contribute to the overthrow of gender and race-based domination or vice versa and the overthrow of which forms of domination would contribute most to human liberty and happiness.

It is hard to argue against the proposition that modern forms of racial domination are founded on economic domination, whether in the form of the slave trade and its aftermath in North America or in the form of immigrant labour in Western Europe or in the various forms of direct and indirect colonialism. While the forms of awareness of and struggle against such domination have been, and will be in the future, culturally varied, it is hard to argue that much dent will be made in domination if black is recognized as beautiful but nothing is done about processes of economic development, unequal terms of trade, global divisions of labour and exclusion from, or marginalization in, labour markets.

Similarly for gender. Again, it would be hard to argue against the proposition that the forms of patriarchy have been profoundly marked by the ways in which the capitalist mode of production has divided the domestic economy from production as a site of waged labour and capital formation, by the ways in which women have been increasingly incorporated into the waged labour force, often and increasingly displacing white male labour, and changes in and struggles over the mode of reproduction and disciplining of labour power. It is plausible to argue, indeed I would argue, that contemporary feminism developed largely as a response to the growing tension between changes in the structure of the labour market and in the mode of reproduction of labour, driven by changes in the mode of production on the one hand and more traditional inherited forms of patriarchy on the other. Again, the cultural forms in which women and their allies come to recognize and struggle against this domination will be varied and of varying efficacy. But I am sufficiently old-fashioned to believe that no empowerment will mean much unless it is accompanied by a massive shift in control of economic resources as between men and women. It is an interesting but open question whether such a shift is compatible or not with the existing class structure of developed capitalism. In short, I would wish to argue that one cannot understand either the genesis, forms or stakes of the struggles around gender and race without an analysis of the political economic foundations and context of the cultural practices which constitute those struggles.

Conclusion

The political economy of culture does not argue, and never has, that all cultural practices are either determined by or are functional for the mode of production of material life. But it has argued, and continues to do so, that the capitalist mode of production has certain core structural characteristics – above all that wage labour and commodity exchange constitute people's necessary and unavoidable conditions of existence. These conditions shape in determinate ways the terrain upon which cultural practices take place – the physical environment, the available material and symbolic resources, the time rhythms and spatial relations. They also pose the questions to which people's cultural practices are a response; they set the cultural agenda.

But, in addition, the process of cultural globalization is increasingly delinking cultural production and consumption from a concrete polity and thus a realizable politics. This has been accompanied by demonstrable signs of political alienation and apathy. We are far from any solution to this problem, but few, I think, would deny that the question of the future of democracy is now central to cultural and communication studies. Cultural studies, having been originally formed in reaction against the regulatory model of social democracy and the structure of party politics that accompanied it, has found it difficult to react with anything except uncritical praise for the local and the forms of identity politics that stem from it to the decline in power of that state and those forms of national politics it always deplored. It has therefore been largely silent in the face of the process of de-regulation and of the trivialization of politics that has accompanied it. Far from empowering the local, this has been a slippage of cultural power from an imperfectly accountable nation state to unaccountable global institutions. By over-stressing the cultural and rejecting structural determination cultural studies has found it difficult to carry out an analysis of the structures, institutions and processes of representative democracy, and the role of cultural processes within them, adequate to the situation in which we now find ourselves.

In particular, cultural studies, with its stress on experience, the local and the everyday, and with its fear of elitism, has found it difficult to confront the problem of representation, in the political sense, in democratic politics and of the division of labour and thus of the cultural mediators in culture. The stress on the active audience, on freedom of interpretation and the rejection of the manipulation model of the relation between producer and consumer has had two disabling effects. First, it has made it difficult, if not impossible, for cultural studies, for all its talk of mediation, to take the mediators seriously as a distinct social group with its own cultural norms, sets of practices and interests and embedded in a distinct labour process, and thus it has nothing to say about how the symbols which circulate in our culture are actually constructed and why or about the possible impact of the current restructuring of the field of cultural production. Secondly, it has tended to collapse both truth and beauty into ideology and thus to abandon any standards by which the cultural mediators could be held to account. Hence the complacency and complicity of much cultural studies in the face of the contemporary developments outlined above. This is particularly disabling where questions concerning the role of the media in democratic politics arise. For here the questions are very simple ones. Why does an increasingly extensive, complex and expensive media and education system fail to provide citizens in general with sufficient accurate and useful information about the world to hold their representatives to account, and is thus accompanied by growing political apathy and alienation, and what might be done about it? Will new electronic systems of information, such as the Information Superhighway, as its proponents promise, help to solve the problem? Or are current trends within the global system of cultural production and exchange driving us inexorably either to 'amuse ourselves to death' or to a new tribalism?

In short, political economists find it hard to understand how, within a capitalist social formation, one can study cultural practices and their political effectivity – the ways in which people make sense of their lives and then act in the light of that understanding – without focusing attention on how the resources for cultural practice, both material and symbolic, are made available in structurally determined ways through the institutions and circuits of commodified cultural production, distribution and consumption. How is it possible to study multi-culturalism or diasporic culture without studying the flows of labour migration and their determinants that have largely created these cultures? How is it possible to understand soap operas as cultural practices without studying the broadcasting institutions which produce and distribute them and in part create the audience for them? How is it possible to study advertising or shopping, let alone celebrate their liberating potential, without studying the processes of manufacturing, retailing and marketing that make those cultural practices possible? How, at this conjuncture, is it possible to ignore, in any study of culture and its political potential the development of global cultural markets and the technological and regulatory processes and capital flows that are the conditions of possibility of such markets? How can one ignore the ways in which changes in the nature of politics and of struggle are intimately related to economically driven changes in the relationship between politics, and the institutions of social communication such as newspapers and broadcasting channels, and to the economically driven fragmentation of social groups and cultural consumers? If this is reductionist or economistic, so be it. It is, for better or worse, the world we actually inhabit. In contemplating the trajectory of cultural studies in recent years I am reminded of Dr Johnson's judgement on the life of Richard Savage, 'nothing will supply the Want of Prudence, and that Negligence and Irregularity, long continued, will make Knowledge useless, Wit ridiculous and Genius contemptible'.

Note

1 Aspects of this argument appeared in an earlier formulation in Garnham (1995a).

5

Dominance and Ideology in Culture and Cultural Studies

Sari Thomas

Recent debate in critical theory has centered on conflict between political economy and cultural studies (Interfaces, 1993; Christians, 1995). In part, this debate might be seen as a contest over who is the rightful heir to critical theory; and, as is typical of dissension within *any* philosophical movement, attention is generally directed to older, safer issues – issues that don't seem to challenge fundamental premises.[1] More specifically, points of contention such as the power of base versus superstructure or the prevalence of false consciousness loom large when political economists debate cultural studies theorists (see, for instance, Garnham, 1995a); however, when surveyed from *outside* these camps – a surveillance which is rarely undertaken or admitted in the literature – other focal points emerge. This chapter is one such outside assessment which focuses on the notion of dominant ideology.

Dominant ideology is an essential and enduring concept in critical theory that remains largely unchallenged. This is not to say that the concept of dominant ideology has never provoked debate among critical theorists, but that such debate routinely circumvents the basic validity of the concept and concentrates instead on secondary issues presupposing dominant ideology's existence. In questioning the basic validity of the concept, this chapter will provide three interrelated arguments. First, despite the scholarly friction between political economy and cultural studies, both approaches rely on a common concept of dominant ideology. Secondly, this commonality is generally denied simply because political economy and cultural studies disagree about the direction and force of dominant ideology. In other words, secondary disagreements routinely overshadow a more important and primary harmony. And, thirdly, acceptance of this dominant ideology concept by cultural studies theorists, in particular, permits their literature to obscure a more complex relationship between ideas and social control. More specifically, it will be argued that much of the cultural contest celebrated by cultural studies' scholars is the result of a faulty, but convenient translation of dominant ideology.

Defining (dominant) ideology

The concept of ideology has been exceedingly prominent in social theory and, not remarkably, its precise meaning remains contested. Ideology is invoked sometimes in reference to false ideas, sometimes to mean class-related ideas, and sometimes just to denote generic beliefs. However, once the term is modified by 'dominant', a more consistent understanding emerges; dominant ideology has routinely indicated an association among three things:

- a set of ideas, world views, central beliefs, discourse, etc.
- an empowered group
- a subordinate group or groups.

The dominant ideology recipe for these ingredients, although not strictly uniform across theories, has a fairly standard rendering: in a society there may be various sets of ideas. One set of ideas, typically theorized as produced by and/or especially associated with the empowered group, is dominant in the sense that it not only represents the interests of the empowered, but that, through the apparatus of ideological transmission, it can incorporate the disempowered and, thereby, contribute to their subjugation. Thus, while a variety of ideological repertoires may be available in society, dominant ideology is the public one – one that is in service to the empowered and which is supposed to serve as an ideological *lingua franca*.[2]

Undeniably, this is a skeletal rendering of dominant ideology when compared to more elaborate characterizations directly or implicitly provided by theorists such as Althusser, Gramsci, Mannheim and Poulantzas. Certainly, these seminal accounts are various and specialized. For the present, though, such amplifications, significant as they may be in other contexts, do not require address; the central problem to be confronted here involves *basic* assumptions embedded in the concept.

The issues traditionally debated

The basic dominant ideology concept described above is common to most critical theory. What is debated, then, is secondary issues – issues that build on this basic, primary premise. Of these secondary issues, the two which most frequently emerge are, first, the base/superstructure debate, and secondly, the debate over the possibility of cultural domination. It becomes important to review briefly these secondary arguments so as to point out subsequently both, the fundamental agreement between political economy and cultural studies, as well as the reason why cultural studies is particularly saddled with problems regarding dominant ideology.

Several 'base/superstructure' questions emerge in examining the critical literature. More recently, for instance, some scholarship sheds doubt on the ability to differentiate between material production and ideas.[3] However, most critical positions *do* accept this basic distinction and much more commonly debate whether base or superstructural forces are causal factors in cultural reproduction. In other words, a critical theorist's position in this base/superstructure debate depends on the extent to which his or her perspective diverges from Marxist economism.

The second matter, cultural domination, is virtually unavoidable in any theory contemplating dominant ideology. The question of cultural domination asks how much a dominant ideology may incorporate and subjugate members of the culture. At first blush, posing this question might seem like flirting with tautology; however, as will be seen, a theory can very well include a dominant ideology concept *without* wholly investing in the idea of cultural domination.

The debates

This portion of the chapter attempts to locate political economy and cultural studies in the larger body of critical theory. By providing this context, it should be easier to see how political economy and cultural studies share a common focus not necessarily incorporated into other branches of critical theory. While the scope of this chapter prohibits an exhaustive or even extensive review of all critical perspectives, it is expected that concentration on the literature's broader assumptions will provide sufficient foundation. What follows is a brief overview that is both chronological and conceptual; although the critical movements identified emerged in the order presented, each continues and evolves.

Political economy

Logically, a description of critical perspectives should begin with political economy. Inasmuch as (revision of) Marx is claimed as a basis for many, if not most, approaches claiming the 'critical' epithet, it might be inappropriate to assign political economy the synonymous label of *the* Marxist approach; still, it is the political economy perspective that is least revised.

On the matter of base/superstructure, political economy theory undoubtedly differentiates labor and mode of production from ideas, and, moreover, provides that economic conditions underlie if not determine ideology. Dominant ideology is thus regarded as a particular set of ideas (possibly among other sets of social-class ideas) which emanate from and uphold the ruling class; however, it is further argued that this set of dominant ideas is, nonetheless, subordinate to supervening economic conditions. It is important to recognize that political economists do not theorize dominant ideology as being at odds with the economic, but rather as a normally reinforcing outgrowth of it.

Stemming from Marx's oft-cited passage from the *German Ideology*, the political economy position does, generally, envision culture domination in connection to dominant ideology; however, this ideology can never be regarded as directly causal:

> The ideas of the ruling class are in every epoch the ruling ideas: i.e., the class which is the ruling material force of society, is at the same time its ruling intellectual force. . . . The ruling ideas are nothing more than the ideal expression of the dominant material relationships grasped as ideas. (Marx and Engels, 1974: 64)

Political economists might vary on the degree to which subordinate 'ideologies' may emerge or how much objective relations and their ruling ideas effectively prevent the development of other forms of consciousness; regardless, from a political economy perspective, dominant ideology is generally seen as substantially prevailing upon subordinate classes which, by definition, are lacking the wherewithal to produce and express an intellectual culture that can compete effectively with the dominant one.

Political economy, then, attributes to materially determined dominant ideology the power of cultural domination, but the theory continues. As characteristic of *critical* perspectives, political economy travels beyond explanatory analysis to prescription (see Wellmer, 1971 and Benhabib, 1986). This shift to a normative level allows for toppling the cultural domination assessed at the explanatory level, and, epistemologically, typically requires a shift from structural to rationalist thought. That is, there is generally an assumption that the personal experience of domination can de-effectuate ideology so that domination can be overthrown.[4]

Modern critical theory

Although many scholars would rightfully claim to cross the line between political economy and what I am labeling modern critical theory, the latter group, despite an overt association with Marxism, is distinguished because of its dissension with the more traditional political economy perspective. Under the rubric of modern critical theory, I very generally include such scholarship as that from the Frankfurt School as well as the less-allied revisionism of Lukács, Gramsci, Althusser and early Habermas. These movements away from more orthodox Marxism may be viewed as formative in the development of later scholarly traditions such as 'mass society theory' (derived from several Frankfurt scholars), the sociology of knowledge (after Mannheim), and various postcritical traditions to be discussed in the next section.

For the present, while the base/superstructure distinction is generally relied upon throughout modern critical theory (see note 3 as it pertains to Althusser), ideology is not treated as derivative of or secondary to the base. The work of modern critical scholars exhibits varying degrees of resistance to economism; although the force of economic conditions is rarely eliminated from the arguments, this body of literature is characteristically infused with ideological interpretation of culture. Indeed, those who followed in this tradition (for example, Godelier, Laclau or Poulantzas) pressed this orientation further.

Modern critical theory also provides a fairly uniform treatment of cultural domination – one which also differs from traditional political economy. In this regard, several interrelated notions emerge in the scholarship. For one, theorists such as Althusser and Habermas argued explicitly that ideology, although compelling, is not deliberately created by one class to subjugate another. Thus, an instrumental interpretation of social structure gives way to a more organistic view of social relations.[5] Moreover, there is also a greater allowance for non-revolutionary consciousness other than that imposed by or shared with the ruling classes. Terms not found in Marx, like 'working-class ideology' appear in reference to alternate world views.

While these shifts away from instrumentalism and unimodal ideology might initially seem to recommend theory that de-emphasizes cultural domination, the reverse is actually true. While such revisions by modern critical theorists gave rise to complex discussion of such phenomena as class antagonisms and resistance (see, especially, Gramsci in this regard), they also provided for social systems at least as oppressive as those envisioned by Marx. Upon closer examination, this makes sense: theories postulating a less centralized but powerful source of control over multiple ideological sites will, ultimately, find it difficult to pinpoint simple mechanisms of emancipation. Especially because modern critical theorists tended to avoid rationalist-psychologism, one finds in their literature assessments of ideological domination that seem even less escapable than that provided by more orthodox Marxist models. Thus, it is not surprising that some modern critical theory (not particularly Gramsci's) and the work that it spawned (especially mass society theory) was later characterized as too 'pessimistic'.

In brief, then, modern critical theory may be distinguished from political economy on both fronts: first, it tends to treat ideas as ontologically separate from economic conditions and, secondly, it tends to endow ideology directly with the power to dominate cultural relations.

Postcritical theory

Probably the last thing social scholarship presently needs is a new label for an academic branch or philosophical position. I offer the term 'postcritical', then, not to recommend a new theory or perspective, but rather as a rubric-of-convenience in which *to collapse* a number of extant movements. Included as postcritical theory is much of what is called poststructuralism, postmodernism and, most notably in the context of this volume, cultural studies. In this arena, I address the work of scholars such as the later Barthes, Baudrillard, Bourdieu, Derrida, Foucault and Lyotard, and, of course, most specifically address those scholars identified with American and British cultural studies.

This grouping, perhaps even more than the groups designated in prior sections, certainly encompasses a range of positions which books are dedicated to comparing rather than collapsing. However, in this context, the overriding postcritical epithet seems apt because of at least two important affinities among the variously named movements.

First, the postcritical work is tied (arguably to varying degrees) to Marx and modern critical theory, not only by overt points of reference (and departure) in the postcritical literature itself, but also because it earnestly shares with earlier critical work certain central concerns with such matters as historical periodization, commoditization and political resistance. However, it is *post-critical* because it both follows from and disengages with traditional critical perspectives.

The second linkage among poststructuralism, postmodernism and cultural studies is a reasonably common orientation to the dominant ideology concept which also illustrates certain disengagements with earlier critical movements. Unlike work in political economy and modern critical theory, there appears in postcritical work some dispute of the base/superstructure distinction. The most intense departure in this context is found in Baudrillard's (1981) challenge to the presumed ontology of major base-related issues such as labor and production. Although the work of others included in this category (for example, Bourdieu or Foucault) is hardly so radical on this issue, truth/falsity/reality concerns do command considerable postcritical attention and, so, it is not in the least surprising that postcritical focus falls on superstructural concerns such as discourse, representation and meaning – and, to the extent that the arguments are influenced by deconstruction, emphasis is given to the alleged transilient nature of these concerns. Moreover, given the significant shift away from the essential Marxist conception of base, postcritical theory generally goes beyond the revision of modern critical theory in discounting economic relations as the determinant of ideological discourse.

However, despite claims of the illusionary, rhetorical and evanescent nature of social forces and relations, postcritical theory does *not* dismiss the notion of dominant ideology. Most notably, cultural studies scholars explicitly make reference to dominant ideology; other postmodernists may avoid the term *per se*, but nonetheless, employ the concept behind it – sometimes even despite competing assertions in the same text.

In the case of cultural studies, Hall frequently addresses dominant ideology in terms of 'preferred readings' (1980c) or unmasking as a strategy of resistance (1986b). Similarly, Fiske's work (1990a: 165–86, for but one example) heavily relies on the dominant ideology concept for explication. Many postmodernists may be less explicit than Hall or Fiske in naming dominant ideology, but it is recognized that the traditional notion is incorporated in many of their explanations, sometimes by what Larrain (1991: 19) labels a 'back-door' entry. Even the more extreme Baudrillard (who otherwise claims that postmodern simulation renders ideological critique impossible) alludes, like Hall, to unmasking dominant ideology. For instance, Baudrillard suggests that the portrayal of Watergate as a *singular* scandal is really a concealment of the American government's broad-based corruption (Baudrillard, 1983; see also Larrain, 1991: 20; and Norris, 1990: 174–5). Likewise, Bourdieu's (1979) analysis of competition in a 'field' as well as Foucault's (1973) periodizing the history of power can be interpreted as relying on the dominant ideology concept.

When turning to the issue of cultural domination, postcritical work diverges from earlier critical movements. More specifically, as noted, the employment of the dominant ideology concept need not demand a corollary acceptance of cultural domination, and the postcritical theorists – especially those in cultural studies – most powerfully exemplify this possible asymmetry.

By focusing on part of Gramsci's hegemony thesis, certain cultural studies' scholars, such as Fiske (1990a), envision a dominant ideology that, while fairly constant in cultural events and materials, is typically accompanied by contradictory ideological elements. Accordingly, ideologically 'closed' events (where only dominant ideology prevails) are rare, whereas more commonly, ideas competing with dominant ones are available and, as a result, give rise to 'resistance' and 'opposition'. Among British cultural studies' scholars, Morley also subscribes to this open textuality of events but suggests the contextual variability of domination or resistance, that is, that an individual will effect opposition to certain events in certain contexts (Morley, 1990: 166). Hall's (1986a) notion of negotiation (as opposed to out-and-out opposition which Hall also recognizes as a response category) indicates a means by which dominant ideology fails fully to dominate in all circumstances.

In terms of general definition, then, postcritical and modern critical theories have in common with political economy a general concept of dominant ideology, although the modern and postcritical assessments are considerably less economistic. However, as discussed more extensively in the next section, political economy *and* postcritical theory, *unlike* modern critical theory, do not 'confer' on dominant ideology the power (directly or fully) to dominate the course of culture production.

Critique of the dominant ideology debates

Abercrombie et al. (1980) have already provided a careful and penetrating critique of dominant ideology, but this work ought not be taken as the last word on the subject. Not only was their work written before the popular advent of postcritical theory, but more importantly, it is largely limited to debating secondary issues. The authors contend that dominant ideology is a concept far too much used in accounting for cultural reproduction; they debate dominant ideology's temporal universality as well as its effectiveness *in comparison to material forces*. Although presented with rigor and sophistication, their arguments are characteristic of those from political economy and Abercrombie et al. centrally address their criticism to *modern* critical theory and related classical social theory. Given the periodization of critical theory suggested earlier, it is only modern critical theory which relies on, as Abercrombie et al. put it, a dominant ideology 'thesis'.[6]

What is important to emphasize here, then, is that neither political economy nor cultural studies adheres to this dominant ideology *thesis*, that is, on the important matter of cultural domination, the two perspectives are kindred: both approaches employ the dominant-ideology concept with which to contrast other phenomena, but neither political economists nor cultural studies' scholars rely on dominant ideology to explain cultural coherence. What political economy and cultural studies debate is *why* the dominant ideology thesis should be rejected. For political economists, dominant ideology doesn't dominate because the base, not superstructure is what is causal; for cultural studies' scholars, dominant ideology doesn't dominate because rational intervention in the forms of opposition, negotiation, play, etc., prevents ideological monopoly.

To reject the notions of either ideology-produced cultural coherence (what political economy rejects) or cultural coherence in general (repudiated by cultural studies), it is very convenient to rely on the concept of a governing set of ideas in contrast to which all other ideas are *non*-dominant – or away from or against the dominant order. That is, it *is* impossible to postulate that any modern culture pivots on a totalizing set of beliefs that are held by and serve what is probably the numerically smallest group in that culture. And, it is likewise impossible to imagine that empowered groups have one, unified set of beliefs. Finally, it is impossible to accept that the stability of a system over time rises and falls on how a monologic is effectively, let alone unilaterally, integrated throughout a complex society. Thus, employing the very concept that *incorrectly* suggests that these conditions *are* possible ironically allows political economists justifiably to abandon idea-based interpretations of culture as well as allows cultural studies' scholars to imagine a less coherent culture in which sites of contest may easily be found and celebrated. In short, the much relied upon notion of dominant ideology has been a sort of theoretical strawperson for political economy and cultural studies.

There is, of course, another version of 'ideological dominance' that may be found in classical sociology and modern critical theory – one that is generally avoided in the theory of political economy and cultural studies. And, as we shall see, this avoidance is far more crucial to a critique of cultural studies than to that of political economy. That is, the classical sociological version of ideological dominance more definitively addresses cultural studies' challenge to the presumption of systematic cultural coherence than it does political economy's emphasis of economics over ideology.

Examination of such canonical scholars as Durkheim, Simmel, Kroeber, Radcliffe-Brown, or Lévi-Strauss yields a significantly different version of social coherence that, on the one hand, doesn't subscribe to the narrow critical theory version of dominant ideology, but, on the other hand, clearly posits an essential relationship between ideas and social control. Although these anthropologists and sociologists consistently observed variation, stratification, and contrast in social structure, their interpretation of such diversity stressed *social integration over incorporation*. More specifically, while incorporation unites components into a unified body or whole, integration brings components together into a relatively stable pattern.

In most classical theories of collective culture, behavioral consistency is not presumed and consensus of ideas is not required for social cohesion. What *is* regarded as necessary in this regard is an aggregate of complementary adjustments of conflicting or diverse elements so that, on the average, a stable pattern of interrelated roles, norms and values result. Thus, when

Lévi-Strauss argues that societies are systematically woven, but *not* to a single center, it is to this concept of integration (not incorporation) that he refers. One can find case descriptions of this notion of integration manifested in, for but a couple of examples, Durkheim's (1947) analysis of variation in totemic systems, or Simmel's (1963) analysis of social conflict.

From this perspective, the notion of a *dominant* social order is a tautology because an 'order' alone is, by definition, an arrangement, a distribution, a patterning, a system, regulation. To order means to engage, to manage, to rule. An order lies over. *An order dominates.* Order, of course, does not have to be understood as linear; it does not have to be defined in relation to a dominant core. Contrary to what Derrida has argued, structure does not presuppose a center of meaning; it presupposes merely a framework of interconnected parts that taken together sustain in mutual support. It is this framework that is the social order; *it is this framework that dominates.*

From this notion of order, it then follows that structural variation (which *is* characteristic of all complex systems) should not be confused with opposition. Variation does not necessarily mean 'at odds with'; it can reflect structural complement. Simmel is very articulate on this matter. He claims that just because we can immediately see social conflict merely in terms of 'its nullifying or destructive sense between the individual elements, the conclusion is hastily drawn that it must work in the same manner upon the total relationship. In reality, it by no means follows' (Simmel, 1963: 262). The imposition of this sort of structural logic, then, in one sense, also rejects the traditional dominant ideology thesis; however, like the traditional thesis, it *does* result in theories linking social coherence to superstructure, as it were. From this, at least two new debates emerge.

The first is a baby/bath water matter. When culturalistic, superstructural, or idea-based theories of social structure are proffered, they cannot be rejected because evidence of unshared values or contradictory beliefs emerges. While theories of ideological *incorporation* may indeed fail to explain diversity and contradiction, this does not mean that *integrational* theory must be surrendered to economistic interpretation. In all fairness, much recent political economy work (see, for example, Murdoch in this volume) is considerably less quick to demand such 'ideological forfeiture'.

Secondly, evidence of unshared values or contradictory beliefs should not likewise evoke characterizations of culture as anarchic or incoherent. Indeed, it is only if we incorrectly posit the existence of a core set of ideas (traditional 'dominant ideology') that we can so easily characterize all other ideas as something else – like resistant or oppositional and, in turn, interpret society as an arena of competing ideologies. Indeed, it is only when we incorrectly conceive of dominant ideology as being one core set of ideas that we can, then, so easily characterize all other ideas (not in that core set) as resistant or oppositional. This problematic characterization, in turn, then allows us to misconstrue society as an arena of competing ideologies. Derrida, who for various reasons is unlikely to be cited in this context, is nonetheless suitable here. Drawing on the Sasseurean concept of simultaneity, Derrida argues that words press up against each other in a simultaneous system – a system whose tendency is toward an equilibrium it can never fully achieve. Derrida's work happens to concentrate on those factors that make it unachievable, but the principles of simultaneity and equilibrium – the pressure of the parts – are eternal and not to be dismissed.

Despite the fact that the history of cultural studies shows consideration of these structural-integrationist arguments (see Hall, 1986c), and that Williams (1977) himself warned about the need to distinguish cultural opposition from meanings that only superficially appear to differ from (to use Williams's terminology) 'the dominant culture', structural–integrationist theory and interpretation *is* otherwise dismissed in this area of postcritical scholarship.

The most common criticism of integrationalist theories such as structural functionalism[7] is voiced by Hall (1980b) who echoes many earlier critics when he claims that the general perspective is highly pessimistic because of (faulty) theoretical premises preventing the discovery of cultural contradiction. The allegation, in other words, is that integrationalist premises invariably lead to interpreting all ideas and practices as systemically normalizing or functional. While I have attempted to contest the validity of this line of criticism elsewhere (Thomas, 1989), there remain terminological and methodological implications pertinent to challenging the idea of dominant ideology.

First, in the context of structural theory, the concept of 'dysfunction' should never, as Hall (1980b: 20) suggests happens, be used as a euphemism for opposition – as lexical subterfuge to disguise cultural contradiction. In fact, to use the term in this way would be quite ironic, for dysfunction is much more severe or radical than conflict or opposition. In a reasonably integrated society, conflicting, contradictory, or opposing sets of ideas or practices may arise that, together (in conflict), might be called ideological in the Marxist sense of that word, that is, together, in opposition, they conceal or distract attention from the social order. The most obvious example of this would be tension between two disempowered groups. Despite normative approaches that might define such situations as 'harmful', the conflict, in this case, might indeed reinforce rather than harm the extant power relations and, thus, be (structurally) 'functional'. In other cases, one might isolate *variations* in ideas or performances that, although unusual or unexpected, are unlikely to challenge how the culture is interwoven. Overall, then, most seeming contests are neither the destructive nor revolutionary collisions observed and celebrated in cultural studies, but rather, instances of structural tension – complimentary pressures that define or support (rather than undermine) the established order (Thomas, 1994). The history of humankind, if it shows anything, demonstrates how social opposition is a routine rather than a radical aspect of cultural life (see, for examples, Sorel or Tarde).

However, an integrational perspective cannot be so specious, as Hall fears it is, to embrace all instances of meaning as somehow exemplifying continuity of the dominant order. When analysed in terms of prevailing social standards and rules, certain ideas or practices *must necessarily* be interpreted as radical inasmuch as their popular diffusion and adoption would significantly alter the standing social structure. To have that effect *and that effect only* would be dysfunctional, that is, dysfunctional events, *unlike* functional contradictions, *change* the order.

Admittedly, dysfunction is not easy to measure, or more to the point, it is better measured retrospectively. When conducting analyses of contemporary culture, the relation of any activity to social stability is anticipated based on familiarity with that culture, with its structure, with its past. In this sense, the type of analysis I am suggesting is invariably time and space specific and comparative. On the other hand, the evaluation of opposition or resistance in relation to a dominant ideology (as conventionally defined) can be considerably less of a methodological problem: one names the dominant belief or practice and determines if the events being analysed are of the same order as the dominant type. Certainly, cultural studies' scholars, like Fiske or Hall, go to considerable lengths to provide descriptively rich rationales for their attribution of contest, resistance, etc. Still, it seems that many such attributions remain problematic because they are measured in terms of their unilinear divergence from a single position of particular establishment standards, that is, the presumed dominant idea, value or practice. Such assessments are troublesome because once a practice is identified as divergent from the dominant practice, there is then no means by which to identify it as nonetheless conservative. Clearly, this is a reversal of Hall's and others' criticism of structural functionalism. While structural functionalism is allegedly incapable of locating contradiction, *this postcritical deployment of dominant ideology makes it impossible to find the conservational value in anything but overtly establishment activities.* My argument here is that the presumption of dysfunction (as defined) at least provides for the option of studying social change while recognizing the compelling nature of social order.

In a compelling assessment, Smelser argues that a view of coherent culture versus one stressing disunity is in large measure 'a function of the vocabulary and theoretical presuppositions of the investigator' (Smelser, 1992: 17). Given the foregoing discussion of structural dysfunction versus cultural contradiction – and, in fact, of how dominant ideology is defined – Smelser's observations could not be more appropriate.

This chapter has attempted to suggest how the very prevalent concept of dominant ideology has created in much critical theory, particularly cultural studies, both descriptive and normative problems. An alternative version of ideological dominance has been offered . . . with admittedly little confidence. More specifically, the intense antagonism otherwise excellent scholars have toward integrationalist (especially functionalist), approaches must be recognized. Thus, when a critique such as this is offered to an audience most likely to endorse either political economy *or* cultural studies, it is unlikely that it will be successfully evangelical. Still, what could be hoped is simply that future discourse relying on the dominant ideology concept entertain some of the foregoing arguments.

Notes

An earlier and abbreviated version of this chapter was delivered at the Annual Meeting of the International Communication Association, Washington, DC, May 1992. The author thanks Lisa Holderman and Mary Pileggi for helping with the library work.

1 Certainly, others (very recently Grossberg, 1995) have lamented stale issues in this line of debate.

2 Unquestioningly, I am not implying here that all concepts of dominant ideology are *precisely* as rendered here. The traditional Marxist version, for instance, would insist that the ideas involved are false and concealing true material relations. In later critical theory, this false-ideas issue is challenged. Still, variations omitted in this chapter should not effect the central arguments.

3 For the most part, these arguments seem to focus on the objective existence of ideological elements, i.e., that ideology is always actualized in the material apparatus. (See Bakhtin and Medvedev, 1985; and Eagleton, 1976.) Certain media-studies scholars (e.g., Gitlin, 1983; Schudson, 1984; and Tuchman, 1978) have treated culture *as* an economic institution. The position is reversed by Althusser and Balibar's (1970) suggestion that economy is inconceivable without ideology and later, Baudrillard's (1981) argument that the material world is illusory.

4 It is this normative evaluation that especially relies on equating ideology with *false* consciousness. The shift to rationalism is marked by the implicit belief that, after the demise of ideology, there exists a level of true or correct human thought that ostensibly is *not* socially determined.

5 It could be argued that the instrumentalism of early critical theory depends on which Marx is read. Subsequent argument in this chapter does not hinge on interpreting the dominant ideology of political economy as a ruling-class conspiracy.

6 To be fair, in reviewing critical theory, Abercrombie et al. (1980) make clear that, rather than imposing a definition, they are borrowing the dominant ideology concept routinely used in the literature. For all intents and purposes, theirs is the same concept employed in this chapter as well. However, as Abercrombie et al.'s review turns to critique, they sustain that definition.

7 The discourse routinely impugning functionalism tends to treat that approach as monolithic, which it is not. The functionalism I refer to here is that influenced on the side of Radcliffe-Brown and Merton; it should not be confused with neofunctionalism. It is my hope and contention that one can revive, explicate, extricate and, when necessary, revise, without inventing a whole other 'school'. With that said, to the extent that the reader interprets the classical literature differently, the arguments should then be attributed to my revision alone.

6

Base Notes: The Conditions of Cultural Practice

Graham Murdock

The absent centre

In Britain, the original impetus behind what came to be called cultural studies, was as much political as intellectual. It was part of a wider struggle to recast democracy in a society where established patterns of experience, division and community, were cracking and shifting. Raymond Williams was a decisive figure in this movement. Re-reading him therefore provides a useful starting point for re-evaluation since his work illustrates, perhaps better than anyone else's, some of the central tensions and silences that have come to characterize the field. His work played a pivotal role in staking out the territory that it was to occupy. His invitation to intellectual transgression and his insistence that culture was always and everywhere implicated in the play of power, was immensely attractive to younger scholars (myself included) who had never felt fully 'at home' in the monastic enclosures of the established disciplines. It offered enticing ways of reconnecting analysis and experience, reflection and intervention. Despite an immediate and abiding kinship with his intellectual and political concerns, however, I found it impossible to accept entirely his conceptual framework or his ways of working. His failure to pursue the logic of his own materialist position and to mount a sustained investigation of the shifting interplay between the economic and symbolic dynamics of contemporary culture was a source of particular disappointment. It limited his analysis and weakened his ability to specify the cultural conditions for complex democracy. If cultural studies is to retrieve this project, and carry it forward, it must address this conspicuous gap.

When Williams began puzzling over the meaning of 'culture' in the years after World War II, it was immediately linked in his mind with four other terms – 'art', 'class', 'industry', and 'democracy'. He saw their connections and collisions forming 'a kind of structure', a field of forces, which he spent his life exploring (Williams, 1976: 11). A number of early texts in cultural studies, including much of Williams's work, can be read as meditations on the transformations of class and class identities in post-war Britain (Gilroy, 1996: 45). This produced a certain tunnel vision. Until a new generation of feminist writers forced the issues on to the agenda, questions around gender received scant attention. Nor was there much engagement with the deep shifts set in motion by Britain's movement from an imperial to a postcolonial polity. At the same time, the fixation with class had one substantial advantage. It focused attention on the myriad ways in which culture was implicated in and shaped by sedimented structures of inequality. It made visible the hidden injuries of exploitation and disregard. This system, and the forces that reproduced it, comprehensively undermined democracy as Williams understood it. By excluding those at the bottom from access to the resources they needed for full social participation, it gave the lie to the promise of universal citizenship, and by concentrating material and symbolic power over people's lives at the top, it deflected and blocked initiatives for change. Williams identified the proliferating industries of communication and culture as one of the centres of this power system but he never analysed their operations in the detail his theory required. This project remained the absent centre of his work, which is paradoxical in many ways, since running through all his writing is an abiding concern with creating an informed, enlightened, and tolerant democratic society in which everyone can participate and 'grow in capacity and power to direct their own lives' (Williams, 1968a: 125–6). He saw very clearly that this required a cultural and communications system that offered the greatest possible range of opportunities for people to speak in their own voice. As he put it in his path-breaking early text, *Communications*, which first appeared in 1962: 'A good society depends on the free availability of facts and opinions and on . . . the articulation of what men have actually seen and known and felt. Any restriction of the freedom of the individual contribution is actually a restriction of the resources of society' (Williams, 1962: 124–5).

The way he pursued this argument was not without its problems. As an 'author' who cared passionately about his own creative life as a novelist and a critic who saw diversity and openness of expression as the bedrock of a democratic culture, he tended 'to view free speech in terms of rights rather than obligations' (Stevenson, 1995: 23). But entitlements to expression also carry responsibilities, not simply to listen to the experiences and views of others, but to refuse the binary notion of the 'other' as someone 'over there', set apart, nothing to do with 'us'. A democratic culture must be marked by the recognition of mutuality as well as the articulation of difference. Williams approached this problem by retrieving and redefining the notion of a common culture.

The problem of how to build a shared culture that spoke to the needs of a complexly divided society, however, could not be properly addressed without a detailed engagement with concrete issues of policy. In Britain in the 1950s, this ambition immediately ran up against the entrenched identification of 'culture' with 'art' (spelt with a capital 'A') which excluded vernacular cultures from serious consideration, and the rising power of communications corporations which continuously pillaged popular cultures for elements that could be sold back at a profit. Both offered versions of a common culture, the one patrician and paternalistic, the other populist. Neither served the interests of complex democracy. Williams set about deconstructing these models and replacing them with a more generous conception of what a shared democratic culture might be and how it might be achieved.

The first piece of Williams's work that I read was his seminal essay 'Culture is Ordinary' written in 1958. Having discovered that much writing on 'culture' was pompous and condescending, its honesty and humanity was refreshing and immediately attractive. It opens with Williams recounting his bus journey home from a visit to Hereford Cathedral to see the Mappa Mundi, one of the great visual codifications of medieval knowledge. The road climbs up from the valley to the landscape nestled beneath the Black Mountains. It was border country, on the administrative divide between England and Wales, and the temporal divide between the agricultural and industrial worlds. As he put it, 'to grow up in that country was to see the shape of a culture, and its modes of change. I could stand on the mountains and look north to the farms and the cathedral, or south to the smoke and the flare of the blast furnaces making a second sunset' (Williams, 1989a: 4). The history of the long, jagged, transition to modernity was 'written visibly into the earth' (ibid.: 5) and inscribed into his family's own history.

The struggle for a common culture engaged in throughout this transition was 'not for some imagined consensus, which we are all supposed to share' but for 'space that allows for a pluralism of perspective and a diversity of contributions; space for a critique of the powerful; space for an awareness that takes us beyond our own nation' (Eldridge and Eldridge, 1994: 110). This effort to construct forms of understanding and solidarity that are hospitable to difference was central to his socialist aim of securing full citizenship rights for all and ensuring that everyone had the resources they needed to participate fully in reshaping the social order in which they lived. At the heart of this enterprise was the fight for rights of access to the greatest possible diversity of information, knowledge and experience, and rights of participation and expression in the central sites of meaning making – the education and communication systems. It addressed people as citizens rather than consumers, members of social and political communities not figures in a marketplace (see Murdock, 1992). For Williams, shared communication was the prerequisite for sustaining these communities and facilitating constructive dialogue on the appropriate balance between sectional interests and the common good. Forging connections based on empathy and tolerance depended on access to communicative networks hospitable to diverse contributions and open debate.

Leaving the anatomy lesson

This political project defined the emerging intellectual enterprise of cultural studies in important ways. Williams had no enthusiasm for the anatomical exercises of semioticians and structuralists that were gaining ground in textual criticism at the time. The purists among them argued that the autopsies they performed on texts must take place behind closed doors to avoid contamination. They had to be, in Olivier Burgelin's words, moments 'of immanent analysis, in which we take account only the internal relations of the system, and exclude all those between the system and man, culture, society – in short the outside world' (Burgelin, 1972: 314). In practice of course, this was an impossible task since no act of interpretation could avoid drawing continually on the reader's reservoirs of social knowledge and cultural capital. As Roland Barthes cheerfully conceded in his essay on photography, connotations are 'not immediately graspable at the level of the message itself . . . but can be inferred from certain phenomena which occur at the levels of the production and reception of the message' (Barthes, 1977: 19). But if interpretation depends on pre-existing social knowledge, how could a structural analysis of a text be 'prior to sociological analysis', as he wished to claim (Barthes, 1977: 15). In retrospect, structuralism's search for the deep patterning of meaning systems is perhaps best seen as a hopeless quest for a double helix of the human sciences, a conception of comparable elegance to the model that Crick and Watson had demonstrated ordered the natural world – an organizational principle that would unite the chaotic surfaces of vernacular cultures into a single, simple, symmetrical system.

There are still some textual essentialists left, but for most people working in cultural studies, the promise of a more rigorous, self-sufficient and 'scientific' study of textual mechanisms has long since faded. Attention has moved from the transhistorical to the contingent and contested, from the rules of language to the ebb and flow of speech. The conceptual edifices erected by structuralism, with their clean binary lines, have been dismantled, deconstructed. Just as architects have learned from Las Vegas to embrace the vernacular and the here-and-now, so textual analysts have delighted in arguing that because every seemingly fundamental division, every hierarchy – 'reality/appearance, clear/uncertain, self/not self' – is 'held in place by discourse . . . they loose their authority as something fixed' (Easthope, 1994: 8). All symbolic patterns are seen as provisional, open to dispute. People have been paroled from the prison house of language and left to roam the open ranges of discourse. Semiotics has been socialized (Hodge and Kress, 1988; Gottdiener, 1995), readers are regarded as the true authors of textual meanings, and studies of everyday interpretative activity are firmly anchored in the dynamics of intimate social encounters.

To this extent contemporary cultural studies has moved closer to Williams's central project. 'We have', he argued, 'to break from the common procedure of isolating the object and then discovering its components. On the contrary we have to discover the nature of a practice and then its conditions' (Williams, 1980: 47). One way to make these connections is to relate specific instances to general structures. This has been a characteristic move in much work in cultural analysis, including much of Williams's own writing. Texts are read as exemplars of new ways of thinking and feeling, produced by changes in social and economic conditions. But there is a link missing in this chain of argument. There is no sustained account of the institutions which mediate between 'remote transformations' and situated practices. Relations are established between texts and contexts, not between practices and conditions.

Hence, Frederic Jameson, in one of the most influential works of recent cultural criticism, can present postmodernist forms as symbolic expressions of the underlying logic of late capitalism, without bothering to show how the life of these forms in society is shaped by the ways that the dynamics of late capitalism work to organize social action in the myriad sites of cultural production and consumption (Jameson, 1991).

Researchers in cultural studies have spent surprisingly little time investigating how the contemporary cultural industries actually operate on a day-to-day basis. This work has been mostly left to sociologists and anthropologists. In contrast, cultural studies has made a substantial contribution to research on practices of consumption, through close-grained studies of the ways people invest cultural objects with meaning and the ways these meanings are remade and argued over in a range of everyday encounters. The problem is that these practices – of sense making, interpretation and expression – are seen as embedded in and sustained by the immediate contexts of action. There is no account of how localized situations are themselves shaped in fundamental but particular ways, by broader, underlying, social and economic dynamics. This produces a paradoxical situation, whereby cultural studies' work on symbolic production tends to look for links between specific texts and macro contexts without investigating mediating practices, while work on consumption focuses on the connections between activity and immediate context with little or no reference to more general forces.

As David Morley has suggested, the analytical challenge is to approach practices of production and consumption as moments in a continual interplay between the specific and the general, the micro and the macro, and to find ways of 'combining interpretative studies of people's "lifeworlds" with attempts to map the contours of the wider formations that envelope and organise them' (Morley, 1992: 272). This moves cultural studies back towards C. Wright Mills's call for an analytical imagination that will 'range from the most impersonal and remote transformations to the most intimate features of the human self – and see the relations between them' (Mills, 1970: 14). This enterprise certainly requires a more comprehensive research agenda. As Angela McRobbie has argued, contemporary cultural studies needs 'a more reliable set of cultural maps, . . . we need . . . graphs, ethnographies and facts and figures' (McRobbie, 1996: 341). This call for 'hard' data is bound to raise methodological hackles among researchers who see the qualitative materials produced by observation, depth interviews and focus groups as the only admissable evidence. As I have argued elsewhere, this is ill-informed and mistaken (Murdock, 1989b: 226–7). But the central issue is not methodological. It is about critical inquiry's philosophical underpinning.

Almost all work in cultural studies belongs squarely in the interpretative tradition within the human sciences. It seeks to explore how people make sense of their social worlds and act on these understandings in their struggles to be recognized and heard. But if a full understanding of how meaning is taken and made in everyday life has to situate grounded practices within the

wider contexts that surround and shape them, we need to move from interpretation to critical realism.

Critical realists do not deny the reality of grounded practices or of discourses and representations, on the contrary, they insist on them. But they
hold that we will only be able to understand – and so change – the social
world if we identify the underlying formations that sustain and organize
everyday activity and expression (see Bhaskar, 1989: 2). The point of this
exercise is not simply to produce a more comprehensive and symmetrical
analysis, but to contribute to the fight for the democratization of culture.
Williams's aim was not just to understand contemporary culture, but to
change it, and because any strategy for change needs to know where to apply
pressure and what to press for, tracing the links between particular practices
and the conditions that sustain them is an indispensable starting point.

In the tea shop

The organization of communications, and particularly of the mass media, was
central to Williams's project, since they provided the major public spaces for
the circulation of experience and interpretation. The battle to democratize
communications was, for him, a long cultural revolution 'comparable in
importance with the industrial revolution and the struggle for democracy'
(Williams, 1968a: 125). But as in all revolutions, there were powerful forces
lined up on the side of things-as-they-are.

Some of these seemed innocent enough, at first sight. He overheard them
talking in a Cambridge tea shop. They were playing the game of distinctions
by displaying 'the outward and emphatically visible sign' of themselves as
'cultivated people'. For them 'culture' was a possession, a trophy, 'they had it,
and they showed you they had it' (Williams, 1989a: 5). Williams's desire to
rescue the culture of ordinary people from condescension was matched by an
abiding contempt for the phoney communality of the commercial marketplace which translated citizens into consumers.

Rushing from judgement

Cultural studies has pursued the ordinary and vernacular with zeal, so that
there is now no cultural practice or production that is not, or could not be,
the focus of scholarly analysis. As one of the assistant professors at Don
Delillo's fictional college-on-the-hill remarks: 'I can understand the music, I
understand the movies, I even see how comic books can tell us things. But
there are full professors in this place who read nothing but cereal boxes'
(Delillo, 1985: 10). At one level this inclusiveness is to be welcomed, since
cereal boxes can indeed tell us things about the ways we live now and our
communal structures of feeling. [1] The problem is one of judgement. Williams
was interested not simply in differences between cultural forms and between
practices, but in 'differences of value'.

As a number of critics have pointed out, contemporary cultural studies has steadily retreated from questions of judgement, and too often lapsed into a happy relativism. Openness has 'become a kind of contempt . . . since it entails a certain indifference' whereby 'no domain of value has anything to say to or about any other' (Frow, 1995: 138). For some commentators this is an unavoidable consequence of the collapse of grand communal narratives and a shared discursive world. For others it arises out of cultural studies' repetitive concentration on the most visible features of popular culture and its lack of points of comparison (Tester, 1994: Chapter 1). Cultural studies' focus on the 'contemporary' has uncoupled it from the analysis of traditional forms 'to the detriment of both' (MacCabe, 1995: 13). To accept this drift is to abandon entirely Williams's critical project. In building a common culture that is responsive to difference but committed to refurbishing the public good, judgements of value must be made. The central question is this: 'Do particular practices or productions provide resources for social participation on the basis of understanding and tolerance and enable "us" to recognise "others" as subjects with equal entitlements to ourselves?' Do they help, in Stuart Hall's words, 'to create a society in which there is enough of a shared culture to mean that we can exist in the same space, without eating each other' (quoted in Sanders, 1994: 18). This involves a continual dialogue with the legacies of cultural inheritance as well as an exploration of emergent forms. The dislocations of contemporary currents of change and the resulting fragmentation and dispersal of established communities and identities makes this task all the more urgent.

Unfortunately, there has been a tendency in recent work in cultural studies to dissolve the notion of the common good in the acid bath of difference. This celebration of 'alterity' and 'otherness' poses substantial problems for the construction of a democratic culture which seeks to negotiate the precarious balance between separation and solidarity. As Christopher Norris has argued: 'it is not much use when it comes to deciding how best to treat others – how to make allowances for their interests, motives, pressures of circumstance, complexities of moral choice – on the only basis we have for such decisions, that of our shared humanity' (Norris, 1995: 35). The focus on difference privileges a cultural politics of recognition, based around the demand to be heard and respected. It has little or nothing to say about a politics of redistribution which is concerned with assigning the resources needed for full expression and participation. But building a democratic culture requires transformations in the deep structures of allocation as well as of symbolic forms (Fraser, 1995). It calls for a political economy of cultural practice as well as critical analyses of the expressive forms these practices produce. To ignore questions of material redistribution is to collude with the conditions that produce the oppressions and exclusions that generate the acts of resistance, defiance and bloody-mindedness that much work in cultural studies has so insistently celebrated. As David Harvey has argued: 'A politics which seeks to eliminate the processes which give rise to a problem looks very different from a politics which merely seeks to give full play to differentiated identities once they have arisen' (Harvey, 1993: 117).

To put the issue in this way is immediately to confront the question of where power over the major public spaces for expression and debate lies. For Williams, building a democratic culture was necessarily a communal enterprise. It had to involve as many people as possible as active participants and contributors. The communications system was central to this project because it is through it 'that the reality of ourselves, the reality of our society, forms and is interpreted' (Williams, 1989a: 22–3). At the heart of this process lay the question of representation, in both its main senses in English – as a system of linguistic and visual devices for picturing the world and interior experience – and as a system of social delegation which nominates some people to speak to and for others. Williams objected particularly strongly to the way the major institutions of public culture – the broadcasting organizations – relied so heavily on professional mediations of popular experience and gave people so little space to speak for themselves. 'Many relationships are possible', he argued, 'in the presentation of talk, but what is most stultifying is the all-purpose presenter, through whom all men and issues flow, and who in the end is a substitute for men and issues' (Williams, 1989b: 45). But who decides who will speak and 'what conventions they have as to what is important and what is not, how they express these'. For Williams, 'these things [were] crucial' (Williams, 1989a: 23). They drew him towards an exploration of cultural power and an engagement with the political economy of culture.

He recognized that a critical political economy of communications was indispensable to his political project, but he never managed to integrate it fully into his theoretical schema. This seriously weakened his ability to demonstrate key points in his argument. It also posed problems for his cultural politics (see Garnham's chapter in this volume). Very few practitioners of cultural studies since have shown much enthusiasm for pursuing this unfinished business, with the result that political economy is generally seen to lie outside the scope of cultural studies' major interests. For some, like John Fiske, this is a simple matter of the division of academic labour. He sees both traditions as 'complementarily engaged in the common critical analysis of capitalist societies in the hope, however slender, of contributing to their change', but he insists that they work with entirely separate theoretical frameworks that cannot be integrated (Fiske, 1994b: 469). For others, like James Carey, critical political economy is 'highly predictable and redundant, and rarely surprising', and politically has been 'on the wrong side of practically everything' that matters (Carey, 1995: 87).

This is difficult to match with my own experience, though admittedly this is rooted in the peculiarities of British intellectual and political life. It is true that some work in political economy has amounted to little more than a description of the circuit boards of cultural power, detailing who owns what, who sits on which board of directors, who has acquired which corporation, and what public regulations are in force. It is also true that this is rarely surprising, but how could it be since the underlying trends are so depressingly constant. But this is not the heart of the enterprise. The central ambition of critical political economy is to trace in detail how the central dynamics of capitalism, and the shifting balances between markets and public provision, shape the making and taking of meaning in everyday life at every level – across the multiple sites of production and consumption – and how they facilitate, compromise, or block the building of a truly democratic common culture. These analyses, in turn, provide an essential resource for debates on which policies and interventions would best underwrite and extend access to the cultural resources required for full citizenship. This project must be an integral part of any version of cultural studies that accepts Williams's invitation to illuminate the conditions and contexts of cultural practice in the service of refurbishing and extending democracy. Simply documenting these practices is an exercise in description. It is not an analysis, and, as such, it has little or no purchase on the levers of change. Any project for intervention must start with an analysis of power.

There was a deep ambivalence in Williams's attitude towards publically funded cultural institutions. He protested their lack of openness and hospitality to diversity at every opportunity. But he did so, as he put it, 'almost against the will of my mind' (Williams, 1989a: 25) since he recognized that, for all their flaws, they represented a major exception to the rapidly rising barrier to complex democracy built out of the 'power of money'.

Williams was convinced, even in the early 1960s, that concentrated ownership of key communications facilities, and the growing importance of advertising, would intensify, and that 'effective control of what people see and hear and read will continue to be in very few hands. New spheres will be invaded' (Williams, 1989a: 28). Thirty years on, their invasion has been massively strengthened by the advocates of privatization, in all its variants.

Formulating a convincing answer to the privateers' question involves two main tasks. First, we need to demonstrate that the capitalist market cannot deliver fully on its promises of choice, diversity, freedom and participation. But, as Williams pointed out, 'it is not enough to state this abstractly. . . . We have to look more specifically into the real failings' (Williams, 1978: 20). Developing detailed, empirically grounded critiques of actually existing market relations, prising open the gaps between promise and performance, is one of critical political economy's central contributions. The other is to help formulate feasible projects for intervention and change that move beyond paternalism and state control.

As Tony Bennett has argued, and as McQuail discusses in this volume, among other things this means that cultural analysts must continually talk and argue with those who control and run the major institutions of public culture and those who decide on their regulation and funding. 'Rather than writing them off from the outset and then, in a self-fulfilling prophecy, criticising them again when they seem to affirm one's direst functionalist predictions', a critical cultural studies has a responsibility to muddy its hands with the practicalities of cultural policies (Bennett, 1992a: 32).

Publics speaking

In the analysis of the shifting definitions of 'culture' in his book, *Keywords*, Williams quotes from Milton's tract, *The Readie and Easie Way to Establish a Free Commonwealth*, published in 1660, in which he advocates spreading 'much more Knowledge and Civility . . . through all parts of the Land, by communicating the natural heat of Government and Culture more distribu- tively' (quoted in Williams, 1976: 78). This was the central project of the public cultural institutions – museums, libraries, adult education – that devel- oped in Britain in the Victorian era and extended into the present century with the foundation of a public broadcasting system. As we noted earlier, Williams was ambivalent about the democratic potential of public broad- casting. He was quick to point to the symbolic violence concealed by the 'silky, persuasive, cultivated, passionless and laughterless' voices of paternal- ism (Muggeridge, 1972: 58) and to the ways in which the BBC's working notions of national interest and national culture too often supported rather than challenged state interests and a politics of conservatism. But a cultural studies interested in the possibilities of building a more democratic public cul- ture cannot afford to give up on existing public institutions so easily, since, for all their faults and failures, they still represent the major alternative to com- mercial populism.

The ideal of public broadcasting rests on four promises that are central to developing a democratic culture. First, its relative, though continually threat- ened, distance from the power of private capital and the power of the state provides a potential space for diverse expression and open debate. Secondly, this space is accessible to everyone without additional charges for particular services. Thirdly, by including a range of experiences, perspectives and argu- ments, within a single stream of mixed programming, it offers an arena in which the politics of difference can be negotiated and a provisional notion of the common good arrived at. And fourthly, it addresses audiences as citizens. It speaks to them as publics. It does not reduce them to consumers. The struggle to defend and extend these promises and to ensure that they are practised is one that anyone committed to a critical cultural studies should actively support.

Williams, however, like many contemporary cultural commentators, saw the potentialities presented by emerging communications facilities, particu- larly the experiments with community cable systems, the embryonic computer networks, and the spread of cheap video cameras as a more attractive arena. These innovations met his two main criteria for democratic communications: they could be owned and controlled in non-capitalist ways, and they allowed audiences to speak as well as to listen, to make programmes as well as to watch them (Williams, 1965: 394). The fact that new means of cultural pro- duction were 'becoming accessible to more diverse, more autonomous, more voluntary and self-organising institutions' marked, for him, a possible break with the existing centralized structures of communications (Williams, 1990: 191). Because these emerging technologies supported horizontal networks

rather than vertical channels of distribution, he felt that they had the potential to become 'the contemporary tools of the long revolution towards an
educated and participatory democracy, and of the recovery of effective communication in complex urban and industrial societies' (Williams, 1974: 151).
This vision was shared by many of the Left who 'dreamt of a Babel-like
explosion in which the cry of protest from the base, transmitted by the new
technologies, would act as to check the unequal linguistic distribution within
society and thus its system of power' (Mattelart and Piemme, 1980: 321). At
the same time, he saw immediately, that because they were being developed
within a communications system which was becoming more concentrated
and more fully capitalized by the day, they also presented potent 'tools of
what would be, in context, a short and successful counter-revolution, in
which, under cover of talk about choice and competition, a few para-national
corporations, with their attendant states and agencies, could reach farther
into our lives, at every level' (Williams, 1974: 151). Again, with the benefit of
hindsight, this has proved a remarkably accurate diagnosis.

The social and cultural practices growing up around these new media offer
a rich new field for studies of meaning-making in everyday life. But if research
is to contribute to the core project announced by Williams, it must do more
than simply analyse practices. It must go on to explore the conditions which
envelop and shape them. And in this enterprise, critical political economy has
a central role to play. Not as an alternative focus, but as a necessary contribution to a full understanding of the constitution of contemporary cultural
life. It is not outside the orbit of cultural studies. It is an integral part of its
overall project. But as soon as we approach the interplay between the economic, social and symbolic dimensions of culture, we walk into the shadow of
Marx's looming metaphor of the base and the superstructure. This way of
looking is undeniably attractive but ultimately disabling. As Williams understood very well, by translating social and cultural systems into terms familiar
from engineering and architecture, it presents them as 'something relatively
fixed and permanent, even hard' (Williams, 1976: 255). It is then very difficult
to introduce a sense of dynamism, process, history. One solution to this problem was to abandon the notion of 'structures' altogether and to think instead
of 'formations' as ensembles created out of collective action and continually
subject to alteration (Murdock, 1989b). But that still leaves the thorny problem of how best to think about the relationship between economic and
cultural formations.

Williams recognized that the power of money could sometimes operate
directly and brutally, without softening or mediation. As he argued, there are
times in cultural analysis when the 'simple' insertion of determinations is 'an
evident advance'. But he immediately added that 'in the end it can never be a
simple assertion' (Williams, 1977: 138). He insisted that 'the analysis of real
determinations' was a matter for careful empirical investigation. It could not
be settled by theoretical dictat. 'We should', he argued, 'not assume in
advance that the basic structural relations between different kinds of activity
form regular uniformities . . . which can then be applied to any specific social

and historical situation' (Williams, 1983b: 41). He was right. If we are look-ing to develop a general approach to the interplay between culture and economy, we have to allow for the fact that the connections are most often both diverse and complex.

It was precisely the denial of this variability in fundamentalist Marxist accounts, that he objected to. For him, determination was 'never . . . a wholly controlling, wholly predicting set of causes' (Williams, 1974: 130). To insist on such a link was, as he saw it, to present culture as a secondary, even derivative, domain, subordinate to the 'real' business of material production. He rejected this construction out of hand, insisting that 'men [*sic*] and societies are not confined to relationships of power, property, and production. Their relation-ships in describing, learning, persuading, and exchanging experiences must be seen as *equally fundamental*' (Williams, 1968a: 18, emphasis added). He felt that the rigid dualism of base and superstructure dismissed 'as merely sec-ondary, certain vital productive social forces, which are in a broad sense, from the beginning, basic' (Williams, 1980: 35). Passionately 'committed to feeling and understanding culture as the place where life was really lived', he 'resited the notion that life was merely superstructured to the hard facts underneath' (Inglis, 1995: 243). His solution was to extend the notion of material forces so that symbolic activities could be reclassified as part of the base, producing a new approach, which he called 'cultural materialism'.

As Terry Eagleton has argued, this move was rooted in a misreading of the base/superstructure metaphor. It is not an ontological thesis about the relative reality and materiality of the two domains. 'It is perfectly possible to concede that . . . pedagogical techniques and sexual fantasies are just as real as steel mills or sterling, just as much a matter of material production' without mod-ifying the essential proposition in the slightest (Eagleton, 1989: 168). The central claim is about the relations between culture and economy. It simply proposes that 'within a multitude of social determinants, some are finally more importantly determinant than others' (Eagleton, 1989: 166).

At other points in his work Williams recognized this. In a late interview he admitted that in the effort of establishing that cultural production was a pri-mary activity, 'I think I sometimes gave the impression . . . that I was denying determinations altogether' (Williams, 1979: 139). Since some conception was essential to his overall project of specifying the conditions of democratic practice in an increasingly commercialized environment, he squared his con-ceptual circle by redefining 'determination'. In this new formulation:

> the reality of determination is the setting of limits and the exertion of pressures, within which variable social practices are profoundly affected but never necessar-ily controlled. We have to think of determination as a process in which the real determining factors – the distribution of power or of capital, social and physical inheritance, relations of scale and size between groups – set limits and exert pres-sures, but neither wholly control nor wholly predict the outcome of complex activity within or at these limits, or under or against these pressures. (Williams, 1974: 130)

This requires us to think of economic dynamics as determining, in Stuart

Hall's phrase, 'in the first instance' (Hall, 1983: 84) and as therefore providing 'a necessary starting point' for any comprehensive analysis of the way the cultural system is structured (Hall, 1986b: 11).

If we accept this formulation, which I for one am happy to do, critical political economy becomes not an optional addition to cultural studies but its missing centre. It is integral to any attempt to explain how and why the cultural system is organized as it is and how it might be changed. Pursuing this project involves two analytical tasks. The first is to chart the contemporary conditions and contexts of cultural practices and to identify the major sources of pressure and opportunity, inertia and movement. Understanding the dynamics of corporate activity is at the heart of this project for the simple reason that in the era of privatization they are more central than ever to the constitution of public culture as an array of representations and spheres of action. They stake out many of the key sites for expression and interchange, and define many of the rules by which the games of distinction and communality, separation and solidarity, are played. The second task is to explore how economic dynamics, operating both within the cultural industries and more generally, structure the distribution of the core resources that support and sustain particular cultural practices. These resources are of three kinds: material – access to money, 'free' time and safe spaces; symbolic – command over forms of knowledge, systems of meaning and cultural rituals; and social – membership of networks of support. From this perspective, realizing the democratic promise of the Internet, for example, immediately faces formidable problems. It is clear that commercial corporations are making concerted moves to mobilize the system as an arena for advertising and marketing and as a medium for distributing information and cultural services, accessible only on payment of a fee. As Bill Gates, the head of Microsoft, recently explained, 'now that the sea of change is becoming apparent, services [including those offered by his own company] are rushing to embrace it. This is exactly the right thing to do. When change is inevitable, you must spot it, embrace it and find ways to make it work for you' (Gates, 1995: 20). The clash between these corporate interests and the ethos of open access and public participation espoused by many Net enthusiasts will be bitter and protracted, and have far-reaching consequences for the construction of a common culture in contemporary conditions (McChesney, 1996; Golding, 1996). Even if substantial public spaces are retained on the Net, there is still the question of who will have access to them, who will be able to use them with confidence? Active participation depends on the possession of the requisite resources and, at the moment, these are very unevenly distributed, in ways that are intimately connected to underlying shifts in the economic system. These are reorganizing patterns of employment, welfare and urban space in ways that have major consequences for everyday cultural practices and choices.

New times/hard times

For an increasing number of people the 'new' times of flux and open horizons, celebrated by some postmodernists, are 'hard' times of narrowing opportunity and the insistent pressures of necessity (see Murdock, 1994). The distribution of discretionary income is becoming more and more unequal, leaving those at the bottom less and less able to enter cultural marketplaces increasing stratified by price (see Murdock and Golding, 1989). At the same time, the vitality of public cultural provision and hence of alternative channels of access to cultural facilities is being progressively weakened by budgetary cuts.

But material costs are not the only blocks to participation. There are the symbolic barriers erected by lack of confidence and the inability to locate oneself imaginatively within the community of users. Public discourses exercise powerful constraints. By constructing the social worlds of technologies in particular ways and privileging particular identities, they simultaneously issue invitations to inclusion and provide grounds for self-exclusion (Murdock et al., 1992). These hesitations and insecurities are further reinforced by transformations in public space and local sociability. De-industrialization and the decay of shared urban spaces have altered patterns of communality and contexts of solidarity. Networks of support, advice and local knowledge are dismantled and not always replaced. However, as some spaces close others open. The complex intersection of shifts in secure employment and changes in the conditions of public subsidy have also provided a basis for new forms of entrepreneurship and self-employment, producing a 'sprawling sector of micro-economies of culture' (McRobbie, 1996: 339).

Close attention to the proliferating repercussions of these overall shifts in the economic formation are central to any proper understanding of the changing conditions of contemporary cultural practice. The critical political economy of culture is not a self-sufficient enterprise, however. It needs to draw on the resources offered by general political economies of late capitalism as well as on more focused studies of the cultural industries. Yet most practitioners of cultural studies see no need to do this. As Robert Hughes, art critic of *Time* magazine, has remarked about recent cultural studies' work on Madonna, the proposition that 'the blonde bombshell explodes the established order of power', 'undermines capitalist constructions' and 'rejects core bourgeois epistemes . . . would certainly be news to my own employers at Time/Warner who recently paid Madonna $60,000,000 for the rights to her work. Some rejection' (Hughes, 1993: 79). He is, of course, bending the stick in the spirit of mischief making, but he has a point. This does not mean that we can understand Madonna solely in terms of transactions in intellectual property. The cultural system is notoriously leaky and contradictory. Neither owners nor stars can guarantee the outcomes of their actions. There are always unintended consequences. But it does mean that any full analysis of the Madonna phenomenon needs to investigate the commercial and industrial dimensions of her enterprise as well as her performances, the images that surround and promote her, and the interpretations and psychic investments of her fans and followers.

As Douglas Kellner has recently argued, we need 'to keep the project of cultural studies open, flexible, and critical, refusing . . . to close off the field in a premature way' (Kellner, 1995: 55). The appetite for theoretical innovation and novelty has certainly been voracious within cultural studies in recent years, yet political economy has been largely excluded from sustained consideration. It has often been seen as stale, *passé*, out of touch with the new times, which is paradoxical since the explosive growth of cultural studies within the academy has coincided almost exactly with the era of privatization and the rapid extension of cultural commodification. Commodities certainly have sign values. They murmur and shout about the kind of people we are and would like to become, and they beckon us to join imagined taste communities. But they also come with prices attached, which organize access and use in important ways. Markets are always systems of economic transaction as well as of symbolic exchange. The trick is to find ways of exploring their interplay.

Turns and returns

There has been a routine assumption within much work in cultural studies that any claim that economic dynamics play a central role in shaping the conditions of cultural practice must involve assertions of reduction or reflection whereby the 'causal agency of the economic base is always written into the very form and content of the cultural superstructure' (Grossberg, 1992: 323). This is a wilful misreading, and one, as we have seen, that Williams rejected. However, in recent work it has licensed a wholesale flight from any engagement with economic processes. As Stuart Hall has noted:

> What has resulted from the abandonment of deterministic economism has been, not alternative ways of thinking questions about the economic relations and their effects, as the 'conditions of existence' of other practices . . . but instead a massive, gigantic, and eloquent *disavowal*. As if, since the economic in the broadest sense, definitely does *not*, as it was once supposed to do, 'determine' the real movement of history 'in the last instance', it does not exist at all! (1996a: 258; emphasis in the original)

This move is bound up with a generalized cultural 'turn' within the human sciences whereby '"culture" has replaced "society" as the preferred object of study in a range of academic fields' (Collini, 1994: 3). The return of the repressed is overdue.

Recent work in the newly fashionable field of 'globalization' is a case in point. It addresses situations marked by the multiple miseries generated by famines, civil wars and crippling debt repayments but has virtually nothing to say about their sources or their consequences. In opposition to Immanuel Wallerstein's influential model of the 'modern world system' as first and foremost an economic formation, commentators such as Malcolm Waters, who are primarily interested in the transnationalization of culture, argue that in the contemporary world 'material and power exchanges in the economic and political arenas are progressively becoming displaced by symbolic ones, that is by relationships based on values, preferences and tastes rather than by material inequality and constraint' (Waters, 1995: 124). In a situation where material inequalities are palpably widening and imposing massive constraints on the freedom of action of citizens and governments in many Third World countries, this is, at best, a substantial misrepresentation. As one critic has caustically observed 'those who deride economic determinism are those whose lives are not economically determined' (Sivanandan, 1995: 20). In the new conceptual world order of cultural globalization, structural inequalities and the systems of exploitation that sustain them slide quietly out of sight. As Terry Eagleton has remarked, in a critique of Homi Bhabha's influential work on postcolonialism, within this discourse 'One is allowed to talk about cultural difference, but not – or not much – about economic exploitation. Post-colonial theory, Bhabha tells us, resists holistic explanations. The truth is that it has hardly any explanation of post-colonial misery at all' (Eagleton, 1994: 13). Williams would have opposed this turn towards texts and insisted on reconnecting work on postcolonial cultures and identities with research on new developments in global capitalism so as to arrive at a fuller understanding of 'late modernity' and its core dynamics (see Hall, 1996: 257).

In the book of his I have returned to most often, *The Country and the City* (1973), Williams fleshes out and extends his conception of a common culture as a mixed inheritance. Alongside the familiar local names – Thomas Hardy, D. H. Lawrence, and the rest – it includes Chinua Achebe, James Ngugi, and a number of other postcolonial writers. He sees their diverse experiences as held together by the threads of a shared passage into a modern world organized around the expansion of capitalism as both a national formation and a global system. 'I have been arguing', he says, towards the end of the book, 'that capitalism, as a mode of production, is the basic process of most of what we know as the history of country and city. Its abstracted economic drives, its fundamental priorities in social relations, its criteria of growth and of profit and loss, have over several centuries altered our country and created new kinds of city. In its final forms of imperialism it has altered our world' (Williams, 1973: 302). Tracing the ways these dynamics have shaped structures of experience and feeling and forms of cultural practice, in different ways at different times and in different places, and contributing to struggles against their destructive, restrictive impacts and for a more equitable, tolerant and democratic social order lay at the heart of his work. Continuing this project, developing and extending it, arguing about how best to accomplish it, remains, for me, the central task and promise of a critical cultural studies.

7

Overcoming the Divide: Cultural Studies and Political Economy

Douglas Kellner

For some decades now, advocates of media studies based in cultural analysis have been at war with those who advocate a political economy approach.[1] In this chapter, I want to argue that the hostility between political economy and cultural studies reproduces a great divide of the field of media studies between two competing approaches with different methodologies, objects of study, and, by now, bodies of texts. This bifurcation pits social science-based approaches that take communications as their object against a humanities and text-based approach that focuses on culture. I will argue that the divide is an artificial one, rooted in an arbitrary academic division of labor, and that media and communications studies are enhanced by drawing on both traditions.

To help overcome the divide, I outline a conception of a multiperspectival cultural studies and criticize approaches to the study of media, culture, and communications that I take to be one-sided or excessively narrow in their methodological and theoretical perspectives. To the question, 'political economy or cultural studies?', I will argue that this is a false dichotomy and that cultural studies should be transdisciplinary and challenge existing disciplines, as well as the dominant society.

Overcoming the great divide

In the early 1980s, the culturalist school of the time was largely textual, centered on the analysis and criticism of texts as cultural artifacts, using methods primarily derived from the humanities. The methods of communications research, by contrast, employed more empirical research strategies, ranging from straight quantitative analysis to more qualitative empirical studies of specific cases or topics, structural analysis of media institutions, or historical research. Topics in this area included analysis of the political economy of the media, empirical studies of audience reception and media effects, or structural analysis of the impact of media institutions in the economy, politics, or everyday life.

These conflicting approaches point to a division of the field of media communications into specialized sub-areas with competing models and methods, and, ironically, to a lack of communication in the field itself. The bifurcation reproduces an academic division of labor which – beginning early in the century and intensifying since the end of World War II – followed the trend toward specialization and differentiation symptomatic of the capitalist economy. The university has followed this broader trend which some theorists equate with the dynamics of modernity itself, interpreted as a process of ever-greater differentiation and thus specialization in all fields from business to education. This trend toward specialization has undermined the power and scope of cultural and communications studies and should be replaced, as I argue in this chapter, by a more transdisciplinary approach.

In regard to the bifurcation of the field of communications, some have suggested a liberal tolerance of different approaches, or ways in which the various approaches complemented each other or could be integrated. Against such pluralism and eclecticism, I wish to argue that it is important to challenge any previously established academic division of labor and to develop a transdisciplinary approach. A critical cultural studies will thus overcome the boundaries of academic disciplines and will combine political economy, social theory and research, and cultural criticism in its project which aims at critique of domination and social transformation. I will accordingly present a model of a multiperspectival cultural studies to illustrate my approach and to criticize one-sided approaches.

The trajectory of cultural studies

British cultural studies was founded as a fundamentally transdisciplinary enterprise and in its very conception attacked established academic institutional practices which neglected the popular in favor of elite culture. Moreover, its boundary-crossing of disciplines and attacks on the detrimental effects of abstracting culture from its socio-political context elicited hostility among those who are more disciplinary-oriented and who believe in the autonomy of culture and renounce sociological or political readings. Against such academic formalism and separatism, cultural studies insists that culture must be investigated within the social relations and system through which it is produced and consumed, and that analysis of culture is thus intimately bound up with the study of society, politics, and economics. Employing Gramsci's model of hegemony and counterhegemony, British cultural studies sought to analyse 'hegemonic', or ruling, social and cultural forces of domination and to seek 'counterhegemonic' forces of resistance and struggle. The project was aimed at social transformation and attempted to specify forces of domination and resistance in order to aid the process of political struggle and emancipation from oppression and domination.

Some earlier programmatic presentations of British cultural studies stressed the importance of a transdisciplinary approach to the study of culture that analysed its political economy, process of production and distribution, textual products, and reception by the audience. For instance, in his now classic programmatic article, 'Encoding/Decoding', Stuart Hall began his analysis by using Marx's *Grundrisse* as a model to trace the articulations of 'a continuous circuit', encompassing 'production – distribution – consumption – production' (1980c: 128ff.). Hall concretizes this model with focus on how media institutions produce meanings, how they circulate, and how audiences use or decode the texts to produce meaning. Moreover, in a 1983 lecture published in 1985/1986, Richard Johnson (1986/87) provided a model of cultural studies, similar to Hall's earlier model, based on a diagram of the circuits of production, textuality, and reception, parallel to the circuits of capital stressed by Marx, illustrated by a diagram that stressed the importance of production and distribution. Although Johnson emphasized the importance of analysis of production in cultural studies and criticized *Screen* for abandoning this perspective in favor of more idealist and textualist approaches (ibid.: 63ff.), much work in cultural studies has replicated this neglect.

I believe that this model delineates the most productive approach to cultural studies, but that it has rarely been pursued. One could indeed argue that throughout its trajectory cultural studies has tended to neglect analysis of the circuits of political economy, production, and distribution in favor of text and audience-based analyses. During the past decade, however, there has been a resolute turning away from political economy within cultural studies, though there has been intense focus on the audience and consumption. This is partly due to a postmodern turn in cultural studies whereby economics, history, and politics are decentered in favor of emphasis on local pleasures, consumption, and the construction of hybrid identities from the material of the popular. This cultural populism replicates the turn in postmodern theory away from Marxism and its alleged reductionism, master narratives of liberation and domination, and statist politics.[2]

In the following analysis, I want to suggest some of the ways that the neglect of political economy truncates cultural studies, arguing for its importance, not only for generally understanding media culture, but also for analysing texts and audience use of media artifacts. I argue that the construction of media texts and their reception by audiences is deeply influenced by the system of production and distribution within which media products circulate and are received. Thus, against the turn away from political economy in cultural studies, I will argue why it is important to situate analysis of cultural texts within their system of production and distribution, often referred to as the 'political economy' of culture. But this requires some reflection on what sort of political economy might be useful for cultural studies.

Production, political economy and cultural studies

The references to the terms 'political' and 'economy' call attention to the fact that the production and distribution of culture takes place within a specific economic system, constituted by relations between the state, the economy, social institutions and practices, culture, and organizations like the media.

Political economy thus encompasses economics and politics and the relations between them and the other central dimensions of society and culture. In regard to media institutions, for instance, in Western democracies, a capitalist economy dictates that cultural production is governed by laws of the market, but the democratic imperatives mean that there is some regulation of culture by the state. There are often tensions within a given society concerning which activities should be governed by the imperatives of the market, or economics, alone and how much state regulation or intervention is desirable to assure a wider diversity of broadcast programming, or the prohibition of phenomena agreed to be harmful, such as cigarette advertising or pornography (see Kellner, 1990).

Political economy highlights that capitalist societies are organized according to a dominant mode of production that structures institutions and practices according to the logic of commodification and capital accumulation so that cultural production is profit- and market-oriented. Forces of production (such as media technologies and creative practice) are deployed according to dominant relations to production which are important, as I shall try to show, in determining what sort of cultural artifacts are produced and how they are consumed. However, 'political economy' does not merely refer solely to economics, but to the relations between the economic, political, and other dimensions of social reality. The term thus links culture to its political and economic context and opens up cultural studies to history and politics. It refers to a field of struggle and antagonism and not an inert structure as caricatured by some of its opponents.

Political economy also calls attention to the fact that culture is produced within relationships of domination and subordination and thus reproduces or resists existing structures of power. Such a perspective also provides a normative standard for cultural studies whereby the critic can attack aspects of cultural texts that reproduce class, gender, racial, and other forms of domination and positively valorize aspects that attack or subvert existing domination, or depict forms of resistance and struggle against them. In addition, inserting texts into the system of culture within which they are produced and distributed can help elucidate features and effects of the texts that textual analysis alone might miss or downplay. Rather than being antithetical approaches to culture, political economy can actually contribute to textual analysis and critique, as well as audience reception and uses and gratifications – as I attempt to demonstrate below. The system of production often determines what sort of artifacts will be produced, what structural limits there will be as to what can and cannot be said and shown, and what sort of audience expectations and usage the text may generate.

Consideration of Stuart Hall's famous distinction between encoding and decoding (1980c), I believe, suggests some of the ways that political economy structures both the encoding and decoding of media artifacts. As the Frankfurt School pointed out, media culture is produced within an industrial organization of production in which products are generated according to codes and models within culture industries that are organized according to industrial models of production.[3] What codes are operative and how they are encoded into artifacts is thus a function of the system of production. In a commercial system of media culture, production is organized according to well-defined genres with their own codes and modes of production.

Film, television, popular music, and other genres of media culture are highly codified in systems of commercial enterprise, organized in accordance with highly conventional codes and formulas. In the system of commercial broadcasting in the United States, for instance, network television is organized into a few dominant genres such as talk shows, soap operas, action-adventure series, and situation comedies. Each genre has its own codes and format, with situation comedies invariably using a structure of conflict and resolution, with the solving of the problem suggesting a moral message or upholding dominant values or institutions. Within the genre, each series has its own codes and formats which are followed according to the dictates of the production company; each series, for instance, uses a manual (or 'story bible') that tells writers and production teams what to do and not to do, defines characters and plot lines, and the conventions of the series; continuity experts enforce the following of these codes rigorously (as do network censors that do not allow content that transgresses dominant moral codes).

Sometimes, of course, the codes of media culture change, often dramatically and usually in accordance with social changes that lead media producers to conclude that audiences will be receptive to new forms more relevant to their social experience. So for some years during the 1950s and 1960s happy, middle-class nuclear families ruled the US situation comedy during an era of unparalleled post-World War II affluence that came to an end in the early 1970s. Precisely then new working-class comedies appeared, such as Norman Lear's *All in the Family*, which focused on social conflict, economic problems, and which did not offer easy solutions to all of the standard conflicts. Lear's subsequent series, *Mary Hartman*, combined situation comedy codes with soap opera codes which endlessly multiplied problems rather than providing solutions. During the protracted economic recession of the 1980s and 1990s, triggered by a global restructuring of capitalism, new 'loser television' situation comedy series appeared featuring the victims of the economic downswing and restructuring (that is, *Roseanne, Married with Children*, and *The Simpsons*). *Beavis and Butt-Head* takes loser television even further, combining situation comedy formats with music video clips and the commentary of two mid-teenage animated cartoon characters without apparent families, education, or job prospects (see the discussion in Kellner, 1995).

Increased competition from ever-proliferating cable channels and new networks led network television in the 1980s and 1990s to break many of the conventions rigorously followed in series TV. Programs like *Hill Street Blues*, *LA Law*, and *NYPD*, for instance, broke previous conventions and taboos of the television crime drama. *Hill Street Blues* employed hand-held cameras to create a new look and feel, multiplied its plot lines with some stories lasting for weeks, and did not always provide a positive resolution to the conflicts and problems depicted. Previous TV police dramas rigorously followed a conflict/resolution model with a crime, its detection, and an inevitable happy ending, projecting the message that crime did not pay and providing ideal-izations of the police and the criminal justice system. But the later police shows mentioned above depicted corrupt members within the law enforce-ment and judicial system, police committing crimes, and criminals getting away with their misdeeds.

Yet even the code-breaking series have their own codes and formulas which cultural analysis should delineate. The relatively young and liberal production team of *Hill Street Blues*, for instance, conveyed socially critical attitudes toward dominant institutions and sympathy for the oppressed marked by the experiences of 1960s radicalism (see Gitlin, 1983's study of the Bochco-Kozoll production team). The team's later series, *LA Law*, negotiates the emphasis on professionalism and rising mobility of the Reaganite 1980s with concern for social problems and the oppressed. Their 1990s series, *NYPD*, reflects growing cynicism toward police, law enforcement, and the society as a whole. The success of these series obviously points to an audience which shares these attitudes and which is tiring of idealized depictions of police, lawyers, and the criminal justice system.

Thus, situating the artifacts of media culture within the system of produc-tion and the society that generate them can help illuminate their structures and meanings. The encoding of media artifacts is deeply influenced by sys-tems of production so that study of the texts of television, film, or popular music, for instance, is enhanced by studying the ways that media artifacts are actually produced within the structure and organization of the culture indus-tries. Since the forms of media culture are structured by well-defined rules and conventions, the study of the production of culture can help elucidate the codes actually in play and thus illuminate what sorts of texts are produced. Because of the demands of the format of radio or music television, for instance, most popular songs are three to four minutes, fitting into the format of the distribution system. Because of its control by giant corporations ori-ented primarily toward profit, film production in the United States is dominated by specific genres and, since the 1970s, by the search for block-buster hits, thus leading to proliferation of the most popular sorts of comedies, action/adventure films, fantasies, and seemingly never-ending sequels and cycles of the most popular films. This economic factor explains why Hollywood film is dominated by major genres and subgenres, explains sequelmania in the film industry, crossovers of popular films into television series,[4] and a certain homogeneity in products constituted within systems of production with rigid generic codes, formulaic conventions, and well-defined ideological boundaries.

Likewise, study of political economy can help determine the limits and range of political and ideological discourses and effects, and can help indicate which discourses are dominant at a specific conjuncture. The rigid production code implemented for Hollywood films in 1934, for instance, strictly forbade scenes showing explicit sexuality, use of drugs, critical references to religion, or stories in which crime did indeed pay. By the 1960s, the production code was thoroughly subverted and eventually abandoned during an era of falling audiences where the film industries broke previous taboos in order to attract audiences to the movie theaters. In addition, the wave of youth and counter-culture films of the 1960s responded to what film studios saw as a new film generation which made up a significant chunk of the audience (Kellner and Ryan, 1988). Low-budget films like *Easy Rider* made high profits and Hollywood spun off genre cycles of such films. Likewise, when low-budget blaxploitation films made high profits, a cycle of films featuring black heroes, often outlaws, against the white power structure proliferated. After consoli-dation of the film industry in the 1970s, however, and megablockbuster hits like *Jaws* and *Star Wars*, Hollywood aimed at more mainstream genre block-buster films, driving more subcultural fare to the margins.

Thus, economic trends in the film industry help explain what sorts of films were made over the past decades. Television news and entertainment and its biases and limitations can also be illuminated by study of political economy. My study of television in the United States, for instance, disclosed that the takeover of the television networks by major transnational corporations and communications conglomerates was part of a 'right turn' within US society in the 1980s whereby powerful corporate groups won control of the state and the mainstream media (Kellner, 1990). For example, during the 1980s all three US networks were taken over by major corporate conglomerates: ABC was taken over in 1985 by Capital Cities, NBC was taken over by General Electric, and CBS was taken over by the Tisch Financial Group. Both ABC and NBC sought corporate mergers and this motivation, along with other benefits derived from Reaganism, might well have influenced them to downplay crit-icisms of Reagan and generally to support his conservative programs, military adventures, and simulated presidency – and then to support George Bush in the 1988 election (see the documentation in Kellner, 1990).

Reaganism and Thatcherism constituted a new political hegemony, a new form of political common sense, and the trend in the 1990s has been for deregulation and the allowing of 'market forces' to determine the direction of cultural and communications industries. Hence, in 1995 megamergers between Disney and ABC, Time-Warner and Turner Communications, and other major media conglomerates were negotiated. Merger mania was both a function of the general atmosphere of deregulation and a Federal Communications Commission ruling under the Clinton administration which allowed television networks to own and produce their own programming (whereas previously independent Hollywood production companies produced programming and the networks distributed it). Relaxing these rules and visions of 'synergy' between production and distribution units has led to an even greater concentration of media conglomerates and will thus probably lead to a narrower range of programming and voices in the future.

Thus, analysis of political economy allows illumination of the major trends in the information and entertainment industries. Furthermore, one cannot really discuss the role of the media in specific events like the Gulf War with-out analysing the production and political economy of news and information, as well as the actual text of the war against Iraq and its reception by its audience (see Kellner, 1992, 1995). Nor can one fully grasp the success of Michael Jackson or Madonna without analysing their marketing strategies, their use of the technologies of music video, advertising, publicity, and image management. Likewise, in appraising the full social impact of pornography, one needs to be aware of the sex industry and the production process of, say, pornographic films, and not just limit analysis to the texts themselves and their effects on audiences.

Yet political economy alone does not hold the key to cultural studies. Important as it is, it has limitations as a single approach. Some political economy analyses reduce the meanings and effects of texts to rather circumscribed and reductive ideological functions, arguing that media culture merely reflects the ideology of the ruling economic elite that controls the culture industries and is nothing more than a vehicle for capitalist ideology.[5] It is true that media culture overwhelmingly supports capitalist values, but it is also a site of intense struggle between different races, classes, gender, and social groups, and is thus better theorized as a contested terrain, open to the vicissitudes of history and struggle, rather than just a field of domination. Thus, in order to grasp fully the nature and effects of media culture, one needs to develop methods to analyse the full range of its meanings and effects.

Textual analysis

I have argued so far that study of the encoding of media texts is enhanced through study of the system of production in which they are generated. In this section, I will provide some examples of how textual analysis is enriched through consideration of production and political economy and how textual analysis that neglects such an approach is vitiated. Cultural studies has traditionally deployed a wealth of critical theories to unpack the meanings of the texts, or to explicate how texts function to produce meaning, rather than deploying just one single method, as is often the case with academic literary schools (that is, semiotics, psychoanalysis, deconstruction, or whatever that take their methods as *the* key to cultural interpretation). Cultural studies has moved beyond literary studies to engage the texts of media culture as well as high culture, and has done so from a variety of perspectives, thus going beyond standard literary criticism in analysing textual meanings, values, symbols, and ideologies.

It is therefore one of the major contributions of British cultural studies to take media culture seriously and to develop a wealth of methods and strategies of analysis to elucidate the full range of meanings and effects of media texts. Quite possibly, one of the reasons for hostility of those in cultural studies against political economy is because of the reductionism and economism of some dominant versions of political economy and the failure of this tradition concretely to engage texts and audiences. The challenge is then to mediate political economy with engagement of actual texts and audiences.

This is impossible to carry out adequately in a programmatic chapter so, in the following discussion, I will merely argue that adequate analysis of the products of media culture require multiperspectival readings to analyse their various forms of discourses, ideological positions, narrative strategies, image construction, and effects.

There have been a wide range of types of textual analysis of media culture, ranging from quantitative content analysis that analyses the number of, say, incidents of violence in a text, to qualitative analysis that analyses images of women, blacks, or other groups. Where cultural studies has traditionally overcome a mere additive eclecticism in its deployment of multiple methods of textual interpretation is in its use of the category of ideology and its expansion of the concept of ideology to include the dimensions of gender, race, and nationality as well as class (see Chapter 13 by Billig and Chapter 5 by Thomas in this volume). The concept of ideology requires analysing texts in terms of specific relations of power and domination and criticizing the ways that cultural artifacts reproduce or resist oppression and subordination. Ideological analysis thus forces one to situate the text within the context of existing systems of domination and struggles against it.[6]

Thus, to capture the full political and ideological dimensions of an artifact of media culture, one needs to view it from the multicultural perspectives of gender, race, and class, and to deploy a wide range of methods to explicate fully each dimension and to show how they fit into textual systems. Each critical method focuses on key aspects of a text from a specific perspective: the specific critical method spotlights, or illuminates, some features of a text while ignoring others. Marxist approaches tend to focus on class, for instance, while feminist approaches will highlight gender, and semiotic approaches will center on codes and the production of meaning. Semiotic analysis is connected with genre analysis and a formalist analysis of how cultural codes and forms help to produce meaning, while narrative analysis displays the construction of stories and the production of cultural myths and ideologies.

In general, the more perspectives one applies to a text to do cultural analysis and critique – feminist, Marxist, generic, semiotics, psychoanalytic, and so on – the better one can grasp the full range of ideological dimensions and ramifications of a text. Some qualifications to this position should be made, however. Obviously, a single reading – Marxist, feminist, psychoanalytic, etc. – may yield more brilliant insights than combining various perspectival readings; more is not necessarily better. Yet the more critical perspectives utilized in a proficient and revelatory fashion provides the potential for stronger (that is, more many-sided, illuminating, and critical) readings.

Each critical method has its own strengths and limitations, its optics and blindspots. Consequently, the more of these critical methods that one has at one's disposal, the better chance one has of producing many-sided critical readings and avoiding one-sided and reductive readings. Marxian ideology critiques have traditionally been strong on class and historical contextualization and weak on formal analysis, while some versions are highly reductionist, reducing textual analysis to denunciation of ruling class ideology. Feminism excels in gender analysis and in some versions is formally sophisticated, though some types are reductive and early feminism often limited itself to analysis of images of gender. Combining Marxism and feminism can enrich cultural analysis by showing relationships between class and gender subordination, or tensions within specific artifacts between progressive and socially critical representations of, say, class and race contrasted to reactionary representations of gender. Or feminism could be articulated with a method like psychoanalysis which calls for the interpretation of unconscious contents and latent meanings in a text, as when the repressed and unhappy mute wife in *The Piano* plays on the instrument as an expression of her latent sexuality and unarticulated feelings. But psychoanalysis can also be reductive and imperious, seeing everything as the expression of the unconscious or sexuality, and thus should be deployed with other critical perspectives.

Using an approach, however, that sees society as a system of relations of domination and subordination and as a contested terrain of struggle against existing forms of hegemony allows the critic to read texts within existing social relations and the system of production that underlies them. Consequently, I am arguing for a political economy approach that does not merely read texts as examples of capitalist or ruling-class ideology, but that takes account of a multiplicity of types of representation, including class, gender, race, ethnicity, nationalism, and so on in analysing the production and distribution of texts. I want to argue that economic analysis can complement and enrich cultural studies' readings and that textual analysis and political economy are therefore not antithetical.

Hall's rich and insightful analysis could be supplemented, however, by analysis of the market reasons why more positive images of people of color and subtle racism have entered the field of media culture. Surveys of US television audiences have indicated that significant numbers of the black population are higher than average TV viewers, and who respond favorably to more positive images of blacks. Advertisers are eager to tap these markets and are supportive of programs that have attractive blacks to draw audiences of color. Yet because black cultural workers have rarely assumed the positions of producers, directors, or writers, programs featuring blacks often project a white fantasy of 'good' blacks, and fears of 'bad' ones, rather than capturing the specificities and concreteness of black culture and personalities. Bill Cosby was one of the most popular US TV personalities precisely because he incarnated the white fantasy of the good black, as well as black fantasies of upward mobility into the middle and professional class. Similarly, audiences of all races were at first incredulous that O.J. Simpson could have killed his ex-wife and her friend because he was projected as a white fantasy of the ideal African-American and role model for black youth. (Although, later, audiences divided along race lines as to his guilt or innocence, showing the importance of history and power as elements in any cultural 'reading'.)

Thus, analysis of how and why images of good blacks were produced and distributed would help explain why suddenly more positive images of people of color began appearing in the 1980s and how these representations too contained a more subtle version of racism. A less dogmatic focus on political economy, therefore, would open itself to issues of textual production of meaning, audience use and pleasures, and the issues concerning the politics of representation. Perhaps the key concept of *articulation* could be deployed to indicate how economics and culture can be combined in doing concrete analyses. Hall defines articulation as 'the form of the connection that *can* make a unity of two different elements, under certain conditions. It is a linkage which is not necessary, determined, absolute and essential for all time' (Hall, 1986a: 53, original emphasis). Hall illustrates the concept to describe how certain ideological elements are articulated in a phenomenon like Thatcherism, but it can also be used to explain how different levels of a social ensemble – such as economics, politics, and culture – are articulated together to produce cultural artifacts and how audiences articulate ideologies or cultural meanings to make sense of their world.

Thus, I believe that consideration of audiences, the production process, and the economic constraints and pressures that lead to one sort of representation or theme rather than another enriches the process of textual analysis. Of course, each reading of a text is only one possible reading from one critic's position, no matter how multiperspectival, and may or may not be the reading preferred by audiences (which themselves will be significantly different according to their class, race, gender, ethnicity, ideologies, and so on). Because there is a split between textual encoding and audience decoding, there is always the possibility of a multiplicity of readings of any text of media culture (Hall, 1980c). Yet readings are more or less valid according to how well they illuminate the actual text in question. Textual analysis cannot always explicate *the* reading preferred by audiences, but it can delineate the parameters of possible readings and offer readings that aim at illuminating the text and its cultural and ideological effects. Such analysis provides the materials for criticizing misreadings, or readings that are one-sided and incomplete. Yet to further carry through a cultural studies' analysis, one must also examine how audiences actually read media texts and what effects they have on audience thought and behavior. Here, too, I want to argue that analysis of audience uses of media texts is enhanced by an understanding of the political economy of the media and of how media culture is produced and distributed within specific systems of production.

Audience reception and use of media culture

It has been a great contribution of cultural studies to stress that all texts are subject to multiple readings depending on the perspectives and subject positions of the reader. Members of distinct groups read texts differently, and cultural studies can illuminate why and how diverse audiences use media culture in a variety of ways and produce disparate readings of texts. It is indeed one of the merits of cultural studies to have focused on audience reception in recent years, though there are also some limitations and problems with dominant approaches.

A standard way to discover how audiences decode media culture is to engage in ethnographic research, in an attempt to determine how texts influence audiences and shape their beliefs and behavior, or provide specific pleasures and resources. Ethnographic cultural studies have indicated some of the various ways that audiences use and appropriate texts, often to empower themselves. Radway's (1984) study of women's use of Harlequin romance novels, for example, shows how these books provide escapism for women and could be understood as reproducing traditional women's roles, behavior, and attitudes. Yet, they can also empower women by promoting fantasies of a different life and may thus inspire revolt against male domination. Or, they may enforce, in other audiences, female submission to male domination and trap women in ideologies of romance, in which submission to Prince Charming is seen as the alpha and omega of happiness for women.

John Fiske (1989a, 1989b) suggests that young teenage girls use Madonna as a resource to inspire gestures of independence and fashion rebellion, and thus empower women to 'express themselves'. Teenagers use video games and music television as an escape from the demands of a disciplinary society. Males use sports as a terrain of fantasy identification, in which they feel empowered as 'their' team or star triumphs. Such sports events also generate a form of community, currently being lost in the privatized media and consumer culture of our time. Indeed, fandoms of all sorts, ranging from *Star Trek* fans ('Trekkers') to fans of *Beavis and Butt-Head*, or various soap operas, also form communities that enable people to relate to others who share their interests and hobbies (Jenkins, 1992).

While this emphasis on audience reception and appropriation helps cultural studies overcome earlier one-sided textualist orientations, it can also lead to simple affirmation of audience pleasures and fandom, thus promoting, rather than critically analysing, media culture. To be sure, audience research can reveal how people are actually using cultural texts and what sort of effects those texts are having on everyday life. Combining quantitative and qualitative research, new reception studies can provide important contributions into how audiences actually interact with cultural texts.

Yet there are several problems with reception studies as they have been constituted within cultural studies, particularly in the United States. First, audiences themselves are a product of the system of media production into which they are enculturated. That is, audiences gain preferences, expectations, and learn ways of interpreting texts according to their experiences of what sort of texts are dominant and most popular. They learn to read the conventions of soap operas and situation comedies, for instance, via experience of the genres. Such experiences create expectations, reinforce preferred modes of reading, and condition audience response. There is no such thing as an innocent audience, unconditioned by its previous experience (except for perhaps cultures not yet exposed to global media culture). Knowing what sorts of systems of production generate what sorts of audiences and ways of decoding can help reception studies gain insight into how audiences interact with texts within very determinate systems.

Indeed, absolute separation of encoding and decoding is a mistake because, as I argued earlier, the types of encoding are determined by the system of production which also habituates its audiences to textual codes that become the familiar lenses through which audiences engage in the activity of decoding texts, producing meanings according to well-established rules – though oppositional readings are also always possible. Thus, to some extent audiences themselves are constructs of the system of production. There are few pure or pristine audiences, and understanding the system of media production dominant in a culture thus provides insight into audience expectations and practices.

For example, audiences come to expect situation comedies to produce solutions to problems and uplifting humor and good cheer. While the viewers' own families may have been dysfunctional and falling apart, audiences seemed to enjoy the idealization of middle-class family life in the classical American television situation comedy. Thus, experience of the codes and conventions of the situation comedy produce viewers that are constructed to enjoy comedy and positive presentation of moral views, and solutions to the problems presented. Yet while in general audiences are conditioned by particular systems of cultural production to react to programs in specific ways (US sitcoms even have laugh tracks dubbed in to signal that it's time for smiles or laughter), different audiences are going to respond differently to specific characters or situations. Younger audiences responded more favorably to the liberal daughter and son-in-law in Norman Lear's *All in the Family* and saw the father character, Archie Bunker, as a reactionary bigot; conservative male audiences, however, often saw Archie as the most popular character and sympathized with him against the other characters. Likewise, working-class audiences felt more sympathy with the beleaguered working-class father than middle- or upper-class audiences.

However, class has frequently been downplayed in audience reception studies in recent years as a significant variable that structures audience decoding and use of cultural texts. Cultural studies in the UK was particularly sensitive to class differences in the use and reception of cultural texts, but in many dissertations, books, and articles in cultural studies in the United States attention to class has been downplayed or is missing altogether. This is not surprising as a neglect of class as a constitutive feature of culture and society is an endemic deficiency in the American academy in most disciplines. And I would argue that neglect of political economy often entails neglect of class, since class analysis is a staple of political economy which necessarily theorizes a class society in which one class owns the means of production, whereas other classes are forced to sell their labor power and submit to class domination. But class too is in part a cultural construct, generated – like gender and race – in the representations produced by media culture, as well as by other institutions. Representations in media culture thus help construct our images of class, race, and gender, or attempt to erase phenomenon like class from audience visions altogether in fantasies of a classless society and a not so benign neglect of class.

In general, the very concept of class – like that of code – articulates the relations between culture and economy and between the levels of analysis I am trying to link. A class that controls the means of representation will help determine what images of class (and gender, race, etc.) will circulate through mainstream culture. Yet class remains a structural constituent of contemporary capitalist societies and so different audiences will use and interpret the representations of media culture differently, requiring reception study to take account of class, which is a crucial variable of consumption, as well as production and the politics of textual representation.

There is also, however, the reverse danger of exaggerating the constitutive force of class, and downplaying, or ignoring, important variables that constitute people's identities and help determine how they use and receive media texts. Staiger (1992) notes that Fiske, building on Hartley, lists seven 'subjectivity positions' that are important in cultural reception, 'self, gender, age-group, family, class, nation, ethnicity', and proposes adding sexual orientation. All of these factors, and no doubt more, interact in shaping how audiences receive and use texts and must be taken into account in studying cultural reception, for audiences decode and use texts according to the specific constituents of their class, race or ethnicity, gender, sexual preferences and so on.

Women, for instance, are usually more sensitive to representations of gender, and in particular negative representations of women, than men, just as African–Americans or members of oppressed racial groups are more sensitive to representations of race. Gays and lesbians are often more sensitive to representations of sexuality and homophobia. But I would warn against a tendency to romanticize the active audience which claims that all audiences produce their own meanings and denies that media culture may have powerful manipulative effects. There is a tendency within the cultural studies' tradition of reception research to dichotomize between dominant and oppositional readings. Hall's distinctions between 'dominant', 'negotiated', and 'oppositional' readings (1980c) is flattened in Fiske's work to a dichotomy between the dominant and the oppositional. 'Dominant' readings are those in which audiences appropriate texts in line with the interests of the dominant culture and the ideological intentions of a text, as when audiences feel pleasure in the restoration of male power, law and order, and social stability at the end of a film like *Die Hard*, after the hero and representatives of authority eliminate the terrorists who had taken over a high-rise corporate headquarters. An 'oppositional' reading, by contrast, celebrates the resistance to this reading in audience appropriation of a text; for example, Fiske (1993) observes resistance to dominant readings when homeless individuals in a shelter cheered the destruction of police and authority figures, during repeated viewings of a video-tape of *Die Hard*.

There is indeed a tendency in cultural studies to celebrate resistance *per se* without distinguishing between types and forms of resistance (a similar problem resides with indiscriminate celebration of audience pleasure in some forms of reception studies). Thus, resistance to social authority by the homeless, evidenced in their viewing of *Die Hard*, could serve to strengthen brutal masculine behavior and encourage manifestations of physical violence to solve social problems. Sartre, Fanon, and Marcuse, among others, have argued that violence can be either emancipatory, directed at forces of oppression, or reactionary, directed at popular forces struggling against oppression. Some feminists, by contrast, see all violence as forms of brute masculine behavior and many people see it as a problematic form of conflict resolution. Resistance and pleasure cannot therefore be valorized *per se* as progressive elements of the appropriation of cultural texts, but difficult discriminations must be made as to whether the resistance, oppositional reading, or pleasure in a given experience is progressive or reactionary, emancipatory or destructive, or a negotiated reading somewhere in-between the two opposites.

To theorize adequately the distinction between dominant and oppositional readings one must analyse existing systems of domination and subordination and contextualize the products of media culture in terms of how they articulate the discourses of domination and resistance in relation to actual social relations. One would need to supplement a class analysis of subordination of the sorts standard with political economy with feminist analysis of gender and multicultural analysis of race and ethnicity. One then discovers that while some texts might resist capitalist domination, or allow, *à la Die Hard*, resistant readings, they might also perpetuate gender or race domination. A multiperspectival reading of resistance and domination thus requires a broad array of critical methods to analyse the complex political effects of cultural texts.

Consequently, while emphasis on the audience and reception was an excellent correction to the one-sidedness of purely textual analysis, I believe that in recent years cultural studies has overemphasized reception and textual analysis, while underemphasizing the production of culture and its political economy. Indeed, there has been a growing trend in cultural studies toward audience reception studies that neglect both production and textual analysis, thus producing populist celebrations of the text and audience pleasure in its use of cultural artifacts (see the critique of cultural populism in McGuigan, 1992). This approach, taken to an extreme, would lose its critical perspective and would lead to a positive gloss on audience experience of whatever is being studied. Such studies also might lose sight of the manipulative and conservative effects of certain types of media culture and thus serve the interests of the cultural industries as they are presently constituted and the dominant social forces which own and control them.

A new way to research media effects is to use the data bases which collect media texts such as Dialogue or Nexis/Lexis and to trace the effects of media artifacts like Rambo, or Madonna, or *Beavis and Butt-Head* through analysis of references to them in the media. Previous studies of the audience and the reception of media privileged ethnographic studies that selected slices of the vast media audiences. Such studies are invariably limited and broader effects research can indicate how the most popular artifacts of media culture have a wide range of effects. In *Media Culture* (Kellner, 1995), I have done precisely this in reference to a large number of cultural artifacts which documented a wide range of very interesting media effects that attest to the power and influence of media culture. Examples include groups of kids and adults who imitated Rambo in various forms of asocial behavior, or fans of *Beavis and Butt-Head* who started fires or tortured animals in the modes practiced by the popular MTV cartoon characters.

My research into the *Rambo* and *Beavis and Butt-Head* effects, for instance, elicited literally hundreds of articles in data bases that demonstrated that these megahits of media culture produced a variety of effects, some quite bizarre. But media culture has more subtle effects in ways that it constructs images of gender, or the warrior hero, or teenage youth. Moreover, computer data bases collect primarily mainstream media articles that operate within the frames of dominant paradigms (that is, representations of violence create violence) and will miss more subtle media effects. It will also miss oppositional uses of shows like *Beavis and Butt-Head* that may help produce positively anti-authoritarian attitudes, or generate critical perceptions of media culture.

Documentation from computer data bases or mainstream research must be supplemented, however, with sophisticated research strategies to understand how audiences actually use cultural texts. But standard ethnographic interview techniques should be complemented by more in-depth questionnaires such as the sort devised by Adorno and his colleagues in their studies of *The Authoritarian Personality* (1950). Audiences often tell interviewers what they want to hear, or think are acceptable answers, and so questions must be devised to try to draw out their responses and penetrate deeper into the mysteries of audience decoding and use of media culture. It was a mistake of some Frankfurt School analysis to assume that audiences were cultural dupes who were simply manipulated by media culture, but it is equally questionable to assume that audiences are always active and creative, produce their own meanings, and transparently communicate their use and interaction with the media to cultural researchers. The actual process of media communication is much more complex and needs accordingly subtle and complex research strategies.

Concluding remarks

To avoid the one-sidedness of reception studies, I am proposing therefore that cultural studies itself be multiperspectival, getting at culture from the perspectives of political economy, text analysis, and audience reception, as outlined above. I also propose that textual analysis utilize a multiplicity of perspectives and critical methods, and that audience reception studies delineate the multiplicity of subject positions, or perspectives, through which audiences appropriate culture. This requires a multicultural approach that sees the importance of analysing the dimensions of class, race and ethnicity, gender, and sexual preference within the texts of media culture and seeing as well their impact on how audiences read and interpret media culture. I also advocate a critical cultural studies that attacks sexism, racism, or bias against specific social groups (that is, gays, intellectuals, the aged, and so on) and that criticizes texts that promote any kind of domination or oppression.

Which perspectives will be deployed in specific studies depends on the subject matter under investigation, the goals of the study, and its range. Obviously, one cannot deploy all the perspectives I have proposed in every single study, but I would argue that if one is doing a study of a complex phenomenon like the Gulf War, Madonna, the Rambo phenomenon, rap music, or the O.J. Simpson trial, one needs to deploy the perspectives of political economy, textual analysis, and audience reception studies to illuminate the full dimensions of these highlights of media culture. In this chapter, I have limited myself to some arguments concerning how considerations of production and political economy can enrich cultural studies, and for a final example of the fruitfulness of this approach let us reflect on the Madonna and Michael Jackson phenomena. There have been a large number of readings of their texts and a vast literature on Madonna's effects on her audiences, but less study of how their mode of production and marketing strategies have helped create their popularity.

My argument would be that Madonna and Michael Jackson have deployed some of the most proficient production and marketing teams in the history of popular music and this dimension should therefore be considered in analyses of their meanings, effects, and uses by their audiences. Just as Madonna's popularity was in large part a function of her marketing strategies and her production of music videos and images that appealed to diverse audiences (see Kellner, 1995), so too has Michael Jackson's media machine employed topflight production, marketing, and public relations personnel. Both Madonna and Michael Jackson reached superstardom during the era when MTV and music videos became central in determining fame within the field of popular music, and arguably became popular because of their look and spectacular presentations in expensive music videos with exceptionally high production values. In both cases, it is arguably the marketing of their image and the spectacle of their music videos or concerts – rather than, say, their voices or any specific musical talent – that account for their popularity. Both deployed top musical arrangers, choreographers, and cinematographers in the production of music videos and performed in highly spectacular and well-publicized concerts that were as much spectacle as performance. Both employed powerhouse publicity machines and constantly kept themselves in the public eye. In particular, both were celebrated constantly by MTV which had entire weekends, and even weeks, devoted to publicizing their work and fame.

Both therefore succeeded because of their understanding and use of the machinery of musical production and promotion by the culture industries. Interestingly, Michael Jackson targeted mainstream audiences from the beginning, attempting to appeal equally to black and white, preteen and teenage, audiences. Indeed, his look erased racial markers as he became whiter and whiter after recurrent plastic surgery; likewise, he cultivated an androgenous look and image that collapsed distinctions between male and female, child and adult, appearing both childlike and sexy, as a naive innocent and canny businessperson, thus appealing to multiple audiences. Madonna, by contrast, targeted first teenage girl audiences, then various ethnic audiences with performers of color and distinct ethnic markers appearing in her music videos and concerts.

Both also appealed to gay audiences, with Madonna in particular pushing the boundaries of the acceptable in music videos, leading MTV to ban a 1990 video 'Justify My Love' with what was deemed excessively extreme sexuality. Both became highly controversial, Madonna because of her exploitation of sexuality and Michael Jackson because of accusations of child molestation. Indeed, the latter created a serious public relations problem for Jackson who had presented himself as a lover of children. But when this image became too literal he needed to refurbish his image. After settling financially with the family of the boy who had claimed that Jackson had sexually abused him, Jackson undertook one of the more successful image refurbishings in years. He married Lisa Marie Presley, Elvis's daughter, thus positioning him as a husband, a father (of Lisa Marie's children by a previous marriage), and as in the lineage of the King of Rock, the successor to the throne. With the 1995 release of *HisStory*, a multi-record collection of his greatest hits and current work, Jackson undertook a massive publicity campaign with Sony records supported with a $30 million budget. The record did not match his earlier sales, but at least brought Jackson back into the limelight as it was accompanied by an unparalleled media blitz in summer 1995, with ABC Television dedicating entire special programs to Jackson and his wife, and to Jackson on-line with his fans in a live Internet interaction. Not to be outdone, MTV devoted an entire week's prime time programming to Jackson.

Yet Jackson and Lisa Marie Presley split up in 1996 and once again rumors circulated that he was continuing to engage in pedophilia, and these rumors and the break-up of his marriage created bad press and retarnished his image. In the midst of this crisis, Jackson declared that a long-time friend was pregnant with his child and he married her in the autumn of 1996, once again, trying to produce a positive image as husband and father. But again, negative media reports circulated and Jackson's image is again in crisis. He who lives by the media can also die by the media, though like old soldiers, media celebrities sometimes just fade away rather than disappear.

Analysing the marketing and production of stardom and popularity can thus help to demystify the arguably false idols of media culture and to produce more critical audience perception. Analysing the business dimension of media culture can thus help produce critical consciousness as well as better understanding of its production and distribution. Such a dimension, I have been arguing, thus enhances cultural studies and contributes to developing a critical media pedagogy that supplements analysis of how to read media texts and how to study audience use of them.

Thus, a cultural studies that is critical and multiperspectival provides comprehensive approaches to culture that can be applied to a wide variety of artifacts from pornography to wartime media management and marketing superstardom, from Michael Jackson and Madonna to the Gulf War and to *Beavis and Butt-Head*. Its comprehensive perspectives encompass political economy, textual analysis, and audience research, and provide critical and political perspectives that enable individuals to dissect the meanings, messages, and effects of dominant cultural forms. Cultural studies is thus part of a critical media pedagogy that enables individuals to resist media manipulation and to increase their freedom and individuality. It can empower people to gain measures of sovereignty over their culture and to struggle for alternative cultures and political change. Cultural studies is thus not just another academic fad, but can be made an integral part of a struggle for a better society and a better life.

Notes

1 In 1995 another futile debate took place between the traditions of political economy and cultural studies in a series of articles and exchanges published in *Critical Studies in Mass Communication* in which the participants talked past each other and often substituted personal attacks for discussion of whether political economy is or is not productive for cultural studies and what their relationship might be. The confrontation thus replicated a long-standing failure of productive debate that might overcome or resolve differences between the traditions, or produce new positions, continuing instead a long legacy of animosity between the two schools; see the symposium in *CSMC* 12 (1995: 60–100).

2 See the discussion of the postmodern turn in Best and Kellner, 1991 and on some versions of a postmodern cultural studies, see Kellner, 1995.

3 For the Frankfurt School analysis of the culture industries, see Horkheimer and Adorno, 1972; for their contributions to cultural studies, see Kellner, 1989 and 1995.

4 Curiously, whereas during the 1970s and the 1980s there were frequent spin-offs of television series from popular movies, in more recent years the trend has reversed with popular classical television series spun off into films like *The Fugitive*, *The Beverly Hillbillies*, *The Flintstones*, *The Adams Family* series, *The Brady Bunch*, and many others.

5 Jim McGuigan suggests that 'the separation of contemporary cultural studies from the political economy of culture' has disabled the field of cultural studies and that the 'core problematic was virtually premised on a terror of economic reductionism' (1992: 40). I agree with both of McGuigan's arguments and am trying to demonstrate here that one can deploy political economy to illuminate media culture and that it can be deployed in non-reductionist modes.

6 Given the centrality of the concept of ideology to textual analysis within cultural studies, John Fiske's rejection of the concept (1993) represents a real break with the earlier tradition (see the criticism in Kellner, 1995). Fiske replicates the rejection of the category of ideology in some versions of postmodern theory (see the discussion in Best and Kellner, 1991).

PART II

ANSWERS AND ALTERNATIVES

8

Theoretical Orthodoxies: Textualism, Constructivism and the 'New Ethnography' in Cultural Studies

David Morley

My concern here is to offer an overview of some recent debates concerning ethnographic audience research within the field of cultural studies. Substantively, one of the major issues concerns the extent to which 'active audience theory' has produced an improperly romanticized image of the media consumer, which tends to ignore institutional questions of cultural power. Its critics have variously dismissed this work as a form of 'new revisionism' (Curran, 1990) or even as 'pointless populism' (Seamann, 1992). In the recent backlash against 'cultural populism', critics such as Frith (1991), Harris (1992) and McGuigan (1992) have tended towards a 'post hoc ergo propter hoc' structure of argument, in which, having identified some particular case in which subcultural/consumer/audience 'activity' is uncritically celebrated by an author with cultural studies allegiances, they then retrospectively declare that this is the kind of (bad) thing to which cultural studies, in general, was bound to lead and that therefore (conveniently reversing the terms of the argument) the whole cultural studies enterprise was, from the start, misconceived, as it has (in fact) led to whatever example of bad practice they have identified.

For my own part, I am happy to agree that some proponents of 'active audience theory' may have (mis)taken evidence of audience activity as an index of audience power (see Ang, 1990, on this point). However, my position is that the arguments of many of the recent critics of cultural studies are misconceived – not least because their criticisms seem designed principally to prepare the ground for a call for a return to the eternal verities of political economy (or classical sociology) as a way out of the blind alley into which cultural studies is said to have (misguidedly) led us. To argue that way is simply to ignore the very real advances made in many branches of cultural studies over the last 20 years. However, this is by no means to argue that cultural studies work on media audiences (or anything else) is problem-free. On the contrary, my other concern here, moving to a more methodological focus, is with the gradual institutionalization of what I view as a damaging set of theoretical/methodological orthodoxies, within some parts of cultural studies.

In recent years, much work in cultural studies has been influenced by debates originating in anthropology, concerning what has been described as 'postmodern' or 'self-reflexive' ethnography (Clifford and Marcus, 1986). Ethnography has become a fashionable buzz-word within the field, and the virtues of its postmodern inflection are now widely assumed to be self-evident, as are those of a constructivist epistemology, and a heavily textualist form of discourse theory, which has little regard for questions of socio-economic determination. This chapter offers a critical examination of these orthodoxies, and argues for a form of cultural studies based on a combination of sociological materialism, epistemological realism and methodological pragmatism. I shall begin with some orienting comments, concerning the recent development of the overall field of cultural studies.

Certainly, as cultural studies becomes increasingly codified and institutionalized, issues of orthodoxy are posed in a particularly sharp manner. Most problematically, in my view, in the context of the North American academy, cultural studies has become almost synonymous with a certain kind of postmodern, deconstructionist literary theory (often referred to, by those involved in it, by the interestingly ex-nominated form, 'Theory'). It is the particular content of the current theoretical orthodoxies of cultural studies with which I am here concerned. Going to conferences in the field, glancing at journals, or talking to graduate students involved in the newest work in cultural studies, one could be forgiven for presuming that all the difficult age-old debates, concerning questions of epistemology which have long bedevilled philosophers, have in fact finally been solved. It would seem, curiously enough, that within much of cultural studies, relativism has been absolutely victorious, to speak oxymoronically.

One part of the motivation for the development of the relativist, self-reflexive orthodoxy which has come to dominate the field has been a quite proper concern with the politics of knowledge, and with taking into account the power relations between subject and object of knowledge. Unfortunately, in my view, the overall effect of much of this has in the end been a disabling one, as a result of which it becomes pretty hard for anyone to say anything about anyone (or anything) else, for fear of accusation of ontological imperialism. Apart from any other considerations, and despite the declared political credentials (and intentions) of much of this kind of work, within cultural studies, this is in fact, politically disabling. It is hard to mobilize around a political platform of principled uncertainty, especially if one of those principles is that it is ultimately impossible to know what is going on.

It is this set of difficulties which this chapter attempts to unravel, by working through current debates concerning both the 'new revisionism' in media audience research and the associated turn towards postmodern ethnography in cultural studies, more broadly. This, I would argue, is a crucial terrain on which to pursue these arguments as, within cultural studies, the employment of a particular self-reflexive form of ethnography has become almost emblematic of the field itself. A commitment to this particular set of epistemological and methodological principles has come to be the doctrinal test of membership of those who are Saved. My argument here is deliberately intended in the spirit of heresy.

From my perspective, one of the crucial features of the American (and predominantly literary) appropriation of British cultural studies has been the loss of any sense of culture and communications as having material roots, in broader social and political processes and structures, so that the discursive process of the constitution of meanings often becomes the exclusive focus of analysis, without any reference to its institutional or economic setting. As Hall (1990b) observes, what we often see is a textualization of cultural studies, which constitutes power and politics as (exclusively) matters of language (or discourse). As Hall notes, in this respect, 'textuality is never enough' and cultural studies must learn to live with 'the tension which Said describes as its affiliations with institutions, offices, agencies, classes, academies, corporations, groups, ideologically defined parties and professions, nations, races and genders . . . questions that . . . can never be fully covered by critical textuality and its elaborations' (Hall, 1990b: 16–17).

Of course, at this point, I have to declare my own position – as one trained initially as a sociologist who has, by virtue of that fact, always had substantial reservations about the successive dominant paradigms (culturalist, structuralist, psychoanalytic, poststructuralist or postmodern) within cultural studies. Thus, from within cultural studies, the major critique of much of my own work has been that it is too essentialist or reductionist, in its sociological emphasis. From my own point of view, the prime objective of the work has been to analyse processes of culture and communication within their social and material settings. I am personally much more worried by what I see as the tendency towards the textualization of cultural studies, which often allows the cultural phenomena under analysis to drift entirely free from their social and material foundations, and it is in this context that I now turn to the consideration of recent debates about media audiences within cultural studies.

The 'new' audience research

As Evans (1990) notes, recent audience work in media studies can be largely characterized by two assumptions: (a) that the audience is always active (in a non-trivial sense) and (b) that media content is always polysemic, or open to interpretation. The questions are what these assumptions are taken to mean exactly, and what their theoretical and empirical consequences are.

Hall's (1980c) original formulation of the encoding/decoding model of communications contained, as one of its central features, the concept of the preferred reading (towards which the text attempts to direct its reader), while still acknowledging the possibility of alternative, negotiated or oppositional readings. This model has subsequently been quite transformed, to the point where it is often maintained that the majority of audience members routinely modify or deflect any dominant ideology reflected in media content, and the concept of a preferred reading, or of a structured polysemy, drops entirely from view. In this connection, I have to confess a personal interest, as I have been puzzled to find some of my own earlier work (Morley, 1980) invoked as a theoretical legitimation of various forms of 'active audience theory'. For any author to comment on the subsequent interpretation of his or her work is plainly an awkward enterprise, and when that work itself is substantively concerned with the ways in which audiences interpret texts, the irony is manifest. Nonetheless, I shall take this opportunity to comment on some recent debates in audience studies, and will argue that much 'active audience' theory is in fact premised on a heavily negotiated reading (if not a misreading) of some of the earlier work which is often invoked as its theoretical basis (see Derrida, 1989; Norris, 1991; and Richards, 1960 for the relevant distinctions between variant readings and misreadings).

For my own part, while I would argue that work such as the *'Nationwide' Audience* project (along with that of Ang, 1985; Liebes and Katz, 1990; and Radway, 1984) offers counter-evidence to a simple minded 'dominant ideology' thesis, and demonstrates that any hegemonic discourse is always necessarily insecure and incomplete, this should not lead us to abandon concern with the question of media power – or as Martín-Barbero puts it, 'how to understand the texture of hegemony/subalternity, the interlacing of resistance and submission, opposition and complicity' (Martín-Barbero, 1988: 462). That was (and remains) precisely the point of studying audience consumption of media texts, a point which now, as the pendulum of media theory swings again (this time towards a dismissal of the more romantic versions of 'active audience theory'), is in great danger of being obscured.

I would agree with Corner (1991) that much recent media audience work is marred by a facile insistence on the polysemy of media products and by an undocumented presumption that forms of interpretive resistance are more widespread than subordination, or the reproduction of dominant meanings (see Condit, 1989, on the unfortunate current tendency towards an overdrawn emphasis on the 'polysemous' qualities of texts in media studies). To follow that path, as Corner (1991) correctly notes, is to underestimate the force of textual determinacy in the construction of meaning from media products, and not only to romanticize improperly the role of the reader, but to risk falling into a 'complacent relativism, by which the interpretive contribution of the audience is perceived to be of such a scale and range as to render the very idea of media power naive' (Corner, 1991: 281).

In a similar vein to Corner, Curran (1990) offers a highly critical account of what he describes as the 'new revisionism' in mass communications research on media audiences. In brief, his charge is that while this 'revisionism presents itself as original and innovative [it] . . . is none of these things' (Curran, 1990: 135), but rather amounts to 'old pluralist dishes being reheated and presented as new cuisine' (ibid.: 151). The history Curran offers is an informative one, alerting us to the achievements of scholars whose work has been unrecognized or neglected by many (myself included) in the past. However, my contention is that this is a particular history which could not have been written (by Curran or anyone else) 15 years ago, before the impact of the 'new revisionism' (of which Curran is so critical) transformed our understanding of the field of audience research and thus transformed our understanding of who and what was important in its history. I would argue that it is precisely this transformation which has allowed a historian such as Curran to go back and re-read the history of communications research in such a way as to give prominence to those whose work can now, with hindsight, be seen to have 'pre-figured' the work of these 'new revisionists'.

However, despite my differences with him about the general terms of his critique, I would agree with Curran that recent reception studies which document audience autonomy and offer optimistic/redemptive readings of mainstream media texts, have often been, wrongly, taken to represent not simply a challenge to a simple-minded effects or dominant ideology model, but rather as, in themselves, documenting the total absence of media influence, in the 'semiotic democracy' of postmodern pluralism.

Budd et al. (1990) argue that much contemporary media audience research now routinely assumes that 'people habitually use the content of dominant media against itself, to empower themselves' (Budd et al., 1990: 170) so that, in their analysis, the crucial message of much contemporary American cultural studies media work is an optimistic one: 'whatever the message encoded, decoding comes to the rescue. Media domination is weak and ineffectual, since the people make their own meanings and pleasures' (ibid.: 170).

While we should not fall back into any form of simplistic textual determinacy, nonetheless we must also avoid the naive presumption that texts are completely open, like 'an imaginary shopping mall in which audience members could wander at will, selecting whatever suits them' (Murdock, 1989a: 236). The equivalence that Newcomb and Hirsch (1987) assert between the producer and consumer of messages, in so far as they argue that the television viewer matches the creator (or the programme) in the making of meanings is, in effect, a facile one, which ignores de Certeau's (1984) distinction between the strategies of the powerful and the tactics of the weak (or, as Silverstone and I have argued elsewhere (1990), the difference between having power over a text and power over the agenda within which that text is constructed and presented). The power of viewers to reinterpret meanings is hardly equivalent to the discursive power of centralized media institutions to construct the texts which the viewer then interprets, and to imagine otherwise is simply foolish.

Between the micro and the macro

The boom in ethnographic media audience research in the 1980s was, in part, the result of the critique of overly structuralist approaches, which had taken patterns of media consumption to be the always-ready-determined effect of some more fundamental structure – whether the economic structure of the cultural industries (Murdock and Golding, 1974), the political structure of the capitalist state (Althusser, 1971b) or the psychic structure of the human subject (Lacan, 1977). However, a number of authors (Curran, 1990 and Corner, 1991) have recently argued that the pendulum has now swung so far that we face the prospect of a field dominated by the production of micro (and often ethnographic) analyses of media consumption processes, which add up only to a set of micro-narratives, outside any effective macro-political or cultural frame. Despite my reservations above, concerning much 'active audience theory', I nonetheless hold that the developing backlash against micro-ethnography is in danger of encouraging a return to macro political issues which is, in fact, premised on a mal-posed conception of the relation between the micro and the macro.

Thus, Corner argues that, in recent research on the media audience, the question of media power has tended to be avoided, and that much of this 'new audience research' amounts to 'a form of sociological quietism . . . in which increasing emphasis on the micro-processes of viewing relations displaces . . . an engagement with the macro-structures of media and society' (Corner, 1991: 269). My own contention would be that this formulation is problematic, in so far as Corner implicitly equates the macro with the 'real' and the micro with the realm of the epiphenomenal (if not the inconsequential). In the first place, Corner's analysis fails to recognize the gendered articulation of the divisions macro/micro, real/trivial, public/private, masculine/feminine, which is what much of the work which he criticizes has, in various ways, been concerned with (see for example, Gray, 1992; Morley, 1986; Radway, 1984). More centrally, Corner seems to invoke a notion of the macro which is conceptualized in terms of pre-given structures, rather than (to use Giddens's phrase) 'structuration', and which fails to see that macro structures can only be reproduced through micro-processes.

It was precisely that realization that drove the initial shift (see Hall, 1977) in cultural studies work, away from any notion of a mechanically imposed 'dominant ideology' towards the more processual model of 'hegemony' – as a better theoretical frame within which to analyse the reproduction of cultural power in its various forms. (Interestingly, neither Harris (1992) nor McGuigan (1992) quite seem to grasp this distinction, and both replicate the confusion instituted by Abercrombie et al.'s (1984) conflation of Althusser and Gramsci.) One important motivation of that shift was to attempt to find better ways to articulate the micro and macro levels of analysis, not to abandon either pole in favour of the other. Nor, as Massey (1991) argues, should we fall into the trap of equating the micro (or local) with the merely concrete and empirical, and of equating the macro (or global) with the abstract or theoretical. In all of this, we could do worse than heed Wright-Mills's (1959) strictures on the need to address the interplay of biography and history, in the 'sociological imagination'.

All of this is, of course, particularly vital in the realm of media consumption, given the media's key role in articulating the public and the private, the global and the local, and in articulating global processes of cultural imperialism with local processes of situated consumption – where local meanings are so often made (see Miller, 1992) within and against the symbolic resources provided by global media networks.

To say that is not to offer any *carte blanche* defence of 'ethnography-as-where-it's-at'. If, as Marcus and Fischer observe, the value of ethnography lies in reshaping our dominant macro-frameworks for the understanding of some structural phenomenon (such as the capitalist world-system, for example) so that we can 'better represent the actual diversity and complexity of local situations' for which our theoretical frameworks try to account in general terms (Marcus and Fischer, 1986: 88) yet, as Fiske cautions, any ethnography 'runs the risk, which we must guard against at all costs, of allowing itself to be incorporated into the ideology of individualism' (Fiske, 1990a: 9). If ethnography is concerned to trace the specifics of general, systemic processes, for instance, the particular tactics which various members of a given society have developed in order to 'make do' with the cultural resources which it offers them still, as Fiske notes, our concern must be with interpreting such activities in the broader context of that 'larger system through which culture and politics intersect' (Fiske, 1990b: 98).

In this context, recent debates within feminist media research and feminist theory offer some interesting parallels. The work of Ang and Hermes (1991), for example, is concerned to criticize essentialist tendencies with feminism, which would too readily invoke the category of gender as an explanatory device, in such a way as to blur all the cross-cutting differences that necessarily exist within that category. At the same time, Walby (1992) and Barrett (1992) raise questions about the potentially negative consequences of a post-structuralist destabilization of categories (such as that of gender) which leads only to the accumulation of micro-narratives of the local, specific and particular, which are theoretically precluded from transposition into any broader form of macro-analysis. While the poststructuralist critique of essentialist tendencies to invoke social categories (whether those of gender, class or race) as the explanatory framework of individual action, functions as a useful corrective to any 'super-structuralist' form of determinism, that critique, nonetheless, itself always runs the risk of falling back into a form of methodological individualism (see Knorr-Cetina, 1981, for an account of a methodological situationist alternative) which leaves one, in the end, able only to tell individual stories of (logically) infinite differences.

From my own perspective, our objective must not be to substitute one (micro *or* macro) level of analysis for the other, but rather to attempt to integrate the analysis of the broader questions of ideology, power and politics (what Hall (1988b) has described as the vertical dimension of communications) with the analysis of the consumption, uses and functions of television in everyday life (the horizontal dimension of communications, in Hall's terms). It is not a question, finally, of understanding simply television's ideological (or representational) role, or simply its ritual (or socially organizing) function, or the process of its domestic (and more broadly social) consumption. It is also a question of how to understand the articulation of micro and macro issues and processes.

Questions of methodology, self-reflexivity and epistemology

The substantive focus in recent years on media consumption as an active process has also had one particularly important methodological consequence, in so far as work in this field has come to employ principally qualitative, and often ethnographic, techniques of enquiry as a means of investigating this process in its natural settings. In the case of American cultural studies, in particular, the identification of qualitative methods with the progressive (politically correct?) wing of communications studies seems to be almost complete, and ethnography, as Lull (1987) has argued, has come to be a fetishised buzz-word in the field.

For my own part, while I have often (though not exclusively) employed ethnographic techniques in my own work, I would want to insist that ethnography, in fact, holds no exclusive claim to methodological adequacy, in so far as it, like any other methodological choice, involves what an economist would call 'opportunity costs'. I would agree with Murdock (1989a) that analytical work can neither be guaranteed nor damned by its methodological choices alone, and I share Corner's (1991) anxieties about the assumption that the provision of 'more context' is always, in itself, the solution to methodological problems, as some proponents of ethnography would seem to believe (see Morley, 1992, Chapter 8 for a fuller version of this argument).

However, despite these disclaimers, I would also want to argue that some of the theoretical debates which have surrounded the practice of ethnography in recent years (cf. Clifford and Marcus, 1986; Geertz, 1988; Marcus and Fischer, 1986) are of considerable importance, not just to anthropology, but also for scholars in the field of media research. In the first place, these debates (initially concerning the relations of power, as well as of knowledge, between representor and represented) concern not only the dilemmas of the white anthropologist who produces forms of knowledge of 'exotic' or 'tribal' peoples. They also concern media researchers, in so far as they too are in the business of investigating and representing others, whether or not those others wear exotic tribal dress: working-class audiences, youth audiences, gendered audiences, ethnic audiences. To that extent, media researchers can also easily fall prey to the dangers of an Orientalism (Said, 1979) in which, as Ang puts it, 'the audience is relegated to the status of exotic "other" . . . objects of study, about whom "we" have the privilege to know the perfect truth' (Ang, 1991: 10), or as Hartley puts it, such audiences 'become the "other" of [our] powerful imperial discourses' (Hartley, 1987: 125). In this context, Trinh T. Minh-Ha's (1989) comments on anthropology as itself an 'anthropophagous' (cannibalistic) discourse, concerned to 'grasp the marrow of native life', or Fiske's comments on the behaviour of the 'ethnographer who descended as a white man [sic] into the jungle and bore away, back to the white man's world, [the] meanings of native life' (Fiske, 1990b: 90) should also give media researchers pause for thought, as they consider their relations with the audiences they research.

Postmodern ethnography

Since the turn towards qualitative, and especially ethnographic, methods of research took hold in cultural studies' work on media consumption, for example, there has been an increasing interest in anthropology as a source of methodological correctives to the perceived dead-ends of the quantitative tradition of social science communications research. The irony here, however, is that, as Probyn observes, 'just as practitioners in other disciplines seem to be drawn to ethnography because of its promise to delve into the concrete (in the hope of finding real people living "real" lives), ethnography is becoming increasingly textual' (Probyn, 1993: 61). Probyn's reference is, centrally, to the influence within anthropology of Clifford and Marcus's collection *Writing Culture* (1986). This book, and the debates which it engendered, laid the basis for a heavily textualist approach to (postmodern) ethnography which has, latterly, also become extremely influential within cultural studies. This approach is heralded as being politically sensitive to questions of representation, to relations of power between researcher and researched, and to the possibility that anthropology as a whole, as the late Bob Scholte put it, may have simply been 'a way Europeans have invented of talking about their darker brothers or sisters' (Scholte, 1987: 25–36). As Fabian (1990: 758) notes, ethnography itself is a word that carries an ideological burden, in so far as, if its denotative meaning can be defined innocently as 'the description of peoples', connotatively, the implication is always that the peoples to be described are Others – non-writers, non-Europeans, non-Christians – 'Them', and not 'Us'.

The contributors to *Writing Culture*, along with Clifford and his collaborators, and their associated works (Crapanzano, Taussig, Nash, Rabinow, Rosaldo, et al.) are centrally concerned with the fact that ethnographies are written: that they are forms of writing and representation which must be scrutinized as such. However, to anticipate my later argument, if it is true that ethnography is a form of writing, it does not follow that it is *only* a form of writing; nor that an address to its textual characteristics will solve all its problems. This emphasis on textuality may well, in fact, also serve to blind us to the non-textual aspects of the frequently oppressive relations between the ethnographer and his or her subjects. As Fabian notes, it is not simply the fact that the would-be postmodern ethnographer's stress on self-reflexivity will not necessarily 'guarantee that [the] oppressors will be less oppressive, just because they are self-conscious' (Fabian, 1990: 768). It is also deeply problematic if 'awareness of the political dimension of writing remains limited to insights about the political character of aesthetic standards and theoretical devices. . . . To be dominated, it takes more than to be written about. . . . Conversely, to stop writing about the other will not bring liberation' (Fabian, 1990: 760). This is Grossberg's point when he notes that one can all too easily 'deconstruct the other into the productivity of the ethnographer's subjectivity – [a deconstruction in which – D.M.] – the very facticity of the other is erased, dissolved into the ethnographer's semiotic constructions' (Grossberg, 1988: 381–2). As Gewertz and Errington argue, it is but a small step from there to a position in which the other is seen as an entirely discursive phenomenon, a position in which, as they put it 'we think, therefore they are' (Gewertz and Errington, 1991: 80), as material otherness is reduced to semiotic difference. As the Native American Indian artist Jimmie Durham scathingly puts it: 'You think you own us. . . . You think I am *your* Other' (Durham, 1993: 138–9).

In saying all this, I am not wanting to decry the importance of the self-reflexive, textual questions posed by much of this recent anthropological work. I would entirely agree that questions of how ethnographic texts are fashioned, constructed and projected, what rhetorical strategies they use to appear persuasive and how their authority is authenticated and legitimated are important issues. Indeed, notwithstanding Geertz's (1988) criticisms of Clifford et al.'s stress on textuality, Hamer (1989) offers a fascinating analysis of the crucial role played by rhetorical and stylistic devices in Geertz's own writing. Equally, the questions Clifford raises as to 'Who speaks? Who writes? When and where? With or to whom? Under what institutional and historical constraints?' (Clifford, 1986: 13) are vital ones. However, while we must take due note of them, they are not the only, or indeed, necessarily the most important, questions. There remains the question of what these ethnographies say and what relation, if any, it is claimed they have to the world outside the text.

Similarly, I would not wish to deny the importance of the questions raised in contemporary anthropological debates concerning the staging of the voices of the ethnographer's subjects, and the relation between these voices and the meta-narrative of the ethnographer who edits and marshalls them. Thus, Marcus (1986) offers a very interesting discussion of the dangers of a kind of ventriloquism in ethnographic writing, using as his example Paul Willis's *Learning to Labour* (1977), in which Marcus argues that, in an undeclared fashion, Willis orchestrates the voices of the 'lads' he studies, in such a way as to give the impression that his analytic discourse is validated and authenticated by being grounded in the voices of his subjects.

Certainly, this is a question to be handled with some circumspection, and self-reflexivity is a useful antidote to any easy naturalization of the particular analytic account offered as the basis of any ethnographic evidence. However, it should be noted that, as Ernest Gellner (1970) argued many years ago in his debate with Peter Winch (1958), the fact that the analyst finally produces an account of his subjects' activities which is not expressed in their own terms, and which may in fact be different from the account they would offer of their own activities, hardly invalidates it, but is perhaps precisely the necessary responsibility of the analyst and this point remains, even if it can be argued that this is a responsibility which Willis himself attempts to displace on to his respondents. The question Marcus poses: 'Does Willis' articulated critical theory of capitalism really come from the lads?' (Marcus, 1986: 184) can, in fact, be answered in the negative – without that necessarily having any of the damning consequences for Willis's work which Marcus seems to presume this would have.

Moreover, as Ullin notes, the response of some contemporary ethnographers to this problem – to choose to foreground their informants' voices, 'does not settle the issue of authority, as these voices are not autonomous, but rather stand mediated by the social conditions of their production' (Ullin, 1991: 81) – conditions in which it is still the ethnographer who chooses, edits and sequences the (often implicit) meta-narrative of the material presented. In this respect it is surely better that the analyst's role in this procedure be explicit, rather than obscured in the editing process, while remaining nonetheless powerful. As Fabian notes 'dialogue, perceived vaguely as an alternative to isolating or domineering monologue' is now much in vogue in anthropological circles, and has 'acquired a non-specific ethical behavioural, oozing goodwill. . . . Who could be against dialogue?' (Fabian, 1990: 763). The problem is that, as Geertz (1988) puts it, the descriptions are still the describer's descriptions and the 'dialogue' is still edited, constructed and presented by the ethnographer – the burden or critical responsibility is, in this sense, inescapable, whether the material is finally presented in monologic or dialogic form. To have recourse to a rhetoric of polyphony, decentred texts, and the principled fragmentation of all meta-narrative, does not necessarily have any of the progressive ethical or political consequences which are often assumed to follow. It can also produce a disempowering incoherence, even if the analyst, in disburdening him – or herself of the responsibility of producing an explicit meta-narrative, is able to step more lightly the while.

Fabian raises the interesting possibility that much early ethnographic writing was not in fact so much realist as 'naively naturalist' (Fabian, 1990: 762) and argues further that 'ethnographic representations that are (or pretend to be) isomorphic with that which is being represented should be met with suspicion; more likely than not, they lack what distinguishes knowledge from mimickry' (ibid.: 765). The point here is parallel to that made by Borges in his story 'Of exactitude in Science' (1972). Purporting to come from an old travel book, the story describes how:

> In that Empire, the craft of Cartography attained such perfection that the map of a single Province covered the space of an entire city, and the map of the Empire itself an entire Province. In the course of time, these extensive maps were found somewhat wanting, and so the College of Cartographers evolved a map of the Empire that was of the same scale as the Empire and that coincided with it point for point. (Borges, 1972: 141)

Unfortunately, of course, while the map was now perfect and complete, it proved a little cumbersome, and soon fell into disuse.

To make these points is, on the one hand, to argue for realism against naturalism, but it is also to argue that the much-discussed 'crisis of representation' in contemporary anthropology (and cultural studies) has to be met by the development of better forms of representation, rather than a rejection of the necessarily realist epistemology of the project of representation itself. As Fabian notes, the only logical alternative is finally 'non-representation, including its most radical form: not-writing, graphic silence' (Fabian, 1990: 761).

At this point, it is of some interest to return to what, for instance, Marcus and Fischer actually claim for their own ethnographies. Despite their espousal of a variety of textual concerns, even they, finally, are concerned with representation. Not only do Marcus and Fischer argue that ethnographies still must refer to and reflect an external reality, but they argue that if they do not, they are without ethnographic value: the value of ethnographic texts, they argue (see Pool, 1991: 321), is finally to be found precisely in their capacity to reflect an external reality. Similarly, notwithstanding the appropriation of the project of *Writing Culture* to a kind of 'anything goes' relativism, in his introduction to that volume, Clifford states clearly that 'the authors in this volume do not suggest that one cultural account is as good as another. If they espoused so trivial and self-refuting a relativism, they would not have gone to the trouble of writing detailed, committed critical studies' (Clifford and Marcus, 1986: 24). This returns us to the question of the relation between the textual and the real. Ullin rightly observes that 'there is much that we can learn from the critical appropriation of communicative or literary metaphor – an appropriation that discloses, as postmodernists and culture theorists alike have agreed, the proximity of [the discipline of anthropology – D.M.] to the art of storytelling' (Ullin, 1991: 82). We are necessarily involved in the telling of stories, and that clearly involves us in question of rhetoric, textuality and writing. This brings us to the question of Deconstruction, or more precisely, to the theoretical consequences of the observation that philosophy is a kind of writing, which constitutes the theoretical foundation of these recent debates about the implications of the recognition of the necessarily textual status of ethnography itself, as one form of writing.

Textuality, rhetoric and the value of truth

In his account of 'Deconstructionist' theory, Norris (1991) offers us an illuminating analysis, which is quite at odds with that, increasingly accepted, reading of the work of Derrida and others which seems to underpin so much postmodern theorizing, in anthropology and elsewhere. Norris argues that, in the writings of 'post-analytical' philosophers such as Richard Rorty (1989), 'Deconstruction' comes to figure as a handy cover-term for everything that points beyond the 'old dispensation of reason, knowledge and truth' (Norris, 1991: 149) and Derrida comes to play the role of the arch-debunker, who dances rings round the earnest philosophical seekers-after-truth. Hence the title of Rorty's essay on Derrida, 'Philosophy as a Kind of Writing' (1978) where he urges that we should give up thinking of philosophy as a specialized activity of thought, with privileged claims on standards of argumentative validity and truth, and think of it simply as just another voice in the 'ongoing cultural conversation of mankind', but one with delusions of grandeur, that can easily be cut down to size by insisting on its necessarily textual status and by pointing to the final 'contingency' of *all* specialist vocabularies, that of philosophy included.

Norris's point is not simply that Rorty has got Derrida wrong; has *mis*-read him, in Richards's (1960) terms. One could not intelligibly even raise questions of interpretative validity and truth if the postmodern, pragmatist argument won out, and philosophy was reduced to the status of just another form of writing (see Gellner's (1992) trenchant critique of 'post-modern relativism' from the point of view of what he calls 'Enlightenment Rationalist Fundamentalism'). More directly, Norris claims, there is a crucial problem of logic with Rorty's argument. It is one thing to show that philosophical writing often mobilizes covert topological figures and sublimated metaphors, and it is of considerable interest to analyse philosophical texts from this point of view. However, there is simply no good reason to support Rorty's unargued assumption that the presence of 'figural' elements in a piece of argumentative writing necessarily impugns its theoretical adequacy or undercuts its philosophical truth claims. Hence, Norris claims, the importance of respecting the distinctive philosophical valences of Derrida's work, and of not going along with the pseudo-Deconstructive, post-textualist or 'levelling' view of philosophy as 'just another kind of writing'. Norris's point is that Derrida's own mode of argument (in 'White Mythology' (1974) for example) is far from endorsing the vulgar Deconstructionist view that all concepts come down to metaphors in the end, or that philosophy enjoys no distinctive status *vis-à-vis* literature, rhetoric or the human sciences at large. Derrida's purpose, in 'White Mythology', as Norris points out, is precisely to deny that we could simply turn the tables on philosophy (or reason) in the name of literature (as metaphor, rhetoric or style): not least because there is simply no possibility, for example, of discussing 'metaphor' without falling back on some concept of metaphor elaborated in advance by philosophical reason. Norris is rightly concerned to counter the widespread, but erroneous, supposition that due regard for the textual (or 'writely') aspects of our work – in itself a beneficial or rewarding perspective – necessarily 'writes off' (*sic*) the traditional concerns of philosophical discourse and reason.

As Norris argues, Deconstruction, properly understood, involves absolutely no slackening or suspension of the standards (logical consistency, conceptual rigour, modes of truth-conditional entailment, etc.) that properly determine what shall count as a genuine or valid philosophical argument. After all, as Derrida himself put it, in his debate with John Searle:

> the value of truth (and all those values associated with it) is never contested or destroyed in my writings, but only re-inscribed . . . in more powerful, larger, more stratified contexts . . . and within those contexts . . . it should be possible to invoke rules of competence, criteria of discussion and consensus, of good faith, lucidity, rigour, criticism and pedagogy. (Derrida, quoted in Norris, 1991: 156)

To put the matter more concretely, this is to argue that the epistemological and ethical difficulties raised by Clifford and others should not be allowed to disable our attempts to produce good accounts of 'what is going on' in various instances of media consumption but can, in fact, enrich our attempt to pursue that project. This is to say that we can recognize the importance of issues concerning the context of the encounter of representer and represented and the context of the writing of ethnography, and yet still conclude, with the late Bob Scholte, that 'while we may never know the whole truth, and may not have the literary means to tell all that we think we know of truth . . . shouldn't we nevertheless keep trying to tell it?' (Scholte, 1987: 39). To take this position is by no means to defend any naively 'naturalist' epistemology, but it is to argue that the importation of anthropology's 'literary turn', into cultural studies, for all its potential benefits, is also capable of producing a form of muddled relativism, which can then function to disable empirical research, by fiat.

Massey (1991) refers, in this connection, to Mascia-Lees et al.'s observation that 'when western white males – who traditionally have controlled the production of knowledge – can no longer define the truth . . . their response is to conclude that there is not a truth to be discovered' (Mascia-Lees et al., 1989: 15). The issue, as formulated by Hartsock (1987) is that:

> it seems highly suspicious that it is at this moment in history, when so many groups are engaged in 'nationalisms' which involve redefinitions of the marginalised others, that doubt arises in the academy about the possibilities for a general theory which can describe the world, about historical 'progress'. Why is it, exactly at the moment when so many of us who have been silenced, begin to demand the right to name ourselves, to act as subjects rather than objects of history, that just then, the concept of subjecthood becomes problematic . . . [that] . . . just when we are forming our own theories about the world, uncertainty emerges about whether the world can be adequately theorised? (Quoted in Massey, 1991: 33)

One (extreme) form of such disabling uncertainty (and relativism) is that developed by Hartley (1987) in his 'constructivist' account of the television audience as a 'fictional object'. Hartley argues that audiences may be 'imagined' empirically, theoretically or politically, but in all cases the product is a fiction that serves the needs of the imagining institution. The argument is that we must recognize the 'constructivist' character of the research process and drop any ideas of 'capturing' the television audience 'as it is', in its totality. From this perspective, the television audience does not so much constitute an empirical object as exhibit an imaginary status, a realm in which anxieties and expectations, aspirations and fantasies, as to the predicaments of modern society are condensed. Thus, Hartley argues that 'in no case is the audience "real" or external to its discursive construction. There is no "actual" audience that lies beyond its production as a category . . . audiences are only ever encountered . . . as representations' (Hartley, 1987: 125). This stress on the institutionalized discursive practices through which television audiences are constructed (for example, in Hartley's argument, the 'paedocratic discourse' through which the television audience is constituted by broadcasters) is of considerable value, as a corrective to any simple-minded 'naive realism' in the research process. However, it is possible to recognize the necessarily constructivist dimensions of any research process without claiming that audiences only exist discursively. To argue otherwise is to confuse a problem of epistemology with one of ontology. Naturally, any empirical knowledge which we may generate of television audiences will be constructed through particular discursive practices, and the categories and questions present and absent in those discourses will determine the nature of the knowledge we can generate. However, this is to argue, contra Hartley, that while we can only know audiences through discourses, audiences do in fact exist outside the terms of these discourses.

Both Tompkins (1986) and Fish (1989) have offered trenchant critiques of the overblown claims often made on behalf of the kind of postmodern, Deconstructionist theories which have now achieved the status of orthodoxy within many areas of cultural studies. Such theories stress the (all) importance of perspectivism ('facts can only be known from some particular perspective') and textualism ('the world is a text capable of infinite interpretation'). The problem, as Tompkins formulates it, is that the effect of bringing 'perspectivism' to bear on a particular area of enquiry (history, in her example; cultural studies in the case I am concerned with) is, effectively, to wipe out its subject matter, and to leave nothing but a single idea: perspectivism itself. Tompkins's argument is that, as long as you think that there are (or could be) some kinds of facts that existed outside of any perspective, then the idea of 'perspectivism' will seem to 'annihilate' any particular fact to which it is applied. However, if one recognizes that there are no facts that are not embedded in some perspective on the world, then the argument that any particular set of facts derives from a perspective (or 'world-view'), no longer constitutes a problem. As she puts it, 'if all facts share this characteristic, to say that any one fact is perspectival doesn't change its factual nature in the slightest' (Tompkins, 1986: 76).

As she goes on to argue, this doesn't therefore mean that one needs to accept any old fact – any 'fact' may, of course, be demonstrated to be false – but it does mean that one is precluded from arguing that what x asserts to be a fact is not 'really' a fact, just because it is 'only' a product of their perspective – since this is, ex hypothesi, true of all facts and thus has no particular bearing on any individual fact. Tompkins thus notes that, while the self-reflexive awareness that all facts are situated within interpretative frameworks is useful when discussing historiography, it has literally no bearing on the facts of any particular case. Her conclusion is heretical, as far as cultural studies' emergent epistemological orthodoxy is concerned: 'what this means is that arguments about "what happened" [in some particular case – D.M.] have to proceed much as they did before post-structuralism broke in, with all its talk about language-based reality and culturally produced knowledge. Reasons must be given, evidence adduced, authorities cited, analogies drawn' (Tompkins, 1986: 76).

For Fish, the key problem facing 'textualist' work in history is how to resolve the logical difficulties that follow from the 'assertion of wall to wall textuality' (Fish, 1989: 303) and the assertion that 'there is no such thing as history in the sense of a referential ground of knowledge' (Hunt, quoted in ibid.: 305). As Fish notes, this (in parallel with Hartley's argument) is to deny that the writing of history could ever 'find its foundation in a substratum of unmediated fact' and the problem is then how to reconcile this radical textualism with the attempt to say anything in particular about a given historical event. As he puts it, 'if you think *that* about history, how can you, without contradiction, make historical assertions?' How can one both 'recognise the provisionality and multiplicity of local knowledge' and yet 'maintain that it is possible to give true accounts of a real world?' (ibid.: 305). How can you at once 'assert the textuality of history and make specific and positive historical arguments?' (ibid.: 307).

Fish's answer to the last of these questions is that it is perfectly possible to square the circle here, as soon as one recognizes that asserting the textuality of history and making specific historical arguments have nothing to do with one another, in so far as they are actions in different practices. As he puts it 'the first is an action in the practice of producing general (i.e. metacritical) accounts of history, the practice of answering such questions as . . . "what is the nature of historical fact?" The second is an action in the practice of writing historical accounts (as opposed to writing an account of how historical accounts get written), the practice of answering questions such as "what happened?"' (ibid.: 307). In parallel with Tompkins's argument, Fish holds that, as the belief that facts are constructed is a general one and is not held with reference to any facts in particular, 'the conviction of the textuality of fact is logically independent of the firmness with which any particular fact is experienced' (ibid.: 308).

Fish's disarming conclusion is that the long road through discourse theory and textualism, in the end, leaves us 'precisely where we always have been', having to make empirical claims 'with reference to evidence, marshalled in support of hypotheses that will be more or less convincing to a body of professional peers' (ibid.: 309), rather than 'brandish[ing] fancy accounts of how evidence comes to be evidence or invok[ing] theories that declare all evidence suspect and ideological', because, as Fish notes, that would be 'another practice, the practice not of giving historical accounts, but the practice of theorising their possibility' (ibid.: 313). Here Fish comes close to Geertz's position, in the debate with Clifford and Marcus, where Geertz notes that, if the traditional anthropological attitude to these theoretical questions ('Don't think about ethnography, just do it') is a problem, nonetheless, to fall (as many would-be postmodern ethnographers have done) into a paralysing (if vertiginously thrilling) trance of 'epistemological nervousness' ('don't do ethnography, just think about it') is no kind of answer. What is needed in this respect, as Haraway puts it, is 'an account of radical historical contingency for all knowledge claims and knowing subjects, a critical practice for recognising our own "semiotic technologies" for making meanings, *and* a no-nonsense commitment to faithful accounts of a "real" world' (Haraway,

1991: 187) – a recognition that the object of our would-be knowledge, while being really 'made up' is nonetheless 'real' for that.

To recap the argument, by the way of conclusion, my concern in this piece has been with the destabilization of two associated theoretical orthodoxies, one concerning the status of the 'active audience' model of media consumption, the other concerning the methodological and epistemological commitments to self-reflexivity and relativism/constructivism, which have come to be widely influential within the field of cultural studies in recent years. My argument has been, in the former case, that some within cultural studies do seem to me to have moved into an unhelpful romanticization of 'consumer freedoms' which forgets the very question of cultural power with which our investigations (or mine, anyway) began. Conversely, I am equally critical of the born-again political economist/sociologists of culture (as manifested, for example, by some of the recent writings of Nicholas Garnham – see his chapter in this volume) who seize upon some of the wilder examples of 'active audience theory' to discredit retrospectively the whole enterprise of cultural studies, on the grounds that they always said it would lead to tears. In relation to the case of the methodological/epistemological orthodoxies which I have identified, clustered around the pole of relativism/self-reflexivity, my argument has been that the seeming contemporary 'closure' of these debates in cultural studies around a set of relativist 'certainties' (sic), and the widespread presumption of the epistemological correctness (and political effectivity) of these currently fashionable positions is, to say the least, ill advised. As I have argued, these positions themselves display significant epistemological and political deficiencies, to which we must attend. To return, in conclusion, to my earlier arguments, if we need to take care both to avoid some of the unproductive excesses of 'active audience theory', and to reconsider our conception of the relation of micro and macro processes, and if our ethnographic accounts of various forms of media consumption are necessarily themselves texts, which must be looked at (as rhetorical constructions), as well as looked through (to such truths as they can reveal), nonetheless, our ultimate ambition must surely still be to develop ethnographies which will, as Geertz (1973: 3–30) famously put it, sort the winks from the twitches (ibid.: 6).

9

Cultural Populism Revisited

Jim McGuigan

During the early 1990s there was a moment of stock-taking in cultural studies which involved both a codification of knowledge for student consumption and a recognition of the diversification of work in the field according to the changing circumstances of theorizing and research that had resulted largely from the 'globalization' of cultural studies (Gray and McGuigan, 1993). It would be tedious to recount yet again these dynamics since they have been so minutely charted, though not always accurately, in a flood of recent literature, a literature which I do not intend to survey here. My intentions are much more specific: to affirm the critique of cultural populism, to further substantiate that critique and to move beyond it.

To recapitulate my original critique of cultural populism (McGuigan, 1992): the old tension between a notion of 'popular culture' derived in one version or another from Herder's 'folk culture', on the one hand, and 'mass culture' in the Frankfurt School sense, on the other hand, has been resolved in much cultural studies in terms of an appreciative and, indeed, celebratory view of 'mass-popular culture'. Popular culture, in the folkish sense, was seen as produced by 'the people', as actively made by them and expressing their distinctive social experiences, attitudes and values. In contrast, the pejorative conception of mass culture, in Left, Right and Centrist versions, stressed media manipulation of popular taste and the passive consumption of commodified culture. This was quite rightly challenged as a form of cultural elitism during the early phase of cultural studies in Britain, a phase which was characterized by a politics of popular culture, particularly rooted in the working class and youth. Both cultural elitism and mainstream media culture were criticized. The unsatisfactory binary opposition between popular and mass culture was more fully deconstructed later, however, by a revaluation of the subordinate term, 'consumption'. From this point of view, consumption was no longer to be seen as the 'passive' moment in cultural circulation but, instead, 'active' and nodal, involving popular appropriation of commodities and differential interpretation of texts. The stress on 'active consumption' had, of course, a legitimate relation to feminism and, more generally, with the populist sentiments, if not necessarily the critical priorities, of earlier cultural studies. Where cultural elitism had viewed popular taste as inferior, ill-educated and lacking in discrimination, latterday cultural populism came to see exactly the opposite. Cultural populism is, I would contend, the binary product of cultural elitism and fatally so, forever tied to it through opposition, directly reversing its values. The decline of cultural elitism, one of the several features of postmodernism, however, calls cultural populism also into question. What started out as a radical and subversive agenda becomes a conventional wisdom and, in that sense, conservative. Furthermore, cultural populism has a close affinity with the ideal of the sovereign consumer in neo-classical economics, the philosophy of the free market, the currently dominant ideology throughout most of the world.

The analysis and critique of populist sentiment in cultural studies was not meant to produce a comprehensive account of the field but, rather, to identify its energizing impulses and to trace how they have transmogrified over time. During the 1980s the widespread drift towards an exclusively consumptionist mode of analysis in cultural studies was focused upon the interpretation of routine and popular consuming practices to the comparative neglect and detriment of critical forms of depth explanation that were concerned with the material conditions of cultural production, such as the political economy of culture. The very idea of explanatory critique became epistemologically unfashionable while postmodernist themes of particularity and contingency contributed to this new relativistic orthodoxy in cultural studies. Theoretical fashion, loss of conviction in progressive politics, New Right hegemony, and the economic and cultural reconstructions associated with what has been called 'post-industrial' or 'post-Fordist' capitalism had a combined yet very complex set of effects on the field of study.

The world had apparently changed dramatically and so had critical theory of culture and society, whereby it scaled down its political expectations and withdrew from commitment to societal transformation. Towards the end of the 1980s these developments were condensed symbolically in the historical metaphor of fallen communism: this, in spite of the fact that the intellectual currents swirling around cultural studies had never been inspired by 'actually existing socialism' in the Soviet communist sense; instead, quite the contrary (compare, for example, Downing's analysis in this volume). Cultural studies was very much the product of that old New Left which had arisen originally during the 1950s in reaction to Stalinism and the normalization of social democracy (Davies, 1995). New Left cultural studies became increasingly marked during its subsequent formation since the 1970s by distinctly 'Western' forms of radicalism, particularly the varieties of feminism, diasporic Black politics and, latterly, 'queer theory'. In recent years, most notably, there has been a belated and characteristic anguishing over its Eurocentric and Atlanticist relation to 'the Other'.

In addition to the populist sympathies of cultural studies, which distinguish it very sharply from mainstream academic disciplinarity, especially in the humanities, cultural studies has been obsessively anti-economistic, distancing itself from the once official Marxist–Leninist doctrines of culture and society, summed up by the reductionism of the so-called 'base-superstructure model'. Economic reasoning was, in effect, repressed in New Left and subsequent cultural studies and simultaneously transposed, in analogical usage, on to the cultural plane, a plane that tended to be seen as almost entirely autonomous from any actual economy and polity. So, we have the idea of a 'cultural' or 'symbolic' economy which consists of exchange relations and significatory flows but with little discernible relationship to something like a 'real' economy that may have a measure of determinacy, however mediated, upon these exchanges and flows. Such a transposition of economic logic on to the plane of the insistently non-economic with no recourse to an economy conceived in terms of the circulation of wealth is a curious form of theoretical repression. This chapter, then, seeks to deepen the critique of consumptionist cultural populism by deconstructing it in relation to the dominant ideology of the recent period, a revived neo-classical economics founded upon the mythology of sovereign consumption. Also, problems of value, analysis and policy are explored that transcend the limits of cultural populism and begin to indicate in particular ways how a fresh critical agenda for work in cultural studies is emerging.

Sovereign consumption

The repressed has a habit of returning in symptoms opaque to the subject's own self-consciousness, as Freudian theory has always insisted. Take, for instance, John Fiske's (1987) claim concerning an actually existing 'semiotic democracy', originally stated with regard to television-viewing as 'producerly' and which was subsequently expanded into a generalized account of popular subversion of what he calls 'the dominant culture' (1989a, 1989b). For Fiske (1991), 'the dominant culture' is one and the same with the approved canon of great works and their supposedly inherent values that are taught in the traditional university curriculum. By contrast, contemporary sources of resistance and opposition somehow derive, according to Fiske, from the popular consumption and meaningful transformation of mass-distributed cultural products in the marketplace. Quite apart from the persistently simplistic binary opposition of dominant and subordinate cultures, with nothing much in-between, Fiske's model, similarly to many academic conceptions of knowledge, vastly overestimates the role of the higher education curriculum in securing cultural power. It is a good deal more plausible to argue, alternatively, that 'the dominant culture', if there is indeed such a phenomenon, is formed most profoundly by prevailing market forces and their legitimating ideologies.

Fiske's semiotic democracy is very similar to Paul Willis's (1990) actually existing 'common culture'. Willis argues that the market has delivered the goods to everyone's satisfaction and especially to the satisfaction of young people, who are making utopian use of cultural commodities here and now in Britain and, when he was writing, before Margaret Thatcher had been deposed due to the failing popularity of her 'authoritarian populism'. The main target of disapprobation for Willis is not so much the university curriculum but, instead, the British system of public arts patronage, which he claims has no relevance at all for the vast majority of people and particularly for the young, although he pays no attention to the universal role of arts and cultural education in the state's schooling system. Rather than the state seeking to enculture youth with community arts projects and the like, Willis calls for an appreciation of the 'symbolic creativity' and 'grounded aesthetics' involved in watching television advertisements, reading mass-market magazines, listening to and remixing popular music, fashion bricolage, and drinking and fighting in pubs.

'Common culture' in the social-democratic tradition was an 'ought' concept which was given a radical and 'productionist' inflection by the New Left (Williams, 1968b). Although of more recent provenance, 'semiotic democracy' would also seem to be a normative ideal, identifying a desirable condition for which to strive rather than an achieved reality. It is conservative theoretically to claim that a condition that, arguably, ought to exist already is; but more than this, in spite of the manifest avoidance, and indeed repression, of political economy in the work of exemplary populist writers such as Fiske and Willis, it is strangely homologous, albeit latently so, in the sense of an homology of structures (Goldmann, 1969), with the right-wing political economy that is founded upon the concept of 'the sovereign consumer'. Before proceeding with this hypothesis, two qualifications need to be made: first, with regard to the potential disjunction between the professed politics of a theoretical position and the underlying logic of that position; and, secondly, with regard to the clearly observable disjunction between conservative cultural theory and right-wing political economy.

There is no doubt that Fiske is on the side of the angels, as his *Power Plays, Power Works* (1993) would readily attest. His sympathies are evidently with the oppressed and their struggles against the powers that be, yet his theorizing, focused so narrowly as it is on the micro-politics of consumption and the local victories and defeats of everyday life, provides little space for transformative struggle of any kind. Willis is also well aware of the material inequalities that obstruct the equitability of consuming pleasures. In his contribution to the 1991 British Arts and Media Strategy debate, while reiterating the critique of publicly subsidized culture, Willis recommended the Dutch idea of a 'culture card' for the poor and unemployed. The problem with local authority 'leisure cards' is that they only provide concessionary access to public facilities, for instance, swimming pools and theatres. However, most people's preferences are for the products of the private sector. Hence, the 'culture card', 'cheapening access to and purchase of the products and services of the cultural industries on a very wide definition: body culture; photo culture; youth culture; home culture; music culture, and so on' (Willis, 1991: 54). Although commercial cinemas, for instance, do quite commonly offer concessionary entrance to the unemployed, pensioners and students to boost box-office takings where audience attendance is flagging, it seems implausible to expect capitalist enterprises to suddenly become genuinely philanthropic on a significant scale of their own volition. Businesses may be forced by local governments to pay a 'percentage for art' when relocating, and companies like McDonald's contribute to charitable activities in the interests of public relations, but more comprehensive voluntary contributions to equitable cultural consumption are less than likely. On reading Willis, I conjure up an image of long queues of unemployed youth snaking into the local music store on a Saturday morning, each member of which, when reaching the counter inside, declares 'I am an unemployed young person. This is my culture card. I claim this week's free chart-topping CD!'

No ideology is ever entirely consistent but it is striking how the neo-classical economics of contemporary conservative parties is diametrically opposed to the traditional forms of conservative cultural thought. The latter tends to be authoritarian, stressing eternal truths and absolute values, while seeing the social value of culture as one of a moral education that abhors relativism of all kinds. In comparison with such cultural authoritarianism, right-wing thought in political economy is downright libertarian and populist. And, when applied to culture, it is cultural populist, rather like Fiske and Willis, in fact. It is hard to see quite how the position represented by Fiske and Willis differs materially on cultural issues from right-wing think tanks such as the Centre for Policy Studies, the Institute of Economic Affairs and the Adam Smith Institute, the very think tanks that provided a steady flow of policy ideas, including cultural policy ideas, for strategic implementation over the past decade and a half of Conservative governmental hegemony in Britain (Desai, 1994). In a North American context, one might similarly refer to the Heritage Foundation, the Cato Institute and the American Enterprise Institute. One has to read beneath the Leftist rhetoric, to which Fiske is especially prone, in order to perceive this theoretical convergence of an exclusively consumptionist cultural populism with right-wing political economy.

As Russell Keat has noted accurately of 'consumer sovereignty', at least in my experience of trying to locate a satisfactory theoretical statement of it, 'one is unlikely to find much explicit discussion of this concept in standard textbook accounts of a market economy' (Keat, 1994: 27). It is, nonetheless, the ideological lynchpin of the neo-classical economics that was so successfully revived politically, if not economically, during the 1980s. That it is not always stated explicitly is perhaps symptomatic of its totemic function in contemporary culture and New Right politics. The concept of consumer sovereignty and its implications for cultural policy were, however, expressed succinctly in the 1986 *Report of the Committee on Financing the BBC* (known as the Peacock Report) on broadcasting, which was originally set up by the second Thatcher government in order to produce a rationale for introducing advertising to the BBC. It did not eventually fulfil the implicit governmental brief because of a fear that this would reduce the advertising revenue of commercial television. Nonetheless, the Peacock Committee did produce a useful articulation of free market ideology in relation to a broadcasting system which had hitherto been regulated according to principles of public service:

British broadcasting should move towards a sophisticated market system based on consumer sovereignty. That is a system which recognises that viewers and listeners are the best ultimate judges of their own interests, which they can best satisfy if they have the option of purchasing the broadcasting services they require from as many sources of supply as possible. (*Report of the Committee on Financing the BBC*, 1986: para. 592)

In such neo-classical economics, the sovereign consumer is a necessary fiction, a construction of an all-rational, calculating subject, forever seeking to maximize marginal utility in consumption choices. Rational consumer decisions, aggregated as demand, are said to trigger supply or, rather, result in success or failure on the supply side in the free market. Nothing should be permitted to interfere with this magical process.

There are two basic criticisms of the ideology of consumer sovereignty that should be mentioned. First, sovereign consumption ideally depends upon perfect knowledge of what is actually or potentially available to consume, in order to facilitate rational choice, since consumption is said to determine production. The counter-argument is that perfect knowledge of what could be consumed is impossible and that demand is not simply aggregated from the sum of rational choices made by consumers, in any case, but is at least partly cultivated by suppliers through advertising and marketing. Thus, production has some determinacy over consumption and the consumer may not be very knowledgeable of how the process actually works in practice. This argument holds, I would suggest, in spite of the selective accounts of production that are now frequently included in the marketing packages of, say, blockbuster movies. The main implication of such an argument for cultural studies is that actually existing consumption patterns are not necessarily a wholly reliable guide to what people might want if they could have it.

The second criticism is similarly well known but is rarely stated with much conviction nowadays. This is that there is a false equalization in the claim that we are all sovereign consumers. Some consumers are more sovereign than others. In effect, it is still a minority of people, according to any universal standards of comparison, who are in a privileged position, by sheer virtue of material advantage, to exercise freedom of choice in consumption and to consume exactly what they want or need. There is also symbolic advantage, resulting from familial habitus and education, which is only partially separable from possession of wealth in shaping the distribution and the various combinations of cultural competence and taste. Fundamentally, if you do not have the money or an appropriately cultivated range of competences, which in the 1990s includes a postmodernist picking and mixing of tastes, high and low, then, your potential choices in consumption are thereby limited.

Two further considerations in connecting this critique of consumer sovereignty to consumptionist cultural populism should be taken into account. These considerations cover both a 'post-Marxist' accommodation to capitalism and the irrationalism of 'postmodern' capitalism. The first consideration is the possibility that a critical view of the symbolic and material economies might still be sustained alongside a commitment to rational choice, which does, after all, attribute a dignified sentience to the human subject, as in 'rational choice Marxism'. However, as Ellen Meiksins Wood has demonstrated powerfully, it is very difficult to produce a convincing critique of the prevailing economic, social and cultural orders out of a mixture of 'neoclassical economics, game theory, methodological individualism, and neo-contractarian philosophy' (Meiksins Wood, 1989: 87), which were such vital ingredients of Reaganomics and Thatcherism. And, as Joan Robinson remarked many years ago in her commentary on the original marginalist economics of Jevons and Alfred Marshall, 'This is an ideology to end ideology, for it has abolished the moral problem' (Robinson, 1964: 53). We are in the presence here of that 'value free' economics which claims merely to describe positivistically how the ineluctable forces of the unfettered market work and, when challenged for its inegalitarianism, is forced to acknowledge the 'naturalness' of inequality and to plead that with the growth brought about by the proper operation of market forces the 'trickle down' effect will, thence, occur.

Secondly, there is the refusal to accept a rationalistic model of the consuming subject and to conceptualize consumption in more visceral and situated ways, which may well be the position that Fiske and Willis would actually subscribe to, although it is difficult to tell for sure from their writings. It is a position which squares quite neatly with prevalent forms of irrationalist theorizing (Larrain, 1994). Here again, there is also a notable correspondence with right-wing political economy, to whit that of Frederick Hayek, whose *The Road to Serfdom* (1944) and his own personal tutoring provided such inspiration for the Thatcherite project which promised to eliminate socialism once and for all from Britain. Hilary Wainwright (1994) has shown how Hayek's version of free market theory differs not only from socialist regulatory rationalism, but also from the rational fictions of neo-classical economics. For Hayek, the consumer does not choose on the basis of rational knowledge of what would maximize utility but, instead, makes decisions purely subjectively without recourse to reason and reliable information since knowledge, for both consumers and economists, is inherently fallible. In a sense, one might argue, Hayek was a postmodernist *avant la lettre* and his belief in the benificence of freely chosen consumption shorn of rationalist illusions is uncomfortably close to consumptionist cultural populism.

During the recent period of New Right hegemony it was only to be expected that the ideologues of the free market would claim, along with Francis Fukuyama (1989), that an ideal cultural polity had virtually been achieved or was in the immediate grasp of right-wing governments. That leading proponents of cultural studies should say something similar is rather more surprising. It is one thing to claim that people make the best use of the cultural products available to them and, therefore, appreciate the ordinary semiotic and symbolic work that this entails, but it is quite another thing to claim that we live in an actually existing 'semiotic democracy' or 'common culture'. If such concepts serve any useful purpose, surely it is to function as a standard of principled criticism by which to measure and find wanting actually existing conditions, not, unwittingly, to endorse the powerful ideologies of think tanks like the Adam Smith Institute.

It should be clear that my critique of an exclusively consumerist mode of analysis in cultural studies is mainly to do with questions of explanation and, in effect, political usefulness. Nevertheless, such a critique may be, and has been, more immediately seen as raising problems of cultural evaluation, particularly in the context of public debate and not only in the academic field of cultural studies.

Value

The call for a return to cultural value has, in Britain, probably quite differently from the USA where issues of 'political correctness' and religious zealotry have predominated, been related to the way in which the aim to 'broaden culture' beyond an authorized aesthetic canon seemed to shift from an oppositional project in the 1960s and 1970s into a market and marketing phenomenon during the 1980s, so that everything became 'culture' under the equivalence of exchange value (see Savage and Frith, 1993). The playwright David Hare's declaration on BBC2's now defunct *Late Show* in October 1991 gave a conservative twist to the cultural value debate among Left-liberal intellectuals in Britain: 'Finally, Keats is a better poet than Bob Dylan'. Hare's comparison was peculiarly inapt and ill-judged. For a start, Dylan's popularity is hardly a hot issue and, besides, he has himself been canonized, if not to quite the same extent as Keats. The comparison was made, presumably, because they are both poets whose texts could be scrutinized for their relative values. We have in this comparison, then, authorship, textual objectivism and finality, key features of 'traditional' aesthetic judgement. That is the first and least satisfactory move in the cultural value debate, in the direction of the aesthetic as a space of fixed standards and once-and-for-all time judgements. It returns to the binary opposition between absolutism and relativism. The more productive tendency in cultural studies, and particularly in populist cultural studies, has been to take a relativistic view of value against exclusionary absolutisms, which evince an unwarranted universalism of value and are not just about art abstracted from social relations but are, in practice educationally and otherwise, implicated in various forms of class, gender, racial and sexual oppression.

Steven Connor, in *Theory and Cultural Value* (1992), has suggested that questions of cultural value typically oscillate between absolutism and relativism: neither extremity is itself tenable. He does not believe that the oscillation between absolutism and relativism should, in the end, be resolved either way. Instead, we would do better to recognize that 'the paradox of value', as he dubs it, pulls both ways. Connor insists on 'the necessity of value', which derives from 'the irreducible orientation towards the better' (Connor, 1992: 2). However, because he is so caught up with respect for the pantheon of great theorists, the proponents of 'Theory' with a capital T, Connor has little distinctive further of his own to offer, except to say, in conclusion, 'the quickening predicament' of value escapes theorizing (ibid.: 255).

The sources of cultural authority that at one time claimed, perhaps with greater credibility than now, to make absolute judgements of value have broken down. As Connor quite rightly indicates, although in an excessively abstract and tortuous fashion, this does not mean that value does not matter. People will value: we make judgements as to quality and worth all the time; and these are not just monetary evaluations. Ordinary human judgement has a great deal to do with social usefulness, a mundane sense of the difference between exchange value and use value. It is the sociality of value which is of prime interest, then, not the remote aporias of aesthetics. Because the aesthetic move is perpetually in danger of dropping off the edge of the theoretical board game, the sociological and the ethical moves in the value debate provide rather more substantial directions for cultural analysis.

To treat questions of aesthetics and cultural value sociologically does not necessarily imply a value-free perspective, as Janet Wolff (1983/93) has argued forcefully. She recommends an approach to value which views evaluation as a social process changing over time and which can be examined from a number of different value positions. The great proponent of such a sociology is, of course, Pierre Bourdieu. His magnum opus, *Distinction – A Social Critique of the Judgement of Taste* (1984), must be the departure point for the sociological move. Bourdieu's original move was to displace the question of value and the principle of 'disinterestedness' in the Kantian aesthetic tradition with the sociological concepts of 'distinction' and 'taste'. In so far as tastes are markers of class, they are bound up with social distinction strategies. Bourdieu analyses this in the hierarchy of distinctions between 'legitimate', 'middle-brow' and 'popular' tastes. His use of extremely elaborate social survey data, much of it gathered as long ago as the 1960s, and the daunting sociologese of some of his prose give Bourdieu's text an objectivist and dispassionate gloss. Although it is sometimes said that Bourdieu displays an Olympian contempt for all the subjects of his research, where his sympathies lie is quite evident, however, with the values of 'the popular aesthetic' and the habitus of his own working-class origins: this is best exemplified in the ethnographic material upon which he draws and in his theorization of the empirical findings.

Bourdieu reserves his greatest contempt for the self-deluding 'independence' of the older avant-garde currents of the bourgeoisie and for the new petite bourgeoisie who 'dream of social flying, a desperate effort to defy the gravity of the social field' (Bourdieu, 1984: 179). From a 1990s' vantage point, Bourdieu's *Distinction* is most suggestive in terms of his prescient remarks concerning these new petite bourgeois agents of 'presentation and representation' (ibid.: 359), which is frequently cited as one of the first formulations of the 'postmodern' class or, at least, identification of that fraction of the professional-managerial class which promotes postmodernism with such self-interested enthusiasm (see Lash and Urry, 1987).

However, it is around the possible postmodernization of the cultural field that Bourdieu's path-breaking work most needs updating (see Wynne and O'Connor, 1995), and which, incidentally, makes Hare's observation so dismally redundant.

It is an open question to what extent cultural hierarchies have actually been flattened and formal boundaries blurred, the principal claims that are made routinely in the postmodernist vernacular. Instead of remaining within a purely theoretical space to debate these matters, which, as Connor was forced to admit, settles very little, there is a need for concrete sociological research, especially in an ethnographic mode. 'The necessity of value' and 'distinction strategies' require scrutiny on the grounds of popular culture itself. With such work, we may find that the populists are flogging a dead horse on behalf of 'the people' against 'the dominant culture' in the university and the publicly subsidized sector. In this respect, Fiske's (1991) idea of 'popular discrimination' is one that needs developing further and Willis's (1990) observations concerning, for instance, 'realism' as a standard of judgement among youthful viewers of soap opera is indicative of what we might discover through empirical research and which, perhaps, runs counter to the 'intellectual' taste inscribed in much critical theory. Thus, the most important questions of value may be to do with 'standards', 'qualities' and 'distinctions' within the field of mass-popular culture and where the boundaries with 'high' and avant-garde culture are no longer so firmly fixed as they once were.

The sociological move may be further supported with an ethical orientation. This is already implied in Terry Eagleton's (1990) bold treatment of the history of aesthetics. He puts the aesthetic in its bourgeois place on the bodily expressive as opposed to the economically instrumental side of capitalism's ideological coin. Having historicized the aesthetic, bringing it down from its ethereal and falsely universalizing pretensions, Eagleton aims to retrieve the aestheticizing promise of better times. He does so mainly via Jurgen Habermas's (1987) theoretical defence of 'the lifeworld' against 'the system' and, similarly to Habermas, Eagleton advocates the radical transformation of 'discourses of reason, truth, freedom and subjectivity' (Eagleton, 1990: 415).

What the move into a Habermasian discourse ethics (see, for instance, Habermas, 1990) might mean in practice can be usefully illustrated with reference to John Mepham's (1991) valuable and, indeed, brave discussion of 'quality' in popular television, which further confirms my criticisms of what Annabelle Sreberny-Mohammadi (1991) has called a 'happy populism' that is hopelessly silent on such matters. Mepham refuses the usual hierarchical way of stating the problem of 'quality' in television as a unitary standard functioning to distinguish 'serious' from 'popular' television. He is concerned with quality within popular television and the qualities of popular television. Mepham outlines a three-point view of quality as, first, 'a social project' with, secondly, 'a cultural purpose' and in, thirdly, 'a normative framework'. For the social project, he defines 'a rule of diversity' in a multicultural and plural society. The cultural purpose of, say, popular television drama is, according to Mepham, to provide 'usable stories', value in use, not just as sign or in exchange. Finally, the normative framework insists upon 'the ethic of truth telling'. In our postmodern times, the stress on truthfulness may seem strangely old hat. However, Mepham makes out a very good case for it: 'It is precisely because there is no Truth, no guaranteed foundation of true principles which could act as a criterion of truth, no certainty derived from access to reality independently from our research and its instruments, that an ethic of truth-telling is essential' (Mepham, 1991: 26).

Because popular culture is so personally and politically important and because television, in particular, is so central to contemporary popular culture, questions of value, quality and truth are necessary to ask, questions that reconnect cultural studies to practical matters of cultural policy. While it is very difficult to make confidently positive judgements, it is not so hard to identify what needs criticizing, as Todd Gitlin makes abundantly clear, yet perhaps a little too clear for some, in his comments on American television:

> Alongside some excellent work, we will see a thin, soulless, nihilist standardization of culture overriding nominal 'diversity'. At the same time, the deep cleavage between class cultures will persist, the wonders of channel-glut being affordable by what might be called a two-thirds society. Heavily (but far from exclusively) because of the televisualization of everyday life, we will continue to be flooded by glibness in speech and style; dazzled by a convergence of information and entertainment; yet at the same time, suspicious and preternaturally savvy. (Gitlin, 1993: 351)

We should, according to such a view, be concerned with the analysis and social critique of cynical values that are represented in multiple and complex ways in communications media, and not only confine ourselves to appreciation of popular resistance, irony and scepticism.

Analysis

The exclusively consumptionist strand of cultural studies has not only been strangely uncritical in its treatment of mass-popular culture due, I believe, to a loss of normative purpose and, in effect, endemic political quietism, but also self-limiting and one-dimensional in its analytical reach. Turning away from the critical perspectives that were inspired by the Frankfurt School and early hegemony theory, media and cultural analysis from the populist perspective became increasingly concerned with how socially subordinate members of the 'active audience' interpreted and used mass-distributed cultural products. This resulted frequently in an insoucient and usually celebratory view of mass-popular cultural consumption and its everyday pleasures, a tendency which was taken to a *reductio ad absurdum* in the work of John Fiske during the 1980s.

Virginia Nightingale (1993: 164) has written of her 'sense of the impossibility of the task so glibly outlined' by Fiske (1987) when he says that the aim of cultural studies is to combine ethnographic audience research with semiotic textual analysis in order to produce a satisfactory account of cultural consumption. From the point of view of a serious anthropology of contemporary culture, the hermeneutic complexities of such a task are so immense that they make Fiske's 'readings' of, say, Madonna seem slight, to say the least. How much more difficult it would be to combine the analysis of consumption with other dimensions and levels of analysis. Yet, nevertheless, it is the near absence of such a combination in populist cultural studies that has come to undermine its analytical and critical powers. The comparative lack of a more rounded or, in the terms used by Steven Best and Douglas Kellner (1991), 'multi-dimensional' and 'multi-perspectival' approach to the field of study can be traced to the abolition of political economy from cultural studies.

This abolition of political economy from cultural studies goes back to the theoretical codifications of Birmingham University's Centre for Contemporary Cultural Studies during the 1970s under the leadership of Stuart Hall. In his seminal article, published in 1980, 'Cultural Studies: Two Paradigms' (1980a), Hall identified not just two paradigms in cultural studies but, in fact, six. In addition to the two of the title, 'culturalism' and 'structuralism', Hall mentioned his own neo-Gramscian synthesis of hegemony theory, Lacanian psychoanalysis, Foucauldian discursive formation analysis and, also, the political economy of communications and culture. These last three were all given short shrift by Hall at the end of the 1970s, which is curious to recall now, since Hall's own recent work, in which he has taken up questions of identity and 'race' in an exceptionally fruitful manner, has become increasingly poststructuralist and even Foucauldian in temper (see, for instance, Hall, 1990a). That, however, is to some extent beside the point for the matters in hand.

Hall was concerned with the specificity of the cultural and so he deemed it necessary to reject political economy for reducing the complexity of meaning in, say, news media to the more or less straightforward expression of prevailing economic and political interests. Alternatively, it was necessary, according to Hall, to draw upon and develop theories that attributed a considerable measure of autonomy to ideological and significatory processes, most notably theories appropriated from the structuralist tradition, in order to account for the specificity of the cultural level. While it is unquestionably so that cultural analysis must deal with language and, more broadly, discourse and also engage routinely in hermeneutic interpretation, it is much less clear how it can do without analytical frameworks to explain how economic and political determinations shape the conditions of production and circulation of cultural commodities. In resisting a pull towards reductionism in the political economy of communications and culture, Hall went much too far and, in effect, gave warrant to a prejudice against, and ignorance of, this crucial dimension of materialist analysis. Hallian cultural studies has persistently sought to do without economics, thereby creating a two paradigm divide, indeed, not so much between culturalism and structuralism but, instead, between cultural studies, on one side, and the political economy of

communications and culture on the other side. It is interesting that while this
schism has characterized much academic theorizing and research on communications and popular culture in Britain, it has been much less
pronounced in the USA, where there are significant examples of synthesis.

In their book, *Postmodern Theory* (1991), Best and Kellner have sought to
resolve similar analytical problems to those raised here with regard to, in
their case, the larger tensions between modern and postmodern social theory.
Although there are important differences between cultural populism and
postmodernist theory, it can, in certain respects, be seen, however, as a particular branch of postmodernism, not least indicative of which is the shared
refusal of political economy and multidimensional forms of explanation. Best
and Kellner take an unusually catholic attitude to contemporary theory, carefully sifting through what they consider to be the strengths and weaknesses of
the varieties of postmodernist social and cultural thought. Among other
things, they call for a reconciliation between cultural analysis in a postmodern mode with modern critical theory and political economy. Best and
Kellner state their general position thus: 'A multi-dimensional critical theory
stresses the relative autonomy of each dimension of society and is thus open
to a broad range of perspectives on the domains of social reality and how
they are constituted and interact. A multiperspectival social theory views
society from a multiplicity of perspectives' (Best and Kellner, 1991: 264). The
social and cultural worlds are so complex, so variously levelled and multiply
dimensioned, that analysis will inevitably take many different and seemingly
incommensurate forms, which does not mean there are no important incom-
mensurabilities of perspective. Best and Kellner warn against an 'eclectic
pluralism' that 'fails to specify what phenomena are most salient in specific
situations and fails to provide distinctive and strong theoretical analysis'
(ibid.: 270). It will not do to say that 'anything goes'. Nevertheless, there is
much to be gained from articulating together a range of perspectives that may
illuminate a multidimensional whole. The value of such an approach can be
illustrated briefly by comparing John Fiske's (1989a) reading of Madonna
with Douglas Kellner's (1995) multidimensional analysis. The case of
Madonna has, it must be said, been overworked to the point of tedium in cultural studies, functioning similarly to the old schools' history problem of the
causes of World War I. Was it due to a spectacular individual act? Was it due
to capitalism in its highest stage of development? Or, was it due to an interlocking set of disparate factors, none of which can be awarded causal
priority? No doubt Madonna would have been studied exhaustively and
exhaustingly in any event: Fiske, however, started it.

Fiske recognizes there is something to be said for a political economy of
the Madonna phenomenon, but not much: 'such an account is inadequate
(though not necessarily inaccurate as far as it goes)' (Fiske, 1989a: 96). The
trouble is that such an approach, says Fiske, treats Madonna's fans as '"cultural dopes"' . . . manipulated at will and against their own interests by the
moguls of the culture industry' (ibid.: 96). Fiske proceeds to quote from a
number of Madonna's 'wanna-be' fans, younger teenaged girls, largely from

published sources, to the effect that her bad girl persona was experienced by them in the mid-1980s as empowering. Fiske also analyses words and images from songs and videos such as 'Like a Virgin' and 'Material Girl' in which he discovers that she is subverting patriarchal systems of representation through various parodic and ironic devices. So, there is a pleasing symmetry, then, between Fiske's 'semiotic' textual analysis and the 'ethnographic' evidence of audience response and identification among young girls. Therefore, as right-thinking (or, is it left-thinking?) people we should think well of Madonna rather than badly of her: she is using the capitalist culture industry to provide young girls with empowering identifications. No contradiction involved.

Alternatively, Kellner (1995) views Madonna as 'a site of genuine contradiction', rather than unification of text and audience response, and traces her career from the mid-1980s into the 1990s as an interaction of semiotic play and experiment with a series of shrewd marketing moves: from 'Boy Toy' through 'Who's That Girl?' to 'Blonde Ambition' and beyond. Kellner reads Madonna's semiosis, her shifting constructions of identity, in relation to the commodification of self that is driven, in the capitalist cultural industries, by the rapid turnover of fashion and the endless search for new target markets. Madonna's cultural and material success owed much to keeping on the move, as capital does, picking up new audiences, differentiated according to age, sexuality, race and ethnicity, while, no doubt, carrying her original fans along too. Kellner's account does not demean the young girls who made Madonna into a star, but it does give a much 'thicker description', in Clifford Geertz's (1973) phrase, than Fiske's admittedly much earlier account.

The combination of interpretive and political economy perspectives also provides a more satisfactory explanation of Madonna's rise and inevitable fall as an icon of the age. To argue for a multidimensional and multiperspectival approach of this kind is not meant to suggest that all forms of analysis should always produce a rounded and totalizing explanation as well as an interpretation. It does have implications, however, for how we think of the field as a whole, by posing a choice between a narrow, exclusionary and enfeebled conception of cultural studies and a broadly conceived and critical field of work that encompasses many different and potentially mutually-informing modes of analysis.

Policy

Whither cultural studies? How much that is a matter of choice or beyond the control of agents in the field is a moot point. In a situation of uncertainty about the future, there is a temptation to clutch at big ideas and sweeping solutions to the accumulating problems of theory, research and education in cultural studies. One such solution that has been proposed is the turn towards policy, advocated by Tony Bennett (1992a, 1992b) and his associates in Australia. While this may seem like a fresh solution for a field of study that has, in the past, been mainly concerned with critical analysis, it is not without precedent. Raymond Williams always maintained a keen interest in policy matters and was greatly disappointed during the 1960s when Harold Wilson's Labour government in Britain chose to ignore him and his arguments concerning the democratic governance of culture (see McGuigan, 1993, 1995).

Although there is considerable disagreement about the scope and the implications of Bennett's specific proposals (see, for instance, O'Regan, 1992), it is quite clear that he is recommending a major overhaul of cultural studies. It is premissed upon a critique of cultural studies, particularly the failure to relate culture and governmentality, which Bennett (1992a) attributes to Williams's misreading of the 'culture and society' tradition. Bennett also questions the politics of cultural studies that has, for him, privileged significatory processes and radical reading, the aim of which is somehow to transform the reading subject as part of a counter-hegemonic project. It is indeed a peculiar kind of politics: learning to read texts radically while neglecting the dynamics of institutional power. Just as seriously problematical as this, perhaps, for Bennett, is the zero sum power game of hegemony theory, whereby winning and losing are symbiotically related to one another. Bennett prefers a more diffuse Foucauldian concept of power as proliferating from multiple sites and flowing in all sorts of minute ways through the capillaries of the body politic. Michel Foucault's (1991) notion of 'governmentality', Bennett stresses, is not reducible to state power but refers to all the mechanisms of social regulation and management in a manner somewhat reminiscent of the Althusserian concept of 'ideological state apparatuses', which was also meant to refer beyond systems of government in the narrowly empirical sense, a similarity, however, that Bennett does not acknowledge and, in fact, denies.

Most controversial are the unusually pragmatic and instrumentalist lessons that Bennett draws from Foucault's work. The task of cultural studies, when engaging with the agents and institutions of policy, museums, public commissions of enquiry, and so forth, is not to challenge and critique but, rather, to produce useful knowledge. For Bennett, 'cultural policy studies' is 'a largely technical matter, . . . tinkering with practical arrangements', instead of pursuing, as cultural studies has done, 'an epic struggle for consciousness' (Bennett, 1992b: 406). In sum, then: 'Cultural studies might envisage its role in the training of cultural technicians: that is, of intellectual workers less committed to cultural critique as an instrument for changing consciousness than to modifying the functioning of culture by means of technical adjustments to its governmental deployment' (ibid.: 406).

Tom O'Regan (1992) objects to Bennett's programmatic reorientation of cultural studies on the grounds that cultural studies is already and widely policy-oriented, but from the point of view of what he calls 'bottom-up' power (populism again) rather than 'top-down' power, concerning itself with the lived effects of policy, not advising the policy-makers on how to be more effective. O'Regan's objection is a reasonable one but it overstates the policy engagement of cultural studies as it is normally practised. Bennett is accurate in suggesting that cultural studies has stood on the sidelines, either indifferent to the policy process, while spouting seminar-room politics and pasting bourgeois academia, or simply deriding the policy-makers as morons and worse. The debate on 'cultural policy studies' further illustrates the curiously hermetic world of cultural studies in general. To suddenly discover policy in this way, albeit in the particular conditions of Australia, which has had a Labour government throughout the 1980s and into the 1990s, is odd when one considers how policy issues have always been paramount in the political economy of communications and culture, revived in recent years over the question of 'information poverty' (Murdock and Golding, 1989), and, to give another example, how cultural policy has played an important role in urban planning and regeneration strategies (Harvey, 1989; Bianchini and Parkinson, 1993). Of the Australian theorists of 'cultural policy studies', Stuart Cunningham (1992, 1993) has been the boldest in reconnecting work in the field of cultural studies with the 'real world' of politics. He has actually said of cultural studies that '[t]he missing link is a social-democratic view of citizenship and the training necessary to activate and motivate it' (Cunningham, 1993: 134). The implications of such a view are to question the role of 'the consumer', which diminishes the role of 'the citizen' and has thus been seriously questioned for that very reason in this chapter, and to engage with the enduring modernist debate about the conditions of 'the public sphere' in relation to culture in all its respects (McGuigan, 1996).

From a policy-oriented perspective, this requires a certain distancing from the immediate contexts of cultural governance. Bennett is right, however, to recommend that cultural studies should enter into dialogue over the micro-processes of cultural policy but, more ambitiously, it should also engage with the macro-processes as well, which are presently very much commanded by the ideologies and material powers of 'the market'. The failures of cultural studies are less to do with faulty volition than with the peculiar conjunction of 'successful' academic institutionalization, occurring simultaneously with the marginalization and confinement of critical thought in the academy. There is no point in simply grumbling about powerlessness and acquiescence with an agenda for purely instrumental usefulness is no way forward. In order to rediscover the sources of an effective and critical praxis, cultural studies must be imaginative, it must propose alternatives, different ways of ordering the social and cultural worlds. And, if this seems unrealistic, one only has to refer back to the unrealism of, say, British right-wing think tanks in the 1970s, who dared to think the unthinkable and had the opportunity to see some of their wildest dreams realized at the cost of great suffering. Cultural studies, then, must be less restricted by its own space, recognizing that cognate work is going on in other spaces, aiming to reinvent the future, instead of becoming too bogged down in cataloguing the consuming pleasures of the present or merely assisting the grinding pragmatics of bureaucratic and economic power.

Note

Earlier versions and parts of this chapter were presented in guest lectures and research seminars at the following universities: De Montfort, Leeds Metropolitan, Liège, Manchester Metropolitan, Sunderland and Warwick. I must thank Tim O'Sullivan, Mike Peters, Sabina Sharkey, John Storey, Yves Winkin and Derek Wynne for providing me with these opportunities to develop my thoughts from *Cultural Populism*.

10

Imagining the Audience: Losses and Gains in Cultural Studies

Joli Jensen and John J. Pauly

Every theory of the media invokes an image of the audience. For the researcher the audience may appear as a market of consumers, a jaded mob, a nascent public, a lumpen proletariat, textual poachers, situated spectators, 'the people'. With each image come assumptions about who the researcher is in relation to the audience – who are 'we' in relation to 'them'?

This question is particularly acute for cultural studies because it hopes to speak in terms other than those offered by the marketplace or traditional social science. Those of us who do cultural studies see the social science tradition of audience research as complicit in a longer line of institutional attempts to scrutinize, package, and control the public. We hope (naively, perhaps) that we, at least, are up to something different. They seek to dominate; we seek to liberate the voice, open avenues of action, or help people articulate their own desires. In this way, we enact our own drama of identity, casting our lot with critical rather than administrative research, and affirming the importance of academic work as a form of political action. But just how does such work help others and the world?

Our chapter interprets the meaning of cultural studies' turn to the audience. Our purpose is not so much to review the audience literature in detail but to name its impulses and capture something of its tone. In particular, we compare two common approaches to audience research. The first approach, far more popular in the USA until recently, has been to treat the audience as a text – or, more precisely, as a subject position articulated by society's competing discourses. This style of work, particularly appealing to researchers trained in literature, attracted a generation of students interested in contemporary culture and politics. This approach constitutes the textual turn. The second approach rejects the traditional tools of audience research – mass surveys and laboratory simulations – in favor of conversational interviews, small-group discussions, and observation. This approach constitutes the ethnographic turn.

We admire the ethnographic turn, and we discuss its possibilities and limits below. Our greatest concern is with the textual turn, especially as practiced in those versions of American cultural studies most influenced by literary and film theory. Though we appreciate researchers' willingness to draw upon diverse traditions and we respect the depth now brought to the analysis of texts, we argue that the textual turn has produced its share of losses, too. These losses appear most obvious in audience research, where the textual turn has signified not just a methodological choice but a preference for European styles of cultural theory that seem indifferent or hostile to popular taste. Our fear is that, in the very act of embracing the audience, researchers may abandon the debate about public life that animated earlier versions of cultural studies. We argue for a style of audience research that respects groups' choices as culturally meaningful and makes better use of American traditions of social thought about the public, democracy, technology, and the mass media. The research we imagine would plausibly draw upon John Dewey for its perspective on media, culture, and democracy, on the Chicago School of Sociology for its approach to inquiry, and on Thorstein Veblen, Lewis Mumford, Harold Innis, and James Carey for its account of the social consequences of technology. It would distinguish itself from both the older behavioral tradition of audience research and from contemporary theories, whether textual or ethnographic, that equate culture with ideology.

The promise of theory

What has made media studies in the USA exciting for students in the past decade is the way it has absorbed Continental theory in combination with new modes of textual analysis. This has been a period of hectic importation, as the language and interpretive methods developed by psychoanalysis and Marxism for the criticism of film and literature have been applied enthusiastically to television and popular music. Because 'cultural studies' seems to describe the relations between texts and the wider world, and because it offers a radical intellectual stance for the researcher, the analysis of media texts via cultural studies seems to offer politically progressive ways to make arguments about contemporary society.

Much of this research addresses more popular and youthful media like television, rather than stolid adult media like the newspaper. Television, as narrative or text, is analysed as film-in-the-home, or as books-with-pictures, in relation to hegemonic processes that are themselves never fully explicated. Researchers round up and question particular shows in order to demonstrate their new techniques of theoretical interrogation. Students gather at conferences to present papers analysing particular shows or genres; dissertations compare narrative styles or devices; the texts of television and popular music join film and literature as terrain waiting to be decoded, or deconstructed, or demystified. All of this is done with the belief (since this is 'cultural studies') that textual analysis is cultural analysis toward progressive social change.

But the rush to analyse media as texts typically neglects the social situation from which those texts emerge – the questions of production, distribution, and consumption that have interested social scientists and political economists; the assumptions about politics, ideology, and history that have defined

British cultural studies; and the concerns with meaning, power, community, and democracy that characterized earlier versions of American cultural studies. In media studies of the 1980s, students and faculty respectfully referenced a few Names in cultural studies, then went on to do sustained and inventive analyses of particular media texts. In this manner, researchers concocted a theoretical bricolage that freely combined assumptions from structuralism, poststructuralism, feminism, Marxism, and reader-response theory – each imported without much reference to its individual intellectual heritage or disciplinary context. In this postmodern mode, researchers have justified their analysis of texts as having something important to say about the constitution of social life, politics, and the economy.

For those in literary studies, where textual analysis has always been the central mode of inquiry, this approach opened exciting new vistas for articles, conferences, departments, institutes, and careers. For those of us in media studies, with a very different heritage of concerns and inquiry, new modes of textual analysis have opened a path, ironically, toward depoliticized intellectualism. While literary critical techniques offer us another way to talk about the content of media forms, they do not, we argue here, offer us ways to think well about media, culture, society, meaning, and power. They offer ways to be sophisticated about textual content, but not about the social worlds we cohabit. Passing references to work by social and cultural theorists cannot connect elaborated readings with the understandings of people, or with the ways in which people engage in practices that construct and sustain everyday life.

Consequences of textualization

When we ask about the role of the audience under this textualized perspective, the limits (and hubris) of this perspective become clear. If the media are a collection of texts, then the audience is a collection of readers. What are the consequences of such a perspective for how we think about our enterprise, and for how we engage the world? Describing any cultural practice as a text, and the audience as readers, inevitably inflects one's subsequent analysis. To conceptualize people who watch television, listen to music, read the newspaper, and generally attend to media events as readers (rather than as social, interpretive actors) is to invoke a much longer heritage of assumptions about texts and their power. Embedded in the term *text* are all our long-contested practices of literacy, education, governance, worship, science, and art.

To speak of the world-as-text is to speak metaphorically. In the hands of careful thinkers like Paul Ricoeur (1991), and when applied to familiar objects of scholarly analysis, that metaphor provocatively suggests parallels between our acts of reading and our larger habits of interpretation. When we apply that metaphor too casually to popular culture, however, we lose track of our own talk. Treating the world as comprising texts that are read is not the same as treating the world as something that is structured and intelligible in the same ways that a text is structured and intelligible.[1] When we collapse the social into the textual, we treat people as if their experiences were *themselves* textual. Life is, we would argue, enacted in experience, not read. To presume that we are best understood as readers of texts, rather than people who act, is to presume that we constantly perform interpretive acrobatics in relation to texts, rather than in relation to other people, and to forget that we encounter others through memory, conviction, plans, and desire.

At times, the literary versions of cultural studies have tried to address the social basis of the audience's interpretations, most notably by describing audiences as 'interpretive communities' (Fish, 1980). In theory, the term *interpretive community* calls attention to interpretation as a social act and readers as inhabitants of a social world. In practice, however, the 'community' described by this approach remains sociologically thin, a world of relations pointed to but rarely explored. To consider the audience an interpretive community is still to locate people through texts rather than through the social processes by which texts influence and engage people in actual circumstances. Because they construct people as readers, text-based approaches will understand family, friendship, and community as secondary or nontextual forces that 'construct' the reader subject, not as the experienced rubric in and through which people read, think, feel, love, and plan.

Culture as social fix

The textualization of media studies has also encouraged researchers to adopt, unreflectively, a set of assumptions about the relationship between culture and society – assumptions that Raymond Williams effectively analysed (and thus hoped to move beyond) in *Culture and Society* (1958a) and *The Long Revolution* (1961). We can briefly sketch a comparable American heritage, one that differs significantly from British concerns because it returns, consistently, to the problems and prospects of participatory democracy.

In discussing the role of culture in democracy, Americans have often debated what would be the 'right' kind of culture for a diverse, experimental, and modernizing nation (Duncan, 1965, 1968; Jensen, 1993). From Alexis de Tocqueville's assumptions about a lively egalitarian literacy, to Walt Whitman's hopes for a redemptive democratic literature, to Lewis Mumford's faith that the arts could counterbalance technics in a holistic synergy, we find a recurring faith in the power of particular forms of culture to transform people and societies.

This faith in the power of cultural forms to change people is, as Jensen (1990, 1994a) argues elsewhere, connected to a deep ambivalence about people's ability to think and act well. Social criticism points to 'bad' culture (advertising, MTV, rap music, comic books) as the reason why people act badly, and 'good' culture (pro-social, uplifting, substantive, imported) as the means either to restore or catalyse good action. In this heritage, readers are the substrate on which the texts 'work', a substrate that social critics seek to protect and improve.

Recent literary criticism would vigorously deny its similarity to older *beaux-arts* or modernist critiques of culture. Yet within literary studies a family resemblance persists: literary critics still make their living telling other people how to read texts. Nineteenth-century critics tutored citizens in the forms of beauty, and twentieth-century New Critics modeled the forms of cosmopolitan irony for their bumpkin brethren. More recently, poststructuralists have perfected the arts of parlor magic, promising to show their apprentices how to make the world disappear in a cloud of self-immolating texts.

Now as ever, literary criticism anoints culture with general social power. It argues that the populace needs the right kind of culture to be the right kind of people, an assumption that we can see, transfigured, in current theorizing about texts. The 'right' kinds of texts are subversive, empowering, marginalized, authentic; the 'wrong' kinds of texts are oppressive, constraining, mainstream, commercial. The assumption is still that the right kinds of texts have the right kinds of effects on readers and society.

Such assumptions of direct social benefit are disguised in contemporary discourse, which presumes that a rupture or suture in a text can both signify and become a rupture or suture in individual understanding or consciousness. In the eclectic sampler of textualized cultural studies, discourse can simultaneously emerge from, cause, and change social conditions. The language of current textual theorizing, with its endless 'interventions' and 'interrogations,' is a language of martial action, mobilized at a theorized moment of text/reader connection, against a backdrop of presumed struggle. This elaborated but occluded analysis of cultural power retains the key unexamined presumption of nineteenth- and twentieth-century literary thought – that textual action is social action.

This intellectual move has proved seductive because it makes writing socially potent, and valorizes intellectuals as social activists. The writing that professors and students do as part of their work is, simultaneously, changing readers and changing the world. While few current theorists make so grandiose a claim for their writing, the implication is always there – my text has power, it does something to the reader, and in doing something to the reader, it is an intervention, doing something to the social formation.

We can see this ideology of powerful texts played out, obliquely, in the critique of American cultural studies as 'banal' because it constantly describes the audience's reading as liberating and empowering (Morris, 1988). American cultural studies, here especially identified with the work of John Fiske, is attacked because it does not account for the ways in which the range of texts is limited. This attack presumes that a fuller range of texts would offer the audience a fuller range of meanings, including access to that which has been occluded or repressed by the dominant order. By this logic, dominant or mainstream texts are 'bad' because they oppress readers, while alternative or marginalized texts are 'good' because they liberate readers.

This critique of American cultural studies further argues that texts might not be read by the average reader in the same way that the critic reads them; what John Fiske sees as empowering in a Madonna video might not be what the average adolescent girl takes from it. This reasonable criticism could justify a turn to more concrete, ethnographic approaches to readership, but until recently it has not. Instead, the researcher imagines readers in an already theorized social order of race, class, and gender, marked by an already understood process of struggle. Fiske is faulted for his individualism, for disembedding readers from the social formation that the critic already knows and understands, rather than for making interpretive claims without empirical evidence. Fiske, and by extension American cultural studies, is attacked (and ultimately dismissed) for refusing to incorporate into the analysis claims about the oppressive social order. That social order is presumed to work, through texts, to subjugate readers.

Theoretical expertise

In the textualized versions of cultural studies, theorists stand in place of evidence. Since Marx, or Freud, or Althusser, or Gramsci, or Foucault, or Derrida have offered us convincing accounts of a social order that the critic already knows to be true, merely quoting theorists can constitute proof of the validity of an interpretation. By this invocation of names, critics deliver a one-two punch, voicing an arrogant, unquestioned faith in their theories, and an unrelenting disrespect for people's understandings of their own experience. The disrespect lies in the presumption that people's understandings are not trustworthy, interesting, or illuminating. The arrogance lies in the belief that, unlike other people, certain theorists have located and articulated what is real and what matters, not just about their own lives, but about everyone else's.

This disdain for vernacular understanding can be found, interestingly enough, among theorists of various stripes – in literary critics' knowing dismissal of readers who naively understand texts as transparent, in critical cultural studies' affirmation of the ultimate power of encoding over decoding, in political economy's complaints about the triviality of cultural as opposed to material forces, in psychoanalytic film theory's obsession with the unconscious. In each case the critic believes that there is something real behind and underneath what people know, something to which the scholar, intellectual, or critic has exclusive access. Thus what audience members have to say about what they understand, dislike, believe, or enjoy about a media text can be (and is) summarily dismissed – people who are not theoretically informed do not have anything interesting to say.

Such a dismissal of non-expert understandings re-enacts the positivist assumption that the world contains immutable truths that can be discovered only through specially trained inquiry. Logical positivism is, of course, considered the antithesis of current critical theory, but it is not. Both positivist and critical perspectives share a belief in the really real, which is hidden from everyday people, but discernible, through special training, by the expert. We are not suggesting that scholars abandon their search for a more systematic knowledge of humans' cultural practices. Rather, we are claiming that all humans theorize their experience at some level, that social theory ought to understand itself as a different rather than a higher form of knowledge, and that in a democratic society the value of any theory, vernacular or academic, must be sustained in public discourse with others who, when it comes to social matters, may not take for granted the superiority of academic modes of analysis.

The literary critical perspective, so enthusiastically adopted in media studies during the 1980s, shares with logical positivism and political economy a certainty about discoverable, underlying systems and processes. Unfortunately, it lacks the humility built into the practice, if not the theory, of positivist inquiry – the humility required by adherence to processes of proof using evidence beyond the theories themselves. Textual approaches claim to be empirical merely through their use of concrete examples from actual texts. Even though all critical readings presume that the texts examined possess social consequence, those presumptions are never empirically examined against anyone's actual experiences.

What the literary critical approach to media leaves us with is a set of professionally useful textual analytic techniques that critics justify as socially and politically powerful interventions by a logic that invokes theorists as if they were evidence. Once inside this approach, a student can spend a career debating interpretations, developing more nuanced and provocative readings, discovering new marginalized texts and previously unnoticed meanings, never meeting, along the way, a colleague or audience member who asks whether any of this matters in anyone's life.

Early hopes of American cultural studies

In short, the literary approach to cultural studies, promoted by researchers who feel most at home in the company of texts, transforms the media audience into yet another text over which researchers can exert their interpretive expertise. In modern societies, which aggressively capitalize cultural production and build their caste systems around the control of knowledge, such battles over interpretive power are inevitable. But cultural studies once hoped for something more. It aimed to combat just such monopolies of knowledge and interpretation. Today the tortuous prose style of literary analysis too often excludes the unanointed. Cultural studies, on the other hand, used to argue for modesty in its claims, and for a spirit of inclusiveness in its conversation. Now the public finds itself excluded from discussions of the very popular cultural worlds that it presumably knows most intimately.

The privileging of the text may be the price media studies pays each time it grows too enamored of literary criticism. Earlier encounters between mass communication research and literary studies produced a similarly ambiguous result. In their own time, the Frankfurt School critique of mass culture and the New Critical analyses of the Leavises both opened and foreclosed discussions of mass communication as a cultural form. Researchers turned to literary criticism for a description of media products and practices as cultural forms. Then, as now, however, literary criticism ultimately derided popular understandings and tastes, condemning them as aesthetically inferior, politically retrograde, or naive. The recent infatuation with European cultural theory rehearses again intellectuals' contempt for the popular and – implicitly – for American life.

Not every intellectual path of the 1960s and 1970s led to a Paris café, however. At that moment, as French intellectuals were transforming their disenchantment with the failed revolution of 1968 into cultural theory, James Carey and his students at the University of Illinois (and, for a time, the University of Iowa) were fashioning an American version of cultural studies. That Illinois style of cultural studies borrowed liberally from American and European traditions. It took its sense of purpose and its arguments on behalf of popular culture from early British cultural studies' scholars such as Raymond Williams, Richard Hoggart, Stuart Hall, and Paddy Whannel. It learned its opposition to structural-functionalism from social scientists like Clifford Geertz, David Reisman, Hugh Dalziel Duncan, C. Wright Mills, Joseph Gusfield, and Murray Edelman. It looked to American studies scholars like R.W.B. Lewis, Henry Nash Smith, Leo Marx, John Cawelti, and Alan Trachtenberg for some of its themes. And it found its tale of origins in the work of a strange collection of visionaries and outcasts loosely connected with the Chicago School of Sociology – John Dewey, Thorstein Veblen, Jane Addams, Robert Park, Lewis Mumford, and Harold Adams Innis.

From the start, Illinois cultural studies imagined itself as a counterweight to the dominant traditions of imperial social science. Carey (1989: 37–68), for example, argued that, in the fluid conditions of American life, social science rather than high culture had made itself the source of authority that governed American institutions. Thus the goal of cultural studies, imagined in this context, was to engage that dominant tradition of social science, rather than merely to displace an earlier version of literary theory. For Carey, as for Mumford, this was an explicitly political task, made more urgent by the fantasies of technological omnipotence being played out in Vietnam, and by communication research's complicity in psychological warfare campaigns following World War II.[2] Carey proposed democratic resistance on a number of fronts: the practice of oral culture as a defense against technophilia (Carey, 1990b), the recovery of journalism as a public art form rather than a profession (Carey, 1987), and the development of qualitative modes of social research as an alternative to reductionist accounts of experience (Carey, 1989). He imagined cultural studies as a democratic social practice rather than an exercise in high theory.[3]

Though often critical of capitalism, Illinois cultural studies did not borrow its central problematic from Marxism.[4] It focused rather on the problems of meaning, group identity, and social change that had so often vexed American thought. It studied the mass media as vehicles of imagination and experience, the reorganization of cultural authority and economic and political power by new communication technologies, the place of journalism in a democratic society, and the significance of symbolic conflicts over cultural style.[5] The teaching of Albert Kreiling particularly influenced Illinois cultural studies in the 1970s. Kreiling argued that expressive style (not content) offers individuals their most powerful and distinctive experience of group identity. He argued that dominant sociology erred by trying to explain away culture by reference to nonsymbolic social forces. His own research focused on the symbolic rituals by which segments of the American middle class endlessly seek to distinguish themselves from one another (Kreiling, 1978). He demonstrated, in his sophisticated but underappreciated work on the African-American press (Kreiling, 1973, 1993) that these dramas of American identity have reproduced themselves in the middle-class segments of marginalized groups as well. Finally, and most provocatively, Kreiling (with Sims, 1981) turned his analysis on the intellectuals from whom he learned the most, showing how the Progressive reformers and intellectuals of Chicago were rehearsing, in their writing and social work, their own dreams of identity.

Audience researchers have never paid much attention to this tradition, for various reasons. Illinois cultural studies imagined itself in opposition to dominant traditions in marketing research, and thus never drew as much on mainstream traditions of sociological fieldwork as British cultural studies did.[6] British audience researchers, generally interested in issues of ideology, power, and reproduction, have preferred structuralist to culturalist theories, and distrusted American traditions such as symbolic interactionism (Moores, 1994: 139). Nevertheless, we think Illinois cultural studies offers a useful way to imagine the meaning and purpose of audience research. Studies such as Kreiling's have often examined middle-class life on its own terrain without snide or supercilious references to 'the bourgeoisie'. Carey and Kreiling have insisted that researchers take seriously the expressive worlds in which individuals participate, even when critics might consider those worlds politically retrograde or commercially corrupted. The goal of cultural studies, imagined in this context, is to open a dialogue about how we, as audiences, use the mass media to structure and articulate our relations with one another and to make the world intellectually meaningful, aesthetically pleasing, and emotionally compelling.

Ethnographic impulses

Recognizing the shortcomings of narrowly textual analysis, in the 1980s a number of researchers turned to fieldwork as a method for studying audience behavior. Within American media studies such methods had often been identified with marketing and behavioral research. In both anthropology and sociology, however, fieldwork had long proven its theoretical value.

Ethnography records an actual social encounter between researcher and sub-ject, in however flawed a way, and that encounter promised to deepen researchers' understanding of the audience. In the USA, a series of studies of news and entertainment production (for example, Tuchman, 1978; Gans, 1979; Gitlin, 1983) encouraged researchers to imagine similar studies of con-sumption. In Britain, interest in the ideological power of the media encouraged researchers to investigate the politics of decoding and subcul-tures' resistance to the dominant order. In both countries, the turn to ethnography promised to restore the balance between literary studies and social theory that had characterized the early years of cultural studies.

Two typical approaches emerged in that period. The first, most promi-nently identified with James Lull (1980, 1988, 1990), has applied traditional sociological methods to study audiences in the field, and even across cul-tures. The second, most prominently identified with David Morley (1980, 1986, 1992; Brunsdon and Morley, 1978), used interviews to elicit the audi-ence's understandings of its own experience, and to situate those understandings in the larger social discourse about gender, nation, and class. We applaud the impulse behind both these traditions, and find these analyses superior to those of narrowly textual approaches. Yet we need to consider some of the limits of this work, as it has been performed so far.

The advantage of fieldwork such as Lull's is that it forces the researcher to engage subjects directly, and to consider a wide range of behavioral evidence. By these methods researchers simply learn more about which people use which media, in what combinations, on what occasions, for how long, with which friends, family members, or strangers. This work demonstrates that the social worlds of the audience encompass far more than their continuing efforts, as a dominated class or situated subjects, to decode the messages sent them by the mass media.

Yet work in this vein reminds us of some of the familiar limits of fieldwork. For one thing such research does not necessarily yield a *cultural* description of the audience's behavior. As in much traditional sociology and anthropol-ogy, researchers often explain symbolic forms by reducing them to nonsymbolic factors such as time budgets, kinship, and technology. Carey and Kreiling (1974) have noted that, at first glance, such functionalist sociol-ogy seems to resemble cultural studies. Both approaches, after all, emphasize the audience as active rather than passive and note the range of people's uses of the media. But important differences remain. In cultural studies, meticu-lous attention to details of social structure is necessary but not sufficient; such details do not fully constitute the object of study. The cultural studies researcher still needs to interpret the audience's lived experience as symbolic practice.

The Morley approach uses familiar social science tools to great advan-tage. Usually, in this model, the researcher conducts in-depth interviews with individual audience members or convenes focus groups to discuss viewing habits or a particular media artifact. Letters published by media organiza-tions or solicited by the researcher, sometimes in conjunction with follow-up interviews, have also provided evidence of the audience's native understandings. By such methods, researchers incorporate the subjects' own voices into the research account, and avoid some of the problems of an omniscient authorial presence. Some of the work that uses these methods, such as Elizabeth Bird's (1992a) study of tabloid newspapers, has been strikingly good.

Not surprisingly, however, the limits of interviewing and small-group research, long familiar to sociologists and psychologists, show up in audience studies, too. Researchers who choose individual interviews risk portraying subjects' interpretations as private and internal, and may not learn enough about the social relations that connect individual subjects, or the social occasions on which individuals express and defend their interpretations to others. Focus groups may better represent interpretation as a social process, but vocal members can easily dominate group discussions and discourage individuals from being forthright about their more idiosyncratic or controversial responses.

Audience researchers may not always take the demands of ethnography seriously enough (Bird, 1992b). Most audience researchers spend little if any time observing subjects' media use or everyday lives, or gathering supplementary materials such as life histories, personal descriptions, or discussions of family problems (as did Bird, 1992a). Within the traditions of sociology and anthropology, by comparison, ethnography has signified just this sort of deep, ambitious commitment to long and labor-intensive work in the field. Researchers' reluctance to spend time in the field means that they will not be present when audiences collaboratively interpret media texts – in the living room, as Morley has documented, but also at the beauty shop, garage, and playground. In this sense, the literature on audiences pales when compared to the best ethnographic work in sociology and anthropology. Our subject pools are small, our time in the field too brief, our descriptions of the audience's lives too scant.

From our perspective, ethnographic research occasionally suffers from the very ideological commitments that make it so attractive to its followers. The temptation to discover domination wherever one looks is great; indeed, as is the temptation to treat subjects as politically or theoretically deficient in their responses. Consider, for instance, the problems of specifying the class character of subjects' responses. In British cultural studies, this problem can be handled more straightforwardly. The history of industrial warfare and aristocracy has deeply scarred British sensibilities and social relations, so that audience members readily imagine their responses to media in terms of social class. In the USA, by contrast, class identity counts for much less in people's self-descriptions. Despite a history of violent labor relations, stunning levels of inequality, and an increasingly class-structured educational system, many (if not most) Americans continue to consider themselves middle-class. A researcher in this situation cannot assume that subjects think about social class in the same way that the researcher does, or that their responses can be easily read as evidence of how the media articulate class distinctions.

The interpretation of ethnographic evidence, like its gathering, can create special dilemmas for the audience researcher. Contemporary theory sanctions the critic's reappropriation of a literary text. But ethnographers today feel more obliged to answer to audiences for their interpretations – one of the features we most admire about this style of research. Subjects' constant exposure not just to a wide range of media but to a popular discourse about 'the media' can easily color their responses. The researcher's questions may invite the audience to reproduce 'what everybody knows' about media effects, meanings, and use. Subjects' responses, taken alone, may tell us little about how they imagine their own experience, and a great deal about their command of the rhetorical strategies by which Americans habitually explain, justify, or condemn their relationship to 'the media'.

Ethnographies of the audience have been surprisingly selective in their choice of informants and topics. For all our theories of race, gender, and class in cultural theory, in practice race remains the least examined of these three forms of audience identity – perhaps because researchers face particular problems getting access to minority audiences or convincing them to participate. Here as elsewhere, forms of cultural identity that are uncomfortable to the Left receive short shrift. As Cornel West (1992) has noted, religion greatly influences the social formation of many African-Americans, but is generally overlooked in postmodern theories of race. Ethnic identity, so important in politics around the world today, receives little attention.

Similarly, ethnographic research by sociologists on television and film has not taken advantage of research on reading. Historians and anthropologists have developed a rich, historically detailed, and carefully argued literature on print and literacy.[7] For instance, anthropologists studying the ethnography of reading have now begun to explore the relationship of orality to reading, the ways in which the practices of everyday speech come into play when readers interpret written texts. Work on television and film, as far as we can see, has not yet made much use of such research.

Conclusion: us and them

For all the research of the last 15 years, audience studies still struggle to convey what Robert Park (1934) used to call a group's 'zest for life' – a feel for the cultural practices that make group life distinctive, meaningful, and worthwhile. In the positivist tradition of ethnography, the danger was always that researchers would lose their objectivity and go native. In both the textual and ethnographic versions of cultural studies, researchers rarely seem tempted to join the other side. After all, if subjects are imagined as deficient in their articulation of their own experience, then there is not much chance that the researcher will personally learn anything from those subjects.

The generally Leftist political commitments of cultural studies' researchers can also get in the way – not so much by coloring the evidence as by deeming some groups too conservative to be worth studying. For instance, much of the world has experienced a religious revival for the last three decades, and American Christians have constructed a system of Christian publications, bookstores, recording companies, radio and television stations, direct mail, and cultural paraphernalia.[8] Yet this world has thus far largely been ignored by cultural studies' researchers. So, too, with consumer worlds that may seem trivial to outsiders but are deeply valued by participants. The subculture of animal fanciers, who number in the tens of millions in the USA, has attracted much less research than a single program like *Star Trek*. Thousands of special-interest magazines, clubs, supply stores, videos, newsletters, and conventions help Americans sustain a world of parasocial relations with their pets. Groups that think of themselves as rooted rather than avant-garde – the elderly, farmers, naturalists, suburbanites – find little voice in audience studies. The postmodern sensibility encourages researchers to focus on the ironic, hip, urban, mobile, and young.

For all its theorizing about pleasure, how rarely does cultural studies speak in a personal, playful tone of voice, the sort of tone found in Susan Douglas's lively autobiographical account of her own media use, *Where the Girls Are* (1994).[9] Most audience researchers conceal their personal tastes, sensibilities, and responses, often revealing no more than a run-of-the-mill positivist would have. The persistent sense is that the audience is them, not us.

The charm of much early work in cultural studies was in how it rejected the artifice of disinterested objectivity. All of Richard Hoggart's work and much of the early work of Raymond Williams has spoken unabashedly of deeply personal experiences like adult education. Robert Park, mentor to an earlier generation of American ethnographers, encouraged his students to re-enter as researchers the social worlds that they had known as participants.[10] Some of the most compelling work on the symbolic worlds inhabited by audiences may be found in contemporary literary journalism. Few academic cultural studies can match the texture and nuance of Jane Kramer's studies (1977, 1994) of Henry Blanton's fondness for cowboy movies or Bronx residents' responses to public art, or of Bill Buford's account (1992) of his morbid curiosity about English soccer clubs, or of Frederick Exley's story (1988) of his own fandom.

Audience research, taken seriously as a democratic task, might make cultural studies' researchers more modest about their theories and more respectful of vernacular accounts of experience. The style of cultural studies we advocate does not presume that there is something distinct from social relations that we can and should locate and describe. Inquiry does not require us to find something lurking behind what we are already up to, in social experience. As scholars and critics, we are not obliged to adopt the hushed and certain tones of those who have penetrated mysteries that inflame and baffle others. Having given up the epistemological conceit of an underlying, explanatory really real, we can also resist the temptation to treat theory as an (ostensibly) neutral language.

In *The Long Revolution* (1961), one of the founding texts of cultural studies, Raymond Williams affirmed the innate creativity of all humans, not just of the specialized class of artists privileged by traditional cultural theory. In a similar way, we might use audience research to close the distance between the habits of intellectuals, scholars, scientists, and critics, and the habits of the rest of us. We all create and sustain explanations and assumptions in order to construct identities, form alliances, make sense of things, and impose meaning and order on to the flux of experience. How we go about doing this, with what consequences, under various conditions – these things matter because different modes of casting up the world have different consequences (Jensen, 1994b). The form of cultural studies we imagine will always focus on the nature and consequences of our interpretations of social worlds.[11]

Doing cultural studies requires the work of heart and hands as well as head. The recent literature on cultural studies makes much of theoretical differences, in part because theoretical complexity marks one's status in the academy. Yet we could choose to signify the meaning of our work in other ways, for other kinds of audiences. Fluency, elegance, passion, candor, delight, and savvy still matter to many readers, and such readers should matter to us. Textual analysis too often remains indifferent to the actual people with whom, in a democratic society, we hope to make common cause. Ethnography, though it contains its own illusions and limitations, at least reminds us of the problems of connecting with the people about whom we write. In cultural studies, the audience should be something more than the stone we use to sharpen our ideological and theoretical prejudices. Audience research ought to bear witness to other people's understandings, struggles, and purposes, and to our own desire to do justice to their stories.[12]

Notes

1 See Jensen (1994b) and Carey (1990a) for a discussion of the consequences of different metaphors of communication.

2 For an account of the politics of mass communication research that Carey would have encountered as a graduate student and young professor in the 1950s and 1960s, see Simpson (1994).

3 In Carey's essays, the intellectual is no friend of democracy. The social scientists who abstract the experiences of the working class, the futurists who hope to use high technology to remake everyday life (Carey, 1989: 173–200), the journalists who identify more with their national professional organizations than with the local communities they cover (Carey, 1969, 1986, 1987), the professors who displace public conversation with their private idioms – all are monopolists of knowledge, all help undermine the possibilities of democratic discourse.

4 This history of resistance to imperial social science should be enough to dispel the frequently heard canard that Carey and other thinkers in the Illinois tradition are indifferent to matters of power. In fact, what Carey has always been indifferent to are the social rituals by which intellectuals code one another as radical.

5 Among the Illinois and Iowa students of that era whose work is likely to be most familiar to readers are Carolyn Marvin, Linda Steiner, Joli Jensen, Norman Sims, Quentin Schultze, John Pauly, Richard Lentz and Douglas Birkhead. Lawrence Grossberg, the best-known Illinois student of that era, has always stood somewhat apart from these influences because of his earlier studies in Britain.

6 Moores (1994) offers an excellent overview of British approaches to cultural studies.

7 For a sampling of this literature, see Kaestle et al. (1991), Boyarin (1993), and Nord (1995).

8 For a brief glimpse at one such Christian media empire – that of James Dobson's Focus on the Family – see Cooper (1995).

9 As editor of *Critical Studies in Mass Communication* from 1987 to 1989, David Eason occasionally used his editor's notes to write brief sketches about his personal experiences of country music and popular culture.

10 See Persons (1987) for a discussion of the strengths and weaknesses of Chicago School ethnic studies.

11 By the term *consequences* here, we simply mean the social and political relations that follow from different modes of addressing one another: what do we become when we think and talk in a particular way?

12 We thank Rob Anderson of Saint Louis University for his thoughtful and generous critique of this chapter.

11

The Es and the Anti-Es: New Questions for Feminism and Cultural Studies

Angela McRobbie

The spectre of humanism

I want to address two questions in this chapter. First, what consequences does recent poststructuralist and postcolonialist writing (notably that of Butler (1990, 1993) and Spivak (1987, 1993)) have for what I might loosely call feminist cultural studies? And secondly, is it possible to use this work to inject some renewed intellectual energy into those areas which cultural studies has, over the last few years, neglected? The most noticeable gaps and omissions in feminist cultural studies have been in the field of 'lived experience'. By this I understand a form of investigation where the impact and significance of empirical changes in culture and in society on living human subjects can be observed and analysed and where these same human subjects are invited to reflect on how they live through and make sense of such changes. I have argued elsewhere that a return to more sociological questions, particularly where these have a relevance for policy, should not be shunned by cultural studies' scholars for whom the politics of meaning have recently taken precedence over the need to intervene in political debates armed with data, facts and figures and 'empirical results' (McRobbie, 1996). Of course there is an important place for the deconstruction of the meaning and significance of what is taken to constitute 'hard facts' and the role these play as a pre-requisite for engagement in certain kinds of political discussion. However, precious little attempt has been made so far to explore how poststructuralism can be made use of more productively in the context of these fields of intervention.

The second question this chapter asks looks, then, not only towards the emergence of a more applied feminist cultural studies, and to a reconciliation of sorts between the poststructuralists and those who consider themselves on the side of studying concrete material reality. It also envisages a return to the 'three Es'; the empirical, the ethnographic, the experiential, not so much *against* as *with* the insight of the 'anti-Es', that is anti-essentialism, poststructuralism, psychoanalysis. While there has been an enormous output of feminist poststructuralist writing of late, there has been some resistance to looking outside 'theory' and asking some practical questions about the world we live in. At every point the spectre of 'humanism' haunts the practice of

those who align themselves with the 'anti-Es'. Ethnography? That truth-seeking activity reliant on the (often literary) narratives of exoticism and
difference? Can't do it, except as a deconstructive exercise. Empiricism? The
'representation' of results, the narrative of numbers? Can't do it either, except
as part of a critical genealogy of sociology and its role in the project of
modernity and science. Experience? That cornerstone of human authenticity,
that essential core of individuality, the spoken voice as evidence of being and
of the coincidence of consciousness with identity? Can't do it, other than as
a psychoanalytic venture.

This leaves us feminists who are concerned with the politics of culture high
and dry when it comes to contributing to political debates outside the academy. It also allows the more practically oriented, down-to-earth feminist
essentialists (Dworkin, 1981; MacKinnon, 1979; Itzin, 1992 and others) to
dominate the terms and the means by which academic feminism filters into
the broader political arena, particularly the media. These new questions that
I put here to feminist cultural studies also have relevance therefore, for how
we conceive ourselves as intellectuals. Feminist cultural studies is not, of
course, a unitary discipline. It intersects with film and media studies and it
also connects with sociology, literature, history and with debates in Marxist,
feminist and postmodern theory. Its interests frequently overlap with those
found in women's studies and there are also shared areas of interest with
feminist psychology and feminist anthropology. The boundaries and limits
drawn in this chapter are admittedly my own. They represent the shaping and
development of my own intellectual formation. This means omitting important but, to me, less familiar work. Within this limited orbit (which I have
chosen to call feminist cultural studies but which could be as easily labelled
feminist media studies or feminist cultural sociology) there has been a substantial difference between those who are concerned with textual meaning,
and whose interest is therefore on issues of representation, and those who are
indeed more focused towards cultural and media policy and whose emphasis
is therefore on more materialist matters.

Feminist materialism, back in the late 1970s, meant drawing on the vocabulary of neo-Marxism to explore how class relations and class struggle
co-existed with patriarchal relations without dissolving the latter into the
former. The second feature of this materialism involved a more specific turn
to class and culture. By looking at the history and culture of working-class
women and girls at home, in the community, in school, in leisure and at work,
a series of ethnographic studies and accounts of lived experience gave testimony to the resilience and to the historical continuity of oppositional class
relations created in this context by women. This work fell under the culturalist framework outlined by Stuart Hall in his seminal 'Cultural Studies – Two
Paradigms' (Hall, 1980a). Within this perspective women and girls were
understood as active class and gendered subjects, doubly subordinated by
class and sex but able to tackle the forces of domination through supportive
networks and through the creation of distinctive but informal cultural forms
and networks which were manifest in the institutions of school, workplace

and community. Ethnographic studies demonstrated both the economic underpinning of these forms and what they achieved in terms of winning space or autonomy for the girls or women involved.

However, it is now so long since this kind of work has had any significant place in feminist cultural studies that its existence has almost been forgotten. This is because work of this type was shown to operate along highly voluntarist lines, as though the girls and women constructed these oppositional cultures unconstrained by other social forces. Little attention was paid to the already existing 'scripts of resistance' which, structuralists argued, were then simply activated by the women in particular pre-defined ways. The transparency of language, as reflective of both consciousness and identity, was most problematic for those who aligned themselves with poststructuralism and psychoanalysis. The spoken testimony of girls and women was here taken as expressive of a full human being, rather than understood as partial, fragmented, articulations of available language codes. Finally, the very category of women or girl used in this kind of work remained unacceptably problematic for most anti-essentialists. It was assumed that there was a direct and unmediated relation between their voices, their identities and their existence as women or girls. Poststructuralists turned this upside down and argued that these were in fact Marxist–feminist representations of the category of working-class woman or girls. Feminist research in these contexts actively produced such subjects. 'She' might have no other recognizable identity outside this particular academic context. Likewise, 'consciousness' could be seen as a particular type of extrapolation, a means by which a specific and partial set of verbal themes are brought together and understood as representing a whole social being, as in 'the consciousness' of working-class women. In fact this was, in itself, a highly edited representation of a certain set of themes from which other discordant themes (such as racism) were carefully removed or ignored.

For all the above reasons the term 'representation' then came to occupy a much more significant place in feminist writing. It was understood mostly in the context of Althusser's usage of the term representation in his theory of ideology (Althusser, 1971a). Drawing both on Freud and Lacan, Althusser argued that representations were not expressive of some prior reality, but were instead actively constitutive of reality. Feminists used this work from the late 1970s onwards to move away from early critiques of the mass media which were concerned with either negative or positive images of women. The question was no longer that images of women were unreal, untruthful or distorted, and that what was required instead were better or more positive images of women which would somehow fit with feminist requirements. The emphasis now shifted to sexual representations as concrete and material accounts of what it was to be a woman. Femininity was nothing more than a set of highly orchestrated representational practices which together produced this coherence of female gender as easy and naturalized. By showing how these signs were grouped together and endlessly repeated across a whole range of female genres (women's magazines, popular romances, melodrama, etc.), feminist media and cultural studies found a stronger theoretical direction for itself. This entailed use being made of Barthesian semiology, Lacanian psychoanalysis, and Foucault's concept of discourse. Representation as a term provides a key link through this work. It informs Laura Mulvey's seminal analysis of women as object of the gaze in classic Hollywood cinema (Mulvey, 1975 reprinted 1989), as it does Judith Williamson's *Decoding Advertisements* (Williamson, 1978), as well as informing Rosalind Coward's contributions to early issues of the feminist journal *m/f* (Coward, 1978). It is thus through the currency of textuality and representation that the field of feminist media, literary and cultural studies acquires for itself a more international dimension. This is partly because of the dominance of the Anglo–American media industries, but it was also because structuralist and poststructuralist methods of analysis could easily be applied to texts independent of context. What was important after all was the genre. So even if American and British magazines, soap operas or popular fictions did not have global distribution, they had frequently spawned local equivalents, allowing feminist media scholars across the world to participate in these discussions. Structuralism and poststructuralism travelled further and faster than their culturalist counterparts.

The effect this theoretical concentration has in feminist media and cultural studies is to push more materialist or indeed culturalist concerns back towards sociology. Socialist–feminist work increasingly accommodates empirical and institutional studies, policy oriented work, studies of employment, discrimination and so on, while poststructuralist feminism concerns itself with subjectivity, difference and meaning. By the mid-1980s, however, this dividing line also begins to crumble as feminists increasingly look to the work of Foucault. Here the emphasis is on how discourses comprising words and statements and other representational forms brought together into a field of coherent textual regularity actively produce social realities as we know them. Thus, institutions are considered not from a viewpoint which asserts their existence as external things, but rather as they are envisaged in discourse – how they are talked about. The emphasis is also on how institutions instigate regularities of conduct and experience, and constitute their subjects accordingly. Even staunchly materialist concerns like rape in fact comprise various competing accounts as to how the scenario and the victim of rape are 'envisaged'. As we know in this respect, some 'bodies' count more than others, and for this reason a good deal is at stake in how the body of the victim is represented in court.

From this point on, a different dividing line comes into being in this now very broad field of feminist scholarship. There are those for whom the category of 'women' represents an unproblematic and fixed set of meanings which are understood as shared by all who count themselves as female (the essentialists), while there are those others who see the category of 'women' as continually contested. Under the influence of Foucault and the poststructuralist critique of humanism, and thus of the coincidence of consciousness with identity, feminists begin to dispute the existence of 'women' *per se*.

Denise Riley and others argue that woman is not an unchanging uniqueness, but instead she is herself the product of particular historical and discursive practices which name and classify her and which give her meaning as a coherent entity which otherwise she would lack (Riley, 1988). Gender discourses rush to fill over all the cracks of fragile unstable sexual identities. They pronounce coherence, as Butler puts it, through 'announcing'; 'It's a girl!' (Butler, 1990). The woman is a subject rather than an agent, and human action is no more than the human enactment of pre-existing scripts and scenarios.

Across the arts, humanities and social sciences, this new vocabulary occupies a more significant place. As Michèle Barrett puts it, there is a shift from 'things to words' (Barrett, 1992). The material existence of women is borne through different, often competing, discursive strategies which in naming, classifying or speaking the truth of 'woman' also bring her into being. Barrett describes the shift of emphasis in feminist scholarship away from 'things' like 'low pay, rape, or female foeticide' to a concern with words, texts and representations. This has come about through the influence of Foucault who 'challenged the familiar hierarchy of value of the materialist perspective, counterposing the "dumb existence of a reality" with the ability of groups of signs (discourses) to act as "practices that systematically form the objects of which they speak"' (Barrett, quoting Foucault, 1992: 203).

I want to conclude this section by suggesting that opposition to the increasing dominance of the 'anti-Es' in feminist scholarship takes a different political form in the USA from what it does in the UK (bearing in mind the limits of these as symbolic geo-political axes). In America the fiercest feminist opposition to the work of Butler, Spivak and others comes from those who assert, against the emphasis on difference, the essential sameness of women's experience. This arises, they argue from female 'bodily matters', from the essential experiences shared by and understood by women, that is childbirth, menstruation, menopause, and female illnesses. In addition, feminists like MacKinnon (1979) and Dworkin (1981) add to this the long catalogue of crimes and violations done to the female body by men, including rape, violence, pornography, sexual abuse and so on. It is around these issues that the modern women's movement comes into being. In America these women occupy a high profile in the media and in the academy, and in many ways have succeeded in defining the terrain of feminism in this context. Their opponents within feminism, including Butler, challenge their unwillingness to take on board differences of ethnicity, class and sexual identity. She and others have argued that difference can be understood in politically positive terms rather than signalling the end of feminism. The threat of fragmentation is too often used as a means of achieving an uneasy, unhappy unity, just for the sake of it. In addition, this writing locates women in a victim-like position from which there is very little opportunity to escape. There is a vicariousness, then, on the part of the successful well-qualified feminist representatives of the women's movement and their 'subjects', who appear to remain trapped in abusive and violent relationships and for whom feminism only seems to confirm the stark dualities of power between men and women without providing hope or opportunity for changing these relations.

This, then, is the materialist–feminist–essentialism against which writers like Butler position themselves. However, in the UK feminist intellectual work has grown out of a more socialist tradition. There has been much less concern to assert gender over and above class and race; instead the emphasis has been on thinking through these relations of difference. Historical materialism rather than bodily materialism has informed much of this work. The socialist feminist tradition has, from the start, recognized that economic inequalities, compounded through the double disadvantage of gender and class, offered a framework for more fully understanding how, in and across different historical moments women have found themselves dependent, powerless or simply subordinate. The socialist feminist refutation of poststructuralism is more muted and confined by and large to occasional interventions and attacks, such as that by Anna Pollert whose real animosity is towards the other 'posts', that is feminist postmodernism and debates around post-Fordism (Pollert, 1988). The 'anti-Es' group in the UK challenges the determining role allocated in Marxist feminist thought to the 'economic', and re-locates materialism to the realm of discourse. It also explores the political consequences of difference and antagonism between women in relation to class, sex and race; it refutes, as described above, the existence of women's consciousness as a thing that can be equated with identity; and it also fully engages with the challenge the unconscious brings to political analysis. So, in a sense, the work of Butler and Spivak perhaps finds more fertile ground in the field of feminist scholarship in the UK, where, in the light of the decline of Marxism, the 'anti-Es' in the arts, humanities and increasingly in the social sciences have almost assumed a position of theoretical dominance.

Feminism as anti-essentialism

Two of the most significant contributors to the debate on anti-essentialism are Judith Butler and Gayatri Chakravorty Spivak. Both these authors force feminism to confront its own, often invisible boundaries and limits as well as those strands in feminism which seek to attribute a 'fixed essence to women' (Grosz, 1995: 47). It will be my contention that the deconstructive exercises of both these writers can be usefully applied to feminist cultural studies. How can this be done? First, by considering their shared concern with feminism as a representational politics, and secondly, by extending Spivak's specific comments on pedagogy and Butler's work on 'gender trouble' to cultural studies, and thirdly, bearing in mind the comments made earlier about the need for applied and policy-focused work, by attempting to revise simultaneously feminist cultural studies to embrace again more fully the 'three Es'. Feminism, from the viewpoint of Butler and Spivak, is required to consider its foundations, its hidden representational remit and its category of woman. Poststructuralist thinking suggests that a range of meanings are invoked around the notion of 'women', while feminism in the past has assumed a simple and single transparency of meaning. Only now is this historical assumption being interrogated. For example, Brunsdon, writing recently on film and TV scholarship, argues that in the 1970s there was a binary divide between feminism and femininity, and that this fuelled feminist analysis (Brunsdon, 1991). The political aim was to pull women away from cultures of femininity (the nail polish) towards feminism. The intellectual aim was to win a legitimate place for gender studies in the academy. The feminist scholar of film and TV studies was inevitably counterposed to the ordinary woman, the housewife watching the soaps.

When feminists talk about women, this too is a representation. It does not automatically and unproblematically refer to and reflect a pre-existing material reality. Instead, it constructs and gives an identity to a social group who might previously have been known as ladies, girls, housewives, or mothers. Feminism creates a category of women which does not reflect a pre-existing reality so much as constitute a new reality. This category now competes with the older categories through which 'women' are known, and in some cases supplants these old titles with this new, political term of representation. Anti-essentialism in feminism recognizes the fluidity of feminism's own categories. As Riley points out, feminism's women also change quite dramatically over time (Riley, 1987). 'The modern "women" is arguably the result of long processes of closure which are hammered out by infinite numbers of mutual references from all sides of these studies and classifications – which are then both underwritten and cross-examined by nineteenth- and early twentieth-century feminisms which adopt, respecify, or dismiss these "women"' (Riley, 1987: 41).

The focus of Riley, Butler and Spivak's work is to dislodge, or at least destabilize, the certainties expressed in a good deal of radical feminism about those qualities which define women. They recognize this as a perhaps necessary political fiction (Spivak talks of the 'strategic use of essentialism') which grants feminism the authority to speak on behalf of a 'global sisterhood', but they also reject it (Spivak with qualifications as we shall see later). No sooner, then, is this essentialism expressed, than it is challenged most specifically by 'other women' who see themselves being spoken of by European white representatives who are not necessarily of their own choosing. They then argue vociferously that this global category of 'women' is one which is based on a Eurocentric confidence which claims to know what all women need to achieve equality, while in fact the charter of universalist feminist aims which has emerged from this movement is informed much more by the specific demands of Western European women. Black feminists have argued that this essentialism has made it all the more difficult for them to engage productively with difference within the category of 'black women'. They, too, have been expected to display characteristics which mark them out through homogenized categories of race and gender.

Poststructuralism posits women as a non-self-evident category. It suggests that feminist essentialism is a strategy of power, an attempt to enclose and foreclose the field of feminism. This can also backfire in policy debates, in that, as Nash points out, to attribute to women a set of essential characteristics or experiences (caring and compassionate, maternal, etc.) can have the effect of reproducing existing inequalities. Feminists therefore can unwittingly 'contribute to the regulation and reification of gender identities, and along pretty traditional lines at that, a regulation and reification that it is surely one of the aims of feminism to disrupt' (Nash, 1994: 69). But if, instead, the category of women is fluid, if it is a 'political signifier', then, argues Butler, the point is to resist the kinds of stabilization which seek to pin women down to something incontrovertible, and instead to 'expand the possibilities of what it means to be a woman' (Butler, 1995: 50). This includes the possibility of re-drafting or of re-designating the self, not in an unproblematically voluntarist capacity, but rather as a process which recognizes gender as more unstable and *potential* than is currently acknowledged in culture. If gender, as Butler argues, is a staging of the body, a performance enacted on a daily basis, if woman is therefore put on, or applied, then there can be no natural female body. Instead the body is only female and feminine to the extent that it is given these meanings right from the start. These acts of gender can, she argues, be re-articulated to broaden out the stagy narrowness of 'men' and 'women'. When poststructuralism uncouples the binary partners of male and female, a range of less rigid sexual possibilities becomes available. Change or agency is here conceived of as taking place within the politics of meaning, that is within the realm of signification. Butler exploits the poststructuralist claim that meaning is never as secure and as tightly tied to its reference point as it seems. Other meanings haunt those which appear to naturally attach themselves to language. The politics of meaning come into play exactly where other more disruptive meanings which haunt, linger or simply hang around the edges of words get sharply eliminated, by the repetitive emphasis: 'Of course this is what a woman is!' The fixing of men and women in this way is a means of guaranteeing the 'heterosexual matrix' in culture. But its own uncertainty can be exploited and gender can be re-scripted.

However, even feminism has opposed this practice of re-signification. It has had to know that its women are really women. Butler explores the theoretical underpinning of this requirement by undertaking a lengthy (and convincing) critique of Lacan, Lacanian feminism, and what has also been called 'New French feminism', that is the work of Cixous, Wittig and Irigaray. Whether they are with or against Lacan, there is a tendency in this work to see women as relegated to some marginal or external zone, to some outside place which is also the only place in which they can speak as women outside the terms laid down by patriarchy (for example, through Kristeva's notion of semiotic or poetic language). Butler disputes this relegation to, and then reluctant occupation of, the outside, particularly since it is also a place to which, in Lacan's writing, the lesbian is expelled. This is a kind of hell, a space of abjection or psychosis, and Butler will have nothing of it.

The force of her argument in *Bodies that Matter* (1993) is that men and women exist as such to guard the sanctity of reproductive heterosexuality. They need not be like this. Gender is a coercion, and it continues to harm and cause immense pain to those who find themselves excluded. There is, overall, a quadruple movement in Butler's writing. She initiates a challenge to normative understandings of sexual difference from an unstable (rather than absolutist and therefore separatist) lesbian position. She confronts the conservatism of Lacan and Lacanian feminism, she positively invokes the 'politics of the signifier' whereby things can be made to mean differently, thus also disputing the deep pessimism of psychoanalytic feminism which almost allows it to turn away from politics. She also then rebukes the more activist forms of feminism for their earlier fantasies of freedom, unity and universal sisterhood. This was a 'phantasmatic signifier', a utopian projection destined to disappoint. But disenchantment with these fantasies of emancipation need not lead to hopelessness or despair. Feminism can instead work through its many differences. It can make coalitions and alliances and, no longer moving resolutely towards some agreed goal, it can also eliminate the older hierarchies which requested that some demands or some issues took precedence over others. Altogether this seems to me the most useful and hopeful critique and analysis to emerge through the dense difficulty of post-structuralist writing.

Back to reality?

Spivak has recently argued for the importance of empirical research informed by the critique of essentialism:

> One has to learn to honour empirical work. Bardhan talks about how stratified the idea of women is in a place like India. In Bardhan's work [she's a development economist] you begin to see how impossible it is to focus, even within endogamous or exogamous marriage lines, on something called a woman. She even diversifies the radicals who can join in the struggle. She diversifies the people who study them. (Spivak, 1993: 17)

Spivak also points to where theory finds itself grounded. She asks that theory recognizes its own place in the classroom. The 'lived experience' of theory is that it is taught to human subjects. Here she does a triple move. She connects theory with the politics of its pedagogic practice, she argues in this context for the 'strategic use of essentialism' and she allows the 'three Es' to be re-cast in the light of her deconstructive techniques, as a strategic gesture. Thus when a student asserts her identity in Gayatri Spivak's seminar, as representative of black or Asian women, Spivak permits this essentialism in that it marks not a closed finality so much as an open opportunity for Spivak to de-essentialize the student's claim. 'Others are many' is how Spivak recalls her response (Spivak, 1993). This takes from the student 'the authority of marginality' (Spivak, 1993: 18). By asking how the community, which the student claims to embody, benefits from this act of representation in the classroom, Spivak also asks the student to consider (and here I paraphrase) 'the coding that has produced you as this subject who can now speak on behalf of your own others?' (Spivak, 1992: 19).

This grounded pedagogic interest on Spivak's part remains unusual in the great portals of theory. In the US context I have only otherwise come across Drucilla Cornell who addresses the connection between poststructuralism, psychoanalysis and empirical research, and she turns the argument around to expose the limits of what is traditionally designated as constituting the researchable. 'Ironically, the lack of emphasis on unconscious motivation and social fantasy in empirical research can itself be analysed as an aspect of a questionable Eurocentric assumption about the "nature" of social reality' (Cornell, 1995: 146). However, this dimension is close to what Valerie Walkerdine has been doing in the UK for some years now. She stands almost alone as a feminist writer influenced by psychoanalysis and poststructuralism but anxious to consider how, in empirical terms, female subjectivities, particularly those of girls and young women, are constituted. Her concern is with the fantasy structures and the enactment of unconscious impulses that are demonstrated in the process of reading girls' comics and magazines, watching television or going to the cinema (Walkerdine, 1990, 1993). Walkerdine's ethnographies are never truth-seeking activities, nor do they claim to be providing a full account. Instead, they are partial, elliptical, interrupted and attentive to the unconscious motivations of the researcher in relation to her subjects. Walkerdine shows how family structures position girls to make them be 'good'. In Foucault's terms, they are continually called upon to become 'docile bodies' even when, as Walkerdine argues, they are being subjected to pain, suffering and also abuse. Walkerdine's work reflects to this extent Butler's concern to 'expose and ameliorate those cruelties by which subjects are produced and differentiated' (Butler, 1995: 141). This interest in the empirical reality of emergent female subjectivities is pursued in a different context by Brunsdon (1991). Instead of asking the students to inspect their own identities or subjectivities (as Spivak does), Brunsdon takes the combative presence of young women in her 'women's genres' seminar as the basis for an interrogation of what happens when feminist analyses become the authoritative texts, when feminism becomes part of the academic canon. The resistance she encounters is complex and worthy of further consideration, she argues. These young women both draw from feminist discourse and repudiate it. Brunsdon queries the implicit assumption in much feminist writing that the aim is either to recruit 'them', or indeed to reproduce ourselves. The girls in question often seem to recoil in horror on being invited to identify with what a previous generation of feminist scholars have labelled 'women's genres', that is melodrama, romance, soap opera and, of course, 'weepies', but neither do they want to take up a recognizably feminist (adult) identity. What Brunsdon's article points to is the often overlooked importance of considering the powerful but also contested subjectivizing process of our own feminist discourse.

Let me now conclude this section by trying to think through how the 'anti-Es' might be brought to bear on a more applied or practical feminist cultural studies. Two short examples, taken from my own research interests, will hope-fully suffice. The first of these is the category of 'single mothers' and the second is that of the 'teenage girl'. In the context of recent inflamed political debates, usually initiated by publicity-seeking Tory MPs, it could be argued that the single mother is the fictive invention of a number of competing and opposing interest groups. These include not just the main political parties, but also self-help groups, feminist groups, local community groups, pressure groups and campaigning organizations. There is therefore no 'single' single mother, but instead many 'single mothers' (as indeed empirically there are). However, the many pejorative accounts of this new social category should not lead us to ignore its performative character. The single mother is no longer simply 'divorced' (that is without a man). Nor is she 'unmarried' (and there-fore helpless). She is single and a mother. This is suggestive of competence, confidence and of a de-stigmatized identity. There is no longer the suggestion of failure, abandonment or dependency. Feminism has made this re-signifi-cation possible, but it cannot control the 'chain of equivalence' set in motion as this social category makes its way through the social and political body (Laclau and Mouffe, 1985). Nor can feminism assume that the category does not have its own exclusionary force. If single is a counterpoint to married, how is the lesbian couple embarking on motherhood designated within the field of maternity and heterosexual parenting?

In the field of political conflict in which the single mother now exists, she is not just talked about, she is also envisaged. Here, too, we see a range of competing representations, with the pressure group and feminist representa-tions suggestive of a female body struggling against poverty but marked by pride, respectability, determination and the desire to work. This is in sharp contrast to the degraded feminine status accorded by the right-wing tabloid press to the young single mother, who is presented as dependent on the state, overweight, unkempt, unattractive, unhealthy, a heavy smoker and usually pictured pushing a buggy against a backdrop of a gloomy council estate. The repudiation of, or by, a husband or father of their children, in the lives of these women can literally be read off from their bodies – theirs is a failed or flawed sexuality. A feminist cultural analysis would consider these circulating definitions in all their complexity and would, in particular, show how women here stand in for and replace questions of poverty, the end of welfare (they are instead, as *The Sunday Times* puts it, 'wedded to the state'), male unemploy-ment, and the escape by women from violent or abusive relationships. The policy implications of an anti-essentialist approach to single motherhood would mean, in the first instance, recognizing that the term has become a 'floating signifier'; it can be and is articulated this way or that by all of the competing political parties. It is no longer a category over which feminism has any control or authority. In this complex field of representation an empirical study of teenage mothers would not so much seek after the truth beneath the media stereotypes as inquire after the impact these many representations have on the self-representations of women who are subjectivized by what Nancy Fraser has called the Juridical–Administrative–Therapeutic apparatus

(Fraser, 1987). What would also need to be taken into account is that feminism, too, has played some role in constituting the possibility of subject positions for these women. We can, as Butler does, re-inflect Foucault to take into account this role. Butler emphasizes the limits and the exclusions of feminist representation, but in this case there was important early work done on de-stigmatizing single motherhood and on making it easier for women to leave violent husbands and survive economically as single parents. British feminism, with its close connections to the left and the Labour Party, has in this instance shaped the space of identification for women across the boundaries of social class.

Bearing in mind the emphasis in Butler's work on the compulsive repetitions of normative heterosexuality, which resonate through the field of culture, and the extent to which feminism has unwittingly confirmed this by leaving uninterrogated the binary divide between men and women, then there is good reason to re-investigate the landscape of the cultures of femininity, including girls' and women's magazines which have informed my own objects of inquiry in the past (McRobbie, 1991). Clearly there was an exclusionary tension which ran across all of these forms of media where active lesbian desire was unspeakable and unrepresentable, all the more so when the subject of interest in these magazines (that is the female body) actually required repetitive, sexualized looking by girls and women at 'other women's bodies'. The precise discursive way in which some currents of desire were legitimated and others repudiated ought to have been the focus of attention, when in fact it was the meaning of heterosexual romance which formed the cornerstones of these and other studies. This is not to negate all such work on romance or more broadly on femininity. Not only was this work attentive to the way in which ideology successfully naturalized what was in fact socially constructed, but it also highlighted the bodily harm and injuries done to women and girls as a result. What was left unquestioned, however, was the extent to which, for all those whom these commercial cultures of femininity drew in, there were and are many whom it brutally excludes, for example black and Asian young women, disabled teenagers and of course gay or lesbian young people. Part of my aim at the very beginning of these studies (back in the late 1970s) was to gain legitimation for areas of research such as commercial cultures of femininity which in the past had been marginalized, ignored or trivialized. However, in the process of doing this what remained unexamined was the very category of 'girl' itself and the way in which this implied a regularity of subjectivities and experiences within which a norm of happy heterosexuality was an unspoken goal. Within this field of adolescent desire lesbianism has only recently appeared as 'no longer a problem'. Indeed, the precise passage through the field of girls' culture of this new articulation of non-heterosexual desire ought now to be an object of feminist analysis.

Having expressed a kind of *mea culpa* position, let me now, very briefly, suggest that some elements within cultural analysis already provide an interesting grounding for Butler's much more theoretical work on re-articulation. Perhaps the attraction of Butler's *Gender Trouble* (1990) is that this is exactly what the sociologist of youth subcultures sees all around her – in the streets, in the shops, in magazines and in the nightclubs. Deviations from the deep binary divide of male and female have been a marked feature of post-war youth subcultures. Hebdige's (1988) use of the concept of bricolage to show how young people reorganize the existing and available codes of cultural meaning to produce new and oppositional relations is not so far removed from Butler's notion of sexual re-signification. In the past I have argued that from within the heartland of commercial culture, new scripts of sex and gender have emerged precisely through this process of creating distinctive and sometimes spectacular subcultural styles. These in turn have then been seen as constitutive of youthful identities which are precisely the subject of the historical tensions of racial, sexual and class differences which are then 'written on the body'. This indicates a line of connection between Butler's theoretical trajectory and that of a particular cultural studies' tradition. Butler's writing evokes, at some subliminal level, memories of the Gramscian Marxism of 'resistance through rituals' (Hall and Jefferson, 1976) through to Hebdige's semiotic account of 'subculture, the meaning of style' from which her own notion of 'gender as performance' seems to unfold quite easily. At each point some note of political hope and some prospect of human agency is squeezed out of a sustained and rigorous poststructuralism.

The strategic use of the Es and the anti-Es?

Can feminist poststructuralism in cultural studies go beyond its function as a critique, as a warning device, a cautionary practice, which relentlessly and inexorably exposes the operations of power manifest in the positions from which we speak as 'feminists'? Can it, as Jeffrey Weeks has put it, be more than a matter of 'tearing apart' (Weeks, 1993) or, as Spivak says, 'looking rather than doing' (Spivak, 1990)? I will argue in this final section that this body of thinking can actually enhance the focus and the clarity of how we might intervene in cultural and social policy issues. So far only Laclau and Mouffe (1985) have begun to spell out how poststructuralist and psychoanalytic ideas can be applied to political practice, though there are also hints and suggestions in Butler's work about the importance of being able to connect or culturally translate between theory and practice. Laclau and Mouffe acknowledge that culture remains underdeveloped as a political space in their work, despite it being the terrain upon which Gramsci developed the concepts of hegemony and articulation, both of which remain critical to the radical democratic politics now envisaged by Laclau and Mouffe.

What, then, can the anti-Es offer empirical, ethnographic or experiential research which facilitates or accelerates a more interventionist mode in the field of feminist cultural studies? I think it allows us to return to these forms of research without embracing them in a totalistic, exclusive or absolutist way. Doing empirical work need not mean becoming an out-and-out empiricist. And given the low profile that empirical research has had in cultural studies over the last 20 years, what this might mean now, in the late 1990s, is not just beginning to do empirical work informed by questions which emerge from a poststructuralist paradigm (for example, exploring the diverse and fluid subjectivities of 'young women'), it might also mean quite simply strategically (or opportunistically) speaking the language of empiricism as and when required. We can perform as empiricists in the public domain when that is appropriate. For example, the strategic (and often critical) deployment of the conventions of empiricism is a not unhelpful tactic for cultural studies' academics who are called upon to comment on political debates about the 'effects' of violence on television or on pornography. It is possible to 'perform' in this capacity and to talk the language of results, data and statistics without necessarily endorsing this as the only way to explore the relations between texts and their readers. This is not a matter of bad faith, disingenuousness or 'falsification'. The particular authority of the empirical mode can be occupied now with greater complexity. It can be both used where appropriate and deconstructed elsewhere for its narratives of truth, its representation of results. Research can therefore be re-written and re-scripted according to the politics of its location. Empirical work can still be carried out even if the feminist researcher no longer believes it to be a truth-seeking activity. Indeed, awareness of this and of the structures and conventions which provide a regulative framework for doing cultural studies' research brings not just greater reflexivity to the field, it also demonstrates cultural studies to be a field of inquiry that is aware of the power which its competing discourses wield in its self-constitution. Cultural studies itself can thus be deconstructed to show how poststructuralist work has occupied a position of authority as 'theory' which has relegated policy-oriented work to the margins of what is in fact an unstable and disputed field. The three Es can then be brought back in from the margins to expand the political potential of the field and to enter a dialogue with those other strands which appear to occupy the high ground.

Ethnographic work has attracted a good deal of deconstructionist attention over the last few years, notably by Clifford and Marcus (1986) and also by bell hooks (1990). The ethnographer is not the unique (and intrepid) self he or she presents him/herself as, but is rather a point deployed in an already existing discourse which produces a set of 'self-effects' in the text. The subjects of ethnography can no longer be exoticized others whose everyday lives are presented in a naturalistic way. But what does this leave? Certainly it provokes a lively and interesting debate about existing ethnographies along the lines of what was left out. How does this particular kind of discourse in cultural studies create the category of 'working-class girls' for example? It also raises the question of doing ethnography differently to allow many voices to mingle so that the authoritative voice of the ethnographer is dislodged, though, as David Morley reminds us, as long as there is an author there is also an authoritative editorial and selective practice embedded in his or her mode of representation (see Morley in this volume).

In fact many of these questions were continually being raised, without the theoretical gloss of the anti-Es, by feminists doing ethnography in the 1970s.

Dorothy Hobson's work on working-class housewives was fully informed by anxieties about speaking on behalf of 'other women' (Hobson, 1978). Later, in the pages of *Feminist Review*, there were furious debates about, for example, whether heterosexual women could 'do' ethnographies of lesbian young women. This debate continues today outside the direct influence of post-structuralism by feminists like Marie Gillespie, carrying out ethnographic research on Asian youth (Gillespie, 1993). So, discussions of power and the rights of representation are not only tabled by the poststructuralists. What is specific to anti-essentialism in these debates is the insistence that there can be no true and authentic account, that the lives and identities being chronicled are necessarily partial, fluid, performed and constituted in the context of that particular ethnographic moment. But this does not negate in an instance the value of the endeavour. Recognition that my own category of 'working-class girls' produced the actual respondents in my research as more fully formed and coherent as individuals than they ever were, does not invalidate the usefulness of the category as a framework for academic feminism to work with and through as part of its own attempt to think both about the politics of representation and also to find a place for already devalued subjects in the academic curriculum. Thinking again about young women, or 'different, youthful subjectivities' (McRobbie, 1994), feminist ethnography, now re-cast in the light of the anti-Es, might accelerate Butler's critique of feminism by illustrating and complexifying the relations between feminism and young women.

This leaves us with the category of experience. It too has been the subject of intense debate in feminist theory over the last few years. Its privileged site in humanist thinking has allowed it to be taken as a cornerstone of truth about the subject – testimony to the existence of a true self or a 'real me', and thus also a clear sign of the appearance of social reality in the context of academic research. However, Foucault's later writings on the 'technologies of the self' permit the category of experience to reappear in poststructuralist feminism through showing agency to be part of the practice of discursive incitement to do or to act (Foucault, 1988). The subject is taught to experience and to expect certain normative experiences. She or he is also endlessly encouraged to 'feel it'. 'Can you feel it?' implores the DJ, 'How did it feel?' asks Oprah Winfrey. The subject is therefore produced as a feeling self and experience is one of the means by which feeling is testified to. This pooling of experience is also, according to Foucault, a means of managing and regulating diverse populations.

But just because experience comes as a pre-packaged set of practices while disguising itself as what is unique and most true about ourselves, this does not mean it cannot find a place in feminist cultural studies. We can stage experience as a way of speaking or writing, as a genre of populist language. Knowing, for example, how the codes of experience work in human-interest sections of national newspapers, or in day-time television programmes, experience can be adopted as a means of lobbying or campaigning so as to connect academic feminist research with a set of policy objectives. My own research 'experience' of reading young women's magazines in great volume and in depth over many years allows me to use this experience and to speak in a certain way in the media to counter the claims by right-wing moral guardians like Lady Olga Maitland that these publications encourage sexual irresponsibility and promiscuity on the part of their readers. That is to say we can temporarily 'humanize ourselves' as feminist academics to speak the more popular language of experience where political goals can be achieved as a result.

Conclusion

The perspectives I have labelled the anti-Es forces us to review and reconsider what we as feminists are doing in our research practices and what relations of power underpin these activities. The anti-Es de-stabilize the 'old' relation between feminists and what used to be called ordinary women by problema- tizing the politics of representation. They also disenchant and disappoint us by removing the possibility of there being a truth of womanhood towards which feminists can encourage women to strive on the basis that unity is a better guarantee of political action and change than the disunity which may follow from the disaggregation of the category of women. However, the more hopeful note in Butler's writing indicates that through the full recognition of difference, new and more sustainable alliances and coalitions can be built. On a more pragmatic level, we have to live with the fragility of such partnerships rather than waiting for a future where unity is somehow miraculously achieved.

If the vocabularies of poststructuralism help us to move feminist cultural studies on in this respect, then it is also important that they, too, are subjected to criticism. The logic of the anti-Es is to resist becoming trapped as a fixed set of meanings. At the same time the open-endedness of meaning proposed by Derrida and others actually legitimates a forceful and even intimidating poetic ambiguity in writing which is underpinned by the strong disciplinary frames of literature and literary theory. Having deconstructed the special place of fiction or poetry in writing, it is possible for poststructuralist literary theorists to intersperse purposefully these modes into their own readings of key literary texts. This gives to poststructuralist criticism the characteristics of a certain playful, meandering or poetic style, one which is much less accept- able as a practice in the social sciences. The commitment to meaning as an endless open chain of signification can be an excuse for producing texts which, to the social scientist, are highly impenetrable. To the sociologist or cultural studies' feminist concerned with making ideas accessible to a wider audience, this can seem like a real abrogation of political responsibility. The language of the anti-Es, in particular psychoanalysis, can appear far beyond an undergraduate readership never mind a wider audience. Thus it can easily be claimed that the anti-Es are as exclusive in their own practice as they are open-ended in the meanings they profess. Indeed, the latter becomes an excuse for the former. It is also the case that the process of actually translating these ideas so that they might have some broader political impact is often overlooked. More attention might therefore be paid to the practical mechanisms through which, for example, Homi Bhabha's or Dick Hebdige's writing is taken up and used in Isaac Julien's films, or for that matter to how Butler's ideas find their way into discussions, debates and interviews in the gay and lesbian press. This at least would demonstrate that high theory can have relevance to cultural and political practice.

Similar questions can also be put to the impact of the anti-Es in feminist cultural studies. Having only recently achieved some degree of institutional recognition in the academy, the experience of being robbed of this authority and of being challenged as to whether it is possible to speak in this context, 'as a woman', is unlikely to be met with a wholly friendly welcome. And to stop thinking universally on behalf of all women runs the risk of retreating into an equally fictive sphere of thinking about 'some women only'. To pursue anti-essentialism uncritically can run the risk of making it a new point of faith, a new kind of thing. And for all the connections and alliances which the anti-Es appear to make possible, there is also the possibility of narrowing down the political field so that it becomes the site of endless dispute and antagonism in a negative rather than in a productive way.

In addition, there is also the danger of re-reification where theoretical journeys, whose own essence or truth can only be grasped by exhaustive reading of a great legacy of philosophers and thinkers, makes it more difficult for 'theory' to consider its own place in contemporary political culture. For these reasons, perhaps the critical task now is to return in feminist cultural studies to the empirical, the ethnographic and the experiential, and to use these tools to explore the social and cultural practices and new subjectivities which have come into being alongside and in relation to what has been happening in the theoretical world of anti-essentialism, psychoanalysis and poststructuralism.

12

Cultural Studies, Communication and Change: Eastern Europe to the Urals

John D.H. Downing

I propose an initial exploration of two closely related themes in this chapter. First, the capacity of the cultural studies' literature to illuminate the economic, political and cultural transitions in Russia, Poland and Hungary[1] that for those nations reached points of no return in 1991 and 1989 respectively, but which self-evidently pre-dated those years and have rolled on since. The second is the other side of the same coin, namely the potential implications of those transitions for our evaluation of cultural studies' approaches.[2]

Let me begin by setting out some of my assumptions and priorities. I take communication research as inherently an integrative exercise, and thus one which poses a challenge to the organization of the study of society conventional in the academy for well over a century, namely its hacking up into anthropology, economics, geography, history, international relations, linguistics, philosophy, political science, psychology, sociology. Of these disciplines, some have no pretension to integration. Indeed, their practitioners rather pride themselves on the solid results they feel they produce from focusing on but one dimension of our social existence. Others sometimes have ambitions toward integration – anthropology, and, in Europe, sociology – and in the hands of their best practitioners, fulfil them. Geography, at the present time, is the only well-established discipline whose practitioners regularly come close to bringing together a full range of foci and methods under one roof.

In the perhaps now waning days of postmodernist analyses, integration and systematic analysis have been rather suspect activities. When only flux and disconnection whirl about one's head like a wild storm of dust, someone seeking out settled patterns and functional interrelations and – worst of all – system, could seem intellectually and even politically on the edge of croaking. Much insight has been produced within postmodernist discourse, yet its alarming dimension has often been the licence provided in the name of attacking the spurious imposition of a rational grid on discombobulated experience, to casual, ill-thought-out (and still more, klutzily articulated) formulations. It has sometimes felt a little like watching an inexperienced and frustrated poker player dawning to the recognition that the game is unpredictable, and then playing at random as though it were utterly unpredictable and any hand or play worth any other.

Simply because any intellectual system is a construct and thus an artificial imposition on our experience, and simply because it will always be contradicted at a series of points where it does not 'fit', this should not be taken to mean that the search for intellectual coherence and connection is itself fatally flawed and counterproductive.

For reasons I will hope to make clear in a moment, the origins of cultural studies' approaches need to be read in this light. They have an affinity, intellectually and politically, with the post-war emergence of social and labor history. On the one hand, that development was and is to be welcomed unstintingly. The avoidance of societal experience in favor of a narrow focus on the elite was analytically absurd, and in a period when there is a gadarene rush to disavow any connection with the marxist tradition, it seems particularly appropriate to honor that tradition for its contribution to broadening our focus. The work of such as Edward Thompson and Eric Hobsbawm, the massive American corpus of writing on slavery in the formation of the United States: these contributions to history writing have decisively expanded our self-understanding.

Cultural studies, in its British inception, bore all the marks of being a translation of that focus from the past to the present. Raymond Williams's and Richard Hoggart's radical challenges to the pretensions of 'high' culture and to the disdain of its *porte-paroles* for the working classes' cultural creativity, are on one level simply the writing of contemporary history from a social/labor history perspective.

The problem has been that quite often, whether in social history or in cultural studies, an exclusive focus on one social class has been replaced by an equally exclusive focus on another. Media and cultural studies' students have gladly junked *passé* and *outré* attention to the elite and the past for the 'now' of now. The growth of postmodernist analysis has assisted, spawning a mass of conference papers – adorned with seemingly obligatory parentheses and hyphens and cutely titled with some tortured pun – on one or other facet of the cultural here-and-tomorrow. A negative aspect of the practice of history, namely the endless replication of minor parish-register research, has been in turn replicated in the practice of cultural studies, as evanescent fads and trends are humorlessly dissected with the aid of a plethora of adjectival nouns.

'No worst there is none', wrote Gerard Manley Hopkins, although it is more than a little unfair to compare the writing I am excoriating, Baudelairean though it might be in its ennui, to his extreme spiritual torment. Nonetheless, I am pitching in no fashion for the abolition of cultural studies (or even of postmodernism – I suppose), but for their integration into a spectrum of systematic analyses of society and communication. The study of popular culture by itself, like the study of communication processes outside their societal contexts, is a complete cul-de-sac. Just as over the last 30 years geography has in some sense reinstated the pre-modern assumption that human society and its physical ecology are indissolubly linked, and has done so in concert with the growing recognition that the last five human centuries have violently accelerated the perils of the planet, so it is high time for communication researchers in particular to overflow the dams created by the nineteenth- and twentieth-century academy's vigorous parcelization of knowledge, and to connect up their research foci.

If not us, who?

The societal changes in Eastern Europe symbolized by the years 1989 and 1991 are a major test for communication researchers, cultural studies specialists or not. Some would argue that these changes are totally unprecedented and deduce accordingly that they are *sui generis*, so attempting to skip out from facing the challenge. But while the specifics of the Soviet experience should not be dissolved into a conceptual ratatouille, partly analogous transitions have taken place in South Africa, South Korea, Taiwan and Latin America, as well as in Southern Europe, and are hopefully under way in China. If communication research has nothing to say on these issues, it should shut up shop. Above all, such transitions confront communication researchers with the demand that they integrate society and power, conflict and change, into the analysis of communication – and likewise that those, such as many in the political science profession, who think they operate comfortably and habitually with power, conflict and change, incorporate communication into their framework, and cease treating social agents simply as mute pieces on a stimulus-response chessboard.

Articulation: a *mot clef* for cultural studies

I will begin, however, with a critique of the term 'articulation' as used by many contemporary cultural studies writers. On the face of it, its frequent use belies my claim that this analytical tradition tends to separate out popular cultural activity from other societal forces, for it does, does it not, zero in precisely on the connections between the eddies and surges of everyday life? Well maybe. Let us see.

It is true that articulation is the only concept used in recent years within the cultural studies' literature that might, on the face of it, have some explanatory force to bring to bear on multiple interconnected factors in socio-cultural analysis (Hall and Grossberg, 1986; Grossberg, 1992: Chs 1–4; Jameson, 1993).

Jameson has indeed asserted that articulation 'stands as the central theoretical problem or conceptual core of cultural studies' (Jameson, 1993: 32). He offers a brief history of its use, but effectively its use within cultural studies' discourse began with Hall. Admittedly, the latter acknowledges a debt to Laclau (Hall and Grossberg, 1986: 53), but the Laclau text cited uses the term without especial definition as equivalent to linkage, and does not even refer to it in the index (Laclau, 1979: 7–13, 34, 38, 42–3, 78, 164, 194–5). Laclau's concern was to explore Althusser's and Poulantzas's statements of the 'relative[3] autonomy' of political and ideological 'instances' from the economic 'instance', whether in relation to rural Latin American economies' linkage with global capitalism, or in relation to fascist and populist ideologies' linkage with class relations.

Hall claims his own use combines the notion of articulation as expression, and articulation as connection or link (as in the tractor–trailer/articulated lorry). He does not explore the truck-metaphor further, although it seems implicitly as though it is only the hitching of one unit to another which he has in mind, rather than the fact that the truck pulls the trailer hitched up to it.

In this combining of meanings he slides conceptually a step beyond Laclau, who described neither populism nor fascism as articulations in the sense of 'expression'. For Hall it seems to be in particular the linkages between ideology and political action that interest him, for instance in his summary remarks on the Rastafarian ideology and movement in Jamaica (Hall and Grossberg, 1986: 54–5). Aside from positing a dual sense to the term, he does not explain how the two senses actually – if I, too, may use the word – articulate with each other. He fudges the two meanings – 'a theory of articulation is both a way of understanding how ideological elements come . . . to cohere together within a discourse, and a way of asking how they do or do not become articulated . . . to certain political subjects' (ibid.: 53) – but does not explain the two meanings' mutual imbrication. Calling them 'absolutely dialectical' (ibid.: 55) increases the resonance in the air, but not much else. In the rest of the interview with Grossberg he effectively only uses the metaphor in its primary sense of joint or linkage.

This is worrying. Any functionalist sociologist knows that elements of social life are interconnected, and the fact that these writers, all strongly influenced by the marxist tradition and by absorption with the flux of multiple ideological currents, would dismiss the functionalist tendency of seeing social integration and stability everywhere, does not give them the excuse to posit linkage, reinvent it as articulation, and leave it at that. Grossberg (1992) does not leave it at that, but it could be concluded it might have been better if he had. It is difficult at times to pin down his fast-flowing use of terms: even he, having defined cultural studies as politicized, conjuncturalist, contextualist and interdisciplinary (ibid.: 18–22), forthwith castigates his definition as 'so obviously too romanticized' (ibid.: 22). However, let us examine further what he endeavors to bring to the notion of articulation. Fairly early on in his argument, articulation retains its primary sense of joint or link:

> The concept of articulation provides a useful starting point for describing the process of forging connections between practices and effects. . . . Articulation links this process to that effect, this text to that meaning, this meaning to that reality, this experience to those politics. And these links are themselves articulated into larger structures, etc. (Grossberg, 1992: 54)

From there he develops the point that articulation forces us to pay attention to context. It 'offers a theory of contexts. It dictates that one can only deal with, and from within, specific contexts . . .' (ibid.: 55). He then proceeds to underscore that simply asserting linkage is insufficient: 'Pointing out that two practices are articulated together, that the pieces "fit" together, is not the same as defining the mode of that articulation, the nature of that fit' (ibid.: 56).

At this point it feels as though we are on the verge of a forward movement, but unfortunately Grossberg immediately dives into a highly indeterminate set of assertions about articulation and causality:

> articulation can be understood as a more active version of the concept of determination; unlike notions of interaction or symbiosis, determination describes specific cause-and-effect relations. But unlike notions of causality and simple notions of determination, articulation is always complex: not only does the cause have effects, but the effects themselves affect the cause, and both are themselves determined by a host of other relations. (Grossberg, 1992: 56)

This formulation regrettably provides the flavor of much of the argument, which ultimately seems to be designed to net Proteus rather than explain him. No statement is provided which is not usually immediately thrown back into a set of unpredictably whirling conceptual dervishes, seemingly to ensure that no reader may assume the analytical game is over. That objective is laudable, but could be achieved satisfactorily while standing still to define terms thoroughly.

A little later, Grossberg comes back to articulation and causality, ascribing substantial causal power to linkages.

> One can conceive of such articulations as lines or vectors, projecting their effects across the field. Each vector has its own quality (effectivity), quantity and directionality. . . . Articulations may have different vectors, different forces and different spatial reaches in different contexts. And they may also have different temporal reaches, cutting across the boundaries of our attempts at historical periodization. (Grossberg, 1992: 60–1)

At this point the term 'articulation' is perilously close to being hypostatized, rather in the way that Hall in the reference already cited[4] sometimes tends to hypostatize the term 'ideology'. It is a common vice of theorists to personify the concepts they most love. But is it the joints themselves that move the arm and the hand? Do they not simply enable movement? Or is Grossberg feeling, not for the elbow, but for the notion of combination, almost of overdetermination, rather than linkage as such? He does not say so, but it might be a way out of what at times seems a conceptual morass.

The project Grossberg sets himself, the dissection of contemporary political conservatism, is interesting and important, and he offers numerous penetrating insights along the way, both conceptual and empirical. The fact that I have attacked some of his and Hall's formulations rather sharply is not meant to distract from that achievement. Indeed, both the book by Hall et al. (1978) on media images of 'mugging' and Britain's 1970s crisis, and this work by Grossberg, do attempt on a certain level the integrated analysis that this chapter argues should be undertaken in order to understand changes in Eastern Europe. The problem I am identifying is that the term articulation is either relatively banal, or bears such a gigantic weight that it cracks under the strain. And both books actually fail, in my view, to link together their constituent parts, Hall's mediatic analysis of 'mugging', for example, sitting rather uncomfortably next to his and his colleagues' macroscopic analysis of the British conjuncture of the time.

One more example may serve to drive home my point about the impossible burden Grossberg places on the term articulation. After having reiterated yet again his continuing caveats against overly tidy ascriptions of causality – 'There are no simple or necessary correlations between, for example, cultural identities and subject-positions . . . and economic or political sites of agent-hood' – Grossberg then writes: 'Individuals must be *won or articulated* into these positions' (Grossberg, 1992: 127; emphasis added).

Seduced or stapled? What *does* this mean?

Conversely, when Jameson offers a formulation of the term articulation, it is in terms which suggest it means conjuncture:

> It implies a kind of turning structure, an ion-exchange between various entities, in which the ideological drives associated with one pass over and interfuse the other – but only provisionally, for a 'historically specific moment', before entering into new combinations, being systematically worked over into something else, decaying over time in interminable half-life, or being blasted apart by the convulsions of a new social crisis. The articulation is thus a punctual and sometimes even ephemeral totalization, in which the planes of race, gender, class, ethnicity and sexuality intersect to form an operative structure. (1993: 31–2)

(Why only these?)

Elsewhere in a recently published book I have suggested ways in which we can theorize these and other problems more adequately (see Downing, 1996). At that point, it will be my critics' turn. For now, all I can do is to stress the necessity of taking into account in the analysis of regime and media transition in Eastern Europe, the full gamut of interlocking factors, from culture and social movements to international relations, that I have identified. I doubt that Hall, Grossberg or Jameson would disagree in principle. Yet their formulations of 'articulation' do not take us any further than I have in this largely empirical essay.

Cultural studies and Eastern European transitions

There are very few works – with the signal exception of the series of brilliant articles by Condee and Padunov (1987, 1988, 1991a, 1991b, 1994, 1995) – that have explicitly adopted any cultural studies framework for the analysis of Russia, Poland or Hungary before, during or since the transitions. This is especially true if the later waves of cultural studies that deploy concepts from Gramsci, Benjamin, Bakhtin, Barthes, and feminist approaches, among others, are taken as the litmus test. In part, this presents a very scathing obituary on the character of Cold War research on the region. 'Politburo' research, supplemented from the 1970s onwards by research into Soviet-bloc economies, dominated completely, reflecting indeed in part the top-heavy character of those polities but in at least equal measure the instinctively elitist sympathies of the mass of sovietologists. Furthermore, if the vigor of conceptual discourse is a yardstick of a field, sovietology was akin to a virgin desert.

The practical effect was the reverse of the cultural studies approach, to privilege either the Soviet-bloc elites, or Western elites, as virtually sole agents in the maintenance or the dissolution of the Soviet structure of power (see, for example, Beschloss and Talbott, 1993; Garton Ash, 1993; Schweizer, 1994). Of this tendency there are many examples.[5] In each instance, we are introduced to the absorbing and intricate story of social agents, enjoying certainly a disproportionate measure of power and engaged (often to their surprise) in the conclusion of the Cold War and the dismantling of the Soviet empire. The role of communication processes, although untapped by these authors in any systematic analytic or conceptual fashion, is plainly central in their narratives, which repeatedly stress the multiple communicative interactions – actual, anticipated or avoided – between elite actors and factions, their media agencies (the 'their' being both perceived and real), and the publics on both sides.

The nearest any of the accounts get to acknowledging the power of other agents than the elite ones they hold in view is when they discuss the deteriorating Soviet-bloc economies and the attempts by bloc regimes to win investment and credits from the West. There is an underlying assumption that at an undetermined but finally inelastic point the Soviet-bloc regimes would have to take serious account of massive public discontent. There is no acknowledgment of popular culture as a steady ongoing internal pressure for substantive change; rather, there is a covert presumption that political anger at economic deprivation would spark some kind of jacquerie that might destabilize, perhaps terminally, through some undefinable miracle, one or more of the regimes in question. It is at this point that the few studies which concentrate on popular culture, whether or not they do so under the explicit aegis of cultural studies, have a major contribution to make to our understanding of how those changes finally came about – and equally, what they entailed.

The point at which I will begin is a paradoxical one, a point of silence, of inactivity. White (1990) studied the House of Culture phenomenon in Russia, Poland and Hungary. The Houses of Culture were institutions set up in Russia under Stalinism, and then transplanted into other East European nations as part of their Sovietization. Their prescribed role was politico-cultural mass enlightenment, as defined and strategized by the Communist Party authorities. White studied the operation of six such agencies during the earlier 1980s in Moscow, St Petersburg, Warsaw, Poznan, Budapest and Debrecen. What was striking, to summarize her study, was that the closer these organizations came to fulfilling their official role, the less they were utilized. Conversely, the more open they became to local community initiatives, the more likely they were to be frequented. This would not have been known from the official figures of participation, which were as mendacious as other published statistics in the Brezhnev era (White, 1990: 44, 135–6).

This pattern should not be ascribed solely to political alienation, since the advent of television and so of home-based sources of leisure recreation certainly also helped to draw people away from them. Nonetheless, the content of television was as capable of producing political alienation as a rote political lecture in the House of Culture, so that the key issue to keep in mind in this situation is the popularity enjoyed by community-originated activities. And, in a curiously powerful albeit indirect fashion, by the end of the Brezhnev era the Soviet Party itself acknowledged the futility of these institutions for its purposes by primarily putting women, often very young women, in charge of their programs (White, 1990: 103, 117, 121–2). This was a dismissive, not a progressive, gesture.

Thus the Party appeared to have given up on the Houses of Culture, albeit without fanfare. Even during the Brezhnev period, they tended to be designed more as locales to crowd out the potential emergence of counter-cultural activities than as places where people's minds could be seduced into soviet loyalism (White, 1990: Ch. 3). In other words, they were there to try to stop the slide rather than to promote the ideal. The cultural 'slide' in question took a variety of forms. Here we will concentrate on four of them, sometimes interrelated: young people's dissent; popular music; social movements; religious expression. The primary aspect of their interrelation was probably the involvement of young people in each one of them, so we will begin with a brief assessment of the cultural and ideological location of youth in late sovietized society. It was a location with profound political implications for these regimes.

Youth

In most cultures, except the most gerontocratic, the future of the society is taken for granted as being bound up with its young people. Within Soviet ideology, given its overwhelming emphasis on the future construction of a utopian society, the official status of young people was especially enhanced. Consequently, their enthusiasm and loyalty were of the essence of the Soviet project. Without those qualities, the Soviet experiment was doomed.

The reality, as is well known, was widely different from the ideology. The main youth organization, the Komsomol, was legendary for the corruption and arrogance of its leading officials (Riordan, 1989), which were vividly depicted in the 1989 film *Che Pe*, a Russian acronymic version of the full title which was *Extraordinary Occurrence at Local Headquarters* (Lawton, 1992: 198–200). The growing disaffection of Soviet youth was acknowledged as a major problem by no less than Marshal Ogarkov, at that point chief of the Soviet general staff, in a book published in 1982, *Always Ready To Defend the Motherland*, in which he vigorously attacked the creeping pacifism, disinclination for military service and pervasive disinterest in the history of World War II among the young (Ogarkov, 1982: Ch. 3). This was in some sense even more unnerving for the *verkhushka*, representing a second phase in which disinterest in Soviet ideals was being joined by a collapse in basic patriotism.

Whatever might be said of this ideological decay among youth in the Soviet context, it could be multiplied many times over in the Polish and Hungarian contexts. To take the single issue of housing as a pointer, the failure of all the East European regimes to provide sufficient housing for their growing populations – especially in Poland – meant that young couples were often forced after marriage to continue living with the bride's or the bridegroom's family, typically in an already cramped apartment. That led to a high early marital breakdown rate and to endless tensions within the primary unit.[6] Nor was there any relief in sight, so that belief in inexorable progress really was a disease of the purblind among young people. To that decay was typically added a comprehensively anti-Soviet nationalism, yet another voracious worm in the bud of the bright Soviet future.

Bachkatov and Wilson (1988) have described in some detail the experiences of many young people in the Soviet Union in the 1980s: disenchantment with the work ethic, involvement with the illegal second economy, a turn to prostitution, petty theft, drugs, gangs, a fascination with the fantastic, whether a mirage version of everyday life in Western societies or even some version of the paranormal.

For the ever more remote *verkhushki* of these regimes, news of these developments was continually more frustrating and perplexing. They had forged their careers in the 1930s and 1940s, when the dramas of collectivization, the anti-Nazi war or of post-war reconstruction had especially harnessed their cohort's energy and vision, more so than any other sector of society at that time. Despite the grimness and the state repression of those decades, at least among their generation there had been at the time a significant number of 'true believers', like the young Lev Kopelev (1980: Ch. 2) or the young Petro Grigorenko (1982: Ch. 6). The attraction of the Cuban revolution to some members of the Soviet leadership during the 1960s and 1970s was due in part to their sense that the revolution they had once committed themselves to in the springtime of their youth was not growing old or out of date, but was springing up elsewhere.

Yet, sooner or later, even some of these dyed-in-the-wool, ossified leaders would find themselves surrounded by dissent, not merely among the would-be hippies or heavy metal rockers or religious converts 'out there', but also in their own homes, voiced by their children or grandchildren. Stites notes how 'the "gilded youth" – or children of the leaders . . . often felt a particular grievance against state culture which they lived so near' (Stites, 1992: 209).

To sum up on the question of the younger generation during the 1980s, it is vital to recognize that the customary Western diagnosis of youth in society – transitional alienation and rebelliousness, combined with energy and creativity – worked neither for the elite nor for youth in late sovietized societies. The only youthful transition process which was imaginable and viable for the elite was equal or greater dedication to the Soviet system. Since this was implausible in any of these nations, the only avenue open to young people was increasing alienation and even rebelliousness, the latter taking many different forms. This rang the tocsin for the system even to the elite, for more and more they were hearing it sounding out from their very own children and grandchildren.

It is against this background that Gorbachev's notable summons should be read at the 27th Party Congress in 1986 in favor of openness, restructuring, and speeding up of technological development (*glasnost'*, *perestroika*, *usko-reniye*), especially his call for an end to the dual reality of Soviet life, the one public and swathed in meaningless self-congratulation, the other private and cynically honest (see Shlapentokh, 1986). Indeed, he spent some considerable time in his address discussing the deterioration of human relationships in Soviet society and what needed to be done about them. In this sense, it is now clear that he was an incurable optimist in thinking it was still possible to rescue the project. As Bachkatov and Wilson put it, 'the parents lost their faith, but the children never had it' (Bachkatov and Wilson, 1988: 2).

Yet the point at issue is this: the impasse reached was such that the solution proposed by antique purist traditionalists in the Politburo, such as Mikhail Suslov or Yegor Ligachev, namely the purification and intensive re-ideolo-gization of the society, had zero chance of success with young people. A prime motivating force in the drive for *glasnost'* and *perestroika* was then that they represented the last and only chance for success in recuperating the Soviet project, for the younger generation simply had to be the target of tar-gets in that drive.[7] In fact, as we now know, but because of the communicative atomization of sovietized societies (see Bahro, 1978: 300–3), neither we nor they were then able to know that the game was already over.

Music

It is at this juncture that it becomes possible to appreciate the significance of new musical movements and expressions as the most tangible of all cultural signals of the alienation of youth in sovietized societies at that time. The first and very powerful underground expression of dissent in musical form came from the so-called guitar-poets or bards, notably Bulat Okudzhava and Vladimir Vysotsky (Smith, 1984; Ryback, 1990: Ch. 3). In some sense they paved the way for the later proliferation of musical styles, many of the latter initially borrowed from Western sources, unlike the bards whose themes and musical style were deeply Russian.

As Ryback underlines, however, rock was much more of a generational phenomenon. As a native phenomenon it developed later in Russia than in Poland, Hungary or other East-Central European countries. Even more so than in the latter region, the cultural bureaucracy in the Soviet Union was very deeply entrenched in the past. Kneejerk denunciations of subversive Western strategies in the musical arena came easily to it, though in turn this was made easier by the generally greater isolation of Russian (though not Baltic) society from its Western neighbors. Whether as a native phenomenon or as an import, however, Ryback recounts instance after instance in almost every Soviet-bloc nation of young people battling with the police, sometimes violently, in order to secure or defend their rights to rock concerts. The right to free musical self-expression was an issue of passionate moment for very many young people.

However, aside from generational clashes of taste on the actual music and its instrumentation, there were profound political divergences between the

Party and Komsomol authorities on the lyrics of many rock-numbers and on the life-styles associated with rock music. In essence, both sides appeared often to agree on one central point: rock music was globally inspired, not Soviet-inspired.

Bushnell (1990: 53–4, 97f., Ch. 4), in his study of graffiti in Moscow around this period, observed how often even Soviet rock groups were generally honored by having graffiti written about them in English, rather than in Russian: 'English words and symbols enjoy prestige and automatically – irrespective of their precise meaning – do the emblem honor' (ibid.: 54). He cites the Burgess novel and the film based upon it, *Clockwork Orange*, as correctly intuiting 'the key role that the language of the ideological and cultural enemy plays in the Soviet subculture', and connects the prestige of English to 'an image of the West as an affluent, energetic and colorful world the opposite of Soviet society in every respect' (ibid.: 240–1).

Not unnaturally, the more the Komsomol bureaucracy and its Eastern European clones inveighed against rock as a decadent imperialist plot, the young discovered there was an ideological Achilles' heel, a point at which they could challenge the system and see it compulsively react. When the same musical moment, a rock concert, was one which, as it did for many people, also meant a moment of positive mental liberation and psychic intensity, then two values fused together into a very powerful commitment.

Interestingly, toward the end of the 1980s, even the Soviet system began trying to co-opt rock groups and give them official space, though at the cost to the groups of having them censor their own lyrics (Easton, 1989). By then, other groups, especially punk rockers and heavy metal bands, had sped past more traditional and melodic rock music, and were the new targets of cultural conservatives and Party officials. In Russia, Poland and Hungary during the 1980s, cultural bureaucrats veered back and forth between allowing punk rockers and others space for concerts and recordings, and trying to rein them in (Ryback, 1990: 11–12, 14). It has to be said that in a few instances the lyrics were of a kind which would draw almost universal repugnance, as in the case of one Hungarian group that called for the extermination of Gypsies, or the banner unfurled by Latvian punks at a concert that read 'Latvian punks will finish what the Germans began', that is the slaughter of Russians in tens of millions (ibid.: 215, 275). Heroizing or homogenizing the opposition is a perilous proposition.

Nonetheless, these forms of popular music effectively became an alternative public sphere (Downing, 1988) for many members of the younger generation in Soviet-bloc countries. It must be recalled, in context, that this was the decade of the second Cold War, a period of very pronounced nuclear tension, a period in which the aggressive militarism of the Reagan administration and the Reagan–Thatcher–Kohl 'front' were endlessly highlighted in Soviet-bloc media. Yet not even the existence of an external enemy armed to the teeth and rattling nuclear sabres was able to be used to deflect the dissident culture and commitments of many young people. Their insistence on honoring and following Western musical forms was not to be interpreted, as did the official press, simply as slavish imitation of a hollow and frenetic commercialism. It was a constant statement to the authorities that the younger generation neither believed in nor cared about a single word they were being fed.

This musically delivered message from below was able eventually to reverberate in the ears of even the most hard of hearing in the *verkhushki*.

Social movements

It is essential to begin with the recognition that in the Soviet-bloc nations autonomous social movements were, by definition, to be excluded from the spectrum of public activities. In Hungary in 1978, for example, supposedly 'the nicest barracks in the socialist camp' as the local saying went, when I asked a feminist (Veres Julia) about the current condition of the Hungarian women's movement, she explained to me that 50 per cent of the movement had recently emigrated to Paris. Which left only her. . . . And went on to point out that any autonomous movement, not a women's movement as such, was intolerable for the party-state.

Recognition of this political communicative reality helps to place in proper focus the extraordinary achievement of *Solidarnosc* for the whole Soviet bloc. And as Goodwyn (1991) and Laba (1991) emphasize, the communicative genesis of that movement is not to be sought in the 'outside agitator' theory of communication, curiously enough shared both by the Polish *verkhushka* and by many Western commentators.

For both these, *Solidarnosc* was the product of one or more of the following: Pope John Paul II's tumultuous visit to Poland in 1979; Radio Free Europe broadcasts; and the advice and leadership for Gdansk and Baltic seaport workers from a small knot of courageous Warsaw intellectuals such as Adam Michnik and Jacek Kuron, leading activists in the tiny organization KOR (Committee for Workers' Self-Defense), founded in 1976. No one is denying the involvement or partial influence of any of these factors in the process as a whole. But no one of them, and no combination of them, actually created *Solidarnosc*.[8]

We need to recognize the way in which this very slowly growing movement on the Baltic coast, coming together over decades, gradually developed its own culture and internal communicative links. Goodwyn in particular traces the transition from endless kitchen-table conversations about the realities people faced – 'we weren't building socialism; we were building shit' (Goodwyn, 1991: 105) – through to the formation of the Inter-Factory Strike Committee that mobilized the Baltic Coast seaport workers and was the cradle of *Solidarnosc*.

It was not that *Solidarnosc* directly inspired labor or other movements in Soviet Russia or Ukraine or Hungary[9] or elsewhere, of which there were a variety (for example, Helsinki Watch, 1987, 1990). As a result of media blackouts on Polish realities, most people were ignorant of the situation there. Its impact on the bloc was through its interpretation by leading elements in both Soviet and Polish *verkhushki*, namely that although limited military actions against civil disobedience were appropriate, sustained and widespread violence to subdue opposition was impossible. If further evidence were needed, the war in Afghanistan supplied it plentifully. Thus the Polish movement, at its height in 1981 numbering ten million members, as contrasted with 2.5 million for the Party and a million in official trade unions (Ost, 1990: 138), was taken by the reform faction in Moscow as prime evidence of why their strategy was right.

Religion

My comments here will be very brief, but two points are of considerable importance. First, that if dissidents in the Soviet Union are to be measured by numbers, then religious dissent was infinitely more significant than those secular figures such as Solzhenitsyn and Sakharov best known in the West, who were known to and represented a tiny constituency up until the late 1980s. Whether considering the Baptist churches, the Ukrainian Uniate church, or a variety of other religious bodies, this form of dissidence was the oldest and most widespread (Jancar, 1975; Alexeyeva, 1985: Chs. 11–14). Judgments vary on the large Muslim populations of the Central Asian republics and Azerbaijan, with some claiming the existence of massive underground dissidence and others arguing that the traditional clans of those regions had effectively colonized the formally Soviet power-structure in their republics, and ironically had developed thereby a more stable version of Soviet power than in the non-Muslim republics.

However, religious dissidence in principle was a primary zone of principled opposition, since it drew its inspiration from ethical absolutes that simply could not co-exist with the Soviet claim to have a lock on the future – a much more significant point of conflict than simply the question of the state's self-designation as 'atheist'. The latter could, in the case of many states, be effectively the same as the United States government's self-designation as constitutionally neutral on the question of religious expression. It was the rival claims to effective total knowledge and ideological supremacy that were irreconcilable, and thus a permanent disturbance of the Soviet cultural project.

The second point is really an extension of the first in a particularly sensitive zone of the bloc. The Polish Catholic church, by virtue of the cultural homogeneity of Poland in its post-World War II borders, and by virtue of its own extremely traditionalist intransigence, was never forced underground. Thus Poland was the only bloc nation with a nationally organized and – however reluctantly – tolerated autonomous entity all through the last years of Stalinism and since. The importance of this entity in sustaining some sense of the possibility of an alternative mode of social life should not be downplayed. Of course, the Catholic church had its own survival at heart, which dominated its strategy in Poland as elsewhere. It was not anxiously beating at the gates of democracy. But it was there, the only organized counterforce to a regime which insisted by force on its own all-sufficiency. It was the only public location where the language was still used unmarred by obfuscation and jargon, a condition hard to imagine for those who have never been inside such a situation.[10]

Thus, during the 1980s, as Jakubowicz (1990) has demonstrated, there were actually three public spheres in Poland: the official governmental one, Solidarity's and the Catholic Church's. While predictably there was considerable friction of various kinds between these zones of public debate, the very fact of having three such meant that in the continuing instability of the Polish situation from early in 1988 onwards, the role of the two oppositional spheres was correspondingly enhanced, and even compelled the official sphere's media to open up their doors to intermittent critique and commentary that would have been difficult to imagine at an earlier date.

In this section, the argument has been made that the major regime transitions in Eastern Europe are only to be understood fully with the aid of a communication focus, rather than a concentration on the *verkhushki*. In the course of the argument, however, it has been clear that not only is this a realm of research rather thinly populated by scholars operating within a cultural studies' framework,[11] but also that those working within the framework have typically not addressed certain major issues that might be expected to fit closely with their concerns, such as social movements or religion. We might also note that the cultural studies' literature has generally not engaged with the Habermas-derived notion of the public sphere. Despite the latter's problematic dimensions (Fraser, 1993; Hanchard, 1995), it offers considerable scope for analytical cross-fertilization, especially in its alternative media implications (Downing, 1988, 1989), that so far still wait to be properly realized by cultural studies' research.

We will now turn to the implications of these regime changes for cultural studies' discourses and propose that they too suggest further typical deficiencies within them.

Eastern European transitions and cultural studies

Accounts of the leading actors on the American and Soviet sides during the period from shortly before Bush's election in 1988 through to the conclusion of the failed putsch of August 1991 offer remarkable insights into the final period of the dismantling of the Cold War (see, for example, Ash, 1993; Schweizer, 1994). What these accounts have in common consists of their focus on (1) the role of certain political agents enjoying a disproportionate measure of power in the international arena, and (2) the extent to which their efforts and schemes were regularly thwarted or were attempted to be outmaneuvered by other highly placed individuals in their own camp ('on their own side' seems sometimes an overstatement).

Although above I argue strongly that such explanations of events are radically incomplete, it is nonetheless the case that these agents of power played an irreplaceable role in the process. Drawing on the data in the texts cited, let us dwell specifically on how this was so. The importance of these considerations, I am proposing, is that they drive us to a much more comprehensive set of considerations than those typically considered by communication researchers or cultural studies' specialists, just as the materials in the previous section are tendentially disregarded by political scientists. It appears that a bedrock reality for Gorbachev and Shevardnadze was that the Soviet system could be reformed without risking disintegration – indeed, that the real threat of disintegration lay in the refusal to reform and to dispel *zastoi* (stagnation).

Simultaneously, US President Bush desired to build on the later (post-Reykjavik) legacy of Reagan, with Secretary of State Baker acting as his chosen instrument. What was decisive at that point was that Baker and Shevardnadze succeeded slowly and in fits and starts in building a rapport of trust and effective communication with each other, which put the circuitry in place to enable a resolution to be successfully generated. The decision to avoid any official US comment upon the Soviet Army's massacre of unarmed demonstrators in Tbilisi in April 1989, the decision in 1990 to act as behind-the-scenes mediator between Gorbachev and Landsbergis, Lithuanian independence leader, during the protracted stand-off between Vilnius and the Kremlin (Beschloss and Talbott, 1993: 51, 196ff.), both decisions calculated with a keen sense of the long-term stakes in a stable and uninterrupted transitional process, are only some instances of this circuitry and its importance.

These factors were, however, only one dimension of the process. For almost two generations, political leadership in the Federal German Republic, despite sometimes sharp conflicts of emphasis between Christian Democrats and Social Democrats, was essentially united in using Germany's medium of power – the deutschmark – to encourage *détente* through intensified economic ties, with a view to fostering eventual reunification of Germany. With this as the leitmotif of foreign policy toward the Soviet bloc, there was a fundamental basis for dialogue between the blocs that operated partly independently of the trajectory of the Cold War stand-off between the Soviet Union and the United States. An example of this German–Soviet process is the recognition of urgent Soviet-bloc need for extra finance, which began its official policy-life as an incentive carrot for peaceful co-existence under the heading of Basket 2 of the 1975 Helsinki Agreement.[12] Implementation of Basket 2 was far more marked in the Federal Republic than in any other nation.

As Ash notes (1993: 104), summarizing the 20 years of West German policy toward the Soviet bloc prior to its dissolution, 'From 1969–70 to 1989–90 the bankers and industrialists preceded and accompanied the diplomats and politicians on their way to Moscow, underpinning and facilitating their work' (ibid.: 365). In the end, he concludes, it was a mixture of Bonn's carrots and Washington's sticks, 'partly intentional and co-ordinated but also partly unintentional and conflictual, which produced the necessary mixture of incentive and deterrent, punishment and reward' (ibid.: 374). On occasion even, what began as a carrot – loans to the Polish State – ended up as a stick in the form of insistence on full and timely repayment during the martial law period 1981–85.

The active support given to *Solidarnosc*, often via Sweden, though unbeknownst it seems as the channel to Polish government officials, rose sharply from under US$200,000 channeled through the AFL–CIO in 1980 to $2 million in 1984, to $8 million in 1985 (Schweizer, 1994: 60, 76, 84–92, 146, 164–5, 184, 225). The amounts, though a miniscule proportion of the US budget, represented a newly aggressive – and dollar-for-dollar, very helpful – support of *Solidarnosc*. Much of the money went on communications equipment of one kind or another, from computers and fax machines to a highly sophisticated military-originated C3I (Command, Communications, Control, Information) installation for the movement's leadership.

The Polish case, however, raises a key question for this chapter's contention, inasmuch as it presents with particular clarity both a cultural and social movement dimension and an international power-struggle dimension. On the one hand, it is evidence for the impact of popular cultural forces;[13] on the other, those forces were enabled to communicate far more effectively through the intervention of an outside strategy, originating in an elite group inside the *verkhushka* of the US superpower.

Conclusions

Cultural studies has frequently been overweening in its ambitions. It has more and more sought to carve out for itself the status of a virtually distinct disciplinary approach, and it has claimed for itself in addition a certain cachet in some circles based on its radical political commitment. About the highly flawed quality of that latter claim I have little to say here, except that the academy generally has its hegemonic revenge over all such scholarly upsurges, including feminist studies, queer studies, postcolonial studies or marxist political economy, and that the uniquely distressing feature of such hegemony is the blithe self-assurance of the *évolué(e)s* in each of these areas that they have evaded its net.

As regards the claim of cultural studies to superior analytical punch, this essay has sought to provide evidence that while its approach is necessary, it is also radically insufficient on its own, empirically or conceptually, to handle societal issues. This is not intended as a body-blow, for the same could be said of political science or political economy. It is simply a much-needed retailoring. In particular, it is an argument that the Foucaultian democratization of power and the postmodernist evaporation of labor process and the cultural studies obsession with academic impressions of the evanescent popular, are all tangents of partial verity whose moments of impact are intermittent. Perhaps a stable, illustrated definition of 'articulation' might help to generate a framework within which the interpenetration and disjuncture of micro and macro, institutional and evanescent, and their intermediate terms, could begin to be theorized.[14]

At all events, much more is needed than simply a contented cow-like pluralism of analytical approaches, treading on no one's academic turf or toes. I would suggest that careful consideration of the data in this chapter underscores unequivocally the folly of treating power without culture/communication or communication/culture without power. To treat culture/communication only at the popular level or only at the elite level or only at the national level, or to treat any of the above without establishing their economic and military interconnections is to renege on our research and theoretical tasks.

Perhaps this is indeed more than one individual researcher can achieve with quality results, but in that case we need to change our approach: effective research needs to be organized in teams. As social scientists, we seem remarkably wedded to the un-sociological logistics of individual endeavor.

Notes

My thanks to Marjorie Ferguson for her editorial patience, and for her intellectual insights over many years; to her and Peter Golding and Vladimir Padunov for their helpful editorial advice; to Doug Kellner for his assistance at a key moment in the preparation of this chapter; and as ever, to Ash Corea for stimulus and support.

1 In a short chapter such as this, it may be difficult not to give an unintentional impression that these three nations were somehow homogenized from top to bottom during the Soviet period. Such an assumption is emphatically invalid, despite the similarity of their formal political and economic structures.

2 It is equally the case that any attempt to homogenize the protean literature of cultural studies is probably doomed to inanition. One could suggest that there are British, US, Latin American and Australian variants, or that there are more politicized versus more anthropological variants, but that is a subject for a different treatment. Here, for practical purposes, I have simply picked out what seems to me to be the kernel of these approaches, namely an intense, tendentially exclusive focus on popular culture and mass culture (see Grossberg et al., 1992).

3 Laclau (1979: 65) insisted the English translation as 'relative' is misleading, signifying 'partial' rather than 'relational'.

4 He says of Rastafarian ideology that 'it functioned so as to harness or draw to it sectors of the population', and a little later, 'One has to see the way in which a variety of social groups enter into and constitute for a time a kind of political and social force, in part by seeing themselves reflected as a unified force in *the ideology which constitutes them*' (Hall and Grossberg, 1986: 55, emphasis added). The fact he then immediately calls this a dialectical process does not help, because the word 'dialectical' still implies, in this setting, a process between two actors or consciously operating forces. To be fair, he also applies the term 'emerges' once to ideology, but this tends to contribute to the confusion, as does his veering back and forth between describing Rastafarian ideology as the product of different 'sectors' and 'other determinations' and yet as unified, product of a 'shared collective situation'.

5 All three books are authored by journalists, not by academic social scientists, but especially in the analysis of changes in Eastern Europe, serious journalism has to date made at least as informative a contribution as the academy, if not more so. While Schweizer's study is not helped by the author's cheerleading for the Reagan and Bush administrations, its data and argument are extremely important.

6 A graphic Russian portrayal of these domestic realities was provided in the 1988 film *Little Vera* (Lawton, 1992: 192–4).

7 Ost puts it rather well: '. . . although totalitarianism is a necessary tendency of a Leninist

party state, it cannot be achieved. And so the Party continually swings between a totalitarian tendency and a reform tendency, which recognizes that the state must interact with civil society rather than try to extinguish it' (1990: 39).

8 For a full analysis, readers are directed especially to the works cited, as well as to Ost (1990).

9 Space forbids a deeper analysis, but Kónrád (1984: 131) has offered some very suggestive comments on the characteristically Hungarian dynamic of the development of an alternative public sphere, sharply different from Poland's. See, too, Haraszti's *The Velvet Prison* (1987), a dissection of artistic self-censorship which perfectly reveals the special character of the Hungarian political dance in those years.

10 For example, the withering up of public communication was felt so intensely by one woman intellectual, an atheist of Jewish descent, that she regularly attended Catholic mass simply to hear a Polish spoken that was unpoisoned by regime-speak (panel, Center for Communication, New York City, 1982).

11 The fine studies by Condee and Padunov already referred to are a major exception to this rule. Their array of specifics and their tracing of shifts and eddies in the process, however, is so detailed that it is hard to address within the confines of a single essay.

12 A package of agreements concerning financial and trade relations, much less publicized than Basket 3, which concerned human rights.

13 There is no space here to explore this issue in detail, but it should at least be recalled that the Polish strike-wave in the first part of 1988, that deeply unsettled the regime, took *Solidarnosc* leaders by surprise. Schweizer's strictly external-factor analysis is reminiscent of those who explain the genesis of *Solidarnosc* by reference to the Pope's visit, or to Radio Free Europe.

14 And then again, perhaps not: a reading of Laclau and Mouffe's Long Tortuous March Out of Marxism (1985), which also deploys the term 'articulation' but not in ways that transcend Grossberg, suggests that perhaps the term should be decently laid to rest.

13

From Codes to Utterances: Cultural Studies, Discourse and Psychology

Michael Billig

Broadly speaking, the topic of cultural studies has been the critical analysis of ideology. Although Marx and Engels, in the *German Ideology*, claimed that the study of ideology should begin with the activity of 'real men' (1970: 42), the pages of cultural studies have tended to be devoid of recognizable women and men. Frequently, the 'culture', to be studied by cultural studies, has been represented by manufactured artifacts, such as magazines, films or academic books. Culture does not appear as something to be lived. The analyses themselves have often appeared remote from life. Stuart Hall, for example, has complained about the barbarous language and the 'overtheoreticism', which tends to 'pile up one sophisticated theoretical construction on top of another . . . without ever once touching ground and without reference to a single concrete case or historical example' (Hall, 1988a: 35; see also Hall, 1992). In consequence, cultural studies has often appeared to be a 'depopulated discipline' (Billig, 1994). Its pages tend not to present readers with the lives of people – their thoughts and feelings.

As will be suggested, cultural studies has not developed a psychological methodology which might be appropriate for studying how consciousness is constituted and reproduced in everyday life. Indeed, cultural studies has avoided the conventional methodologies of the social sciences. Certainly, surveys and other forms of inquiry requiring statistical analyses have been rare, almost to the point of non-existence. For much of its history, cultural studies has been suspicious of ethnography. Paul Willis alluded to this bias when he included a defensive justification of ethnography in his classic study, *Learning to Labour* (1977); it was as if he expected readers from a cultural studies' background to have taken against his type of investigation. An analysis of the television programmes, which Willis's 'lads' might have watched, or of the books which they would not have read, might have been in order. But hanging around with them, chatting and watching, was at that time theoretically suspect.

Now there seems to have been a reaction with, at last, a turn to ethnography. Feminist theorists, for example, have stressed the importance of the lived life, and the need to oppose the dominating abstractions of masculine rationalism with the details of women's oppressed lives (see, for example, Smith,

1991). Similarly, a number of analysts studying the mass media are recognizing that it is insufficient to 'read' audience reactions from the content of films and television programmes. Instead, the voices of audiences have to be directly heard (see, for example, Morley, 1993; Ang, 1991; Brunt, 1992; Moores, 1993). The suspicion against ethnography as a non-critical activity seems to have receded in cultural studies. The sort of defence, which Willis felt impelled to make nearly two decades ago, no longer appears necessary.

The turn to ethnography, however, should not be exaggerated; nor should it be thought to be a solution to all the problems of cultural studies. In the first place, ethnography is still very much a minority preoccupation. Virtually any issue of the journal *Cultural Studies* will confirm that the occasional ethnographic article is far outnumbered by theoretical and/or textual studies. This is unsurprising. The newly trained students in cultural studies are often better equipped to engage in critical literary analysis than to use the empirical methods of the social sciences. Furthermore, it takes far more time to immerse oneself in another way of life, than to comment on magazines or films. On occasions, the term 'ethnography' is being used loosely. Some of today's 'ethnographic' studies are barely ethnographic in the classic sense of being the product of extensive field work. Focus groups and interviews are also being bracketed as ethnographic. But, no matter: one should not quibble. The voices of people should be welcomed into the texts of cultural analysis, whether they are brought express via focus groups or on the luxury liners of ethnography.

The turn to ethnography brings into focus another set of problems, which, in broad terms, can be classified as defined as psychological. So long as cultural studies avoided studying people and their lives, it had little need to develop a critical psychology. Ethnographic analyses involve the investigation of people, rather than cultural products. As studies move from the products themselves to the role that such products play in the lives of consumers, then, in the broadest sense, psychological dimensions will become apparent. This is especially true for studies which seek to investigate the relations between audiences and media products. Such investigations will examine the ways that people think, speak and react. To do this satisfactorily, they will need some sort of social psychological frameworks of analysis.

To date, cultural studies has not evolved an adequate social psychology. Orthodox social psychology does not offer a framework that is adequate to the critical purposes of cultural studies: it tends to assume that psychological factors are theoretically predominant, rather than constructed within ideology. Nor can psychological questions be properly addressed merely by using smatterings of psycho-analytic terminology, imported via the opaque pages of Lacan. It will be suggested that those concerned for the future of cultural studies could do worse than pay attention to some of the new intellectual movements in social psychology. There are a range of new social psychologies, which are explicitly adopting a social constructionist view, insisting that psychological states, including both thoughts and emotions, are socially created (Gergen, 1994, 1995; Harré and Gillett, 1994; Shotter, 1993a, 1993b, 1995;

Moscovici, 1984, 1988). One particular variant of this social constructionist perspective is discursive or rhetorical psychology. This places particular emphasis upon the role of language in constructing psychological phenomena. As will be argued, the intellectual roots of this approach have more affinity with Bakhtin's approach to language, than with the sort of theorising derived from Foucault or Lacan that is currently popular within cultural studies. Moreover, this approach examines the operations of language in practice, rather than speculating abstractly. In consequence, this form of psychology, using the methodological techniques of discursive and conversational analyses, offers ways of investigating the detailed processes by which ideological consciousness is constituted within, and reproduced by, the ordinary language of life.

Language, utterance and psychology

The editors of the recent compendium *Cultural Studies* list a variety of methodologies which, they claim, are used within cultural studies. Their list is interesting for both what it includes and what it omits. The editors mention 'textual analysis, semiotics, deconstruction, ethnography, interviews, phonemic analysis, psychoanalysis, rhizomatics, content analysis, survey research' (Nelson et al., 1992: 2). As is apparent, there is no mention of psychology, or specifically psychological methodologies, although there is a reference to 'psychoanalysis', which itself bears further consideration. The few psychologists who have worked within the cultural studies' framework were largely ignored within the *Cultural Studies* compendium (see, for instance, how few and patchy are the references to the work of Valerie Walkerdine or Chris Griffin, and the scant attention paid to *Changing the Subject*, written by Henriques et al. (1984)).

By contrast, Nelson's list is heavy with methodologies for the study of language. This is unsurprising. A major theme in cultural studies has been to show how ideology is embedded and reproduced within discourses. Moreover, when cultural artifacts are treated as 'texts', then they can be analysed as if they were linguistic productions: their ideological grammar and syntax can be explored. Nevertheless, the methodologies of language, cited by Nelson et al., are revealing for their partiality. The included methodologies are not those which are devoted to analysing the specific usage of language, rather than language as a system. They do not take the utterance – or the speech-act – as their object of study. Even phonemic analysis, although based upon the study of speech, is not really concerned with analysing utterances, as, for example, made in everyday conversations. Conversation analysis, pragmatics, ethnomethodology, rhetoric and discursive psychology find no place in the editors' list. Nor do they figure in the compendium's various contributions, which, as the editors explain, were selected in order 'to identify the dimensions of cultural studies and its varied effects' (Nelson et al., 1992: 1). To use the famous Saussurian distinction, *la langue* is well represented, but *la parole*, or the use of language in practice, is absent. In this, the structuralist heritage of cultural studies is revealed.

The neglect of the utterance (as compared with the emphasis upon the 'structure' of language or discourse), taken together with the general neglect of psychology, seems to leave discursive psychology well outside the project of cultural studies. In discursive psychology, the utterance is of major significance, for it is through the study of utterances, as made in particular rhetorical contexts, that investigators can directly study the social constitution of psychological states. Although it is not possible to summarize here the various strands of discursive and rhetorical psychology, several key assumptions of this approach can be mentioned (for discussions of discursive psychology, see, *inter alia*, Antaki, 1994; Billig, 1991, 1996a; Edwards and Potter, 1992, 1993; Harré, 1995; Harré and Gillett, 1994; Potter and Wetherell, 1987; Shotter, 1995; Wetherell and Potter, 1992):

1 Discursive psychology assumes that language is of key importance in social life. Without language it would not be possible for humans to have the forms of life which they do; and without language these forms of life could not be reproduced.
2 Language is not to be construed as an abstract system, based upon hypothesized 'rules of grammar'. Language, above all, is something which is to be used. Thus, the conventional distinction between 'words' and 'actions' is misplaced. Most utterances in social life are actions.
3 Analysts of language should seek to examine what actions are being performed by particular 'speech-acts', and, also, how, in social life, actions are accomplished through utterances. Conversation analysis, for example, has shown how even routine, and apparently inconsequential, utterances can be accomplishing actions. For example, racists, in uttering racist remarks, are not merely representing an internalized schema of hatred, but they are doing things with their racist words (Billig, 1991; van Dijk, 1992; Wetherell and Potter, 1992).
4 In order to study 'speech-acts', it is necessary to study the use of language in its contexts, for utterances are context-bound, or 'occasioned'. The meaning of utterances, whether spoken or written, is bound up with their rhetorical contexts, especially if the utterances are involved in the business of justification and/or criticism. In this sense, utterances are not to be considered as unproblematic reflections of wider discourses or internal states, but their meaning is dependant upon their occasioned use.
5 Psychological states should not be presumed to lie *behind* the language but *within* it. Language, in fact, is used to constitute what are known as 'psychological states'. Therefore, in order to understand the constitution of psychological states, one should examine in detail the use of 'psychological' language. For instance, one might wish to study the social constitution of 'identities'. One should not presume that an identity is a hidden psychological state, as if there is a wordless, psychological or neurological state of 'having an identity'. Instead, investigators should examine how

people make claims about themselves – the groups to which they claim to belong and those to which they claim not to belong. Investigators should pay particular attention to what people are doing when making such claims (Billig, 1997a; Widdicombe and Wooffitt, 1995). In this respect, discursive psychologists urge investigators not to search for hidden, unobservable psychological entities, but to observe outward patterns of interaction and utterance.

6 There is a further development in discursive psychology, which could have significant implications for cultural studies and the critical examination of ideology. Language not only constitutes consciousness, but it also constitutes the unconscious. Thus, utterances are not only expressive, but they can also be repressive. It should be possible to examine routine uses of language in order to reveal how discursive habits enable certain things to be said, and others to be left unsaid. In this respect, patterns of speech can have repressive functions, constituting a 'dialogic unconscious', which can be observed directly in patterns of social interaction (Billig, 1997b).

Those working within the field of cultural studies might look askance at a psychology which seems to derive much of its impact from micro-sociological traditions, such as ethnomethodology and conversation analysis, which have generally avoided discussing ideology. Certainly, the majority of conversation analysts, and even some discursive psychologists, might not see their work as contributing specifically to the sorts of questions addressed by cultural studies. Nevertheless, some connections between the two strands of work can be made. This can be accomplished by using the ideas of Bakhtin as a link, especially those ideas to be found in *Marxism and the Philosophy of Language* (1973), published under the name of Volosinov, but thought by many to be the work of Bakhtin (see Clark and Holquist, 1984; Holquist, 1990; and Morris, 1994 for discussions of the authorship of *Marxism and the Philosophy of Language*). This book emphasized how both language and consciousness are created through ideological processes, and, therefore, the study of ideology involves examining how consciousness is constituted through the practical activity of communication. Bakhtin, like today's discursive psychologists, advocated constructing a psychology on the basis of the detailed analysis of actual language-usage.

Although most conversation analysts do not directly link their own work to Bakhtinian ideas, nevertheless those in cultural studies have sometimes claimed a Bakhtinian heritage, without always appreciating the full scope of Bakhtinian ideas in relation to psychology. Recently, Stuart Hall has suggested that *Marxism and the Philosophy of Language* had a 'decisive and far-reaching impact' on the work of the Birmingham Centre for Contemporary Culture Studies (Hall, 1996b: 295). He goes on to state that the book was appropriated 'narrowly' within cultural studies (ibid.: 298). According to Hall, cultural studies tended to take up the themes that ideology is semiotic and that language differences do not simply map on to class differences. On the other hand, Bakhtin's ideas about carnival were overlooked.

Hall might have added that two further themes tended to be neglected: these were the claim that consciousness was constituted through language, and the advocacy of studying utterances in detail in order to create a materially based social psychology. With the new developments in discursive psychology, it will be suggested that this social psychological project, whose outlines are to be found in *Marxism and the Philosophy of Language*, may now be more realizable than ever before. Moreover, this is occurring just at a moment when cultural studies, with its own ethnographic turn, needs an appropriate psychology.

Cultural studies and the neglect of utterances

There is little doubt that cultural studies was deeply influenced by the works of structuralist thinkers such as Althusser, Foucault and Lacan. The structuralist project, broadly speaking, searches for the hidden structures of social formations, which may not be apparent in the messiness of everyday interactions. A model of grammar informs many structuralist notions. Speakers of languages may not be able to articulate the grammatical rules which they follow in order to speak. Nevertheless, behind all speech performances lie the grammatical structure of the language. This grammatical structure permits the particular speaker to make utterances. It is not difficult to see why structuralist notions were attractive to Marxist thinkers. The analogy of grammatical structure could be applied to a hidden social structure. All societies have a structure, or an underlying economic grammar, which determines the details of life and culture. Once one can understand this grammar, then one can see its determining influence in particular cultural artifacts. Just as the texts of a society are surface productions of a deeper linguistic grammar, so they are also products of that society's underlying economic and class grammar.

The analogy has been a productive one, but its limitations can be seen in the structuralist treatment of language, which is very different from the approach taken by discursive/rhetorical psychology. Years ago, Bakhtin/Volosinov identified an 'idealist' tendency in the Saussurian approach to language: the details of language usage are overlooked, as the analyst searches for the hidden, unobservable codes or grammars. This tendency can be observed, for example, in the works of Foucault and Lacan. Both writers, despite their interest in language, neglect the utterance and this hinders Foucauldian and Lacanian analyses from filling the psychological gap (see Billig, 1996a, for a discussion of the ways rhetorical psychology differs from Foucauldian and Lacanian approaches).

Foucault, as is well known, takes 'discourses', and their historical creation, as his central topic. He writes of the 'dispersal' of discourses, such as those of economics, psychiatry, medicine, showing how these 'discursive formations' create their own regimes of truth and objects of knowledge. Rarely, however, does his analysis descend to the level of the utterance, in order to analyse particular speech-acts in their social and historical context. He himself is interested in wider patterns, especially the underlying structure of the discourses. Nevertheless, Foucault recognizes that the 'discourses' themselves are based upon statements: unless utterances are made, then there can be no identifiable discourses. In *The Archeology of Knowledge*, Foucault claims that 'we must grasp the statement in the exact specificity of its occurrence, determine its conditions of existence, fix at least its limits, establish its correlations with other statements that may be connected with it, and show what other forms of statement it excludes' (Foucault, 1974: 28). Despite this, Foucault's own *modus operandi* was situated at a much more general level, searching for the general 'discourse' which supposedly gives meaning to the specific statement. In this respect, Foucauldian notions of the 'discourse of economics' or the 'discourse of psychiatry' suggest that there is a discursive structure, a hidden *langue*, lying behind all the diverse utterances which might be made by economists or psychiatrists. It also suggests that this *langue* in some way produces, or determines, the utterances, which are surface manifestations of the deeper structure.

It is easy to assume that the discourse is the hidden agent, which determines, controls and positions the speaker. This discourse can never be apprehended directly – like *la langue*, it is only manifest in utterances. For example, a Foucauldian, who rather untypically recommends the social psychological analysis of utterances, writes that 'it would be misleading to say that we ever find discourses as such' for 'we find discourses at work in *texts*' (Parker, 1991: 6). The analyst looks for the coherent, structures of meaning in the text. By elaborating 'coherent statements out of the texts', the analyst is able to construct the discourses which 'inhabit' the texts (Parker, 1991: 16). If the analyst constructs the discourses out of textual statements, then it is circular to presume that these discourses determine the textual statements.

The problem was well expressed by Bakhtin in his criticism of Saussure's notion of *la langue*. In his essay 'The Problem of Speech Genres', Bakhtin accused linguistic theory of ignoring the '*real unit*' of speech communication', which was 'the utterance'. He explained: 'Speech is always cast in the form of an utterance belonging to a particular subject, and outside this form it cannot exist' (Bakhtin, 1986: 71, emphasis in original). Thus, the notion of a code, or a discourse, or a *langue*, existing as the determining cause of utterances, but only knowable through those utterances, is an idealist fiction. Due attention needs to be paid to the utterances – whether spoken or written – and the ways that these utterances always belong to particular, material contexts.

When Nelson et al. (1992) included psychoanalysis in their list of methodologies used within cultural studies, they were not referring to it as a therapeutic technique. No leading exponents of cultural studies are practising psychoanalysts. The 'psychoanalysis' to which Nelson et al. refer is a tendency to use psychoanalytic concepts, especially in textual analysis. Above all, Lacan is the psychoanalytic theorist who tends to be cited. The popularity of Lacan in cultural studies is an interesting topic in its own right, especially in the light of the debate among feminist writers whether his writings are radical or reactionary. There is no doubt that Lacan's writings have their own textual style, which is abstract, allusive and very different from Freud's. Freud, in his writings, presented his patients and their utterances. For example, in the famous case of 'Dora', Freud produces, albeit in a rhetorically directed format, the character of his patient, her circumstances and her words, together with his own interpretations, as well as Dora's own reactions to these interpretations (Freud, 1995). Dora, as well as her family, leap from the pages, as if characters in a novel. The descriptions and the reported speech, along with other accounts of the psychoanalytic conversations, provide the evidence for the claimed existence of the hidden subconscious world. Because of the details of persons and their words, later analysts, including Lacan himself, can offer further interpretations, rebutting or developing Freud's interpretations (see, for example, Bernheimer and Kahane, 1985).

Lacan's writings are very different from Freud's. His texts are aridly 'depop-ulated', remarkable for their lack of case studies. He rarely presents individuals. One can read page after page of Lacan without ever coming across a patient, nor, most crucially, anything a patient ever says. Thus, Lacan's evidence for his claims about hidden psychological structures is itself hidden from readers in a way that Freud's evidence is not. Significantly, Lacan's reinterpretation of Dora's case concentrates on elaborating the quadrilateral structure of relationships binding Dora, her father, her father's mistress and the latter's husband, who is a friend of Dora's father and con-stant harasser of Dora (Lacan, 1985; see also, Lacan, 1993: 90–2 and 175f.). Only someone who searches for hidden structures and overlooks the surface humanity could describe Dora – the youngest, most vulnerable of the four, bullied by her father and stalked by his friend – as a 'procurer' for her father (Lacan, 1979: 38). Whatever difficulties Freud may have had in listening to Dora's story, Lacan, encountering Dora as a textual creation of Freud's, is even deafer.

Lacan, in a famous phrase, claims that 'the unconscious is structured like a language' (Lacan, 1979: 20). The structure of language, to which Lacan refers, is not the structure of particular, analysable utterances. The structure of *la langue*, or language in general, is presumed to lie behind *la parole*, or uttered speech. Significantly, Lacan illustrates his famous dictum by citing Lévi-Strauss to suggest that anthropological sciences show that the structure of society exists before any individual or collective experiences. In the same pas-sage, he claims that the science of linguistics, 'which must be distinguished from any kind of psycho-sociology', reveals the structure of language and 'it is this linguistic structure that gives its status to the unconscious' (Lacan, 1979: 20–1). The activities of speech are not Lacan's concern: 'when he speaks the subject has the entire material of language at his disposal, and this is where concrete discourse is formed' (Lacan, 1993: 54). The entire material of language (which is the structured *langue*) is presumed to form the concrete discourse (or utter-ance). This entirety of language cannot be apprehended directly, yet it also matches the hidden structures of the unconscious. It is small wonder that Lacan's texts are so obscure and filled with poorly explicated diagrams and quasi-formulae. It is as if Lacan were trying to transcend uttered language in order to discover a hidden structure which is reflected in the hypothetical mirror of yet another hidden structure. And all the time, the only tools at his disposal are mere utterances. The study of the unconscious does not require such abstraction: it is possible to stay with the detail of actual utterances in order to explore the social creation of repression and the 'dialogic unconscious' (Billig, 1997b).

It is not immediately clear why such an abstracted thinker as Lacan should have been so influential in cultural studies. There is an ahistorical element in Lacanian thinking, especially when writing about the ways that individuals are created through being absorbed into the structure of language. The person is trapped by forces, which are presumed to be universally repeated, rather than which are the product of specific historical processes. As Stuart Hall (1988a) has written, Lacan's ideas address issues about language in general, rather than specific ideologies: 'There is all the difference in the world between the capacity to use Language *as such* and the appropriation and imaginary identity with particular *languages* and their specific ideological and discursive universes' (Hall, 1988a: 50). In consequence, argues Hall, specific political phenomena, such as Thatcherism and its ways of denoting Englishness, cannot be adequately explained 'by the transhistorical speculative generalities of Lacanianism' (ibid.: 50).

Lacan's sort of psychoanalytic theorizing offers the prospect of a de-psychologized psychology, or a psychology without people. Writers in cultural studies have not been slow to take advantage of this possibility. The unconscious, the mirror stage, *le petit autre*, can all float free, to be spotted in a film or television quiz show. This is part of a wider trend within cultural studies, not merely related to the adoption of Lacanian ideas. Instead of locating psychological feelings or thoughts with individuals, there has been a tendency to 'read off' psychology from cultural products. Texts are psychologized, as the analyst's reading postulates the psychological characteristics of (other) readers. For example, Kaplan (1987), having studied the content of MTV videos, presented a psychologized portrait of the viewer. She writes of 'a decentred, a-historical model spectator that mimics the cultural formation of contemporary teenagers appearing to live in a timeless but implicitly "futurized" present' (Kaplan, 1987: 27). The model spectator can be described as de-centred without any actual spectator appearing in the text and without knowing exactly what an actual spectator would have to say or do to count as being 'de-centred'.

Some of the most notable examples of such de-psychologized psychologizing occur in the writings of Frederic Jameson. On the basis of analysing contemporary cultural products, such as films, art and architecture, Jameson talks of a 'waning of affect' and the 'decentering' of the subject in the postmodern world (see, for example, Jameson, 1991 and 1992). The inference is made without analysing whether the citizens of the postmodern world are to be characterized by decentred egos or shallow emotions. It is as if the psychology inheres in the textual products themselves. One major contribution of

a turn to ethnography, especially if accompanied by a psychological awareness, will be to throw into doubt this sort of speculation about the psychology
of the postmodern world. 'Decentered egos' and 'waned affect', if they exist
anywhere, will exist in the actions and utterances of those who inhabit this
world.

The polysemic reaction against structuralism

The decentring of the ego is becoming an increasingly popular concept in
recent cultural studies. It marks a shift away from the abstracted psychology
of structuralist thinking to the equally abstracted psychology of poststructuralism. If the structuralist assumptions tended not to be rooted in close
observation of culture-as-lived and language-as-used, then nor are the poststructuralist assumptions. However, there has been a marked shift in one
important respect: the underlying force of ideology has been theoretically
weakened.

At the core of all ideology critique lies a dilemma. To the extent that ideology is depicted as being powerful, the dominated recipients of ideology
will appear as helpless dupes, being engulfed by that ideology. On the other
hand, the more that the recipients are depicted as showing independence of
mind, the feebler the powers of ideology will appear. The Foucauldian
approach loads the balance in favour of the powers of ideology. If discourses
are said to position subjects and to limit their powers of utterance, then those
subjects, whose very subjection is created through the prestructured discourses, appear as moulded dupes with few degrees of freedom. Their
utterances and their bodily responses are mere instantiations of the unseen,
controlling discourses. Similarly, Lacanian psychoanalysis points to the controlling force of the structure of language itself, creating the unconscious
which, in turn, determines conscious life.

There has been an understandable reaction within cultural studies against
this sort of determinism. Hall suggests that it is no longer acceptable to view
the masses as 'the dupes of history', for 'ruling or dominant conceptions of
the world do not directly prescribe the mental content of the illusions that
supposedly fill the heads of the dominated classes' (Hall, 1988a: 44). The
structuralist assumption that behind utterances there is a determining structure has been challenged by poststructuralist, deconstructionist theorists.
Language is seen as open-ended, not closed; texts are polysemic; the readers
create their own readings. The consumers of ideology, far from being rigidly
controlled in their thinking and speech, are now seen to be able to engage in
a free play of signification. Because analyses tend to be grounded neither in
a close observation of the use of language, nor in a realistic psychology, there
has been little to moderate this shift to the opposite theoretical extreme. The
cultural dupe exits left stage and, entering from the right, come the free
heroes and heroines of the semiotic consumer democracy.

John Fiske has championed this polysemic view of contemporary, popular culture. In *Understanding Popular Culture*, he suggests that popular culture cannot have a single meaning, but must permit different readings by different 'readers': 'To be popular, *Dallas*, for example, must offer complex and contradictory meanings about Americanness, about class, gender, and family, to name only a few' (Fiske, 1989b: 170). Cultural products will stimulate talk: 'The media and other cultural resources such as sport or shopping malls form one of the most common subjects of conversation in homes, the workplaces, social organizations, bars, or anywhere else people meet face to face' (ibid.: 174). Such talk is selective and productive, and, according to Fiske, it 'is read back into the media, so that the meanings and pleasures of a TV show, a football game, or a shopping trip are in part produced by conversation, both before and after the event, with others in one's social formation' (ibid.: 174).

Fiske goes on to suggest that there is a 'semiotic democracy', in which audiences appropriate their own meanings from the media (Fiske, 1987, 1989a, 1989b and 1992). Viewers, far from being the dupes of programmers, have the sovereign power to determine media meanings (for criticisms, see Morley, 1993, and his chapter in this volume; Murdock, 1989a). In *Reading the Popular*, Fiske discusses music videos. These, he argues, contain 'syntagmatic gaps'; 'readers' have to perform a vast amount of 'writing' to fill in the gaps. This places the reader 'in a more empowered authorial relationship with the text' (Fiske, 1989a: 121). The reader is able to shift the meanings of a text so that 'she produces her meanings and pleasure at the moment of reading the text' and 'this production is a direct source of power' (ibid.: 122). In this image of the powerful reader, ideology's power is correspondingly receding into the distance.

Nevertheless, the image of ideological power is not totally absent. The structuralist assumptions are shifted from audience to author. In *Reading the Popular*, Fiske discusses the limitations of authorship. Following Foucault and Barthes, Fiske declares the author, if not exactly dead, to have restricted powers. Authors merely rearrange a discourse which pre-exists them: 'The deep structure of the narration is determined, the outcome preset, and the author's authority limited to the transformations through which the deep structure is manifest and the outcome achieved' (ibid.: 89–90). In this way, the authorial utterance is downgraded, and the powers of deep structure promoted. Authorship is declared an illusion: 'Our postromantic culture still ascribes to the author a degree of power and self-determination that is both false and widely believed in' (ibid.: 90). Just a few pages later, when the focus has turned from writers to readers, authorship is not so impossible. Readers can be authors of their own readings; but authors cannot be authors of their own texts.

There are problems with such a stance. One sort of utterance (the authored text) is treated differently from other utterances (those of 'readers'). Intricate readings are performed by analysts in order to show how authored texts are limited by their deep structure. The conversational utterance, which is presumed to occur in the workplace, home or shopping mall, is not treated in the same way. Somehow, this talk, unanalysed in any detail, is presumed to signify power and freedom. But what if such talk still reflects the illusions of our 'postromantic culture' – if speakers reveal that they believe in the traditional powers of authorship? Can such illusions be empowering?

If, as Bakhtin (1986) claimed, speakers are authors of their utterances, and, indeed, through their utterances, people are authors of their own lives, then is not the authorship of ordinary life just as ideologically limited – or as ideologically free – as the authorship of texts? Might there not also be a parallel illusion? Speakers might falsely think that they are the masters of their own words in conversations. Through the talk about shopping, football and mass-produced television programmes, the sounds of ideology might be heard, at least if analysts were listening. On the other hand, might not such conversations also show the spark of creativity, for people are continually saying things, and thereby formulating thoughts, which neither they, nor others, have ever uttered before?

Clearly, there are issues which are unresolved in Fiske's images of speakers' semiotic democracy and writers' imprisonment within the constraints of discourse. That the same author can formulate both images – and within a few pages of the same piece of writing – suggests that it is the nature of verbal communication itself which may have been untheorized. If that is the case, then such issues will only be capable of resolution by paying close attention to the nature and rhetoric of utterances, both spoken and written.

Ideology, psyche and language

Fiske's contrasting images of author and speaker express both sides of the basic dilemma of ideological analysis. To the extent that ideology is seen to be a powerful code, its subjects appear as robotic dupes. If the subjects are depicted as freely creative, then the power of ideology is theoretically diminished. Far from being something which is abstractly remote, this dilemma is reproduced in the very act of utterance. Any speaker, in using language for a speech-act, must repeat words which are not of their making; yet in speaking, people are formulating their own utterances, saying things which have never been said before in response to new conversational situations. Barthes wrote that the speaker is 'both master and slave' of language. Within each sign there 'sleeps that monster: a stereotype'. The speaker, in using the words of language, cannot but reawaken the sleeping monsters. Yet, the speaker does more than repeat stereotypes: 'I am not content to repeat what has been said, to settle comfortably in the servitude of signs: I speak, I affirm, I assert *tellingly* what I repeat' (Barthes, 1982: 460).

Volosinov argued that the material study of ideology necessitated the study of language in action, for the word is 'the most suitable material for viewing the whole of this problem (i.e. ideology) in basic terms' (Volosinov, 1973: 19). Therefore, to understand ideology, the analyst should study 'unofficial discussions, exchanges of opinion at the theatre or a concert or at various types of social gatherings, purely chance exchanges of words . . .' and so on (ibid.: 19–20). These exchanges, which mirror Fiske's conversations at the workplace or in the shopping mall, would, according to Volosinov, reveal 'ideological creativity' (ibid.: 19) and would exhibit 'an extraordinary sensitivity to all fluctuations of social atmosphere' (ibid.: 20).

In such remarks, Volosinov was expressing a number of themes which are directly relevant to the contemporary study of ideology. He was affirming the importance of language in ideology – or that 'the word accompanies and comments on each and every ideological act' (ibid.: 15). Language is not an abstract, static system but it exists through use. By usage it is constantly changing, for speech-acts do not exactly reproduce previous acts. This implies that ideology, because it is realized in acts of language, is also in a state of constant change, or creativity. Yet, at the same time, these acts of language are shaped by the social and historical context.

There is a further, psychological theme, which Volosinov stressed. The study of ideology was also the study of consciousness. To understand this, it was necessary to be clear about the relations between language and consciousness. Language did not reflect inner psychological states, which were themselves unobservable. Instead, psychological states, and consciousness, were socially and materially constituted through the acts of language and, thereby, through ideology. In this way, psychological phenomena were not internal events, which could not be studied directly. As Volosinov argued, 'social psychology in fact is not located anywhere within (in the 'souls' of communicating subjects) but entirely and completely *without* in the word, the gesture, the act' (ibid.: 19). As such, social psychology is 'made up of multifarious *speech performances*', such as those of little, unofficial conversations (ibid.: 19, emphasis in original).

Such remarks contain a crucial insight about the sort of social psychology which can reveal the workings of ideology in everyday patterns of behaviour and thought. This psychology should be rooted in the study of language use. It should not presume that the psychological elements of ideology are constituted within unobservable, inner psychic structures, which are forever locked within the head of the person. Quite the reverse: the inner life is constituted by the outer activity of communication.

Precisely the same assumptions are made by contemporary discursive and rhetorical psychologists, who argue that the topics of social psychology are not mysterious, inner 'processes' or 'structures' which accompany outer behaviour. Instead, the traditional topics of psychology are, by and large, constituted within social and discursive activity. Thus, 'attitudes', which have dominated the subject matter of social psychology, are not internal schemata, but are outwardly displayed stances in matters of controversy. Psychologists, interested in 'attitudes' should be studying the ways in which people offer opinions and what they are doing when opinions are offered (Edwards and Potter, 1993; Billig, 1991; Potter and Wetherell, 1987). The focus is shifted from hypothetical psychological events, supposedly taking place within the isolated individual psyche, to historically situated and socially created psychological states. Thus, to understand a particular individual's attitudes, one must understand the public controversies, about which people might be socially expected to 'hold attitudes'. In this way, individual psychology becomes socially situated. The same is true for other psychological topics. For example, to understand memory, one should not presume that remembering takes place within a series of unobservable, inner 'memory structures', located within the individual's head. Psychologists should be examining how in everyday life people conduct the social activities which are said to constitute 'remembering'; how memories are contested; what people are doing when they claim to remember and to forget and so on. In this way, it is possible to understand the social creation of remembering and to appreciate how this creation takes place, above all, through the use of language (Edwards and Potter, 1993; Billig and Edwards, 1994; Billig, 1996b; Middleton and Edwards, 1990). This is particularly important for the study of collective memory, as, for example, when a nation, in its rituals, claims to remember jointly, or co-memorate, its national past (Billig, 1995).

By the same token, the processes of thinking are not to be considered as inherently unobservable. They can, for instance, be observed directly in conversational dialogue, where the interchange is so immediate that it is unrealistic to presume that each utterance is the reflection of an inner, formulated thought (Billig, 1991). There is a further point which ties the new discursive psychology to Bakhtinian ideas. Internal thinking is intimately connected with dialogue, being itself modelled upon publicly observable dialogue and frequently taking the form of an internal debate. In this sense, much thinking can be said to be inherently rhetorical and dialogic (Billig, 1996a; Shotter, 1992, 1993a, 1993b). In addition, in talking of one topic, one is not talking, by definition, of other topics. Through the shared moral codes which underwrite dialogue, one can observe how the routines of talk can function to keep certain matters from the discursive agenda. In this respect, the processes of repression can be seen to be dialogically based (Billig, 1997b). Given that ideology functions to make the contingent world appear as 'natural' and inevitable, then the repressive aspects of dialogue are as ideologically important as the expressive ones.

The implication is that mental states – including emotional ones, and possibly unconscious ones too – are socially and ideologically constituted. The social construction of psychological states should be a key assumption for any sort of psychology, which is suitable for cultural studies, especially in relation to the study of media. Such a psychology should guard against the temptation to assume that the 'real' psychological business is always occurring just out of sight (or earshot). For example, ethnographers may ask people what they think and feel when they watch particular programmes. The researchers might then feel tempted to treat these accounts as signs of what was *really* going on in the mind of the person at the precise moment of reception – as if the presumed 'coding' of information, received through the senses, were the real locus of psychological events. The ethnographer may even attempt to record the moment of reception, paying attention to any remarks which viewers might spontaneously utter when watching their programmes. Again, there is the temptation to treat the remarks as the outward signs of the hidden internal events, as if the internal event, at the very moment of reception, held the key to understanding the power of the media.

Volosinov's remarks on the nature of social psychology – together with the outlook of contemporary discursive psychologists – should caution against tendencies to search for hidden psychological 'processes'. Utterances and accounts should be considered in themselves: they are the phenomena of social psychology, not the second best approximations for the 'real', but hidden, psychological events. Take, for instance, someone exclaiming 'I think that's rubbish', while watching a television programme. The remark is not usually understood as the report of an inner event: an individual, making such a remark, is not typically reporting that they have had a particular experience – the sensation of rubbishness – which they are now informing others about. What the speaker is doing depends on the context of utterance, including the interaction with those addressed by the remark; the remark needs to be understood in relation to previous and subsequent conversational utterances. For example, the remark might be addressed to fellow family-members who are enjoying the programme. A discourse analyst would pay particular attention to the words uttered by the fellow watchers to examine whether the remark is being 'heard' as a criticism of themselves and whether subtle family-business is being done. In such exchanges, as Volosinov well appreciated, ideology will scarcely be absent.

It should be said that some important concepts of cultural studies bear traces of the very sort of 'psychic idealism', against which Volosinov argued. Stuart Hall's imaginative and influential analysis of the encoding and decoding of television programmes is a case in point (Hall, 1980c). As Morley (1993) has pointed out, there is a lack of clarity about the central notions of 'code' and 'coding'. Because subsequent analysts have tended to take the notions of 'codes' and 'decoding' without relating them to the practices of audiences (or what Volosinov called 'behavioural ideology'), the ambiguities have not been resolved. For example, it is not clear whether the decoding is intended to refer to mental processes. Decoding would then be understood psychologically in terms of the matching of media messages to what Hall calls 'meaning structures' (another ambiguous term). These 'meaning structures' are presumably internalized codes of some variety or another. 'Coding', thus, would not be an activity which was observable in itself, but would only be hypothesized from participants' accounts about their reactions to programmes. Inevitably, such a notion of encoding is drifting towards the sort of processes which orthodox cognitive psychologists assume to lie behind outward behaviour. And just as inevitably, the resulting psychology drifts into the sort of psychic idealism, which Volosinov challenged over half a century ago and which discursive psychologists are criticizing today.

It would be no improvement to give 'code' a discursive interpretation, by suggesting that the code is the deep structure of the discourse, and that particular texts (or utterances, or media programmes) need to be matched to the code. This would seem to invite a 'linguistic idealism', which also opens the door to psychological idealism, should actual audiences ever be considered. It would suggest that audiences understand programmes by decoding the particular utterances into the underlying discursive code, and that their accounts about their viewing are themselves manifestations of this code. Instead, the accounts should be taken as the topic themselves. They are not signs of encoding or interpreting. They *are* interpretations – and their meaning needs to be understood in relation to the contexts of their utterance. As such, it might be simpler all round to omit the notion of 'code' and 'codings' and to concentrate upon 'accounts' and 'accountings'.

In the accounts which participants give about television programmes, analysts should not be expecting to find either the pure freedom of a polysemic democracy or the total, uncreative reproduction of an orthodox ideology. Both images misunderstand the nature of communication and ideology. Instead, there is in every utterance, as Volosinov/Bakhtin constantly emphasized, a dialectic of constraint and creativity. Bakhtin, in *The Dialogic Imagination* (1981), was to characterize this dialectic as the opposition between centripetal (conformist) forces and centrifugal (creative) ones. Both forces, he argued, are present in every utterance. As such, each utterance is not to be labelled as either purely conformist or radical, conservative or creative; instead, the analyst must show the contrary forces, or the basic dialectic of communication within each utterance. No theoretical guide can calculate the balance of the dialectic for any actual act. The constraints and creativities must be weighed in their particularities on each occasion.

The resulting analyses should be simultaneously psychological and ideological, for the details of discursive interaction can reveal ideological thinking in practice. For example, accounts about the reception of media can be informative, not as true or false descriptions about the hypothetical moments of reception, but in terms of the ways which audiences represent themselves and their own relations to the media. Billig (1992) describes a study in which British families talked about the Royal Family, often arguing among themselves as they did so. In talking of the media, people often gave 'methodological accounts' about how they themselves read the newspapers. Frequently, they claimed to be critical readers who 'read between the lines'. The point is not whether or not these accounts were accurate records of the way the speakers actually read the papers. Their value lies in what the speakers were doing when making their claims. Above all, they were claiming a critical independence for themselves, while they criticized the 'bias' of the media. Yet, in making these claims they were demonstrating that they were absorbing the very information which they claimed to distrust: often they warranted their knowledge about royalty by claiming that they had read the 'fact' in the papers. Typically, such speakers contrasted themselves with 'others', the uncritical readers, who might be identified as other members of the family or members of classes, conceived to be lower in the social hierarchy. In such utterances, the speakers were claiming for themselves an independent ego – itself a highly ideological and historical construct. As they were making such claims, they were reproducing ideological notions which were locating themselves not as pure independent, critical spirits, but as subjects within a monarchy and within a wider commercial market, in which, typically, they themselves occupied disadvantaged places. That is not all. At the same time, these remarks, uttered in the family home, would be accomplishing little bits of family business – the remarks about uncritical 'others' might be accompanied by sly digs about gender and age intended for targets close to home. In this way, a whole complex of ideological themes – messy, contradictory and highly rhetorical – were contained within, and reproduced by, these little remarks.

Context and ideology

Volosinov emphasized that utterances need to be understood in terms of their immediate context. Bakhtin, in his self-ascribed works, developed the point by stressing that utterances are typically responses to other utterances. In this respect, they are dialogic, in that their meaning depends upon the wider dialogue in which they occur. The meaning cannot be 'read off' from a 'structure' or 'code' considered in isolation from actual dialogues. This position has methodological implications. Utterances should be studied in relation to their immediate, dialogic context, in order to see what conversational, or dialogical business, the utterer is performing.

At this point, students of cultural studies might have misgivings. Such a methodological injunction might be seen to be drawing attention away from the sort of critical and historical analyses, and replacing them by detailed interpersonal analyses. By such a change of focus, the critical edge of cultural studies might be lost. After all, it might be said that experts in conversation analysis and ethnomethodology, by concentrating on the details of interpersonal communication, rarely produce the socially critical analysis to which cultural studies has always aspired. As Heritage (1984) has claimed, conversation analysis has put the details of interaction under the sociological microscope. The question is whether the broader, historical sweep, which is so necessary for critical ideological analysis, can be captured, mounted and stained upon the microscope's slides.

However, the very question implies that there is inevitably a methodological – and indeed theoretical – conflict between analyses of the immediate and the ideological contexts of utterances. There is no need to presume the inevitability of such a conflict. Volosinov wrote that all utterances are conditioned simultaneously 'by the social organization of the participants involved and also by the immediate conditions of their interaction' (Volosinov, 1973: 21). The message is not that one has to choose to study one or the other form of context. Rather it is that both forms have to be understood in relation to each other.

All too often in cultural studies, this is not appreciated. Utterances sometimes are taken out of their immediate context, in order to be ascribed ideological significance, in terms of a hypothesized ideological discourse or code. The result is a less ideological analysis than would have been achieved had the utterance been studied in terms of its immediate, dialogic context. An illustration can be briefly given; it comes from an author who recognizes the necessity of studying utterances in their context. John Hartley (1992) has accused David Morley of reifying and decontextualizing the accounts given by television audiences (Morley, 1980; see also, for example, Brunt, 1992; Jancovich, 1992). According to Hartley, Morley discounts the situation in which audiences were viewing and speaking about their programmes in order to read 'class-codes' into their comments: 'For Morley, the "cultural and linguistic codes a person has available to them" is not a matter affected by the "situation" in which those persons are watching a programme' (Hartley, 1992: 107). It may be justified to claim that Morley did not pay sufficient attention to the situated nature of his respondents' accounts (and Morley (1993) himself has offered a careful reassessment of his study). However, Hartley's own analysis reveals the lack of a framework for studying the situated nature of utterances. Using the Foucauldian notion of 'regime', Hartley claims that television executives have a 'paedocratic regime': the professionals 'paedocratize' audiences, treating them as childlike. In evidence, Hartley cites, at second-hand, several comments by producers and directors. Significantly, he makes no attempt to situate these comments in order to examine the contexts of their utterance. Hartley does not attempt to reconstruct the rhetorical meaning of the comments: this would involve situating them in their dialogic context and showing the counter-positions (or antilogoi) against which the producers' utterances might have been rhetorically directed (Billig, 1996a). As such, Hartley shows what Bakhtin termed the 'disregard for the active role of the other in the process of speech communication' (Bakhtin, 1986: 70).

Hartley treats the decontextualized comments as if they were signs for the existence of the 'regime'. He ignores the very real possibility that the same speakers will talk about audiences in very different ways under other circumstances. The rhetorical variability of speech is one of the key assumptions of discursive psychology, separating it from traditional attitude theory, which presumes that social actors tend to have limited ways of responding (Billig, 1991, 1996a; Edwards and Potter, 1992, 1993; Potter and Wetherell, 1987). In Hartley's example, one might imagine what the producers might have said had their own work been threatened by censorship, or if they were appearing face-to-face in front of approving audiences. Then, they might be able to switch from the dismissive metaphors of audience-childishness to talk about audience-discernment. It would be just as methodologically unsound to dissociate such utterances from their dialogical contexts, and then to claim them as evidence for the existence of an 'adultocratic regime'.

The immediate context of an utterance is not something which necessarily stands outside ideology. If the dynamics of power operate within ideology, so too they can be observed on a micro-level. This is something which was stressed by Foucault and which, of course, is a central theme of much feminist analysis within the social sciences. An analysis of ethnographic accounts can reveal the micro-processes of power, but this would require a more sustained analysis of contexts than is typical in cultural studies. For this, some of the techniques of conversation analysis might be useful. In her analysis of the audiences of the television soap, *Crossroads*, Dorothy Hobson (1980) presented parts of her interview transcripts with women talking about the television programmes that they watched (see also Hobson, 1982). Unusually, Hobson used some of the transcription notations of conversation analysis. One of her arguments was that women rejected programmes which they saw as being masculine, such as news programmes. They felt that their husbands had a right to watch such programmes. It would be possible to reinterpret some of the material, adding insights from conversation analysis which treats pauses and hesitations as conversationally meaningful (Atkinson and Heritage, 1984). The reinterpretations would place the utterances in their own discursive context, and enrich, rather than undermine, the ideological analysis of power.

In this case, one can see how the dynamics of class might affect interaction, reproducing working-class uncertainty in the face of bourgeois cultural confidence. 'Anne' recounts, in answer to a question, the programmes she watches. The interviewer comments: 'This is all on ITV, isn't it?' There is a long pause, followed by: 'Yes, er . . . yes, that's another programme. *Whose Baby?*' (Hobson, 1980: 110). When asked whether she watches the news, there are again hesitations, followed by a lengthy justification of why she does not watch the news. Here is not the place to re-analyse the interview, except to say that conversation analysts have often seen hesitations as signs of 'dispreferred responses', and justificatory answers as indications that questions are being taken as bearing criticisms (Potter and Wetherell, 1987; Edwards and Potter, 1992, 1993; Heritage, 1988; Pomerantz, 1984). The interview may not merely provide evidence of what occurs in Anne's home when the television set is switched on. The details of the transcript can be understood as showing the difficulties, or the embarrassments, of a working-class woman discussing her preferences with a middle-class academic, albeit a sympathetic woman. The question about 'ITV' can be read as an implicit challenge, as if the interviewed woman has revealed that none of her preferred programmes are on the higher status BBC: her hesitant response, and offering of another programme, suggests that the question was being heard to bear an implicit criticism. It must be emphasized that the 'real' intentions of the interviewer are irrelevant to this analysis. If this is correct, then the ideological downgrading of working-class women's tastes is instantiated in the uttering of the accounts themselves; indeed, the working-class woman herself is collaborating discursively in this downgrading. In this way, ideology marches through the hesitations and the pauses of utterances.

Recoding codings

It was suggested earlier that there might be theoretical advantages in shifting from the notion of 'codes' to that of 'accounts'; the analyst would not seek the audience's potentially unobservable 'encodings', but would attempt to analyse the accounts given by the audience. The notion of code was central to Stuart Hall's classic paper published in 1980. One of the major strengths of Hall's encoding paper was its insistence that audiences do not find themselves on a level field of interpretation: not all 'decodings' of media products are equally likely. There are 'preferred readings' (the parallel with the conversation analytic concept of 'preferred responses' remains to be explored). Hall, in developing a distinction proposed by Parkin (1972), distinguished between three different codes: the 'dominant code' which represented the view of the *status quo*, the 'negotiated code' which expressed a limited challenge, and the 'oppositional code' which constituted a direct opposition to the established order. Since it is not completely clear what a code is, it might be simpler to retranslate codes into accounts, so that one might distinguish between dominant, negotiated and oppositional accounts.

The division between the three different sorts of accounts should be treated as a rough heuristic. They should not be seen as mutually exclusive 'systems of discourse'. To use Bakhtinian terms, language is never a straightforward 'code' or 'system'; but in its usage it is marked by 'heteroglossia' or a multiplicity of voices. The same language embraces different genres, themes, moods etc., permitting the expression of contrary themes and enabling argumentation to occur. Discussions, whether in the workplace or the home, are only possible because speakers of the same language can use that language to make contrary utterances (Billig, 1996a). As Volosinov stressed, it is not the case that some members of society will speak one code, with its particular set of ideological meanings, and another will speak a totally separate code, for the 'various classes will use one and the same language' (Volosinov, 1973: 23). Instead, each ideological sign bears the characteristic of 'multiaccentuality' for 'each living ideological sign has two faces' (ibid.: 23). Volosinov explained: 'any current curse word can become a word of praise, any current truth must inevitably sound to many other people as the greatest lie' (ibid.: 23).

By the same token, the notion of an all-exclusive, dominant ideology is a simplification, if it is understood as a force which drives all other possibilities and meanings from consciousness. It is a mistake to think of ideologies as unitary constructions. Ideologies contain contrary themes, for if they were unitary, they would not provide ideological subjects with the means of rhetoric, discussion and thought: for the 'subjects' of ideology think *within* the ideology, rather than fail to think at all (Billig et al., 1988; Steinberg, 1994). The dialogic nature of ideology is reflected in the detail of utterances. Again Bakhtinian notions about the dialogical and rhetorical nature of utterances may help guard against reification. Bakhtin stressed that utterances were not 'pure', but contained mixed themes and meanings. Each utterance is typically a response to another, and thus bears its traces. A rhetorical theory of meaning is suggested: the meaning of any utterance, or piece of logos, must be understood in terms of its dialogical context, and this means in terms of the anti-logos, which it seeks to counter (Billig, 1996a).

In consequence, 'dominant accounts' will not simply be dominant messages, as expressions of a powerful, unitary 'code'. They will be utterances, produced for particular purposes by powerful forces; they will have dialogic functions, seeking to combat or refute opposing accounts. In this, they will bear traces of the messages which they seek rhetorically to exclude. As such, accounts have the characteristic of 'intertextuality', echoing other accounts, other meanings, and thereby revealing themselves as not utterly dominating (Fairclough, 1992). The dominance – or rather the depth – of an ideology may be revealed in the unnoticed, small words which seem beyond rhetorical challenge and which are routinely and widely repeated; for example, the assumptions of nationhood are daily transmitted and discursively reproduced in little words, which themselves are routinely beyond the focus of conscious attention, rather as the flag hanging outside a public building is unnoticed by the passing crowds (Billig, 1995).

In some respects, the threefold division into dominant, negotiated and oppositional accounts may be more suited for societies in which dominating segments have a greater social and ideological stability than is the case in advanced capitalism. Certainly, the condition of advanced capitalism, strengthening its position globally, has not been marked by the growing triumph of a single mode of thinking. The media today testify to the existence of an expanding, market-driven heteroglossia. An unprecedented Babel of different voices can be heard nightly on television sets; it is available to audiences regardless of class background. Never before in history do people hear such discursive variety so regularly. It is no wonder that the same person can effortlessly switch, in the course of a conversation, from radical to conservative themes, for both are part of the contemporary kaleidoscope of common-sense (Billig, 1992).

In this situation, the appearance of debate and controversy is not necessarily a sign of opposition; nor is negotiation necessarily a challenge to dominance, albeit of a limited kind. The sounds of negotiation, argument and rhetorical creativity are part of the economic ordering. The media, far from attempting to create uncritical responses, frequently seek to create debate, for the 'controversial' argument is very much part of television programming (Livingstone and Lunt, 1994). In this way, polysemy can be the programmed intention, which itself responds to the market forces of the media. In giving their accounts, speakers may present themselves as critical egos, challenging orthodoxies and contrasting themselves with imagined, docile others. Mass circulation tabloid newspapers, whose sales are crucial to the commercial fortunes of international multi-media empires, encourage such responses. They frequently invite readers to take stances in debates, whose terms and limitations are presented; moreover, they present their own editorial voices as being iconoclastic and controversial, while simultaneously claiming to be guardians of the national heritage (Taylor, 1991).

The construction of 'polysemy', or the 'polyphonia of controversy' should not be surprising. The noisy appearance of controversy and radicalism is being produced through economic structures which constantly need to revolutionize their own products and their means of production. New voices, new controversies, new attacks on the old-fashioned are constantly demanded. In a world where the market structures must be revolutionized to be maintained, the rhetorics of conservatism and radicalism will not be neatly separated. Conservatives will claim the rhetoric or revolution, while socialists, on occasions, will present themselves as the defenders of tradition. The claims and counter-claims will echo each other. Denunciation is not necessarily a rhetorical force for radicalism. As Murray Edelman (1977) wrote in a brilliant analysis, which has been unjustly ignored by cultural studies, today's politicians deplore injustice, not to change things, but to maintain them.

In the face of such a Babel, the analyst needs to keep a sense of proportion. It is important not to be swept along by delight that today we have so many heteroglossic, or polysemic, possibilities, as if all has become free and unrestrained. On the other hand, it would wrong to see the hidden force of a constraining structure behind the heteroglossia: more voices mean more argumentative possibilities. In itself, this is nothing new, although the extent and speed of change might be unprecedented. The basic conditions were acutely described by Gramsci over 60 years ago. The mass of humanity, he wrote, does not have a consistent, unified conception of the world. Instead, their thinking is filled by diverse and contradictory bits and pieces of common-sense: 'It contains Stone Age elements and principles of a more advanced science, prejudices from all past phases of history at the local level and intuitions of a future philosophy which will be that of a human race united the world over' (Gramsci, 1971: 324). The last phrase is crucial and needs to be stressed: the Babel, somewhere in the din of its speaking voices, contains the rhetorical seeds of its own transcendence.

Bibliography

All references and citations are included. Where authors have cited different editions, both are included for reference.

Abercrombie, N., S. Hill and B.S. Turner (1980/84) *The Dominant Ideology Thesis*, 2nd edn. London: George Allen and Unwin.

Adorno, T.W., E. Frenkel-Brunswick, D.J. Levinson and R. Nevitt Sandford. (1950) *The Authoritarian Personality*. New York: Norton.

Alasuutari, P. (1992) 'I'm ashamed to admit it, but I have watched Dallas', *Media, Culture and Society* 14 (4): 561–82.

Albats, Y. (1994) *The State Within a State: The KGB and its Hold on Russia – Past Present and Future*. New York: Farrar, Straus, Giroux.

Alberoni, F. (1972) 'The powerless elite: theory and sociological research on the phenomenon of the stars', pp. 75–98 in D. McQuail (ed.), *Sociology of Mass Communications*. Harmondsworth: Penguin.

Alexeyeva, L. (1985) *Soviet Dissent: Contemporary Movements for National Religious and Human Rights*. Middletown, CT: Wesleyan University Press.

Althusser, L. (1971a) 'Ideology and ideological state apparatuses', pp. 121–80 in L. Althusser, *Lenin and Philosophy and Other Essays*. London: New Left Books.

Althusser, L. (1971b) *Lenin and Philosophy and Other Essays*. London: New Left Books.

Althusser, L. and E. Balibar (1970) *Reading Capital*. New York: Pantheon Books.

Anderson, B. (1983) *Imagined Communities: Reflections on the Origin and Spread of Nationalism*. London and New York: Verso.

Ang, I. (1985) *Watching Dallas*. London: Routledge/New York: Methuen.

Ang, I. (1990) 'Culture and communication: towards an ethnographic critique of media consumption in the transnational media system', *European Journal of Communication* 5 (2): 239–60.

Ang, I. (1991) *Desperately Seeking the Audience*. London: Routledge.

Ang, I. and J. Hermes (1991) 'Gender and /in media consumption', pp. 307–29 in J. Curran and M. Gurevitch (eds), *Mass Media and Society*. London: Edward Arnold.

Antaki, C. (1994) *Explaining and Arguing*. London: Sage.

Arendt, H. (1958) *The Human Condition*. Chicago: University of Chicago Press.

Ash, T.G. (1993) *In Europe's Name: Germany and the Divided Continent*. London: Jonathan Cape.

Atkinson, J.M. and J. Heritage (1984) *Structures of Social Action*. Cambridge: Cambridge University Press.

Atkinson, P. (1990) *The Ethnographic Imagination: Textual Constructions of Reality*. London: Routledge.

Bachkatov, N. and A. Wilson (1988) *Les enfants de Gorbatchev: la jeunesse Soviétique parle*. Paris: Calmann-Lévy.

Bahro, R. (1978) *The Alternative in Eastern Europe*. London: New Left Books.

Bakhtin, M.M. (1981) *The Dialogic Imagination*. Austin: University of Texas Press.

Bakhtin, M.M. (1986) *Speech Genres and Other Late Essays*. Austin: University of Texas Press.

Bakhtin, M.M. and P.M. Medvedev (1928/1985) *The Formal Method in Literary Scholarship: A Critical Introduction to Sociological Poetics*. Cambridge, MA: Harvard University Press.

Barker, M. and A. Beezer (1992) 'Introduction: what's in a text?', pp. 1–20 in M. Barker and A. Beezer (eds), *Reading into Cultural Studies*. London and New York: Routledge.

Barnhurst, K. and E. Wartella (1991) 'Newspapers and citizenship: young adults' subjective experience of newspapers', *Critical Studies in Mass Communication* 8 (2): 195–209.

Barrett, M. (1992) 'Words and things: materialism and method in contemporary feminist analysis', pp. 201–20 (261–79) in M. Barrett and A. Phillips (eds), *Destabilising Theory: Contemporary Feminist Debates*. Oxford (Cambridge): Polity Press.

Barthes, R. (1977) *Image, Music, Text*. London: Fontana.

Barthes, R. (1982) 'Inaugural lecture, College de France', pp. 457–78 in S. Sontag (ed.), *A Barthes Reader*. London: Jonathan Cape.

Baudrillard, J. (1981) *For a Critique of the Political Economy of the Sign*. St Louis, MO: Telos Press.

Baudrillard, J. (1983) *Simulations*. New York: Semiotext.

Bell, D. (1976a) *The Coming of Post-Industrialist Society*. Harmondsworth: Penguin.

Bell, D. (1976b) *The Cultural Contradictions of Capitalism*. London: Heinemann.

Benhabib, S. (1986) *Critique, Norm and Utopia: A Study of the Foundations of Critical Theory*. New York: Columbia University Press.

Bennett, T. (1992a) 'Putting policy into cultural studies', pp. 23–37 in L. Grossberg, C. Nelson and P.A. Treichler (eds), *Cultural Studies*. London: Routledge.

Bennett, T. (1992b) 'Useful culture', *Cultural Studies* 6 (3): 395–408.

Bennett, T. (1996) 'Out in the open: reflections on the history and practice of cultural studies', *Cultural Studies* 10 (1): 133–53.

Bernheimer, C. and C. Kahane (1985) *In Dora's Case: Freud – Hysteria – Feminism*. London: Virago.

Beschloss, M. and S. Talbott (1993) *At the Highest Levels: The Inside Story of the End of the Cold War*. Boston, MA: Little Brown and Company.

Best, S. and D. Kellner (1991) *Postmodern Theory: Critical Interrogations*. London and New York: Macmillan and Guilford Press.

Bhaskar, R. (1989) *Reclaiming Reality: A Critical Introduction to Contemporary Philosophy*. London: Verso.

Bianchini, F. and M. Parkinson (eds) (1993) *Cultural Policy and Urban Regeneration – The West European Experience*. Manchester: Manchester University Press.

Billig, M. (1991) *Ideology and Opinions: Studies in Rhetorical Psychology*. London: Sage.

Billig, M. (1992) *Talking of the Royal Family*. London: Routledge.

Billig, M. (1994) 'Repopulating the depopulated pages of social psychology', *Theory and Psychology* 4 (3): 307–35.

Billig, M. (1995) *Banal Nationalism*. London: Sage.

Billig, M. (1996a) *Arguing and Thinking: A Rhetorical Approach to Social Psychology*. Cambridge: Cambridge University Press.

Billig, M. (1996b) 'Discursive, rhetorical and ideological messages', in C. McGarty and A. Haslam (eds), *Message of Social Psychology: Perspectives on Mind in Society*. Oxford: Blackwell.

Billig, M. (1997a) 'Remembering the particular background of social identity theory', in P. Robinson (ed.), *Groups and Identities: A Festschrift for Henri Tajel*. London: Butterworth Heinemann.

Billig, M. (1997b) 'The dialogic unconscious: discourse analysis, psycho analysis and repression', *British Journal of Social Psychology*.

Billig, M. and D. Edwards (1994) 'La construction sociale de la memoire', *Recherche* 25: 742–5.

Billig, M., S. Condor, D. Edwards, M. Gane, D. Middleton and A.R. Radley (1988) *Ideological Dilemmas: A Social Psychology of Everyday Thinking*. London: Sage.

Bird, E.S. (1992a) *For Enquiring Minds: A Cultural Study of Supermarket Tabloids*. Knoxville: University of Tennessee Press.

Bird, E.S. (1992b) 'Travels in nowhere land: ethnography and the "impossible" audience', *Critical Studies in Mass Communication* 9 (3): 250–60.

Blumler, J.G. (ed.) (1992) *Television and the Public Interest*. London: Sage.

Bogart, L. (1995) *Commercial Culture: Media Systems and the Public Interest*. New York: Oxford University Press.

Borges, J.L. (1972) 'Of exactitude in science', p. 141 in J.L. Borges, *Universal of History*. London: Allen Lane.

Bourdieu, P. (1979) 'The field of cultural production', *Poetics* 12: 311–56.

Bourdieu, P. (1984) *Distinction – A Social Critique of the Judgement of Taste*. London: Routledge.

Boyarin, J. (ed.) (1993) *The Ethnography of Reading*. Berkeley, CA: University of California Press.

Brunsdon, C. (1991) 'Pedagogies of the feminine: feminist teaching and women's genres', *Screen* 32 (4): 364–81.

Brunsdon, C. and D. Morley (1978) *Everyday Television: 'Nationwide'*. London: British Film Institute.

Brunt, R. (1992) 'Engaging with the popular: audiences for mass culture and what to say about them', pp. 69–80 in L. Grossberg, C. Nelson and P.A. Triechler (eds), *Cultural Studies*. New York: Routledge.

Budd, B., R. Entman and C. Steinman (1990) 'The affirmative character of American cultural studies', *Critical Studies in Mass Communication* 7 (2): 169–84.

Buford, B. (1992) *Among the Thugs*. New York: W.W. Norton.

Burgelin, O. (1972) 'Structural analysis and mass communication', pp. 313–28 in D. McQuail (ed.), *Sociology of Mass Communication*. Harmondsworth: Penguin.

Burgelman, J.-C. (1986) 'The future of public service broadcasting', *European Journal of Communication* 1 (2): 173–202.

Bushnell, J. (1990) *Moscow Graffiti: Language and Subculture*. Boston, MA: Unwin Hyman.

Butler, J. (1990) *Gender Trouble: Gender and the Subversion of Identity*. New York: Routledge.

Butler, J. (1993) *Bodies that Matter: On the Discursive Limits of 'Sex'*. New York: Routledge.

Butler, J. (1995) 'For a careful reading', pp. 127–45 in S. Benhabib, J. Butler, D. Cornell and N. Fraser (eds), *Feminist Contentions*. New York: Routledge.

Carey, J.W. (1969) 'The communications revolution and the professional communicator', *Sociological Review Monograph* 13: 23–38.

Carey, J.W. (1986) 'Journalists just leave: the ethics of an anomalous profession', pp. 5–19 in M.G. Sagan (ed.), *Ethics and the Media*. Iowa City: Iowa Humanities Board.

Carey, J.W. (1987) 'The press and public discourse', *Center Magazine* 20 (2): 4–32.

Carey, J.W. (1989) *Communication as Culture: Media Myths and Narratives*. Boston, MA: Unwin Hyman.

Carey, J.W. (1990a) 'The language of technology: talk, text and template as metaphors for communication', pp. 19–39 in M.J. Medhurst, A. Gonzalez and T.R. Peterson (eds), *Communication and the Culture of Technology*. Pullman, WA: Washington State University Press.

Carey, J.W. (1990b) 'Technology as a totem for culture', *American Journalism* 7 (4): 242–51.

Carey, J.W. (1994) 'Communications and economics', pp. 321–36 in R. Babe (ed.), *Information and Communication in Economics*. Boston, MA: Kluwer Academic Publishers.

Carey, J.W. (1995) 'Abolishing the old spirit world', *Critical Studies in Mass Communication* 12 (1): 82–9.

Carey, J.W and A. Kreiling (1974) 'Popular culture and uses and gratifications: notes toward an accommodation', pp. 225–48 in J.G. Blumler and E. Katz (eds), *The Uses of Mass Communications: Current Perspectives on Gratifications Research*. Beverly Hills, CA: Sage.

Chen, K.-H. (1996) 'Not yet the postcolonial era: the (super) nation-state and trans*nationalism* of cultural studies: response to Ang and Stratton', *Cultural Studies* 10 (1): 17–70.

Christians, C. (ed.) (1995) 'Colloquy in critical studies', *Mass Communication* 12: 62–100.

Clark, K. and M. Holquist (1984) *Mikhail Bakhtin*. Cambridge, MA: Harvard University Press.

Clifford, J. (1986) 'Partial truths', pp. 1–27 in J. Clifford and G. Marcus (eds), *Writing Culture: The Poetics and Politics of Ethnography*. Berkeley, CA: University of California Press.

Clifford, J. and G. Marcus (eds) (1986) *Writing Culture: The Poetics and Politics of Ethnography*. Berkeley, CA: University of California Press.

Collini, S. (1994) 'Escape from DWEMsville: is culture too important to be left to cultural studies?', *The Times Literary Supplement* (27 May): 3–4.

Condee, N. and V. Padunov (1987) 'The outposts of official art: recharting Soviet cultural history', *Framework* 34: 59–106.

Condee, N. and V. Padunov (1988) 'The cultural combat zone: where is the DMZ?', *Soviet Union/Union Soviétique* 15 (2–3): 167–85.

Condee, N. and V. Padunov (1991a) '*Makulaluk'tura*: reprocessing culture', *October* 57: 79–103.

Condee, N. and V. Padunov (1991b) '*Perestroika* suicide: not by bred alone', *New Left Review* 189: 69–91.

Condee, N. and V. Padunov (1994) 'Pair-a-dice lost: the socialist gamble, market determinism, and compulsory postmodernism', *New Formations* 22: 72–94.

Condee, N. and V. Padunov (1995) 'The ABC of Russian Consumer Culture: Readings, Ratings and Real Estate', pp. 130–69 in N. Condee (ed.), *Soviet Hieroglyphics: Visual Culture in Late Twentieth Century Russia*. Bloomington, IN: Indiana University Press.

Condit, C.M. (1989) 'The rhetorical limits of polysemy', *Critical Studies in Mass Communication* 6 (2): 103–22.

Connor, S. (1992) *Theory and Cultural Value*. Oxford: Basil Blackwell.

Cooper, M. (1995) 'God and man in Colorado Springs', *Nation* 260 (2): 9–12.

Cornell, D. (1995) 'Rethinking the time of feminism', pp. 145–57 in S. Benhabib, J. Butler, D. Cornell and N. Fraser (eds), *Feminist Contentions*. New York: Routledge.

Corner, J. (1991) 'Meaning, genre and context: the problematics of public knowledge in the new audience studies', pp. 267–85 in J. Curran and M. Gurevitch (eds), *Mass Media and Society*. London: Edward Arnold.

Coward, R. (1978) 'Sexual liberation and the family', *m/f* 1: 7–25.

Cunningham, S. (1992) *Framing Culture – Criticism and Policy in Australia*. Sydney: Allen & Unwyn.

Cunningham, S. (1993) 'Cultural studies from the viewpoint of policy', pp. 126–39 in G. Turner (ed.), *Nation, Culture, Text – Australian Cultural and Media Studies*. London: Routledge.

Curran, J. (1990) 'The new revisionism in mass communication research: a reappraisal', *European Journal of Communication* 5 (2/3): 135–64.

D'Amico, P. (1981) 'Dewey and Marx: on partisanship and the reconstruction of society', *The American Political Science Review* 75: 654–66.

Davies, I. (1995) *Cultural Studies and Beyond. Fragments of Empire*. London: Routledge.

de Certeau, M. (1984) *The Practice of Everyday Life*. Berkeley, CA: University of California Press.

Delillo, D. (1985) *White Noise*. London: Picador.

Derrida, J. (1974) 'White mythology', *New Literary History* 6 (1): 7–74.

Derrida, J. (1976) *Of Grammatology* (translated by G.C. Spivak). Baltimore, MD: Johns Hopkins University Press.

Derrida, J. (1989) *Limited Inc* (2nd edn). Evanston, IL: Northwestern University Press.

Desai, R. (1994) 'Second-hand dealers in ideas – think tanks and Thatcherite hegemony', *New Left Review* 203 (January–February): 27–64.

Dewey, J. (1927) *The Public and its Problems*. New York: Henry Holt.

Douglas, S.J. (1994) *Where the Girls Are: Growing up Female with the Mass Media*. New York: Random.

Downing, J. (1988) 'Alternative public realm: the organisation of the 1980s anti-nuclear press in West Germany and Britain', *Media, Culture and Society* 10 (2): 165–83; also in P. Scannell, P. Schlesinger and C. Sparks (eds) (1992), *Culture and Power*. London: Sage. pp. 259–77.

Downing, J. (1989) 'Computers for political change', *Journal of Communication* 39 (3): 154–62.

Downing, J. (1994) 'East European change and conceptual priorities for media research', *Electronic Journal of Communication/La Revue Électronique De La Communication*.

Downing, J. (1996) *Internationalizing Media Theory: Transition, Power, Culture*. London: Sage.

Drotner, K. (1991) 'Intensities of feeling: modernity, melodrama and adolescence', *Theory, Culture and Society* 8 (1): 57–87.

Duncan, H.D. (1965) *Culture and Democracy: The Struggle for Form in Society and Architecture in Chicago and the Middle West During the Life and Times of Louis H. Sullivan*. Totowa, NJ: Bedminster Press.

Duncan, H.D. (1968) *Communication and Social Order*. London: Oxford University Press.

Durham, J. (1993) *A Certain Lack of Coherance: Writings on Art and Cultural Politics*. London: Kala Press.

Durkheim, E. (1947) *The Elementary Forms of the Religious Life*. Glencoe, IL: The Free Press.

Dworkin, A. (1981) *Pornography: Men Possessing Women*. London: The Women's Press.

Eagleton, T. (1976) *Criticism and Ideology*. London: Verso.

Eagleton, T. (1989) 'Base and superstructure in Raymond Williams', pp. 165–75 in T. Eagleton (ed.), *Raymond Williams: Critical Perspectives*. Cambridge: Polity Press.

Eagleton, T. (1990) *The Ideology of the Aesthetic*. Oxford: Basil Blackwell.

Eagleton, T. (1994) 'Goodbye to the enlightenment', *The Guardian* (2 August): 12–13.

Eagleton, T. (1996) 'The hippest', *London Review of Books* 18 (5): 3,5.

Easthope, A. (1993) 'The death of literature – Anthony Easthope on cultural studies', *Literature Matters* 14: 7.

Easthope, A. (1994) 'The practice of theory', *The Sunday Times Books* (18 September): 8–9.

Easton, P. (1989) 'The rock music community', pp. 45–82 in J. Riordan (ed.), *Soviet Youth Culture*. Bloomington: Indiana University Press.

Edelman, M. (1977) *Political Language*. New York: Academic Press.

Edwards, D. and J. Potter (1992) *Discursive Psychology*. London: Sage.

Edwards, D. and J. Potter (1993) 'Language and causation: a discursive action model of description and attribution', *Psychological Review* 100: 23–41.

Eldridge, J. and E. Eldridge (1994) *Raymond Williams: Making Connections*. London: Routledge.

Ellul, J. (1980) *The Technological System*. New York: Continum Books.

Evans, W. (1990) 'The interpretative turn in media research', *Critical Studies in Mass Communication* 7(2): 145–68.

Exley, F. (1988) *A Fan's Notes*. New York: Random.

Fabian, J. (1990) 'Presence and representation: the other and anthropological writing', *Critical Inquiry* 19(4): 753–72.

Fairclough, N. (1992) *Discourse and Social Change*. Cambridge: Polity Press.

Feyerabend, P. (1978) *Science in a Free Society*. London: Verso.

Fish, S.E. (1980) *Is There a Text in This Class?: The Authority of Interpretive Communities*. Cambridge, MA: Harvard University Press.

Fish, S.E. (1989) 'The young and the restless', pp. 303–17 in H.A. Veeser (ed.), *The New Historicism*. London: Routledge.

Fiske, J. (1987) *Television Culture*. London: Methuen.

Fiske, J. (1989a) *Reading the Popular*. Boston, MA: Unwin Hyman.

Fiske, J. (1989b) *Understanding Popular Culture*. Boston, MA: Unwin Hyman.

Fiske, J. (1990a) *Introduction to Cultural Studies* (2nd edn). London: Routledge.

Fiske, J. (1990b) 'Ethnosemiotics', *Cultural Studies* 4 (1): 85–100.

Fiske, J. (1991) 'Popular discrimination', pp. 103–16 in J. Naremore and P. Brantlinger (eds), *Modernity and Mass Culture*. Bloomington, IN: Indiana University Press.

Fiske, J. (1992) 'Cultural studies and the culture of everyday life', pp. 154–73 in L. Grossberg, C. Nelson and P.A. Treichler (eds), *Cultural Studies*. New York: Routledge.

Fiske, J. (1993) *Power Plays. Power Works*. New York and London: Verso.

Fiske, J. (1994a) *Media Matters: Everyday Culture and Political Change*. Minneapolis, MN: University of Minnesota Press.

Fiske, J. (1994b) 'Radical shopping in Los Angeles: race, media and the sphere of consumption', *Media, Culture and Society* 16 (3): 469–86.

Fiske, J. (1996) 'Down under cultural studies', *Cultural Studies* 10(2): 369–74.

Foucault, M. (1970/1973) *The Order of Things: An Archaeology of the Human Sciences*. London: Tavistock/New York: Vintage Books.

Foucault, M. (1974) *The Archeology of Knowledge*. London: Tavistock.

Foucault, M. (1985) *The Use of Pleasure*. Harmondsworth: Penguin.

Foucault, M. (1988) 'The political technology of individuals', pp. 143–65 in L. Martin, H.

Gutman and P. Hutton (eds), *Technologies of the Self: A Seminar with Michel Foucault*. London: Tavistock.

Foucault, M. (1991) 'Governmentality', pp. 87–104 in G. Burchill, C. Gordon and P. Miller (eds), *The Foucault Effect. Studies in Governmentality*. Hemel Hempstead: Harvester Wheatsheaf.

Fox, E. (1996) 'Media and culture in Latin America', pp. 184–205 in J. Corner, P. Schlesinger and R. Silverstone (eds), *International Media Research: A Critical Survey*. London: Routledge.

Fraser, N. (1987) 'Women, welfare and the politics of need interpretation', *Thesis* 11(17) Australia.

Fraser, N. (1992) 'Rethinking the public sphere: a contribution to the critique of actually existing democracy', pp. 109–42 in C. Calhoun (ed.), *Habermas and the Public Sphere*. Cambridge, MA: MIT Press.

Fraser, N. (1995) 'From redistribution to recognition? Dilemmas of justice in a "Post Socialist" age', *New Left Review* 212 (July/August): 68–93.

Freud, S. (1995) 'Fragment of an analysis of a case of hysteria ('Dora')', pp. 172–239 in P. Gay (ed.), *The Freud Reader*. London: Vintage.

Frith, S. (1991) 'The good, the bad and the indifferent: defending popular culture from the populists', *Diacritics* 21 (4): 102–15.

Frow, J. (1995) *Cultural Studies and Cultural Value*. Oxford: Clarendon Press.

Fukuyama, F. (1989) 'The end of history?', *National Interest* 16 (Summer): 3–18.

Gans, H. (1979) *Deciding Whats News*. New York: Random.

García Canclini, N. (1993) *Transforming Modernity: Popular Culture in Mexico* (translated by L. Lozano). Austin, TX: University of Texas Press.

García Canclini, N. (1995) *Hybrid Cultures: Strategies for Entering and Leaving Modernity* (translated by C. Chippari and S. Lopez). Minneapolis, MN: University of Minnesota Press.

Garnham, N. (1995a) 'Political economy and cultural studies: reconciliation or divorce', *Critical Studies in Mass Communication* 12 (1): 62–71.

Garnham, N. (1995b) 'Cultural studies vs political economy– is anyone else bored with this debate – abolishing the old spirit world – reply to Grossberg and Carey', *Critical Studies in Mass Communication* 12 (1): 95–100.

Gates, B. (1995) 'Tycoons watch *Tomorrow's World*', *The Guardian* (20 July): 20.

Geertz, C. (1973) *The Interpretation of Cultures*. New York: Basic Books.

Geertz, C. (1983) *Local Knowledge*. New York: Basic Books.

Geertz, C. (1988) *Works and Lives*. Cambridge: Polity Press.

Gellner, E. (1970) 'Concepts and society', pp. 18–50 in B. Wilson (ed.), *Rationality*. Oxford: Basil Blackwell.

Gellner, E. (1992) *Postmodernism, Reason and Religion*. London: Routledge.

Genovese, E.D. (1994) 'The question', *Dissent* 41 (3): 371–6.

Gerbner, G. (1995) 'Marketing global mayhem', *Javnost/The Public* 2 (2): 71–6.

Gergen, K.J. (1994) *Toward Transformation in Social Knowledge* (2nd edn). London: Sage.

Gergen, K.J. (1995) *Realities and Relationships*. Cambridge, MA: Harvard University Press.

Gewertz, D. and F. Errington (1991) 'We think therefore they are? On occidentalising the world', *Anthropological Quarterly* 64 (2): 80–91.

Gillespie, M. (1993) '*The Mahabharata* – from Sanskrit to sacred soap: a case study of the reception of two televisual versions', pp. 48–74 in D. Buckingham (ed.), *Reading Audiences: Young People and the Media*. Manchester: Manchester University Press.

Gilroy, Paul (1996) 'British cultural studies and the pitfalls of identity', pp. 35–49 in J. Curran, D. Morley and V. Walkerdine (eds), *Cultural Studies and Communications*. London: Edward Arnold.

Gitlin, T. (1983) *Inside Prime Time*. New York: Pantheon.

Gitlin, T. (1987) *The Sixties: Years of Hope, Days of Rage*. New York: Bantam.

Gitlin, T. (1993) 'Glib, tawdry, savvy and standardized – television and American culture', *Dissent* 40 (3): 351–5.

Gitlin, T. (1995) *The Twilight of Common Dreams: Why America is Wracked by Culture Wars*. New York: Metropolitan Books/ Henry Holt.

Golding, P. (1996) 'World wide wedge: division and contradiction in the global information infrastructure' *Monthly Review*: 70–85.

Goldmann, L. (1969) *The Human Sciences and Philosophy*. London: Jonathan Cape.

Goodwyn, A. (1991) *Breaking the Barrier: The Rise of Solidarity in Poland*. New York: Oxford University Press.

Gottdiener, M. (1995) *Postmodern Semiotics: Material Culture and the Forms of Postmodern Life*. Oxford: Basil Blackwell.

Gramsci, A. (1971) *Prison Notebooks*. London: Lawrence and Wishart.

Gray, A. (1992) *Video Play Time: The Gendering of a Leisure Technology*. London: Comedia/Routledge.

Gray, A. and J. McGuigan (eds) (1993) *Studying Culture*. London: Edward Arnold.

Gray, J. (1995) *Enlightenment's Wake*. London: Routledge.

Grigorenko, P. (1982) *Memoirs*. New York: W.W. Norton.

Grossberg, L. (1988) 'Wandering audiences, nomadic critics', *Cultural Studies* 2 (3): 377–92.

Grossberg, L. (1992) *We Gotta Get Out Of This Place: Popular Conservatism and Postmodern Culture*. London and New York: Routledge.

Grossberg, L. (1993) 'Can cultural studies find true happiness in communication?, *Journal of Communication* 43 (4): 89–97.

Grossberg, L. (1995) 'Cultural studies vs political economy: is anybody else bored with this debate?', *Critical Studies in Mass Communication* 12 (1): 72–81.

Grossberg, L.C, C. Nelson and P.A. Treichler (eds) (1992) *Cultural Studies*. New York: Routledge.

Grosz, E. (1995) *Space, Time and Perversion*. New York: Routledge.

Gusfield, J.R. (ed.) (1989) *Kenneth Burke on Symbols and Society*. Chicago: University of Chicago Press.

Habermas, J. (1987) *The Theory of Communicative Action Vol. 2 – The Critique of Functionalist Reason*. Cambridge: Polity Press.

Habermas, J. (1990) *Moral Consciousness and Communicative Action*. Cambridge: Polity Press.

Hall, S. (1977) 'Culture, the media and the ideological effect', pp. 315–48 in J. Curran, M. Gurevitch and J. Woollacott (eds), *Mass Communication and Society*. London: Edward Arnold.

Hall, S. (1980a) 'Cultural studies – two paradigms', *Media, Culture and Society* 2 (2): 57–72; also in T. Bennett, G. Martin, C. Mercer and J. Woollacott (eds) (1981), *Culture, Ideology and Social Process*. London: Batsford Academic. pp. 19–42.

Hall, S. (1980b) 'Cultural studies and the centre: some problematics and problems', pp. 15–47 in S. Hall, D. Hobson, A. Lowe and P. Willis (eds), *Culture, Media, Language*. London: Hutchinson.

Hall, S. (1980c) 'Encoding/decoding', pp. 128–38 in S. Hall, D. Hobson, A. Lowe and P. Willis (eds), *Culture, Media, Language*. London: Hutchinson.

Hall, S. (1983) 'The problem of ideology: Marxism without guarantees', pp. 57–185 in B. Matthews (ed.), *Marx: A Hundred Years On*. London: Lawrence and Wishart.

Hall, S. (1986a) 'On postmodernism and articulation: an interview with Stuart Hall', *Journal of Communication Inquiry* 10 (2): 45–6.

Hall, S. (1986b) 'Media power and class power', pp. 5–14 in J. Curran (ed.), *Bending Reality: The State of the Media*. London: Pluto Press.

Hall, S. (1986c) 'Cultural studies and the centre: some problematics and problems', pp. 15–47 in S. Hall, D. Hobson, A. Lowe and P. Willis (eds), *Culture, Media, Language*. London: Hutchinson.

Hall, S. (1988a) 'The toad in the garden: Thatcherism among the theorists', pp. 35–57 in C. Nelson and L. Grossberg (eds), *Marxism and the Interpretation of Culture*. Basingstoke: Macmillan.

Hall, S. (1988b) 'Introductory address', International Television Studies Conference. London, July.

Hall, S. (1990a) 'Cultural identity and diaspora', pp. 222–37 in J. Rutherford (ed.), *Identity – Community, Culture, Difference*. London: Lawrence and Wishart.

Hall, S. (1990b) 'Cultural studies: now and in the future'. Paper presented to conference of that name. University of Illinois, April 1990; reprinted in L. Grossberg, C. Nelson and P.A. Treichler (eds) (1992), *Cultural Studies*. New York: Routledge.

Hall, S. (1992) 'Cultural studies and its theoretical legacies', pp. 277–86 in L. Grossberg, C. Nelson and P.A. Treichler (eds), *Cultural Studies*. New York: Routledge.

Hall, S. (1996a) 'When was the "Post Colonial"? Thinking at the limit', pp. 242–60 in I. Chambers and L. Curti (eds), *The Post Colonial Question: Common Skies, Divided Horizons*. London: Routledge.

Hall, S. (1996b) 'For Allon White: metaphors of transformation', pp. 287–305 in D. Morley and K.-H. Chen (eds), *Critical Dialogues in Cultural Studies*. London: Routledge.

Hall, S. and L. Grossberg (1986) 'On postmodernism and articulation: an interview with Stuart Hall', *Journal of Communication Inquiry* 10 (2): 45–60.

Hall, S. and T. Jefferson (eds) (1976) *Resistance Through Rituals: Youth Subcultures in Post-War Britain*. London: Hutchinson.

Hall, S., I. Connell and L. Curti (1976) 'The "unity" of public affairs television', pp. 51–93 in *Working Papers in Cultural Studies, Vol. 9*. Birmingham: Centre for Contemporary Cultural Studies, University of Birmingham.

Hall, S., C. Critcher, T. Jefferson, J. Clarke and B. Roberts (1978) *Policing the Crisis: Mugging, the State, and Law and Order*. London: Macmillan.

Hamer, M. (1989) 'Review of Clifford Geertz's works and lives', *Textual Practice* 3 (3): 456–9.

Hampden-Turner, C. and A. Trompenaars (1993) *The Seven Cultures of Capitalism*. New York: Doubleday.

Hanchard, M. (1995) 'Black Cinderella?: race and the public sphere in Brazil', *Public Culture* 7 (1): 165–85.

Hárászti, M. (1987) *The Velvet Prison*. New York: Basic Books.

Haraway, D. (1991) *Simians, Cyborgs and Women*. London: Free Association Books.

Harré, R. (1995) 'Discursive psychology', pp. 143–59 in J.A. Smith, R. Harré and L. Van Langenhove (eds), *Rethinking Psychology*. London: Sage.

Harré, R. and G. Gillett (1994) *The Discursive Mind*. London: Sage.

Harris, D. (1992) *From Class Struggle to the Politics of Pleasure. The Effects of Gramscianism on Cultural Studies*. London: Routledge.

Hartley, J. (1987) 'Television audiences, paedocracy and pleasure', *Textual Practice* 1 (2): 121–38.

Hartley, J. (1992) *Teleology: Studies in Television*. London: Routledge.

Hartsock, N. (1987) 'Rethinking modernism', *Cultural Critique* 7: 187–206.

Harvey, D. (1989) *The Urban Experience*. Oxford: Basil Blackwell.

Harvey, D. (1993) 'Class relations, social justice and the politics of difference', pp. 85–120 in J. Squires (ed.), *Principled Positions: Postmodernism and the Rediscovery of Value*. London: Lawrence and Wishart.

Hayek, F. (1944) *The Road to Serfdom*. Chicago: University of Chicago Press.

Head, S. (1996) 'The new ruthless economy', *New York Review of Books* February 29.

Hebdige, D. (1978/1988) *Subculture: The Meaning of Style*. London: Routledge.

Helsinki Watch (1987) *From Below: Independent Peace and Environmental Movements in Eastern Europe and the USSR*. New York: Helsinki Watch.

Helsinki Watch (1990) *Nyeformaly: Civil Society in the USSR*. New York: Helsinki Watch.

Henriques, J., W. Hollway, C. Urwin, C. Venn and V. Walkerdine (1984) *Changing the Subject*. London: Methuen.

Heritage, J. (1984) *Garfinkel and Ethnomethodology*. Cambridge: Polity Press.

Heritage, J. (1988) 'Explanations as accounts: a conversation analytic account', pp. 127–44 in C. Antaki (ed.), *Analysing Everyday Explanation*. London: Sage.

Herman, E. and N. Chomsky (1987) *Manufacturing Consent*. New York: Pantheon.

Hermes, J. (1995) *Reading Women's Magazines*. Cambridge: Polity Press/London: Routledge.

Hobson, D. (1978) 'Housewives: isolation as oppression', pp. 79–96 in Women's Studies Group (eds), *Women Take Issue*. London: Hutchinson.

Hobson, D. (1980) 'Housewives and the mass media', pp. 105–14 in S. Hall, D. Hobson, A. Lowe and P. Willis (eds), *Culture, Media, Language*. London: Hutchinson.

Hobson, D. (1982) *'Crossroads': The Drama of a Soap Opera*. London: Methuen.

Hodge, R. and G. Kress (1988) *Social Semiotics*. Cambridge: Polity Press.

Hoggart, R. (1957/1970) *The Uses of Literacy*. London: Chatto and Windus/New York: Oxford University Press.

Holquist, M. (1990) *Dialogism: Bakhtin and his World*. London: Routledge.

Hook, S. (1987) *Out of Step*. New York: Harper and Row.

hooks, b. (1990) 'Representing whiteness in the black imagination', pp. 338–47 in L. Grossberg, C. Nelson, P.A. Treichler (eds), *Cultural Studies*. New York: Routledge.

Horkheimer, M. and T.W. Adorno (1972) *Dialectic of Enlightenment*. New York: Seabury.

Howe, S. (1994) 'Colony Club', *New Statesman and Society* 25 February: 40.

Hughes, R. (1993) *Culture of Complaint: The Fraying of America*. Oxford: Oxford University Press.

Inglis, F. (1995) *Raymond Williams*. London: Routledge.

Interfaces (1993) 'Interfaces: culture and structure in communication research'. Panel presented at the International Communication Association meeting, May.

Itzin, C. (ed.) (1992) *Pornography: Women, Violence and Civil Liberties*. Oxford: Oxford University Press.

Jakubowicz, K. (1990) 'Musical chairs? The three public spheres of Poland', *Media, Culture and Society* 12 (2): 195–212.

Jameson, F. (1991) *Postmodernism or the Cultural Logic of Late Capitalism*. Durham, NC: Duke University Press.

Jameson, F. (1992) *The Geopolitical Aesthetic*. Bloomington: Indiana University Press.

Jameson, F. (1993) 'On "Cultural Studies"', *Social Text* 34: 17–52.

Jancar, B.W. (1975) 'Religious dissent in the Soviet Union', pp. 191–230 in R. Tőkés (ed.), *Dissent in the USSR: Politics, Ideology, and People*. Baltimore, MD: Johns Hopkins University Press.

Jancovich, M. (1992) 'David Morley, the "Nationwide" studies', pp. 134–47 in M. Barker and A. Beezer (eds), *Readings into Cultural Studies*. London: Routledge.

Jenkins, H. (1992) *Textual Poachers*. London and New York: Routledge.

Jensen, J. (1990) *Redeeming Modernity: Contradictions in Media Criticism*. Newbury Park, CA: Sage.

Jensen, J. (1993) 'Democratic culture and the arts: constructing a usable past', *Journal of Arts Management, Law and Society* 23 (2): 110–20.

Jensen, J. (1994a) 'Culture for democracy: intellectuals and the arts in American social thought'. Unpublished manuscript.

Jensen, J. (1994b) 'The consequences of vocabularies', pp. 75–82 in M. Levy and M. Gurevitch (eds), *Defining Media Studies: Reflections on the Future of the Field*. New York: Oxford University Press.

Johnson, R. (1986/87) 'What is cultural studies anyway?' *Social Text* 16: 38–80.

Kaestle, C.F., H. Damon-Moore, L.C. Stedman, K. Tinsley and W.V. Trollinger Jr (1991) *Literacy in the United States: Readers and Reading since 1880*. New Haven, CT: Yale University Press.

Kaplan, E.A. (1987) *Rocking around the Clock*. London: Methuen.

Keat, R. (1994) 'Scepticism, authority and the market', pp. 23–42 in R. Keat, N. Whiteley and N. Abercrombie (eds), *The Authority of the Consumer*. London: Routledge.

Kellner, D. (1989) *Critical Theory, Marxism and Modernity*. Cambridge, Polity Press/Baltimore, Johns Hopkins University Press.

Kellner, D. (1990) *Television and the Crisis of Democracy*. Boulder, CO: Westview Press.

Kellner, D. (1992) *The Persian Gulf TV War*. Boulder, CO: Westview Press.

Kellner, D. (1995) *Media Culture: Cultural Studies, Identity and Politics Between the Modern and the Postmodern*. London and New York: Routledge.

Kellner, D. and M. Ryan (1988) *Camera Politica: The Politics and Ideology of Contemporary Hollywood Film*. Bloomington: Indiana University Press.

Knorr-Cetina, K. (1981) 'Introduction: the micro-sociological challenge of macro-sociology', pp. 1–47 in K. Knorr-Cetina and A. Cicourel (eds), *Advances in Social Theory and Methodology*. London: Routledge.

Kónrád, G. (1984) *Antipolitics: An Essay*. New York: Henry Holt and Company.

Kopelev, L. (1980) *The Education of a True Believer*. New York: Harper and Row.

Kramer, J. (1977) *The Last Cowboy*. New York: Harper and Row.

Kramer, J. (1994) *Whose Art is it?* Durham, NC: Duke University Press.

Kreiling, A. (1973) 'The making of racial identities in the black press: a cultural analysis of race journalism in Chicago, 1878–1929'. Unpublished PhD dissertation, University of Illinois at Urbana-Champaign.

Kreiling, A. (1978) 'Toward a cultural studies approach for the sociology of popular culture', *Communication Research* 5 (3): 240–63.

Kreiling, A. (1993) 'The commercialization of the black press and the rise of race news in Chicago', pp. 176–203 in W.S. Solomon and R.W. McChesney (eds), *Ruthless Criticism: New Perspectives in US Communication History*. Minneapolis: University of Minnesota Press.

Kreiling, A. and N. Sims (1981) 'Symbolic interactionism, progressive thought and Chicago journalism', pp. 5–37 in J. Soloski (ed.), *Foundations for Communication Studies*. Iowa City: Center for Communication Study, School of Journalism and Mass Communication, University of Iowa.

Krugman, P. (1996) *Pop Internationalism*. Cambridge, MA: MIT Press.

Laba, R. (1991) *The Roots of Solidarity: A Political Sociology of Poland's Working Class Democratization*. Princeton, NJ: Princeton University Press.

Lacan, J. (1977) *Ecrits*. London: Tavistock.

Lacan, J. (1979) *The Four Fundamental Concepts of Psycho-analysis*. Harmondsworth: Penguin.

Lacan, J. (1985) 'Intervention on transference', pp. 92–104 in C. Bernheimer and C. Kahane (eds), *In Dora's Case*. London: Virago.

Lacan, J. (1993) *The Psychoses*. London: Routledge.

Laclau, E. (1979) *Politics and Ideology in Marxist Theory: Capitalism–Facism–Populism*. London: Verso.

Laclau, E. and C. Mouffe (1985) *Hegemony and Socialist Strategy: Towards a Radical Democratic Politics*. London: Verso.

Larrain, J. (1991) 'Stuart Hall and the Marxist concept of ideology', *Theory, Culture and Society* 8 (4): 1–28.

Larrain, J. (1994) *Ideology and Cultural Identity*. Cambridge: Polity Press.

Lasch, C. (1995) *The Revolt of the Elites and the Betrayal of Democracy*. New York: W.W. Norton.

Lash, S. and J. Urry (1987) *The End of Organized Capitalism*. Cambridge: Polity Press.

Lawton, A. (1992) *Kinoglasnost: Soviet Cinema in our Time*. Cambridge: Cambridge University Press.

Lee, B. (1995) 'Critical internationalism', *Popular Culture* 7 (3): 559–00.

Liebes, T. and E. Katz (1990) *The Export of Meaning*. New York/Oxford: Oxford University Press.

Lipset, S.M. (1996) *American Exceptionalism: A Double-Edged Sword*. New York: W.W. Norton.

Livingstone, S. and P. Lunt (1994) *Talk on Television: Audience Participation and Public Debate*. London: Routledge.

Lowenthal, L. (1961 [1943]) 'The triumph of mass idols', pp. 109–36 in L. Lowenthal, *Literature, Popular Culture and Society*. Palo Alto, CA: Pacific Books.

Lull, J. (1980) 'The social uses of television', *Human Communication Research* 6 (3): 197–209.

Lull, J. (1987) 'Audience texts and contexts', *Critical Studies in Mass Communication* 4 (3): 318–22.

Lull, J. (ed.) (1988) *World Families Watch Television*. London: Sage.

Lull, J. (1990) *Inside Family Viewing: Ethnographic Research on Television's Audiences*. London: Routledge.

MacCabe, C. (1995) 'Tradition too had its place in cultural studies', *Times Literary Supplement* (26 May): 13.

McChesney, R. (1995) 'Is there any hope for cultural studies'. Paper presented to 'Across Disciplines and Beyond Boundaries: Tracking American Cultural Studies' Conference. University of Illinois, November.

McChesney, R.W. (1996) 'The Internet and US communication policy-making in critical and historical perspective', *Journal of Communication* 46 (1): 98–124.

McGuigan, J. (1992) *Cultural Populism*. London and New York: Routledge.

McGuigan, J. (1993) 'Reaching for control – Raymond Williams on mass communication and popular culture', pp. 163–87 in J. Morgan and P. Preston (eds), *Raymond Williams – Politics, Education, Letters*. London: Macmillan.

McGuigan, J. (1995) '"A slow reach again for control" – Raymond Williams and the vicissitudes of cultural policy', *European Journal of Cultural Policy* 2 (1).

McGuigan, J. (1996) *Culture and the Public Sphere*. London and New York: Routledge.

MacKinnon, C. (1979) *The Sexual Harassment of Working Women. A Case of Sex Discrimination*. New Haven, CT: Yale University Press.

McRobbie, A. (1991) *Feminism and Youth Culture: From Jackie to Just Seventeen*. Basingstoke: Macmillan.

McRobbie, A. (1992) 'Post marxism and cultural studies: a postscript', pp. 719–30 in L. Grossberg, C. Nelson and P.A. Treichler (eds), *Cultural Studies*. New York: Routledge.

McRobbie, A. (1994) *Postmodernism and Popular Culture*. London: Routledge.

McRobbie, A. (1996) 'All the world's a stage, screen or magazine: when culture is the logic of late capitalism', *Media, Culture and Society* 18 (2): 335–42.

Manent, P. (1994) *An Intellectual History of Liberalism*. Princeton, NJ: Princeton University Press.

Marcus, G. (1986) 'Contemporary problems of ethnography in the world system', pp. 165–93 in J. Clifford and G. Marcus (eds), *Writing Culture: The Poetics and Politics of Ethnography*. Berkeley, CA: University of California Press.

Marcus, G. and M. Fischer (1986) *Anthropology as Cultural Critique*. Chicago: University of Chicago Press.

Martín-Barbero, J. (1988) 'Communication from culture', *Media, Culture and Society* 10 (4): 447–65.

Martín-Barbero, J. (1993) *Communication, Culture and Hegemony: From the Media to Mediations* (translated by E. Fox and R. White). London: Sage.

Marx, K. (1974) *Political Writings Volume II: Surveys from Exile*. New York: Vintage Books.

Marx, K. and F. Engels (1970/1974) *The German Ideology*. London: Lawrence and Wishart.

Mascia-Lees, F.E., P. Sharpe and C.B. Cohen (1989) 'The postmodernist turn in anthropology: cautions from a feminist perspective', *Signs* 15 (1): 7–33.

Massey, D. (1991) 'Flexible sexism', *Environment and Planning (d): Society and Space* 9 (1): 31–57.

Mattelart, A. and J.-M. Piemme (1980) 'New means of communication: new questions for the left', *Media, Culture and Society* 2 (4): 321–38.

Meiksins Wood, E. (1989) 'Rational choice Marxism – is the game worth a candle?', *New Left Review* 177 (September–October): 41–88.

Mepham, J. (1991) 'Television fictions – quality and truth-telling', *Radical Philosophy* 57 (Spring): 20–7.

Middleton, D. and D. Edwards (1990) 'Conversational remembering: a social psychological approach', pp. 23–45 in D. Middleton and D. Edwards (eds), *Collective Remembering*. London: Sage.

Miller, D. (1992) '*The Young and the Restless* in Trinidad: a case study of the local and the global in mass consumption', pp. 163–82 in R. Silverstone and E. Hirsch (eds), *Consuming Technologies*. London: Routledge.

Miller, J. (1993) *The Passion of Michael Foucault*. New York: Simon and Schuster.

Mills, C.W. (1970) *The Sociological Imagination*. Harmondsworth: Penguin.

Milner, A. (1993) *Cultural Materialism*. Melbourne: Melbourne University Press.

Minh-Ha, T. (1989) *Woman, Native, Other*. Bloomington: Indiana University Press.

Minnow, N. (1991) 'How vast the wasteland now', *Media Studies Journal* 5 (4): 67–81.

Moores, S. (1993) 'Satellite TV as a cultural sign: consumption, embedding and articulation', *Media, Culture and Society* 15 (4): 621–39.

Moores, S. (1994) *Interpreting Audiences: The Ethnography of Media Consumption*. Thousand Oaks, CA: Sage.

Morley, D. (1980) *The 'Nationwide' Audience: Structure and Decoding*. London: British Film Institute.

Morley, D. (1986) *Family Television: Cultural Power and Domestic Leisure*. London: Comedia.

Morley, D. (1990) 'Texts, readers, subjects', pp. 163–73 in S. Hall, D. Hobson, A. Lowe and P. Willis (eds), *Culture, Media, Language*. London: Hutchinson

Morley, D. (1992) *Television, Audiences and Cultural Studies*. London and New York: Routledge.

Morley, D. and K.-H. Chen (eds) (1996) *Stuart Hall, Critical Dialogues in Cultural Studies*. London: Routledge.

Morley, D. and R. Silverstone (1990) 'Domestic communications: technologies and meanings', *Media, Culture and Society* 12 (1): 31–55.

Morris, M. (1988) 'Banality in cultural studies', *Discourse* 10 (2): 3–29.

Morris, P. (1994) 'Introduction', pp. 1–24 in P. Morris (ed.), *The Bakhtin Reader*. London: Edward Arnold.

Moscovici, S. (1984) 'The phenomenon of social representations' in R.M. Farr and S. Moscovici (eds), *Social Representations*. Cambridge: Cambridge University Press.

Moscovici, S. (1988) 'Notes towards a description of social representation', *European Journal of Social Psychology* 18: 211–50.

Muggeridge, M. (1972) *The Thirties: 1930–1940 in Great Britain*. London: Fontana Books.

Mukerjee, C. and M. Schudson (eds) (1991) *Rethinking Popular Culture*. Berkeley, CA: University of California Press.

Mulhern, F. (1995) 'The politics of cultural studies', *Monthly Review* July–August: 31–40.

Mulvey, L. (1975/1989) 'Visual pleasure in narrative cinema', *Screen* 3 (16): 6–18.

Murdock, G. (1989a) 'Cultural studies: missing links', *Critical Studies in Mass Communications* 6 (4): 436–40.

Murdock, G. (1989b) 'Critical inquiry and audience activity', pp. 226–49 in B. Dervin, L. Grossberg, B.J. O'Keefe and E. Wartella (eds), *Rethinking Communication, Volume 2: Paradigm Exemplars*. London/Newbury Park, CA: Sage.

Murdock, G. (1992) 'Citizens, consumers and public culture', pp. 17–41 in M. Skomand and K.C. Schroder (eds), *Media Cultures: Reappraising Transnational Media*. London: Routledge.

Murdock, G. (1994) 'New times/hard times: leisure, participation and the common good', *Leisure Studies* 13: 239–48.

Murdock, G. and P. Golding (1974) 'For a political economy of mass communications', pp. 205–34 in R. Miliband and J. Saville (eds), *The Socialist Register 1973*. London: Merlin Press.

Murdock, G. and P. Golding (1989) 'Information poverty and political inequality – citizenship in the age of privatized communications', *Journal of Communication* 39 (3): 180–95.

Murdock, G., P. Hartmann and P. Gray (1992) 'Contextualising home computing: resources and practice', pp. 146–60 in R. Silverstone and E. Hirsch (eds), *Consuming Technologies: Media and Information in Domestic Spaces*. London: Routledge.

Nash, K. (1994) 'The feminist production of knowledge: is deconstruction a practice for women?', *Feminist Review* 47: 65–78.

Nelson, C., P.A. Treichler and L. Grossberg (1992) 'Introduction', pp. 1–22 in L. Grossberg, C. Nelson and P.A. Treichler (eds), *Cultural Studies*. New York: Routledge.

Newcomb, H. and P. Hirsch (1987) 'Television as a cultural forum', pp. 455–71 in H. Newcomb (ed.), *Television: The Critical View* (4th edn). Oxford: Oxford University Press.

Nightingale, V. (1993) 'What's "ethnographic" about ethnographic audience research?', pp. 164–77 in G. Turner (ed.), *Nation, Culture, Text – Australian Cultural and Media Studies*. London: Routledge.

Nord, D.P. (1995) 'Reading the newspaper: strategies and politics of reader response, Chicago, 1912–1917', *Journal of Communication* 45 (3): 66–93.

Norris, C. (1990) *What's Wrong with Postmodernism: Critical Theory and the Ends of Philosophy?* Baltimore, MD: Johns Hopkins University Press.

Norris, C. (1991) *Deconstruction: Theory and Practice* (Rev. edn). London: Routledge.

Norris, C. (1995) 'Culture, criticism and communal values: on the ethics of enquiry', pp. 5–40 in

B. Adam and S. Allan (eds), *Theorizing Culture: An Interdisciplinary Critique After Postmodernism*. London: UCL Press.

Ogarkov, N. (1982/1984) 'Toujours prêt à défendre la patrie', translated in *Stratégique* 30 (1984): 7–75.

Oppenheimer, C. and L. Harker (1996) *Poverty: The Facts*. London: Child Poverty Action Group.

O'Regan, T. (1992) '(Mis)taking policy – notes on the cultural policy debate', *Cultural Studies* 6 (3): 409–23.

O'Regan, T. (1993) *Australian Television Culture*. Sydney: Allen and Unwin.

Ost, D. (1990) *Solidarity and the Politics of Anti-Politics: Opposition and Reform in Poland since 1968*. Philadelphia, PA: Temple University Press.

Park, R. (1934) 'Introduction', pp. ix–xxii in C.S. Johnson (ed.), *Shadow of the Plantation*. Chicago: University of Chicago Press.

Parker, I. (1991) *Discourse Dynamics*. London: Routledge.

Parkin, F. (1972) *Class Inequality and Political Order*. London: Routledge.

Parsons, T. (1949) *The Structure of Social Action*. Glencoe: The Free Press.

Patten, J. (1993) 'Must think harder', *Spectator* (2 October): 14–15.

Persons, S. (1987) *Ethnic Studies at Chicago, 1905–45*. Urbana: University of Illinois Press.

Pollert, A. (1988) 'Dismantling flexibility', *Capital and Class* 34 (Spring): 42–75.

Pomerantz, A. (1984) 'Agreeing and disagreeing with assessments: some features of preferred/dis-preferred turn shapes', pp. 57–101 in J.M. Atkinson and J. Heritage (eds), *Structures of Social Action*. Cambridge: Cambridge University Press.

Pool, R. (1991) 'Postmodern ethnography', *Critique of Anthropology* 11 (4): 309–31.

Potter, J. and M. Wetherell (1987) *Discourse and Social Psychology*. London: Sage.

Press, A. (1991) *Women Watching Television*. Philadelphia: University of Pennsylvania Press.

Price, M. (1994) 'The market for loyalties: electronic media and the global competition for allegiances', *The Yale Law Review* 104 (3): 667–705.

Probyn, E. (1993) *Sexing the Self: Gendered Positions in Cultural Studies*. London and New York: Routledge.

Radway, J. (1984) *Reading the Romance: Women, Patriarchy and Popular Literature*. Chapel Hill: University of North Carolina Press.

Real, M. (1989) *Supermedia*. London: Sage.

Report of the Committee on Financing the BBC (Peacock Report 1986) Cmnd 9824. London: HMSO.

Richards, I. (1960) 'Variant readings and misreadings', pp. 241–53 in T. Sebeok (ed.), *Style in Language*. Cambridge, MA: MIT Press.

Ricoeur, P. (1991) *From Text to Action: Essays in Hermeneutics*. Evanston, IL: Northwestern University Press.

Riesman, D. (1950) *The Lonely Crowd*. New Haven, CT: Yale University Press.

Riley, D. (1987) 'Does sex have a history?', *New Formations*, Spring: 5–35.

Riley, D. (1988) *Am I That Name? Feminism and the Catogory of 'Women' in History*. Basingstoke: Macmillan.

Riordan, James (ed.) (1989) *Soviet Youth Culture*. Bloomington, IN: Indiana University Press.

Robinson, J. (1964) *Economic Philosophy*. London: Penguin.

Rorty, R. (1978) 'Philosophy as a kind of writing', *New Literary History* 10: 141–60.

Rorty, R. (1989) *Contingency, Irony and Solidarity*. Cambridge: Cambridge University Press.

Ryback, T. (1990) *Rock Around the Bloc*. New York: Oxford University Press.

Said, E. (1979) *Orientalism*. Harmondsworth: Penguin.

Sandel, M. (1996a) *Democracy's Discontent: America in Search of a Public Philosophy*. Cambridge, MA: Harvard University Press.

Sandel, M. (1996b) 'America's search for a new public philosophy', *The Atlantic Monthly* 277 (3): 57–74.

Sanders, C. (1994) 'A leading indicator', *The Times Higher Education Supplement* (13 May): 17–18.

Savage, J. and S. Frith (1993) 'Pearls and swine – intellectuals and the media', *New Left Review* 198 (March–April): 107–16.

Schlesinger, P. (1987) 'On national identity', *Social Science Information* 25 (2): 219–64.

Scholte, R. (1987) 'The literary turn in contemporary anthropology', *Critique of Anthropology* 7 (1): 33–47.

Schudson, M. (1984) *Advertising: The Uneasy Persuasion*. New York: Basic Books.

Schwarz, B. (1994) 'Where is cultural studies?', *Cultural Studies* 8 (3): 377–93.

Schweizer, P. (1994) *Victory: The Reagan Administration's Secret Strategy that Hastened the Collapse of the Soviet Union*. New York: Atlantic Monthly Press.

Seamann, W.R. (1992) 'Active audience theory: pointless populism', *Media, Culture and Society* 14 (2): 301–11.

Shattuck, R. (1995) 'Second thoughts on a wooden horse', *Salmagundi* 106–107: 23–30.

Shlapentokh, V. (1986) *Soviet Public Opinion and Ideology: Mythology and Pragmatism in Interaction*. New York: Praeger.

Shohat, E. and R. Stam (1994) *Unthinking Eurocentrism: Multiculturalism and the Media*. New York: Routledge.

Shotter, J. (1992) 'Bakhtin and Billig: monological versus dialogical practices', *American Behavioral Scientist* 36 (1): 8–21.

Shotter, J. (1993a) *The Cultural Politics of Everyday Life*. Milton Keynes: Open University Press.

Shotter, J. (1993b) *Conversational Realities*. London: Sage.

Shotter, J. (1995) 'Dialogical psychology', pp. 160–78 in J.A. Smith, R. Harré and L. Van Langenhove (eds), *Rethinking Psychology*. London: Sage.

Silverstone, R. (1994) 'The power of the ordinary: on cultural studies and the sociology of culture', *Sociology* 28 (4): 991–1001.

Simmel, G. (1963) 'The sociology of conflict', pp. 260–319 in H.M. Ruitenbeek (ed.), *Varieties of Classical Social Theory*. New York: E.P. Dutton.

Simpson, C. (1994) *Science of Coercion: Communication Research and Psychological Warfare, 1945–1960*. New York: Oxford University Press.

Sivanandan, A. (1990) *Communities of Resistance: Writings on Black Struggles for Socialism*. London: Verso.

Sivanandan, A. (1995) 'La trahison des clercs', *New Statesman and Society* (14 July): 20–1.

Smelser, N.J. (1962) *Theory of Collective Behaviour*. London: Routledge and Kegan Paul.

Smelser, N.J. (1992) 'Culture: coherant or incoherant', pp. 3–28 in R. Münch and N.J. Smelser (eds), *Theory of Culture*. Berkeley, CA: University of California Press.

Smith, D.E. (1991) 'Writing women's experience into social science', *Feminism and Psychology* 1: 155–69.

Smith, G.S. (1984) *Songs to Seven Strings: Russian Guitar Poetry and Soviet 'Mass Song'*. Bloomington: Indiana University Press.

Spivak, G.C. (1987) *In Other Worlds: Essays in Cultural Politics*. London and New York: Methuen.

Spivak, G.C. (1990) 'An interview', *Radical Philosophy* (Spring): 32–40.

Spivak, G.C. (1993) *Outside in the Teaching Machine*. New York: Routledge.

Sreberny-Mohammadi, A. (1991) 'The global and the local in international communications', pp. 118–38 in J. Curran and M. Gurevitch (eds), *Mass Media and Society*. London: Edward Arnold.

Staiger, J. (1992) 'Film, reception and cultural studies', *The Centennial Review* 35 (1) (Winter): 89–104.

Steele, J. (1994) *Eternal Russia: Yeltsin, Gorbachev and the Mirage of Democracy*. London: Faber.

Steinberg, M.W. (1994) 'The dialogue of struggle', *Social Science History* 18: 505–41.

Stevenson, N. (1995) *Understanding Media Cultures: Social Theory and Mass Communication*. London: Sage.

Stites, R. (1992) *Russian Popular Culture: Entertainment and Society since 1900*. Cambridge: Cambridge University Press.

Taylor, S.J. (1991) *Shock! Horror! The Tabloids in Action*. London: Corgi.

Tester, K. (1994) *Media, Culture and Morality*. London: Routledge.

Thomas, S. (1989) 'Functionalism revised and applied to mass communication study', pp. 376–96 in B. Dervin, L. Grossberg, B. O'Keefe and E. Wartella (eds), *Paradigm Dialogues in Communication, Vol II*. Beverly Hills, CA: Sage.

Thomas, S. (1994) 'Artifactual analysis in the study of culture: a defense of content analysis in a postmodern age', *Communication Research* 21 (6): 683–97.

Thompson, E.P. (1963) *The Making of the English Working Class*. New York: Pantheon.

Thompson, E.P. (1978) *The Poverty of Theory and Other Essays*. London: Merlin Press.

Tompkins, J. (1986) 'Indians: textualism, morality and the problem of history', pp. 59–78 in H.L. Gates (ed.), *'Race', Writing and Difference*. Chicago: Chicago University Press.

Tuchman, G. (1978) *Making News: A Study in the Construction of Reality*. New York: The Free Press.

Ullin, R. (1991) 'Critical anthropology twenty years later', *Critique of Anthropology* 11 (1): 63–89.

van Dijk, T.A. (1992) 'Discourse and the denial of racism', *Discourse and Society* 3: 87–118.

Volosinov, V.N. (1973) *Marxism and the Philosophy of Language*. Cambridge, MA: Harvard University Press.

Wainwright, H. (1994) *Arguments for a New Left*. Oxford: Basil Blackwell.

Walby, S. (1992) 'Post-post-modernism? Theorising social complexity', pp. 31–52 in M. Barrett and A. Phillips (eds), *Destabilising Theory*. Cambridge: Polity Press.

Walkerdine, V. (1990) *Schoolgirl Fictions*. London: Verso.

Walkerdine, V. (1993) '"Daddy's gonna buy you a dream to cling to (and mummy's gonna love you just as much as she can)": young girls and popular television', pp. 74–89 in D. Buckingham (ed.), *Reading Audiences: Young People and the Media*. Manchester: Manchester University Press.

Waters, M. (1995) *Globalization*. London: Routledge.

Watt, I. (1957) *The Rise of the Novel*. Berkeley, CA: University of California Press.

Weber, M. (1946) *From Max Weber: Essays in Sociology*, edited by H. Gerth and C. Wright Mills. New York: Oxford University Press.

Weeks, J. (1993) 'Rediscovering values', pp. 189–211 in J. Squires (ed.), *Principled Positions: Postmodernism and the Rediscovery of Value*. London: Lawrence and Wishart.

Wellmer, A. (1971) *Critical Theory of Society*. New York: Continuum.

Wertsch, J. (1991) *Voices of the Mind*. Hemel Hempstead: Harvester/Wheatsheaf.

West, C. (1992) 'The postmodern crisis of the black intellectuals', pp. 689–705 in L. Grossberg, C. Nelson and P.A. Treichler (eds), *Cultural Studies*. New York: Routledge.

Wetherell, M. and J. Potter (1992) *Mapping the Language of Racism*. Hemel Hempstead: Harvester/Wheatsheaf.

White, A. (1990) *De-Stalinization and the House of Culture: Declining State Control over Leisure in the USSR, Poland and Hungary, 1953–89*. London: Routledge.

Widdicombe, S. and R. Wooffitt (1995) *The Language of Youth Subcultures*. Hemel Hempstead: Harvester/Wheatsheaf.

Williams, R. (1958a) *Culture and Society, 1780–1950*. London: Chatto and Windus/New York: Columbia University Press.

Williams, R. (1958b) 'Culture is ordinary', pp. 74–92 in N. McKenzie (ed.), *Conviction*. London: MacGibbon and Kee/New York: Monthly Review Press (1959).

Williams, R. (1959) 'The culture of politics', *Nation* 188 (1): 10–12.

Williams, R. (1961) *The Long Revolution*. London: Chatto and Windus.

Williams, R. (1962/1968a) *Communications*. Harmondsworth: Penguin.

Williams, R. (1965) 'Towards a socialist society', pp. 367–97 in P. Anderson and R. Blackburn (eds), *Towards Socialism*. London: Fontana.

Williams, R. (1968b) 'The idea of a common culture', reprinted in R. Gable (ed.) (1989), *Resources of Hope: Culture, Democracy, Socialism*. London: Verso. pp. 32–8.

Williams, R. (1973) *The Country and the City*. London: Chatto and Windus.

Williams, R. (1974) *Television: Technology and Cultural Form*. London: Fontana.

Williams, R. (1976) *Keywords: A Vocabulary of Culture and Society*. London: Fontana.

Williams, R. (1977) *Marxism and Literature*. Oxford: Oxford University Press.

Williams, R. (1978) 'The press we don't deserve', pp. 15–28 in J. Curran (ed.), *The British Press: A Manifesto*. London: Macmillan.

Williams, R. (1979) *Politics and Letters: Interviews with New Left Review*. London: New Left Review Editions.

Williams, R. (1980) *Problems in Materialism and Culture: Selected Essays*. London: Verso.

Williams, R. (1983a) *Keywords*. New York and London: Oxford University Press.

Williams, R. (1983b) 'Culture', pp. 15–55 in D. McLellan (ed.), *Marx: The First 100 Years*. London: Fontana.

Williams, R. (1989a) *Resources of Hope: Culture Democracy, Socialism*. London: Verso.

Williams, R. (1989b) *Raymond Williams on Television* (edited by A. O'Connor). London: Routledge.

Williams, R. (1989c) *The Politics of Modernism: Against the New Conformists*. London: Verso.

Williams, R. (1990) *What I Came To Say*. London: Hutchinson.

Williamson, J. (1978) *Decoding Advertisements*. London: Marion Boyars.

Willis, P. (1977) *Learning to Labour*. Farnborough, Hants: Saxon House.

Willis, P. (1978) *Profane Culture*. London: Routledge and Keagan Paul.

Willis, P. (1990) *Common Culture*. Milton Keynes: Open University Press.

Willis, P. (1991) 'Towards a new cultural map', *National Arts and Media Strategy*. London: Arts Council of Great Britain.

Winch, P. (1958) *The Idea of a Social Science*. London: Routledge and Kegan Paul.

Wright Mills, C. (1959) *The Sociological Imagination*. London: Oxford University Press.

Woodward, B. (1987) *Veil: The Secret Wars of the CIA 1981–1987*. New York: Simon and Schuster.

Wolff, J. (1983/1993) *Aesthetics and the Sociology of Art*. London: Macmillan.

Wynne, D. and J. O'Connor (1995) 'City cultures and the "new cultural intermediaries"'. Leicester: British Sociological Association Annual Conference: April.

Index